PORTFOLIO MANAGEMENT FOR NEW PRODUCTS
2ND EDITION

ROBERT G. COOPER,

SCOTT J. EDGETT,

ELKO J. KLEINSCHMIDT

BASIC BOOKS

A Member of the Perseus Books Group
New York

Many of the designations used by manufacturers and sellers to distinguish their products are claimed as trademarks. Where those designations appear in this book and Basic Books was aware of a trademark claim, the designations have been printed in initial capital letters.

Cataloging-in-Publication data for this book is available from the Library of Congress.
ISBN-13: 978-0-7382-0514-4
ISBN-10: 0-7382-0514-1

Text design by Reginald Thompson
Set in 10-point Times Roman by Perseus Publishing Services

EBC   20 19 18
First printing, December 2001

Books published by Basic Books are available at special discounts for bulk purchases in the U.S. by corporations, institutions, and other organizations. For more information, please contact the Special Markets Department at the Perseus Books Group, 11 Cambridge Center, Cambridge, MA 02142, or call (800) 255–1514 or (617) 252–5298 or email special.markets@perseusbooks.com.

Find us on the World Wide Web at
http://www.basicbooks.com

Contents

Exhibits

Acknowledgments

No research is possible without financial support. Over the years our research has benefited from three generous benefactors. In alphabetical order they are

- Esso Chemical Canada Ltd. (Exxon in Canada), in particular Bill Brennan, who has been a constant source of financial support and encouragement for our research efforts for many years
- Innovation Research Centre (Chris Bart, Director) at the Michael G. DeGroote School of Business, McMaster University, which has repeatedly supported our research into new products and portfolio management
- The Industrial Research Institute, Washington, DC, for allowing us to research their member firms, and in particular Chuck Larson, Executive Director, IRI; Miles Drake (Air Products), Chairman of the Research-on-Research Committee (IRI), and Bob Burkett

A special thanks to Barbara Pitts, Michelle Jones, Robert Prior, and Dina Stoyles—all of the Product Development Institute—for their input and support. Also Jens Arleth, Managing Director of U3 Innovation Management, Copenhagen, Denmark, who offered valuable suggestions for Chapters 9 and 10. Jens also provided a major European test setting for the proposed techniques profiled in this book. In addition, we would like to thank Dr. Angelika Dreher of SIMMA & Partner, Austria, who also made helpful suggestions.

A number of other people and organizations have also kindly helped us in writing this book. Companies and people that provided us with insightful comments and their views on portfolio management included Richard Albright of Lucent Technologies; Martin Brennan and Mike Harley of Reckitt-Benckiser; Tony Brophy and Brian Crean of Guinness Breweries Ireland; Tom Chorman of Procter & Gamble; Adrian Dale, formerly of Unilever; Randy Englund, formerly of Hewlett-Packard; Dave Erlandson of Sopheon; Patricia Evans of Strategic Decisions Group; Charles Gagnon of Hydro-Quebec; Robin Karol of DuPont; Ray Kilminster of Hoechst U.S.; Wolf-Rudiger Lange of Rhode & Schwarz; Robert McCarthy of Roche Molecular Biochemicals; John Noonan of Inco Ltd.; Dan Panfil of English China Clay; Ro Pavlick and Dodge Bingham of Thomson Corporation; Kathryn Sachse and Marg Kneebone of the Royal Bank of Canada; Charles Shephard of NCR Financial Solutions Group; Barry Siadat of AlliedSignal–Honeywell; Erik Lahn Sorensen of Danish Technological Institute; Fred Squires of Specialty Minerals; Ron Taylor of Bayer Polyurethanes; Yutaka

Tashiro of Dainippon Ink & Chemical; Gary Tritle of 3M; Per Velde formerly of
Telenor Privat (Norwegian Telephone System); Mike Wolfe, editor of *Research-Technology Management*; Bob Wood, James Barrett, and Ed Bartkus (retired) of
Rohm and Haas.

We also thank our editor at Perseus Publishing, Nick Philipson, for his continued support for our books.

A final and heartfelt thanks to our families for their continued support and
help throughout this time consuming exercise, especially Linda, Ruth, and Barb.

Robert G. Cooper
Scott J. Edgett
Elko J. Kleinschmidt

CHAPTER 1

The Quest for the Right Portfolio Management Process

New products are vital to the success and future prosperity of the modern corporation. Witness the stunning successes that have been achieved in just the last decade in everything from wireless Internet and genetic engineering through to Pfizer's Viagra and Heinz's green ketchup. While some executives still look to cost cutting as the way to improve bottom lines, these periodic downsizing exercises have proven ineffective in the long run. Senior executives are finally sobering up to the reality that no corporation ever shrank itself to greatness.

As we begin this new millennium, the growth game is still on—faster and more competitive than ever. Front and center is the desire for new products—successful, significant, winning new products. Driven by rapidly advancing technologies, globalization of markets, and increasing competition at home and abroad, effective new product development is emerging as the major corporate strategic initiative of the decades ahead. Corporations that succeed at new product development will be the future Pfizers, HPs, 3Ms, and Microsofts; those that fail to develop excellent new products will invariably disappear or be gobbled up by the winners.

A vital question in this new product battleground is, How should corporations most effectively invest their R&D and new product resources? That is what portfolio management is all about: resource allocation to achieve corporate new product objectives. Much like stock market portfolio managers, senior executives who optimize their R&D investments—define the right new product strategy for the firm, select the winning new product projects, and achieve the ideal balance of projects—will win in the long run. This book is about how winners manage their R&D and new product portfolios, and about the lessons your company can put into practice in order to achieve higher returns from R&D investment.

Example: Before moving ahead, consider the plight of this major company heading for trouble:

The U.S. division of a multinational pharmaceutical company was almost blindsided by problems with its new product portfolio. True, the company had launched some huge winners over the years, but blockbuster products like these were becoming harder to come by. And senior management was increasingly impatient with R&D's inability to get next-generation products to market. Some executives were even questioning the wisdom of continuing high spending on R&D. A new product task force was put together to assess the problem. Here's what they discovered:

Although there were a few solid projects in the development pipeline, there were far too many substandard ones as well—projects that were pet projects of executives, or poor projects that should have been killed some time ago. Clearly, the reviews were not doing the job of weeding out poor projects.

There were a great many projects underway that seemed to be all over the place—in too many disease areas and market segments. Strategically, it was a scattergun effort. The company did not even sell to some of these markets, and others were way off strategy. There was simply no rhyme or reason to the list of projects—there was no focus at all.

Some market segments (disease areas) seemed to be consuming inordinate proportions of R&D and new product launch resources in relation to their potential value to the company. Although many of these projects were good ones, the company was spending large amounts of money in some areas and leaving other areas that were good strategic fits desperately short of resources.

Many projects were taking far too long. Some had been in the pipeline for years longer than they should have been. Even the smaller projects seemed to take forever. When queried, the standard answer was that new drug projects do take years, and that project teams were working as hard as they could. A closer inspection revealed that project teams were stretched across too many projects. The result was pipeline gridlock: too many projects in the pipe.

There were too many small projects in the pipeline. An accounting of resource allocation showed that more than 75 percent of R&D resources were going to improvements, tweaks, extensions, fixes, and modifications—low-risk, low-payoff projects. There was a real shortage of significant high-reward and longer-term projects—the kind that had built the company.

In summary, while there were some promising projects, the portfolio as a whole was in bad shape! It was unfocused, contained too many projects, and resources were spread too thinly. There were too many projects of marginal value in the portfolio; thus, it was poorly balanced. Finally, the portfolio did not support the business strategy very well.

What Is Portfolio Management?

Portfolio management and the prioritization of new product projects has become a critical management task in the past decade.[1] Portfolio management and project prioritization are about resource allocation in the firm. That is, which new product projects from the many opportunities the corporation faces will it fund? And which ones will receive top priority and be accelerated to market? It is also about business strategy, for today's new product projects decide tomorrow's product/market profile of the firm. An estimated 50 percent of a firm's sales today come from new products introduced to the market within the previous five years.[2] Finally, portfolio management is about balance: about the optimal investment mix between risk versus return, maintenance versus growth, and short-term versus long-term new product projects.

Before charging into the topic of what techniques work best, let us stand back and reflect on what portfolio management is. We formally define portfolio management as follows:

Portfolio management for new products is a dynamic decision process wherein the list of active new products and R&D projects is constantly revised. In this process, new projects are evaluated, selected, and prioritized. Existing projects may be accelerated, killed, or deprioritized and resources are allocated and reallocated to the active projects. The portfolio decision process is characterized by uncertain and changing information, dynamic opportunities, multiple goals and strategic considerations, interdependence among projects, and multiple decision makers and locations.

The portfolio decision process encompasses or overlaps a number of decision-making processes within the business, including periodic reviews of the total portfolio of all projects (looking at the entire set of projects and comparing all projects against each other); making ongoing Go/Kill decisions on individual projects; and developing new product strategies for the business, complete with strategic resource allocation decisions across business units and strategic arenas.

The point is that portfolio management is a pervasive and all-encompassing topic. It is more than project selection, although that is part of it; it is certainly much more than annual budgeting or resource allocation across projects; it goes beyond simply developing a prioritized list of projects; it is more than strategizing and trying to arrive at the best set of projects to meet strategic needs, although strategy and strategic imperatives are certainly key components. Finally, it is more than corporate resource allocation—allocating R&D resources across various business units—although this corporate planning exercise should involve or interface with portfolio management. Portfolio management includes all these.

Done properly, portfolio management is multifaceted and complex. But one cannot duck the issue—refuse to deal with portfolio management—just because it's complex and challenging, since portfolio management is vital to new product success.

One problem is that everyone sees portfolio management a little differently: The strategist sees it as allocating resources across businesses, or perhaps developing a strategically correct portfolio to support the corporation's vision and mission. The financial person looks to portfolio management to allocate scarce financial resources efficiently and optimally to achieve maximum shareholder value. The technical community looks to portfolio management to pick the right projects and foster the right kind of innovation. Meanwhile, the marketing person hopes that portfolio management yields better priorities and faster times to market. And the CEO prays that portfolio management will deliver big winners with positive financial impacts—and soon!

What Happens When You Lack Effective Portfolio Management

Companies without effective new product portfolio management and project selection face a slippery road downhill (see Exhibit 1.1). Indeed, many of the problems that beset product development initiatives in businesses can be directly traced to ineffective portfolio management. The pharmaceutical company described earlier in this chapter provides an example of only some of the problems that arise when portfolio management is lacking. Here are some of the agonies firms endure when they do not have proper portfolio management.

First, weak portfolio management translates into a strong reluctance to kill new product projects. Go/Kill criteria are ineffective or nonexistent and there is no consistent mechanism for evaluating and, if necessary, culling weak projects. Projects seem to take on lives of their own, running like express trains past review points. Further, new projects simply get added to the "active" list with little appreciation for their resource requirements or impact on other projects. The result is a total lack of focus: far too many projects for the available resources.

The problems don't stop here. A lack of focus and too many active projects mean that resources and people are too thinly spread. As a result, projects end up in a queue, there are serious logjams in the process, and cycle time starts to increase. Suddenly there are complaints about projects taking too long to get to market. But worse, with resources and people thinly spread, everyone starts to scramble—too many balls in the air. The result is predictable: Quality of execution starts to suffer. For example, the essential up-front homework is not done, and needed market studies designed to build in the voice of the customer are left out due to lack of time and people. Poor-quality execution of these and other

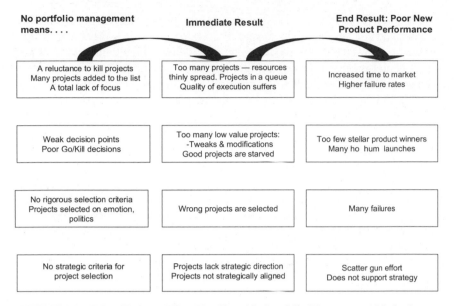

No portfolio management means. . . .	Immediate Result	End Result: Poor New Product Performance
A reluctance to kill projects Many projects added to the list A total lack of focus	Too many projects — resources thinly spread. Projects in a queue Quality of execution suffers	Increased time to market Higher failure rates
Weak decision points Poor Go/Kill decisions	Too many low value projects: -Tweaks & modifications Good projects are starved	Too few stellar product winners Many ho hum launches
No rigorous selection criteria Projects selected on emotion, politics	Wrong projects are selected	Many failures
No strategic criteria for project selection	Projects lack strategic direction Projects not strategically aligned	Scatter gun effort Does not support strategy

EXHIBIT 1.1   What Happens When You Have No Portfolio Management Method

steps in the new product process means an increase in failure rates.[3] So, not only are projects late to market, but their success rates drop!

There's even more. Lacking effective portfolio management, there are no rigorous and tough decision points, which in turn leads to poor project selection decisions. One common result is too many mediocre projects in the pipeline: too many extensions, minor modifications, and defensive products, which yield marginal value to the company. So, many launches yield disappointing and "ho-hum" results. There is a noticeable lack of stellar new product winners. Even more insidious, the few really good projects are starved for resources, so that they're either late to market or never achieve their full potential. And that creates a huge opportunity cost, which never appears on the profit-and-loss statement.

The problems don't end there. Without a rigorous portfolio method, the wrong projects often get selected and for all the wrong reasons. Instead of decisions based on facts and objective criteria, decisions are based on politics, opinioneering, and emotion. Too many of these ill-selected projects simply fail!

The final negative result is strategic: Without a portfolio management method, strategic criteria for project selection are missing, so there is no strategic direction to the projects selected. After all, new products are the leading edge of business strategy. They define tomorrow's vision of your company! But without a portfolio method, projects are not aligned with the strategy, and many strategically unimportant projects find themselves in the pipeline. The end result is a scattergun effort that does not support the business's strategic direction.

The price for not having an effective portfolio management and project selection method for new products is very high. If your business faces any of these problems—few stellar new products, long cycle times, high failure rates, or poor strategic alignment—perhaps they can be traced back to the root cause of ineffective portfolio management. So read on and find out what others are doing about the challenge and, most important, what your company can do!

A Roadmap of the Book

1. The balance of this chapter highlights the importance of portfolio management. It helps shed light on why so many firms face difficulties in their attempts to allocate R&D resources and what the major challenges and problems in managing development portfolios are.
2. Much has been written over the years on the topic of portfolio management, so Chapter 2 provides some useful background: It probes the literature, identifies the main generic types of portfolio management tools proposed in the literature, and defines the requirements for an ideal portfolio management approach. The chapter ends with a look at the three goals in portfolio management.
3. In chapters 3–5 we provide a close look at the methods that leading corporations employ to manage their new product project portfolios and allocate their R&D resources:

   - approaches used to maximize the value of a portfolio (Chapter 3)
   - approaches used to achieve a balanced portfolio (Chapter 4)
   - approaches used to develop a strong link to strategy (Chapter 5)

THE RESEARCH THAT UNDERLIES THIS BOOK

Many of the techniques, approaches, insights, and performance results outlined or reported in this book are based on our extensive and widely published investigations into portfolio management practices and performance in industry. Phase I of the study looked at 35 leading firms' portfolio management approaches; companies were singled out for in-depth analysis on the basis of the uniqueness and proficiency of their portfolio management approaches. The results of this study were reported in several journal articles as well as in the first edition of this book.[4]

Phase II of our research looked at 205 companies and focused on what methods were being used and what results were achieved. Because of the larger sample size in this study, we were able to correlate performance results with methods used, in order to provide insights into which methods seem to work best in terms of specific performance metrics.[5]

Phase III of the research consisted of case studies to probe some of the difficulties uncovered in portfolio management and what some companies are doing to address these difficulties.[6] The 40 companies in Phase III were chosen because we had prior knowledge of their approaches and because they were actively addressing portfolio management issues. Further, they are more representative of industry at large.

4. Chapter 6 lowers the microscope on portfolio performance: We reveal the performance results achieved by each portfolio management method and how users rate the various methods.
5. In Chapter 7, observations are made on what appears to work in portfolio management and what doesn't and on the pitfalls, hurdles, and concerns managers are addressing. We also identify some of the major problems and challenges that firms have encountered as they attempt to implement portfolio management.
6. The methods are only as good as the data they rely upon. So integrity of the data for all portfolio methods is a major issue and is the focus of Chapter 8. Here we propose methods for improving estimates for such things as market and revenue forecasts, pricing, costing, and probabilities of success.
7. Next we recommend ways in which portfolio management can be made more effective in your organization, and we propose some techniques and methods to make this happen (Chapters 9 and 10). Our recommended Portfolio Management Process, along with a number of alternatives to consider, is outlined in these two chapters.
8. The final chapter deals with the thorny issue of implementation—moving forward toward designing and installing an effective Portfolio Management Process.

Throughout the book, we use examples drawn both from our extensive research studies and from companies with which we have worked. These we hope yield additional insights and help clarify this challenging topic. In addition, we provide "Points for Management to Ponder" in the hope that you will put the book down for a moment and think about how the material you have read applies to your own business.

Portfolio Management Is Vital

Portfolio management is fundamental to successful new product development. Portfolio management is about resource allocation—how your business spends its capital and human resources, and which development projects it invests in. Portfolio management is also about project selection—ensuring that you have a steady stream of big new product winners! And portfolio management is about strategy: It is one method by which you operationalize your business strategy.[7]

Recent years have witnessed a heightened interest in portfolio management, not only in the technical community, but in the CEO's office as well. Portfolio management is a critical senior management challenge, according to our best practices survey of Industrial Research Institute (IRI) members. Exhibit 1.2 shows how various functional areas rate the importance of portfolio management.[8] Note how important the topic is rated by senior executives as well as senior technology people. In addition, higher-performing businesses tend to rate the importance of portfolio management much higher than lower-performing ones.

Portfolio management is important to your business for three main reasons:

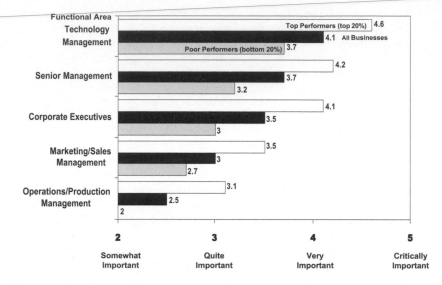

EXHIBIT 1.2   Importance of Portfolio Management by Functional Area

Exhibit shows how important various functions rated portfolio management to be. Note the significant differences between top and poor performers: Top-performing firms rate portfolio management to be much more important.

SOURCE: R.G. Cooper, S.J., Edgett, and E.J. Kleinschmidt, "Best Practices for Managing R&D Portfolios," *Research-Technology Management* 41, 4 (1998): p. 24.

rate the importance of portfolio management much higher than lower-performing ones.

Portfolio management is important to your business for three main reasons:

1. A successful new product effort is *fundamental to business success.* This logically translates into portfolio management: the ability to select today's projects that will become tomorrow's new product winners.
2. New product development is the *manifestation of your business strategy.* One of the most important ways you operationalize strategy is through the new products you develop. If your new product initiatives are wrong—the wrong projects, or the wrong balance—then you fail at implementing your business strategy.
3. Portfolio management is about *resource allocation.* In a business world preoccupied with value to the shareholder and doing more with less, technology and marketing resources are simply too scarce to allocate to the wrong projects. The consequences of poor portfolio management are evident: You squander scarce resources on the wrong projects, and as a result, starve the truly deserving ones.

Specific reasons for the importance of portfolio management, derived from the best practices study, are[9]

- to yield the right balance of projects and investments
- to communicate project priorities both vertically and horizontally within the organization
- to provide greater objectivity in project selection.

Every company we interviewed in depth believed the portfolio management, project selection, and resource allocation problem to be critical to new product success. Virtually all companies had experienced considerable problems with project selection and resource allocation. Further, the desire to see the business strategy reflected in portfolios of R&D investments is another driver of improved portfolio management techniques. As a result, many of the firms we studied are devoting considerable amounts of effort to solving the portfolio problem.

POINTS FOR MANAGEMENT TO PONDER

Have you identified portfolio management for new products as a key issue in your business? And does the leadership team of your business play an active role in these portfolio decisions? If new products are vital to your future, then the most important decisions your business faces concern portfolio management—how you allocate your new product resources. Senior management must lead here! Make it a top-priority issue.

Much Room for Improvement

How well is project selection, program prioritization, and portfolio management working in industry? This is both a fundamental and a vital question, and a question we posed in our large sample study of IRI firms. Portfolio performance is a multi-faceted concept, so six metrics were constructed to capture how well a business portfolio is performing. These metrics include: decision effectiveness and efficiency, having the right balance of projects, high value projects, and a strategically aligned portfolio (see Exhibit 1.3 for a complete listing). All are metrics that emerged as goals in Phase I of our study.

Portfolio management appears to be working in a *moderately satisfactory fashion* on average in our sample of businesses. Mean scores across the six performance metrics are typically midrange—not stellar, but not disastrous either—although there are some differences across metrics. (See Exhibit 1.3: The bars show mean performance values across all firms.) The results indicate that:

- Businesses on average obtain *fairly good alignment* between their portfolio of projects and the business strategy.
- Portfolios contain *moderately high-value projects* on average.
- Spending breakdowns (across projects) *reflect business strategy fairly well*, on average.

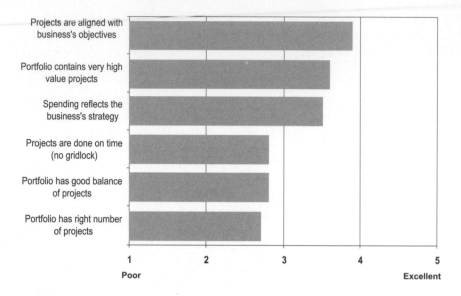

EXHIBIT 1.3   Portfolio Performance Results on Six Key Metrics
Performance metrics are rank-ordered according to mean scores.

But portfolio performance is markedly lower, on average, in terms of the *right number of projects* and *project balance*, namely

- Project gridlock exists in the portfolio pipeline, on average, with *projects not being done on time*!
- Businesses tend to *lack a balanced portfolio* of projects (balance in short-term versus long-term, high-risk versus low-risk, and so on).
- Businesses have *too many projects underway*, given the resources available (which might explain the gridlock and timeliness problem above). Performance on this metric is the weakest of the six.

The conclusion is that, on average, firms are performing satisfactorily on some portfolio metrics and not so well on others. Of course, many of the firms in the study were performing well below these averages. Overall, there is much room for improvement in portfolio management practices and performance.

Major Challenges for Portfolio Management

Our investigation identified specific problems in project selection and portfolio management, problems that are creating a sense of urgency. Let's now consider some of the challenges that are immediately evident—conclusions regarding project selection and some of the problems these companies faced.

The portfolio of projects does not reflect the business's strategy: Many businesses (business units, BUs or SBUs) we investigated had enunciated business strategies. In some cases, they had even developed new product strategies that defined the goals for new products (for example, "by year four, 32 percent of our sales revenue will be generated by products we do not now have"). The role product development would play in achieving overall business goals was also defined in some cases (for example, "60 percent of our SBU's growth will come from new products, another 30 percent from market developments, and 10 percent from market size increases"). Strategic arenas of focus were even identified—what product types, markets, and technologies (or platforms) would generate these new products. The problem lies in linking these strategies—business and new product—to spending on R&D projects. The breakdown of R&D spending by project type often revealed serious disconnects between the goals/strategies of the business and where the money was spent.

POINTS FOR MANAGEMENT TO PONDER

Does your portfolio reflect and support your business's strategy? Find out by doing what management in the pharmaceutical company did earlier in this chapter. Undertake a portfolio review of all your active projects. Are they all on strategy—that is, within product, market, or technology areas defined as areas of focus? Then undertake a breakdown of spending on the projects. Do the resulting splits reflect your strategic priorities? Are your spending breakdowns consistent with your business strategy?

Poor-quality portfolios: A number of executives are displeased with, or at best doubtful about, their firms' current portfolio of projects. Many new product projects are thought to be weak or mediocre; others are considered unfit for commercialization; and success rates in the marketplace are less than adequate. As one executive put it, "We implemented our portfolio management approach (a risk-reward bubble diagram model), and the first thing that became evident was that half our projects were in the wrong quadrants, including some of our big ones! By the end of the year, the list of projects had been cut in half." Similar audits have resulted in similar cuts in other firms.

MORE POINTS FOR MANAGEMENT TO PONDER

What is the quality of your portfolio? Are most of the projects solid ones? Are they of high value to the business? Is the economic value of your total portfolio considerably higher than what you've spent on it? Perhaps it is time to undertake a critical portfolio review, place a value or "economic worth" on each project, and cull out the mediocre ones.

We have tunnels, not funnels: Another related problem is that Go/Kill decision points—the gates in new product processes—are often perceived to be ineffective. In too many companies, projects tend to take on lives of their own. Little can stop them once they gain momentum. In one leading firm, an internal audit of 60 current projects revealed that 88 percent resembled an express train, "slowing down at stations (project reviews), but never with the intention of being stopped!" Only 12 percent were handled in a thoughtful way with rigorous Go/Kill decision points. Even when killed, some projects had a habit of being resurrected, perhaps under a new name.

We observed that criteria for making Go/Kill decisions were inadequate or not used, and that a mechanism for rating, prioritizing, or even killing projects was often lacking. As one frustrated manager exclaimed, "We talk about having a funneling process which weeds out poor projects; heck, we don't have a funnel, we have a tunnel. Ten concepts enter the process, ten go into development, ten go to launch—and one succeeds!"

STILL MORE POINTS FOR MANAGEMENT TO PONDER

Do you have a portfolio funnel? Do you start with a number of concepts and then via successive, tough screens at multiple stages in your new product process do you narrow the list down to the very best projects—skimming the cream off the top? Or, once projects start, is there very little chance they'll ever be killed? If the latter is the case in your company, review the attrition curve of projects. If you keep records of project decisions, go back and find out how many projects (what proportion) were actually killed at each of your Go/Kill decision points. If very few were killed, then you have a tunnel, not a funnel!

Scarce resources and a lack of focus: Resources are too scarce to waste on the wrong projects. Indeed, a common complaint is that product development suffers from lean resources, especially in areas such as marketing and manufacturing/operations. Most firms confessed to having far too many projects for the available resources. The result is that resources are spread very thinly across new product projects, so that even the best projects are starved for people, time, and money. The end result is that projects take too long to reach the market. Many key activities—up-front homework, getting sharp, early product definition, and building in the voice of the customer—are not executed as well as or as consistently as they should be. The bottom line is a lack of focus, which creates a plethora of other problems—not the least of which is poor resource allocation.

Trivialization of product development: A final problem brought on by a lack of resources (or a lack of focus) is the trivialization of product development in some firms. The quest for cycle time reduction, together with the desire for more new products than ever, when coupled with the resource constraint, leads many firms to do the obvious: pick "low-hanging fruit" projects that can be done quickly, easily, and cheaply. Often these projects are trivial (modifications or extensions) while the significant products, which are the ones needed to yield real competitive advantage and major breakthroughs, are placed on the back burner. The net result is a portfolio of projects that is very short-term, while projects designed to create tomorrow's winners or technology platforms for growth are missing.

Some Definitions

Before we lower the microscope on leading firms' current portfolio practices, here are some definitions of terms we use throughout this book:

Business Strategy: This specifies the goals, direction, and areas of focus for the business unit (defined below).

Business Unit (BU) or (SBU): This is the smallest unit in the company for which portfolio management is undertaken. Usually a BU (or SBU—strategic business unit) is a semiautonomous, self-contained business with its own goals, strategy, and resources. For example, a BU likely has its own R&D budget. For smaller firms, the BU may be the entire company.

New Product Strategy: This is a component of (or flows from) the business strategy. It specifies the new product goals, direction, and areas of focus (that is, areas in which product development efforts will focus). It may even specify desired levels of R&D and new product spending in specific arenas of focus (for example, how much to spend in certain markets or product categories).

Portfolio Management Process (PMP): This is the entire method of project selection and portfolio management. It includes a gating or Stage-Gate™ process,* portfolio reviews, resource allocation, and portfolio models.

Portfolio Models: These are the specific models or tools used to select projects or review the portfolio. They include scoring models, bubble diagrams and maps, charts, financial models, and strategic approaches. These are outlined in Chapters 2 to 5.

Portfolio Review: This is the periodic review of the portfolio of all projects. It may take place annually, semiannually, or quarterly. Here all projects—active projects and even those on hold—are reviewed and compared against each other. The portfolio review often uses portfolio models to display lists or maps of the current portfolio. Vital questions in the portfolio review are these: Are the active projects the right ones? Is this the right combination or mix of active projects? Is this really where the company's money should be spent?

Resource Allocation: This is the decision process by which development resources (R&D, marketing, capital) are allocated to certain activities, projects, or even businesses. At the micro or 500-foot level, resource allocation might amount to an R&D head assigning certain people to work on certain projects or even tasks within projects. At the 5,000-foot level, resource allocation involves creating a prioritized list of projects in rank order for resource eligibility using predefined and agreed-upon ranking criteria. At the 50,000-foot, or macro, level, resource allocation can be as broad as a decision on how many resources are allocated to each business unit in the corporation.

*Stage-Gate™ Process:** This is the formal process, or road map, that firms use to drive a new product project from idea to launch. This process has multiple stages, together with gates or decision points. A Stage-Gate™ process has many variants; it is also called the new product process, gating process, or phase-review process. Such a process is important to portfolio management because the gates are where Go/Kill decisions are made on individual projects; hence, where many of the resources are allocated. If your company has a Stage-Gate process, then it must be included as an integral facet of the total portfolio approach.

* Stage-Gate is a registered trademark of R.G. Cooper & Associates Consultants, Inc., a member company of the Product Development Institute. See www.prod-dev.com.

CHAPTER 2

Three Decades of R&D Portfolio Methods: What Progress?

The concept of portfolio management for new product development is not new. Over the decades, the topic has surfaced under various guises, including "R&D project selection," "R&D resource allocation," "project prioritization," and "portfolio management." By the early 1970s, dozens of articles had appeared on the topic, with most authors making only small stabs at the subject before moving on to more fruitful fields. The majority of these early proposed methods involved management science optimization techniques. To the management scientist, the portfolio management problem was one of constrained optimization under conditions of uncertainty: a multiproject, multistage decision model solved by mathematical programming. Thus, the original portfolio selection models were highly mathematical and employed techniques such as linear, dynamic, and integer programming. The objective was to develop a portfolio of new and existing projects to maximize some objective function (for example, the expected profits), subject to a set of resource constraints.

Anyone familiar with these programming techniques will immediately recognize the hurdles that the mathematician and management scientist would have to overcome before solving this portfolio problem. Further, in spite of the many methods proposed in the early days, there was a remarkable lack of follow-up. For example, few authors ever described attempts to actually implement their methods and to gauge their feasibility; indeed, the articles appear to be largely the result of academics writing to and for each other. In spite of the importance of the topic, no guru or "dominant school of thought" emerged, perhaps an indication of the frustrations faced in seeking solutions.[1]

Recent Advances in Portfolio Management Methods

More recently, a number of proposed new product portfolio methods have been described in various articles and books.[2] Some are described below and may prove useful in your firm. So let's now look at what the more recent literature says about how to select projects and the methods to use in managing your portfolio of new products.

Financial or Economic Models

These models treat project evaluation much like a conventional investment decision. Traditional computation approaches, such as payback period, break-even analysis, return on investment, and discounted cash flow (DCF including Net Present Value (NPV) and Internal Rate of Return (IRR)) methods are used, as well as various financial ratios (such as the Productivity Index).[3]

According to our research, such methods are used in one of two ways in portfolio management:

1. The metric is determined for each project (for example, the NPV) and then compared to a cutoff criterion (example, the NPV must exceed x). This forms the basis of the Go/Kill decision at gates. Via this method, projects that promise weak financial payoffs are killed and weeded out. Applied in a disciplined fashion, the net effect is to increase the overall economic attractiveness of the portfolio of remaining projects.
2. A metric is determined for each project (for example, the NPV), and it is used to rank projects. Resources are allocated to projects by rank until there are no more resources available. Those projects beyond that point are either killed (if the metric is negative) or put on hold (if the metric is positive but resources are unavailable).

Although we recommend the use of some financial methods—namely payback, DCF, decision trees, and sensitivity analysis at some gates in a gating process and in portfolio management—we recognize their weaknesses too! Their main deficiency is *simply the lack of solid, reliable financial data*. See more on these models in the next chapter.

Scoring Models and Checklists

Scoring models and checklists fall into the general category of "benefit measurement techniques." They require a well-informed management group to assess the project on a variety of characteristics.[4] Such methods typically rely less on conventional economic data—such as projected sales, profit margins, and costs—and more on subjective assessments of strategic variables, such as fit with corporate objectives, competitive advantage, and market attractiveness.

Like the financial models above, the metrics or "project scores" generated by checklists or scoring models can be used in one of two ways: either against some absolute standard or cutoff criterion to make Go/Kill decisions; or simply to rank projects against each other to allocate resources until they run out.

Benefit measurement techniques recognize the lack of concrete financial data at earlier stages of the project and the fact that financial analysis is likely to yield unreliable results. So they rely primarily on subjective inputs of characteristics that are likely to be known. These techniques are most useful at the earlier points in a project, for example, at the initial idea screen and even the "go-to-development" decision point.

Probabilistic Financial Models

Financial and economic models (above) have been modified to better handle the element of risk and uncertainty evident in most development projects. Two main approaches are recommended:

Monte Carlo simulation: Monte Carlo simulation creates multiple scenarios representing the possible financial outcomes of a project.[5] Instead of merely inputting single estimates for each financial variable, the user is required to provide multiple inputs for each; for example, a pessimistic, an optimistic, and a most likely estimate. The computer model takes these data (which reflect the probability distribution for each financial variable), and using random number simulation, generates multiple scenarios of what might happen to this project. From these many scenarios, a distribution of financial outcomes is generated. Two commercially available Monte Carlo software models are *At Risk* and *Crystal Ball.*[6]

Decision tree analysis: In decision tree analysis, the project is reduced to a series of decisions, activities, and outcomes in a tree-and-branch format.[7] Probabilities of each branch or outcome occurring at each decision point or activity are noted on the branches, along with the financial consequences of each outcome. The expected value is simply the probabilities of the outcomes times their financial consequences.

Options pricing theory (or real options): Options pricing recognizes that investments in new product projects are made in increments rather than in an all-or-nothing fashion; management "buys" the project a piece at a time.[8] This is analogous to buying options in the stock market. The ability to buy options instead of making the full investment reduces the risk of the project; hence it has a monetary value (which is ignored in traditional financial methods). The true value of the project can be approximated using a decision-tree approach. More on this relatively new method in the next chapter.

Behavioral Approaches

These techniques are designed to bring managers to a consensus and include a variety of methods such as:

Modified Delphi method: The Modified Delphi method provides a formal and systematic way of integrating the collective wisdom of a decision-making group. This is a facilitated behavioral process wherein a group of decision makers engages in open discussion, followed by individual decision making. After each round, the decisions or best guesses of each participant are displayed to the entire group. More discussion ensues, again followed by individual decision making. A series of such rounds usually leads to consensus.

The Q-sort method: Users claim that Q-sort is one of the simplest and most effective methods for rank-ordering a set of new product proposals, especially at the idea-screening gate.[9] Each participant is given a deck of cards, each card describing a project. Following a discussion on all the projects, each member then sorts and resorts the deck into five categories, from a "high" group to a "low" group (or into simple "Yes" or "No" categories), evaluating each project according to a prespecified criterion. The results are anonymously tallied on a chart and displayed to the entire group. The procedure is repeated, and by the third round, the group usually moves to consensus on the ranking of projects.

Paired comparison models: The argument in paired comparison models is that it is often more revealing to make choices between pairs of projects than to assess a project on its own merits or against some absolute standard. These methods allow a decision-making group to select a subset of projects from a larger list, or to rank a list of projects. Analytic Hierarchy Processes (AHP) are a general class of such models.[10] Through a series of pairwise comparisons, a group of decision makers derives priorities for both the decision criteria and the projects.

AHP methods force choices between pairs of criteria in order to determine the relative importance of each criterion; they then force choices between a number of pairs of projects on these criteria. For example, suppose a decision-making group were trying to rank-order five projects—A, B, C, D, and E. The group would be shown pairs of projects (A versus B; B versus C; C versus A; and so on) and asked to indicate which project was better in terms of some key characteristic (such as strategic fit). The group's many decisions reveal their preferences. These decisions are analyzed by a sophisticated computer model, which provides the rank order of the projects and the strength of preferences. AHP models, such as *Expert Choice,*[11] are often viewed as decision support systems (below).

Mathematical Optimization Procedures

Mathematical optimization models (MOMs) are also called operations research or search for optimal solutions, and were referred to as the original portfolio models at the beginning of this chapter. MOMs are mathematical routines that attempt to find the optimal set of projects in order to maximize some objective (such as profit), subject to a set of resource constraints (such as person-days or money). They include techniques such as linear and mathematical programming, statistical decision theory, game theory, and probability theory (such as Markov processes).[12] They find solutions only under severe restrictions with very little flexibility, and they have special limitations on the kind of alternatives to be considered. Objectives usually must be quantifiable and specific (e.g., profits or costs). Judgment and experience do not factor into mathematical optimization procedures.

Decision Support Systems (DSS)

Decision support systems have seen much development work and visibility in publications in recent years. They promise a new wave of portfolio management tools. A DSS is essentially a mathematical model that allows management's intervention. More formally: "A decision support system is an interactive system that helps people make decisions, use judgment, and work in areas where no one knows exactly how the task should be done in all cases."[13] Compared to mathematical optimization approaches (above), DSSs are much more flexible because they include the decision maker as part of the system. DSSs provide information, models, and/or tools for manipulating data; these systems solve part of the problem and help isolate places where management judgment and experience are required.

Basic DSS concepts, such as interactive problem solving, grew out of dissatisfaction with the limitations of mathematical optimization approaches (MOMs), which were often inflexible and unable to provide the information managers needed. DSS is intended to support managers who are doing largely analytical work in less structured, nonroutine situations with unclear criteria for success. DSS supports general management work by providing flexible, user-controlled methods for displaying and analyzing data and formulating and evaluating alternative decisions.

DSSs rely on statistical methods, simulation, and optimization models to guide management through the decision process. An excellent DSS example is the PASS system (Project Analysis and Support System) developed by Ghasemzadeh and Archer.[14] The optimization model is applied to the portfolio decision and considers resource limitations, timing, balancing criteria, and interconnectedness among projects and then maximizes the total portfolio benefit. Managers then adjust the portfolio to meet their concerns. The model overcomes problems with other systems (unreasonable constraints, lack of flexibility, user unfriendliness). Other DSS examples are cited in the end notes.[15]

For portfolio management applications, DSS methods frequently include mathematical simulation or optimization routines. These methods require considerable detailed analytical understanding and work (data input) on the part of the decision makers. This may explain the limited use of DSS today, since executives typically prefer receiving the results of analyses done by others but rarely spend much time doing analytical work themselves.

Mapping Approaches

Mapping approaches are typically bubble diagrams that display projects on an X-Y plot. They are essentially extensions of the original strategic business unit portfolio models (the Boston Consulting Group model: stars, cash cows, dogs, wildcats; or the GE/McKinsey model). Various parameters are plotted against each other in a bubble diagram format. A typical portfolio map or bubble diagram plots reward from each project against the probability of project success.[16] Bubble diagrams and other more traditional plots display portfolio balance well and are the topic of Chapter 4.

Where Portfolio Management Stands Today

In spite of the many challenges, much progress in portfolio management models has thus been made. Here's where we stand. First experts recognize that no one model gives the right answer. Instead, hybrid approaches are being developed that permit a more tailored approach to portfolio selection. Here are some further thoughts on the models outlined above.

Classical methods, such as scoring and sorting models, have been modified and adapted to become more relevant as portfolio selection aids. Scoring models in particular have been refined and validated over the years and now are seen as effective tools for prioritizing projects. However, while useful for ranking projects on financial, strategic, and other criteria, scoring models often fail to capture concerns about the right balance of projects in the portfolio.

New mapping approaches and bubble diagrams have gained adherents because they greatly simplify the portfolio problem and provide a visual representation of the choices faced. Mapping is perhaps too new for us to be able to assess its impact, but there are already some problems. Mapping projects on a two-dimensional matrix may be a little too simplistic (after all, portfolio management is a complex problem, difficult to boil down to a few maps and a handful of dimensions). The maps that focus on financial rewards have been criticized for being too financially driven, while maps that consider numerous strategic and other qualitative factors are far too numerous for executives to digest.

Mathematical portfolio and project selection models have become more realistic in recent years. Such models are now able to integrate multiple constraints, multiple time periods, different goals and objectives, and other parameters into a single-choice model.

Major Gaps between Theory and Practice

In spite of all the proposed solutions, management has been slow to adopt new and better portfolio management approaches. One of our benchmarking studies points to project selection and project prioritization as the weakest facet of all new product management activities.[17] Management in the 161 business units we studied rated themselves very low on:

- achieving the right balance between the number of active projects and available resources (too many projects)—a poor "proficiency rating" of 51 points out of a possible 100
- undertaking solid ranking and prioritization of projects—an even poorer proficiency rating of only 49 points out of 100.

One result of poor portfolio management is that projects tend to take on lives of their own! In too many companies we investigated, projects moved too far along in the process without being subjected to serious scrutiny. And it was only as these projects approached commercialization that the hard truths were recognized: that the market wasn't quite as large as expected, or that manufacturing costs were higher than anticipated, or any number of other reasons why the project should have been scrapped long ago.

Example: As one executive in a major biotechnology firm observed: "We claim to have a process with lots of screens or gates; we even show our new product process in the shape of a funnel—it's supposed to weed out poor projects along the way. But that's not happening. Once a project receives an initial 'Go' decision, nothing can stop it.... Project reviews aren't Go/Kill decisions; they're progress review meetings! Nothing stops the project."

The lack of tough Go/Kill decision points means too many product failures, resources wasted on the wrong projects, and a lack of focus. The result is too many marginal projects in the pipeline, while the truly deserving projects are starved.

There is a major gulf between theory and practice in portfolio management. While the literature over the past 30 years has outlined many approaches for portfolio management and project selection, there is very little evidence on the actual transfer of these techniques into management practice. It is not surprising to find that companies continue to flounder here. Thus, the question remains: How should companies select the appropriate portfolio of new product investments?

POINTS FOR MANAGEMENT TO PONDER

Does your company have effective new product project selection and portfolio management? Or do you suffer from many of the same ailments we found in our benchmarking studies? Do you have explicit criteria for making Go/Kill and prioritization decisions on projects at various points in the process from idea to launch? Or does your new product process resemble the biotechnology firm cited above, with no projects ever killed once they receive initial approval? If you're uncomfortable about the answers to these questions, then perhaps it's time to find out why: Undertake a retrospective analysis of past projects:

- Identify a number of new product projects undertaken in the past few years in your company.
- Assemble the project teams that worked on each project.
- Have each team map out from beginning to end what happened on the project—from idea to launch.
- Require that they rate the proficiency with which each major activity was done and all the key Go/Kill decision points in the process (pay special attention to the decision points).
- Determine where decision points were substandard, or missed altogether, and find out why.
- Identify where activities or stages were weak, and find out why (for example, poor prioritization, lack of focus, too many projects and not enough time, lack of resources).

Portfolio Management: It's Not So Easy

New product portfolio management sounds like a fairly deliberate exercise of decision making and resource allocation. Why, then, has the goal of an effective portfolio management process been so elusive? One reason is that there are many unique facets of the problem that make it, perhaps, the most challenging decision-making task faced by businesses today.

- Unlike traditional portfolio approaches, which allocate resources across business units (for example, the BCG or GE/McKinsey models), R&D portfolio management focuses on what might be: new opportunities, new products, new ventures. We witnessed some confusion between traditional portfolio methods (the well-known "stars, cash cows, dogs" models) and portfolio models for R&D or new product projects. The confusion is compounded because some of the diagrams, such as bubble diagrams, look much the same for both. But that is where the similarities end! Note that traditional portfolio models focus on existing businesses or BUs and allocate resources across these businesses. They plot well-known metrics such as "business position" versus "market attractiveness"—metrics for which years of data are readily available. By contrast, new product portfolio models plot products that do not even exist yet and allocate resources to these. Because new product portfolio management deals with future events and opportunities—unlike traditional portfolio models—much of the information required to make project selection decisions is at best uncertain and at worst very unreliable. But even with this doubtful information, the resource allocation decisions still must be made!

- The decision-making environment is dynamic. The status of, and prospects for, projects in the portfolio are ever-changing, as results of new studies become known, market or technical tests are completed, and new competitive and market information emerges. What looked like an excellent project just six months ago may suddenly be not so promising. In addition, new opportunities are constantly being discovered that vie for resources with existing projects.

Example: A major Boston telecommunications hardware and software firm undertakes fairly high-risk and exciting projects whose outcomes are often quite uncertain. Projects are commissioned with the full expectation that they will be successful. But some months later, after the market studies are undertaken and the technical appraisals are completed, a very different picture often emerges: The market is smaller than anticipated, pricing is problematic, there are unforeseen and costly technical challenges, and so on. This new information dramatically changes the relative attractiveness of projects and may even result in deprioritization or outright cancellation. The point is that this company's portfolio is in a constant state of flux as the result of new information.

- Projects in the portfolio are at different stages of completion. Some are at the early stages, where little is known about them. Others are approaching commercialization and launch, where forecasts and data are somewhat more reliable. The dilemma is that all projects compete against each other for resources, so that comparisons must be made between projects at different stages, each with information at varying degrees of completeness and reliability.

Example: At one firm, we sat in on a portfolio review meeting in which management was trying to select and prioritize new product projects. Projects under consideration ranged from those well into the development and commercialization stages to projects at the idea stage; some were little more than a gleam in people's eyes. It was an almost impossible task to compare the merits of the ill-defined, early-stage projects with those at later stages. Management quickly discovered that, with differing amounts and quality of information, idea-stage projects cannot be directly compared with or prioritized against later-stage projects. But resources must still be allocated!

- Competition for resources is complicated by the fact that money, people, and time are limited. A decision to fund one project may mean resources must be taken away from another. What complicates the decision even more is that projects are not totally independent of each other. For example, the talents needed to work on one project may also be vital for another. Finally, some resources are not infinitely flexible: Unlike money, people cannot always be immediately transferred between projects in a seamless fashion.
- Projects are interconnected in a new product portfolio. By contrast, in a stock market portfolio, investments are independent of each other. For example, buying Stock A does not make it easier, faster, or cheaper to buy Stock B. Not so in new product portfolio management. Undertaking one project may actually facilitate another—there are synergies between projects. For example, Project A and Project B may share a common component or common technology. Still other projects are linked in a compulsory way: Project C requires Project D to be done first because the output of one project is essential for implementing the next.

Example: At Caterpillar, the heavy equipment manufacturer, the development of a new vehicle often requires development of a number of new components: engine, transmission, drive mechanisms, etc. And these may require development of new subcomponents: The new engine requires new electrical components, for example. Thus a large set of projects and subprojects—each with its own team and leader— are linked together and are interdependent. The decision to kill or delay one affects the rest, and so the decision-making process can become more complex.

- Portfolio management is critically important to the business. At one time, new product project selection and allocation of R&D resources were thought to be "an R&D thing" and were left largely in the hands of the technical community. Not so today, as senior management recognizes that new products are the leading edge of business strategy; in this environment, new product choices are virtually synonymous with strategic choices.

Requirements for Effective Portfolio Management

The lackluster performance of most portfolio approaches, coupled with the reluctance of industry to adopt prescribed methods, has yielded a long list of recommendations about what the ideal portfolio management method should be and do. The literature, while short on practical tried-and-proven solutions, offers many suggestions and insights into portfolio management requirements. Reflect for a moment on some of these requirements, especially as we get set to review the many portfolio methods in use in industry in the next three chapters.

1. *Corporate goals, objectives, and strategies must be the basis for new product (or R&D) portfolio selection.*[18]
   More than ever, the management of technology and R&D is viewed as strongly linked to corporate strategy and a firm's competitive success.[19] This is especially

true for multinational corporations, which face a much broader scope of possible strategic directions. Portfolio management must be congruent with the overall strategy of the business;[20] indeed, it is the embodiment of the strategy! Portfolios in many Japanese firms, for example, tend to stress continual technological improvement (a long-term strategy) aimed at constant product improvement (incrementalism, a major aspect of the R&D effort), which have resulted in positive performance.[21] It cannot be said too often that portfolio analysis and resource allocation must be intimately linked to strategy formulation.[22]

2. *Senior management is the driver of strategy and must be closely involved in new product (or R&D) project selection decisions.*[23]

This is a parallel theme to the first point above. Traditionally, senior management has been involved in R&D to the extent of periodically reviewing research programs, projects, and staff to assess progress and determine the contribution that each makes to the corporate goal.[24] Today, however, there is a *need to go beyond this*, given that technology and strategy are inseparable.[25] Thus, the organizational context in which R&D project selection and resource allocation occurs must be considered in developing appropriate project selection methods.[26] This means that the cooperation and active involvement of top management, who direct the long-term strategy, are essential if R&D efforts are to be properly focused. This implies that a commitment, both in terms of time and actions, is needed.[27]

3. *Good communication and understanding must exist between senior corporate management and R&D management.*[28]

One problem with the adoption of some of the more sophisticated and quantitative portfolio models is the gulf between R&D management and senior corporate management. Senior executives often lack a strong research background, while R&D personnel lack the skills to communicate with senior executives in an understandable and credible fashion. This communication gap mandates a portfolio selection method that not only effectively selects projects, but also manages R&D programs and projects and their communication to top management.[29] Senior personnel must have consensus on key issues (for example, new product goals or project priorities)—something that is often lacking—and ensure that this common position is understood lower down in the firm.[30]

4. *Portfolio methods must mesh with the decision framework of the business.*[31]

The organizational context in which new product or R&D project selection and resource allocation occurs is a fundamental consideration in the development of appropriate decision methods.[32] For example, there is growing recognition that project selection tools should be used to ask questions of the entire organization. "Picking the right projects" is a meaningless exercise unless the whole organization is involved and emotionally committed to the final set of selected projects.[33] For large multinational corporations, the problem is even more complex. Here portfolio decisions must be made seeking buy-in from multiple business units, across geographic boundaries, and at the corporate level.[34] One way to involve senior management in the decision process is by integrating selection models into interactive decision support systems.[35]

5. *Portfolio methods should be used for information display only and not yield an optimization decision.*[36]

This conclusion almost flies in the face of logic. In the early days, the assumption was that management wanted the portfolio model to yield a decision recommendation (for example, a prioritized list of the right projects). The fact is that managers are less interested in the final result of the method than in the process itself. The value for them is in systematically stepping through each project and assessing its status and how it fits with the corporate strategy and objectives.[37] For example, a risk-reward (or risk-return) map or matrix, often obtained via highly subjective methods, does not yield an optimum solution or even an analytical tool to arrive at a solution. But it is recommended as an effective tool and guideline for managers— a visual representation of the entire set of possible projects—for use throughout the whole process of portfolio selection.[38] Other recommended approaches, which combine optimization methods with management interaction and intervention, are DSS models, described above.[39] Yet another recommended approach is fuzzy modeling, whose flexibility permits switching from maximizing behavior to satisfying behavior with respect to some or all goals.[40] This method permits the manager to investigate, in an interactive fashion, different scenarios in response to various new product aspirations.

6. *The selection method must accommodate change and the interaction of goals and players.*[41]

Portfolio methods must be able to deal simultaneously with resource interaction, benefit interaction, and outcome interaction among and between projects. To date, no operational model has been proposed that can do all three.[42] Further, the system must be flexible. It must adapt to the reality that goals, requirements, and project characteristics change during the lifetime of projects.[43] For example, if the manager modifies his or her aspirations, the system must adjust and compute a new compromise solution.[44] Finally, the system must enable managers to plan how the active project list evolves over time: which new projects are added to the list, when, and what role each should play in the total portfolio.[45]

7. *The portfolio selection method must accommodate decision making at different levels in the organization.*[46]

Project selection decisions are made at different levels in major corporations. Some projects conducted within business units are independent or stand-alone efforts; others, such as platform programs or cross-SBU projects, involve several business units or divisions, and so subprojects within each business unit are highly interdependent. Clearly, the selection approach must be able to handle both types.[47] The choice of project selection methods must also consider the organization structure and the nature of the decision-making process used for these various types of projects.[48]

8. *Risk must be accommodated by the selection technique.*[49]

One facet of strategy is deciding on the acceptable risk level within a chosen portfolio and then finding ways to minimize (or manage) it.[50] Therefore, risk, uncertainties, and probabilities of success must be somehow built into the portfolio model and be visible in the project selection process.[51] Another way of handling risk is via diversity, and so diversity or portfolio balance must also be a consideration.

9. *Organizational structure and appropriate support systems are required.*[52]

A solid organizational support structure is needed to enhance internal communications.[53] Increasing awareness and standardized portfolio procedures can be achieved by leveraging internal support systems. Information management (as a process to connect all players, share knowledge—both formally and informally—and share the results) goes a long way in helping management to create buy-in and understanding of the goals they are trying to achieve in portfolio management.

What the Leaders Do:
Three Goals in Portfolio Management

While the portfolio methods vary greatly from company to company, the common denominators across firms are the goals management is trying to achieve. One or more of three high-level or macro goals dominate the thinking of each firm we studied, either implicitly or explicitly. The goal most emphasized by the firm seems to influence the choice of portfolio method. The three broad goals are:

1. *Maximization of Value*: To most firms, the principal goal is to allocate resources so as to maximize the value of the portfolio in terms of a major company objective (e.g., long-term profitability, return on investment, or likelihood of success). This is an admirable goal, at least in theory; but in practice, how does one place a value or economic worth on a portfolio of projects that are still underway and may never become commercial successes?

Example: One major U.S. consumer goods firm uses a relatively simple financial index to rate, rank, and prioritize new product projects: NPV/investment. This is the ratio of the project's NPV to the total investment remaining in the project (R&D, capital, and launch costs). The finance person in product development was quick to point out that this method of trying to maximize the portfolio's value is fraught with deficiencies, but at least it did place some of the obvious higher-value projects at the top of the list. These maximization of value methods are discussed in more detail in Chapter 3.

---

2. *Balance:* Here the main concern is to develop a balanced portfolio—to achieve a desired balance of projects in terms of a number of parameters. For example, the right balance in terms of:

   - long-term projects versus short, fast ones
   - high-risk long shots versus lower-risk sure bets
   - the various markets the business is in (don't target all resources at one market)
   - different technologies or technology types (for example, embryonic, pacing, base)

- different project types: new products, improvements, cost reductions, fundamental research.

Portfolio methods aimed at securing the right balance of projects are the topic of Chapter 4.

Example: One SBU at Mobil Chemical uses four categories* of development projects:

- Type I: cost reductions and process improvements
- Type II: product improvements, product modifications (visible to the customer), and customer satisfaction projects (product changes in response to customer requests)
- Type III: new products
- Type IV: new platform projects and fundamental/breakthrough research projects.

Two additional categories of work are also identified: plant support and technical support for customers. Senior management in this business unit reviews the spending split across these six types (what is) and compares this to the target breakdown (what should be).

---

3. *Strategic Alignment*: The main focus here is to ensure that, regardless of all other considerations, the final portfolio of projects is strategically aligned and truly reflects the business's strategy. Chapter 5 highlights these strategically oriented portfolio methods.

Example: The Privat division of Telenor, Norway's national telephone company, sells a multitude of products in many market segments. In order to help direct the division's new product portfolio, the new product strategy was developed first. This included a product/market matrix, identifying many possible strategic arenas on which to focus new product efforts. These arenas were prioritized using traditional planning and portfolio techniques. Some arenas, such as Internet services to the small office/home office (SoHo) segment, were accorded top priority.

The company also employs a Stage-Gate new product process, with gates acting as Go/Kill decision points. Important criteria at these gates include "strategic alignment" and "strategic importance." As a result, new product projects that are targeted at the Internet/SoHo arena score more points; hence, they have a higher likelihood of passing each gate and are also prioritized higher on the active list. Periodically, management also conducts a portfolio review to ensure that spending across projects reflects strategic priorities (for example, that the funding for projects within the Internet/SoHo arena adds up to a substantial proportion of total project funding). Although some of these processes are quite new at Telenor, over time the new product project portfolio is slowly achieving strategic alignment.

---

* Slightly disguised project categories.

What becomes clear is the potential for conflict among these three high-level goals. For example, the portfolio that yields the greatest NPV or ROI may not be a very balanced one. It may contain a majority of short-term, low-risk projects, or it may be overly focused on one market. Similarly, a portfolio that is primarily strategic in nature may sacrifice other goals, such as likelihood of success. What also became clear in our interviews with companies is that, although executives did not explicitly state that one of the goals took precedence over the other two, the nature of the portfolio management tool elected by that firm certainly indicated a hierarchy of goals. This is because certain portfolio approaches are much more applicable to some goals than to others. For example, the visual models (such as maps or bubble diagrams) are most amenable to achieving a balance of projects (visual charts being an excellent way of demonstrating balance); scoring models tended to be very poor for achieving or even showing balance but are most effective if the goal is maximization of value against an objective. Thus, the choice of the "right" portfolio method depended on the goal upon which management had explicitly or implicitly focused.

POINTS FOR MANAGEMENT TO PONDER

How does your current portfolio of new product or R&D projects rate against these three goals?

1. maximization of value
2. balance
3. strategic alignment

Has your business consciously considered its goals for the new product portfolio? What methods have been adopted to achieve these goals?

CHAPTER 3

Portfolio Management Methods: Maximizing the Value of the Portfolio

Goal 1: Maximizing the Value of the Portfolio

The first goal of most firms we studied was to maximize the value of the portfolio of projects against one or more business objectives (such as profitability, strategy, acceptable risk, and so on). A variety of methods are used to achieve this maximization goal, ranging from financial methods to scoring models. Each has its strengths and weaknesses.

The end result of each maximization method in this chapter is a rank-ordered list of projects. The projects at the top of the list score highest in terms of achieving the desired objective(s). Projects are typically ranked on this list until resources run out. Using these approaches, the value of the portfolio against that objective is maximized for a given resource expenditure—at least in theory.

This sounds easy, but there are many challenges. One challenge, of course, is determining a consistent, valid, and reliable method for valuation of projects: If one cannot figure out the value or economic worth of each project, then it is difficult to speak about maximizing the value of the entire portfolio. A second and related challenge is to arrive at the appropriate criteria and method for rating and ranking the projects. This chapter provides the approaches.

Throughout this chapter, we refer to two decision processes: project Go/Kill decisions, or gate decisions (here the focus is on individual projects), and portfolio reviews (where the entire portfolio of projects is considered—all projects together). There is an important distinction between the two that is sometimes missed.

Using Net Present Value to Get Bang for Buck

Perhaps the most straightforward value maximization tool to use is the Net Present Value (NPV) of each project as the decision criterion. After all, most firms'

new product processes require the calculation of the NPV, certainly as part of
the development of the business case. Usually this calculation takes place just
before the project enters the heavy-spending stage, namely development (that is
at Gate 3, perhaps even as early as Gate 2 in our standard Stage-Gate™ model in
Appendix A). The timing of the NPV calculation is indeed convenient, because
that is just about the time resource expenditures on projects are significant
enough to require portfolio management to kick in. Up to this point in the life of
the project, resource requirements have been quite low; hence resource allocation and portfolio management are not burning issues.

The use of the NPV at gate decision points is quite a well-known procedure.
The project's NPV along with its sister calculation, the IRR (internal rate of return), are compared to cutoff criteria in order to make the Go/Kill decision. Usually the criteria are that the NPV must be positive and the IRR must be greater
than a risk-adjusted hurdle.

In portfolio reviews, however, where all projects are considered together and
against each other, the procedure is a little more complex. The NPV of each
project is displayed, along with the resource requirements (see Exhibit 3.1). Any
projects with poor NPVs are flagged and removed from the list. Resource requirements in Exhibit 3.1 are defined in terms of dollars or person-day amounts.
These may be expressed in terms of the most critical or most important resource, often R&D dollars or R&D person-days per project. And resources are
defined for the entire project as well as for the next allocation time period. Both
are important.

The goal is to maximize the total NPV or economic value of the entire portfolio, subject to a resource constraint. If resources were unlimited, the decision rule
would be simple: Do all projects whose NPVs are positive. Add these NPVs up,
and that is the economic value of the entire portfolio. It is also the maximum possible value of the portfolio.

But resources are always constrained. Let us assume that the constraining resource is R&D dollars—that there is a fixed R&D quarterly budget available for
new and improved product development.* Exhibit 3.1 lists the projects under
consideration (column 1) along with their NPVs (column 2) and their total resource requirements (R&D dollars remaining to be spent on the project in column 3). In addition, the immediate resource requirements for the project are
shown in column 5—in this case, the R&D dollars required for each project for
the quarter, assuming a Go decision.

How does one maximize the value of the portfolio? The problem is that some
projects—for example Oven Fresh with Ammonia in Exhibit 3.1—are great projects and have huge NPVs, but they consume a lot of resources, making it impossible to do other less attractive but far more efficient projects—they have lower

---

*Note that we use a quarterly budget figure here. For most businesses, especially fast-paced ones,
the traditional annual budget or one-year time frame is too long for resource allocation decisions
and project choices. In spite of this, we saw considerable evidence of firms attempting to allocate
the entire annual budget to specific projects; that is, to plan the portfolio for the entire year.

1 Project Name	2 NPV ($M)	3 Resource Requirements Remaining ($M)	4 Bang-for- Buck Index	5 Immediate Resource Requirements (Next Quarter)
Instant Oven Fresh	52.0	9.5	5.5	3.2
New Tidalwave	30.0	3.1	9.7	0.3
Dishwasher Soap 4	8.6	2.1	4.1	1.4
Bathtub Supreme Care	42.0	3.8	11.1	2.5
Counter Top Finish	48.5	7.0	6.9	1.3
Improved Kitchen Cleaner	43.8	5.0	8.8	1.5
Wrench Soap for Men	37.5	8.3	4.5	3.8
Better Air Freshener	3.0	1.0	3.0	0.7
Car Wax with Lemon	9.5	2.5	3.8	0.5
Spray & Rinse Car Wash	6.2	0.8	7.8	0.8
Fresh House	4.5	1.4	3.2	1.2
Oven Fresh with Ammonia	55.0	5.0	11.0	5.0

EXHIBIT 3.1   Listing of Projects, NPVs, and Resource Needs

NPVs but can be done using relatively few resources. How does one decide? It's simple: The goal is to maximize the bang for buck. The way to do this is to take the ratio of the item one is trying to maximize (in this case, the NPV) divided by the constraining resource (the R&D dollars required) to determine the bang for buck. The Bang-for-Buck Ratio, or Index, is shown in column 4.

$$\text{Bang for Buck Index} = \frac{\text{NPV of the project}}{\text{Total resources remaining to be spent on the project}}$$

Now it is time to sort the list of projects again. But first consider the constraint: Let us assume an R&D spending constraint of $15 million for the quarter for new products. Now, simply reorder the project list, ranking projects according to the Bang-for-Buck Index (See Exhibit 3.2). Then go down the list until resources for that quarter are exhausted. Note that column 6 shows the cumulative resource expenditure for the quarter. Resources run out after project Instant Oven Fresh.

A horizontal line is drawn at the point where the resource capacity is reached. Projects above the line are designated "Go," or active projects; those below the line are "on hold"—good projects, but with no resources. Note that killed projects have previously been removed from the list. The end result is a first cut at a portfolio listing of projects—one that promises to yield the maximum economic return, measured by NPV, for a limited set of resources. We note that this is a "first cut" because there may be other considerations, such as strategic issues or project balance, that may result in adjustments to the list of active projects.

1 Project Name	2 NPV ($M)	3 Resource Requirements Remaining ($M)	4 Bang-for-Buck Index	5 Immediate Resource Requirements (Next Quarter)	6 Cumulative Immediate Resource Requirements ($15 M)
Bathtub Supreme Care	42	3.8	11.1	2.5	2.5
Oven Fresh with Ammonia	55	5.0	11.0	5.0	7.5
New Tidalwave	30	3.1	9.7	0.3	7.8
Improved Kitchen Cleaner	43.8	5.0	8.8	1.5	9.3
Spray & Rinse Car Wash	6.2	0.8	7.8	0.8	10.1
Counter Top Finish	48.5	7.0	6.9	1.3	11.4
Instant Oven Fresh	52	9.5	5.5	3.2	14.6
Wrench Soap for Men	37.5	8.3	4.5	3.8	18.4
Dishwasher Soap 4	8.6	2.1	4.1	1.4	19.8
Car Wash with Lemon	9.5	2.5	3.8	0.5	20.3
Fresh House	4.5	1.4	3.2	1.2	21.5
Better Air Freshener	3.0	1.0	3.0	0.7	22.2

EXHIBIT 3.2   Rank-Ordered List of Projects

($15 Million R&D Spending Constraint)

Some important notes and caveats in this exercise:

- The time frame of resource requirements is always problematic. Note that the total resource requirements for each project must be considered (which might include expenditures over several years), as well as the immediate resource requirement (for the next time period). One is trying to juggle both—get the biggest return from total resources spent over the lives of projects, as well as maximizing productivity from resources spent in the next quarter. Note that if only the immediate resources were used in Exhibits 3.1 and 3.2, the resulting rank-ordered list would be different; and the same is true if only the total resources required per project were considered.

- The problem of which resources to consider is an issue. Some firms consider all resources: typically R&D, marketing and launch, and capital. In other firms, capital requirements for projects are usually minimal, so R&D and, perhaps, marketing person-days or dollars become the definition of resources. Some companies admit that when it comes to people, only R&D resources are measurable. Finally, it is possible to use one resource measure for immediate resources (such as R&D person-days required per project) and another measure for the total resources over the project's life (perhaps the total dollar cost of the project remaining to be spent).

- Another important subtlety of the value maximization method is that only resources yet to be spent on projects are considered. Money already spent on the project—sunk costs—is irrelevant to the decision to move ahead. As in any financially based decision, the question of which costs to consider in the calculation depends on what decision is being made. Here the decision is Go/Kill; thus, only resources yet to be spent should be considered. The fact that you may have already sunk a million dollars into the project is not an input to the decision (other than a political or psychological consideration). In contrast, if the exercise were an analysis of past projects to see which ones were profitable, then clearly the total costs—beginning to end costs—of each project must be considered.

- A thorny issue is: "What about projects that are already well underway—perhaps halfway through development? Won't this method potentially kill these, and thus many projects will never get completed?" This is a concern, and it is exacerbated by the fact that projects often look better at the beginning of development than they do partway through. Taken to an extreme, this decision model might result in no project ever getting through development—resources would always be taken from mature projects to fund the more promising new projects! And nothing would get to market.

   This dilemma is handled in two ways. First, the bang-for-buck approach considers only resources remaining to be spent. Thus, projects that are halfway completed usually have less money remaining to be spent on them. So the denominator in the Bang-for-Buck Index is smaller for mature projects, thus favoring them. Of course partially completed projects merit funding, but only as long as they remain good projects. A second solution is to identify the "must do" projects as the portfolio review begins—projects that are far along and whose business cases remain sound. Then remove these projects and their immediate resource needs from consideration. In effect, these projects move to the top of the list in Exhibit 3.2.

- A final issue concerns launch timing. When NPVs are calculated on a spreadsheet, year 1 is typically the first year on the market, while all development and investment takes place in Year 0. Not true! The clock is ticking right now. If the project will take three years to get to market, determine the NPV back to today, not just to launch date. This more realistic approach will penalize projects that are years away from launch—and rightly so.

This NPV and bang-for-buck approach has many adherents, and we saw a number of firms using this method or a variant of it. It has many positive points. First, the method requires that all significant projects in the portfolio have an NPV calculation undertaken. We are always surprised by how difficult it is to get NPV values on all projects, especially when each project is supposed to have had a business case already prepared. Invariably many of the projects somehow slipped into the process without tough financial analysis undertaken. So the method brings about some consistency, discipline, and rigor to the process.

Second, the method requires that the project team face financial realities before their project becomes a major development initiative. This means they must seek market size and market acceptance information, debate pricing issues, and determine costs and capital requirements. This exercise in itself may be a great leap forward in many companies.

Third, the bang-for-buck approach will yield an economically attractive portfolio of projects. In theory, it should, indeed, maximize the value of your portfolio. An added benefit is that the method recognizes that some projects are more efficient than others and it takes into consideration the ratio of bang to buck (not just the NPV numerator).

The NPV method has a number of other tactical advantages:

- It considers the time value of money.
- Projects that are years away from launch are penalized.
- Projects that are halfway through development are favored, all other things being equal.
- The method considers immediate resource requirements (e.g., next quarter's) as well as the total resources required for each project.

Alas, the world is not a perfect place, and neither is the NPV and bang-for-buck approach. The biggest drawback is that the method relies exclusively on financial analysis, which is only as good as the data input. And financial estimates for new product projects, especially in the earlier stages of development, are notoriously inaccurate. See more on this major deficiency in "The Dark Side of the Financial Approaches to Project Evaluation" later in this chapter. A second deficiency is that the method assumes only financial goals. Admittedly financial goals are usually very important. But there may be other considerations, such as strategic fit and seeking the right balance of projects. Finally, an important input to the calculation is resource estimates—both immediate ones and those remaining to be spent during each project. These, too, are typically inaccurate. Project teams seem to have great difficulty making reliable estimates of the resource requirements—dollars and person-days—needed to complete the project or even a stage in the project.

POINTS FOR MANAGEMENT TO PONDER

Is your company financially oriented? If it is, you will be able to check off these points:

- good financial data and profitability estimates are available fairly early in the life of a project
- there is a major constraining resource.

If you checked these points, then the NPV and bang-for-buck method has merits for your company. In spite of deficiencies, NPV and bang for buck are a good place to start if you have no other effective means for ranking projects.

Expected Commercial Value

The Expected Commercial Value (ECV) method seeks to maximize the *expected* value, or *expected* commercial worth, of the portfolio, subject to certain budget constraints. The key word here is *expected*. One weakness of the NPV and bang-for-buck method above is that it fails to consider risk. Probabilities of technical and commercial success are simply not factored into the model.

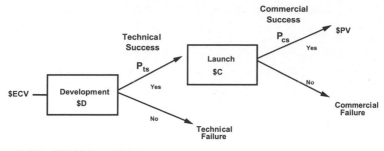

$$ECV = [(PV * P_{cs} - C) * P_{ts}] - D$$

ECV = Expected Commercial Value of the project
P_{ts} = Probability of Technical Success
P_{cs} = Probability of Commercial Success (given technical success)
D = Development Costs remaining in the project
C = Commercialization (Launch) Costs
PV = Net Present Value of project's future earnings (discounted to today)

EXHIBIT 3.3   Determination of Expected Commercial Value of Project
ECC uses a slightly modified version of this exhibit.

Expected Commercial Value

The Expected Commercial Value (ECV) method seeks to maximize the *expected* value, or *expected* commercial worth, of the portfolio, subject to certain budget constraints. The key word here is *expected.* One weakness of the NPV and bang-for-buck method above is that it fails to consider risk. Probabilities of technical and commercial success are simply not factored into the model.

The ECV method overcomes this weakness and is one of the better thought out financial models we have seen. It is an extension of the NPV and bang-for-buck method but features several new twists that make it particularly appropriate to portfolio management. We found it in use at English China Clay:

Example: English China Clay, plc (ECC), is the world's largest producer of clay and clay-related products. U.S. operations are headquartered in Atlanta, Georgia. Clay products have myriad markets and applications, including fine paper (clay is what makes paper white and bright) and extenders and fillers for plastics, paints, and other materials.

In the ECV method, English China Clay determines the value or commercial worth of each project to the corporation, namely, its expected commercial value. This approach is based on a decision tree as shown in Exhibit 3.3; it considers the future stream of earnings from the project and the probabilities of both commercial and technical success, along with both commercialization and development costs. ECC's version of the ECV method also incorporates the strategic importance of the project, a feature the company added to the general ECV model in Exhibit 3.3.

Project Name	PV	Probability of Technical Sucess	Probability of Commercial Sucess	Development Cost*	Commercial-ization Cost*	ECV
Alpha	30	0.80	0.50	3	5	5.0
Beta	63.75	0.50	0.80	5	2	19.5
Gamma	8.62	0.75	0.75	2	1	2.1
Delta	3	1.00	1.00	1	0.5	1.5
Echo	50	0.60	0.75	5	3	15.7
Foxtrot	66.25	0.50	0.80	10	2	15.5

* Development cost (or Commercialization cost) remaining in project.

EXHIBIT 3.4   ECC's Determination of Expected Commercial Value

- But this PV income stream assumes commercial success, which is not 100 percent. Therefore it must be multiplied by the probability of commercial success, P_{cs}. So the ECV is now $PV \times P_{cs}$.
- But to get to market, the firm must commercialize the project (represented by the launch box in the exhibit). The firm must spend C dollars on commercialization costs—perhaps capital and market roll-out costs. The ECV is now $(PV \times P_{cs}) - C$.
- But before commercialization can occur, the product must be a technical success— the development effort must yield the right product at an appropriate cost. Thus the ECV value above must be multiplied by the probability of technical success, P_{ts}. The ECV equation is now $[(PV \times P_{cs}) - C] \times P_{ts}$.
- But to get to a technical success, the firm must spend money on development, designated by the development box or development stage in the exhibit. Development costs D dollars, and so the ECV must be reduced by that amount. Based on this decision tree analysis in Exhibit 3.3, the resulting formula for the ECV is:

$$ECV = [(PV \times P_{cs} - C) \times P_{ts}] - D$$

where

$$
\begin{aligned}
&ECV &&= \text{the expected commercial value of the project} \\
&PV &&= \text{the present value of the cash flow, after launch (none of the} \\
& && \quad \text{project costs—development, capital, and so on—have been} \\
& && \quad \text{subtracted from this stream; this PV is strictly the income} \\
& && \quad \text{stream)} \\
&P_{cs} &&= \text{the probability of commercial success (a number from} \\
& && \quad \text{0 to 1.0)} \\
&C &&= \text{commercialization or launch costs remaining to be spent on} \\
& && \quad \text{the project (capital costs, customer trials, marketing costs, etc.)} \\
&P_{ts} &&= \text{the probability of technical success (again a number from} \\
& && \quad \text{0 to 1.0)} \\
&D &&= \text{development costs remaining to be spent.}
\end{aligned}
$$

Note that the illustration in Exhibit 3.3 is based on a convenient two-stage model. You may choose a three- or a four-stage model, with each stage having its own costs and probabilities of success. For example, an extra stage may be validation, with the likelihood of success of the beta tests or field trials being the relevant risk and probability.

A sample calculation is given in Exhibit 3.4, with disguised projects from the company. Note how different the ECV is from the simple NPV; for example, Project Alpha's PV is $30 million; after subtracting development and commercialization costs, its value or NPV becomes $22 million. Thus, at first glance, one might be tempted to place a commercial worth of $22 million on Project Alpha. But not so, according to the ECV method: the real value of the project is only $5 million—a major difference from the $22 million! The point is that merely rating or ranking projects according to NPV could be very misleading.

Our illustration company, ECC, adds a new twist by introducing the strategic importance of the project. They simply adjust the PV by multiplying it by a Strategic Importance Index (SI):

SI = Strategic Importance Index, which has three levels, depending on the strategic importance of the project (high, medium, low = 3, 2, 1).

This is ECC's way of recognizing that strategic considerations as well as financial value are important, and that a project's strategic value can enhance its overall value to the company.

In order to arrive at a prioritized list of projects, ECC incorporates elements of the bang-for-buck approach and considers resource constraints. In their case, capital is thought to be the constraining resource (note that many of ECC's projects are very capital-intensive; some, for example, require new plant equipment). Other companies may choose to use R&D personnel or work-months, or R&D funds, as the constraining resource, as in Exhibit 3.3. Most firms have a finite annual R&D budget and a finite number of people. In the example borrowed but disguised from ECC, we have used R&D dollars as the constraint and have set a budget of $15 million as a dummy figure.*

ECC then takes the ratio of what it is trying to maximize (the ECV) divided by the constraining resource (the annual R&D spending proposed per project). Projects are rank-ordered according to this ratio, thereby ensuring the greatest bang for buck; that is, the ECV is maximized for a given R&D budget. Exhibit 3.5 shows the final prioritized list, with a horizontal line noting the point where the budget of $15 million is exceeded. Projects above the line are considered "active and in the portfolio"; those below the line are placed on hold.

Note that had ECC's projects simply been rank-ordered according to the ECV alone (rather than the ECV/R&D ratio), the prioritized list would have been quite different. And, most important, the value of the total portfolio would have been inferior: that is, the resulting project list would have yielded a lower total ECV value for a given R&D budget!

---

*The company uses exactly the same routine to maximize the portfolio's value, except with capital as the constraint.

Project Name	ECV	Development Cost (Dev)	ECV/Dev	Sum of Dev
Beta	19.5	5	3.90	5.0
Echo	15.7	5	3.14	10.0
Alpha	5.0	3	1.67	13.0
Foxtrot	15.5	10	1.55	(23.0)
Delta	1.5	1	1.50	14
Gamma	2.1	2	1.05	15

EXHIBIT 3.5   ECC's Rank-Ordered List According to ECV/Dev

(Total Development Budget of $15 Million)
Criterion: Ratio of what you are trying to maximize divided by constraining resource (yields maximum "bang for buck").

This ECV model has a number of attractive features. It boasts all of the advantages of the NPV and bang-for-buck method described earlier:

- It introduces discipline and financial rigor.
- It does not consider sunk costs—only remaining costs count.
- It considers the time value of money and starts the clock ticking right away.
- It recognizes constrained resources and attempts to maximize the value of the portfolio in light of this constraint.
- It yields the maximum value portfolio.

But the greatest advantage is that the ECV method considers risks and probabilities—both commercial and technical—which the usual NPV and spreadsheet calculations do not. For most firms and for most significant projects, the probabilities of success are less than 100 percent. Ignoring this fact, as traditional NPV approaches do, tends to overvalue projects and hence overvalue the entire portfolio. And the differences are often large. Note the huge differences between the traditional NPV numbers and the EVCs for the same projects in Exhibit 3.4.

A second major, but more obscure, benefit is that because this method is based on a decision-tree approach, it recognizes that if a project is halted partway through, certain expenses are not incurred, and that the Go/Kill decision process is a stepwise or incremental one. In other words, it recognizes the options nature of investing in projects—that projects are "purchased" a piece at a time. For example, the simplistic route adopted by some—multiplying the NPV of a project by its probability of success—fails to capture this subtlety. The latter method distorts the value of projects, and in particular, overpenalizes projects with high capital or commercialization costs and low probability of technical success. Even

Monte Carlo simulation methods miss the options nature of the decision-making process. The ECV method recognizes that management has Go/Kill options along the way; that these options reduce the risk of a project; and that the "correct valuation" of a project should be via a decision-tree approach, as in Exhibit 3.3 (see the section entitled "Options Pricing Theory").

A final positive feature is that the model, as ECC employed it, introduced a Strategic Importance Index. As a result, although largely financially based, the ECV as modified does consider the strategic importance of projects.

A careful review of the equation in Exhibit 3.3 and the rank-ordering models in Exhibit 3.4 and 3.5 reveals that certain types of projects will be appropriately favored by this ECV model. Projects that will be prioritized more highly:

- are closer to launch
- have relatively little left to be spent on them
- have higher likelihoods of success (commercial and technical)
- have higher streams of earnings
- utilize less of the constraining resource.*

The major weakness of the method is the dependency on financial and other quantitative data. For example, accurate data on all projects' future streams of earnings, on their probable commercialization (and capital) expenditures, development costs, and probabilities of success must be available. Often these estimates are unreliable, leading to doubts about the validity of the ranking method. Or these estimates are simply not available early in the life of a project; hence, the method can only be used for projects past a certain point in the process (for example, after a full financial business case has been developed).

A second weakness is the treatment of probabilities. How does one quantitatively estimate probabilities of success? This amounted to little more than pulling numbers out of the air in some companies; yet, the impacts that these probability estimates have on the valuation of projects is high. These probability numbers are, in effect, multiplied by each other and then multiplied by the PV or NPV of projects. Modest errors in probability estimates can produce huge errors in project valuation figures! One seasoned executive took great exception to multiplying two very uncertain probability figures together, noting that it results in a very inaccurate, often small number: "This will always unfairly punish the more venturesome projects!"

A third weakness is that the method does not look at the balance of the portfolio—at whether the portfolio has the right balance between high- and low-risk projects, or across markets and technologies. A final weakness is that the method considers only a single criterion—the ECV—for maximization (although, admittedly, the ECV comprises a number of parameters).

---

* In ECC's case, projects with smaller R&D annual costs and lower capital requirements. But this could be any constraining resource, such as person-days or months, as explained in the bang-for-buck approach earlier.

The first two weaknesses above—the need for accurate financial estimates, and the need for estimated commercial and technical success probabilities—are important and problematic issues. We devote Chapter 8 to the challenge of obtaining more reliable estimates as inputs to these models.

The Productivity Index (PI)

The Productivity Index (PI) is a variant of the ECV method described above in that it considers risks and probabilities of projects; thus, it shares many of the ECV's strengths and weaknesses. The PI also tries to maximize the financial or economic value of the portfolio for a given resource constraint. We saw the method in a medical products firm in the United States and a nuclear firm in the United Kingdom. The method has been popularized by Strategic Decision Group (SDG).[1]

The Productivity Index is

$$PI = [ECV \times P_{ts} - R\&D] / R\&D$$

where

ECV	=	the expected commercial value of the project (adjusted for commercial risk)
P_{ts}	=	the probability of technical success
R&D	=	the R&D costs remaining in the project.

Note that this ECV is quite a different number from the ECV presented in the previous section. Here the ECV of the project is simply the NPV adjusted for commercial risk only. More specifically, the authors define this ECV as the probability-weighted stream of cash flows from the project, discounted to the present. This ECV assumes technical success and must be multiplied by P_{ts}, the probability of technical success. And similar to the bang-for-buck approach,

R&D is the R&D expenditure remaining in the project (note that R&D funds already spent on the project are sunk costs and hence are not relevant to the decision). Projects are rank-ordered according to this index in order to arrive at the preferred portfolio.

Example: In a U.K. nuclear firm, each project has its Productivity Index calculated according to the above formula. The projects are then rank-ordered on a list, those with the highest PIs at the top. Lower-ranked active projects are flagged for immediate review. Several projects with lower PIs had already been canceled within months of implementation of the method.

Example: A major U.S. consumer goods firm uses a variant of the Productivity Index. Here the denominator, instead of being only R&D costs, includes all investment remaining in the project (R&D, capital, and launch costs). While considered a sound technique for driving obvious high-value projects to the top of the list, management is concerned that dramatic breakthroughs with uncertain estimates will not score well using this method. According to one senior executive, one of the firm's major success stories in the hair care field would likely never have made it through to development had this Productivity Index been rigorously applied.

In order to calculate the Productivity Index, the probability-weighted cash flow of each project (the ECV) is required. This can be determined in one of several ways. The simplest way is to multiply or weight the possible financial outcomes of the project (the cash flows, present-valued) by their respective probabilities of occurring. A more elegant approach is to employ a Monte Carlo simulation, which generates multiple random financial scenarios for the project.

POINTS FOR MANAGEMENT TO PONDER

Have you determined the economic value or worth of your new product or R&D portfolio? Most senior executives have a fairly good idea of how much they have spent on the portfolio over the past few years, but ironically they have very little idea of its current value. An analogy would be stock market portfolio managers knowing how much they paid for the shares they own, but having no idea of their current value. We'd fire them!

Many businesses are guilty of a similar crime: They have no idea what the economic value of their portfolio of projects is. If your company is one of these, perhaps it is time to undertake this task now. Assess the economic worth of each project in the portfolio, using the NPV and bang-for-buck approach (Exhibits 3.1 and 3.2) or the ECV method (Exhibits 3.3 and 3.4), or the probability-weighted NPV seen in the PI method above. Then add up the valuations of the projects. You may be shocked at the worth of your portfolio versus what you've spent to get there!

A variety of other techniques is employed for building risk and uncertainty into NPV calculations (more on this topic in the next chapter).

Options Pricing Theory (OPT)

In recent years, some financial experts have recognized that the assumptions underlying discounted cash flow analysis (DCF), including NPV and IRR, are invalid in the case of new product investments. The net result is that NPV analysis *unfairly penalizes* certain types of projects, particularly risky ones, and by a considerable amount. Here's why.

In a DCF or NPV analysis, the assumption is that the project is an "all or nothing" investment decision—a single and irreversible expenditure decision. In reality, however, investments in new product projects are made in increments: that is, management faces a series of Go/Kill decisions along the way. As new information becomes available during the course of the project, decisions are made to invest more or to halt the project. This is the basis for the stages and gates of the Stage-Gate process described in Appendix A.[2]

These Go/Kill options, of course, reduce the risk of the project versus the "all or nothing" approach. In effect, management is able to purchase options on the project, rather than investing all its money at the outset. As in the stock market, the ability to purchase options reduces risk. And the risk-reducing nature of the incremental decision process has monetary value that is ignored in traditional NPV calculations. Put more formally, when DCF is used, this lost option value is an opportunity cost that should be incorporated when the investment is analyzed.[3]

By contrast, options pricing theory (OPT), or the real options method, recognizes that management can kill a project after each incremental investment is made. OPT is, thus, claimed to be the correct valuation method, and a number of pundits have argued that NPV or DCF is "misused." Senior management at Eastman Kodak go further and state "the use of options pricing theory concepts brings valuable insights into the R&D valuation process" and "an options approach often yields a substantially higher valuation than a traditional DCF approach."[4] We have done a number of simulations comparing the results of the options pricing approach to results obtained with NPV and conclude that the Kodak view is correct: When the project is high-risk one—that is, when the probability of technical or commercial success is low and the costs to undertake the project are high (as is often the case in a breakthrough project)—then the DCF and NPV considerably understate the true value of the project. This means that a company will tend to kill otherwise valuable projects if it uses traditional NPV!

Details of the theory and computation of options pricing theory are fairly complex and beyond the scope of this book. Fortunately, one can come very close to an OPT valuation by simply structuring the decision problem in the form of a decision tree, as in the ECV method and Exhibit 3.3, according to Kodak. At least the ECV method incorporates the notion of a stage-wise process with options, along with probabilities of outcomes. Thus it comes considerably closer to OPT and the correct valuation than does the NPV method. A more detailed representation of the decision situation than the ECV illustration in Exhibit 3.3 would include:

- using three, four, or five stages with multiple Go/Kill decision points along the way
- considering more than just two possible outcomes of each stage—success or failure; for example, a range of possible outcomes (for commercial outcome, the possibilities might be major success, fair success, marginal success, breakeven, and so on, each with their own financial consequences.)
- including financial consequences of failure (for example, opportunity costs of lost future spinoff projects, loss of reputation in the marketplace, and so forth).

The OPT approach is a fairly new concept. Insufficient research data are available to assess its use and results. Nonetheless, at a recent forum of CTOs of major U.S. firms, virtually every firm attending indicated that it was now using OPT, or real options approaches, to evaluate higher risk and larger, longer-term, and platform projects.[5]

Dynamic Rank-Ordered List

The final financial method overcomes the limitation of relying on only a single criterion to rank projects. We've labeled it the dynamic rank-ordered list approach, although Company G simply called it their "portfolio model." The advantage of this method is that it can rank-order projects according to several criteria concurrently, without being as complex and time-consuming as a full-fledged, multiple-criteria scoring model. The criteria can include, for example, profitability and return measures, strategic importance, ease and speed, and other desirable characteristics of a high-priority project. Exhibit 3.6 provides an illustration using disguised projects and data from Company G. The four principal criteria used by this company are:

1. *The NPV of the project's future earnings, less all outstanding expenditures.* This NPV value is considered an important objective by Company G, in that it captures both the fact that the project exceeds the acceptable hurdle rate and denotes the sheer magnitude or impact of the project on the company—the "bang." Note that the NPV has built into it probabilities of commercial success.
2. *The IRR is calculated using the same data as the NPV but gives the percent return.* This is an equally important criterion for Company G, as it captures the efficient utilization of capital.
3. *The strategic importance of the project*—how important and how aligned the project is with the business's strategy—is a key criterion for ranking projects at Company G. Importance is gauged on a 1–5 scale, where 5 is "critically important."
4. *The probability of technical success* is also an important consideration in ranking projects for Company G, as some projects are very speculative technically.

Project Name	IRR* (%)	NPV ($ millions)	Strategic Importance**	Probability of Technical Success
Alpha	20%	10.0	5	80%
Beta	15%	2.0	2	70%
Gamma	10%	5.0	3	90%
Delta	17%	12.0	2	65%
Epsilon	12%	20.0	4	90%
Omega	22%	6.0	1	85%

EXHIBIT 3.6   Company G: Dynamic Rank-Ordered List

*The Hurdle rate is 10% IRR.

**Strategic importance scale is a 1–5 rating, where 5 = critically important.

How are projects prioritized or ranked on four criteria simultaneously? First, the probability of technical success is multiplied by both the IRR and the NPV to yield an adjusted IRR and adjusted NPV (see Exhibit 3.7). Next, projects are ranked according to each of the three criteria: IRR adjusted, NPV adjusted, and strategic importance. Exhibit 3.7 shows this procedure, with the numbers in parentheses showing the rank orders in each of the three columns. The overall rankings—the far right column in Exhibit 3.7—are determined by calculating the mean of the three rankings. For example, for Project Alpha, which scored first on strategic importance and second on both the IRR and the NPV, the mean of these three rankings is 1.67, which places Alpha at the top of the list. Simple perhaps, but consider the disguised list of projects in Exhibit 3.7 and try to come up with a better ranking yourself—one that maximizes against all three criteria!

The major strength of this dynamic list is its sheer simplicity. Evaluate your projects on each of several criteria and rank them, then take the means of the rankings. Another strength is that the method can handle several criteria concur-

---

POINTS FOR MANAGEMENT TO PONDER

Are there several different financial and strategic goals in your portfolio management approach? If so, do consider the dynamic rank-ordered list approach to evaluation. It certainly is simple, and it considers not only the NPV but also the efficiency of funds employed, namely, the IRR. Strategic importance and probability of success are also built in. We suggest that, if this method is of interest, you consider modifying it by considering key ratios (such as NPV/R&D costs) rather than just NPV to do the ranking (much like the bang-for-buck, ECV, and PI methods do).

Project Name	IRR X PTS	NPV X PTS	Strategic Importance	Ranking Score**
Alpha	16.0 (2)	8.0 (2)	5 (1)	1.67 (1)
Epsilon	10.8 (4)	18.0 (1)	4 (2)	2.33 (2)
Delta	11.1 (3)	7.8 (3)	2 (4)	3.33 (3)
Omega	18.7 (1)	5.1 (4)	1 (5)	3.67 (4)
Gamma	9.0 (6)	4.5 (5)	3 (3)	4.67 (5)
Beta	10.5 (5)	1.4 (6)	2 (4)	5.00 (6)

EXHIBIT 3.7   The Six Projects Rank-Ordered

Both IRR and NPV are multiplied by probability of technical success. Projects are then ranked according to the three criteria. Numbers in parentheses show the ranking in each column. Projects are rank-ordered until there are no more resources.
**The final column is the mean across the three rankings. This is the score that the six projects are finally ranked on. Project Alpha is number 1 and Project Beta is last.

rently without becoming overly complex. A major weakness is that the model does not consider constrained resources (as did the bang-for-buck and ECV models, although conceivably Company G could build this into its rank-ordering model). Like the NPV, ECV, and PI models, this method relies on financial data that is uncertain and often unreliable. Finally, it fails to consider the appropriate balance of projects.

The Dark Side of the Financial Approaches to Project Evaluation

Virtually all the firms we interviewed employ financial methods of one form or another—either at gate reviews or at portfolio review meetings—for project valuation and to attempt to maximize the economic value of the portfolio. The rigor and toughness of financial methods, coupled with the fact that the assessment boils down to a few key numbers, are positive features.

One concern that was consistently heard in our study, however, is that an overreliance on strictly financial data and criteria may lead to wrong portfolio decisions, simply because the financial data are often wrong! And there is indeed evidence to support this view.

More and Little's study of companies' abilities to estimate expected new product sales revenues showed that there were orders-of-magnitude errors, on average.[6] Another study echoes the concerns of overreliance on net present value techniques.[7]

One company had tracked NPV estimates over the life of a project for a set of 30 projects.[8] (Most managers in other firms had no idea how accurate their NPV and financial estimates had been!) In that firm, the sum of the NPVs across the 30 projects showed a marked decline as the projects progressed from predevelopment through to postlaunch. On average, financial prospects are very much overestimated! Unfortunately, while the average NPVs of the 30 projects followed the shape of a predictable, smooth curve downward, plots of individual projects' NPVs over time were more erratic, which rules out the use of a standard "correction factor" that could be applied to early NPV estimates.

The proof is in the results, however. Here, too, financial methods fare very poorly. In spite of the fact that financial methods are theoretically correct, the most rigorous of all methods, and the most popular of all tools, of all the methods we studied in the large sample survey of practices versus results, they yielded the *poorest results on just about every portfolio performance metric.*[9] See more on this in Chapter 6. Again we conclude it is not because the methods are wrong; it is because the data on which these financial methods rely is so terribly in error. The sophistication of these methods far exceeds the quality of the data!

One reason for unreliable financial information is the continuing reluctance on the part of senior management to insist that solid upfront homework and good market information be part of every project at the "Go to Development" decision point. (Our benchmarking studies reveal that upfront homework and solid market information remain critical weaknesses.)[10] Some senior people seem to be in such a hurry that they are prepared to sacrifice quality of execution, and then they are surprised and disturbed when everything starts to go wrong! Other reasons are that many financial variables remain uncertain until later stages of a project and well into the development stage (for example, manufacturing costs or capital requirements). Because the integrity of the data is such a key issue, we delve into ways to improve this data—including estimates of revenue and probabilities of success—in Chapter 8.

A second and more subtle concern about an overreliance on financial data to make project Go/Kill and portfolio decisions is the realization that major breakthrough projects will be penalized, while minor modifications and small, low-risk initiatives will score higher. One reason for this is the "all or nothing" investment assumption made in traditional NPV calculations. In reality, however, management has multiple Go/Kill options in projects. Options reduce the risk of projects and hence portray particularly high-risk projects in a more favorable economic light than does NPV (see the section "Options Pricing Theory"). Another reason why breakthrough projects are penalized is that the expected outcomes and payoffs are harder to quantify and prove, especially in a project's early days.

Valuation Methods: Scoring Models

A number of characteristics of new product projects are strongly correlated with success and hence become excellent predictors or proxies for success and profits.

> **POINTS FOR MANAGEMENT TO PONDER**
>
> If you rely solely on financial data and criteria to make Go/Kill and portfolio decisions in the early stages of a project, you're using a very rubbery meter stick. Not surprisingly, many of your decisions will be wrong ones! With the exception of close-to-home, well-defined projects, financial estimates made for many new product projects are highly uncertain, especially when made before the development phase begins. The dilemma is that this is precisely when portfolio and project selection decisions are required.
>
> Suggestions:
>
> - Do consider financial data and criteria at these early decision points. But don't base the entire decision on these. Go beyond the financial methods and use some nonfinancial methods to gauge reward and make decisions on projects. These are outlined in the rest of this chapter and in the next.
> - Try to improve the quality of information—especially market information—notably at the "Go to Development" decision point. Insist on solid upfront homework!
> - Start tracking your financial estimates over the life of a project. Be sure to build in a postlaunch review (perhaps 12 to 18 months after launch), when the actual results can be compared to those forecast when the project was approved. This way you can determine the reliability of financial estimates made early in the life of a project and improve these over time.

For example, over the years, many investigations have probed what makes a winning new product. These studies have compared and contrasted hundreds of new product successes and failures. In so doing, they have identified the critical success factors.[11] Some of the more important success factors that are correlated with the profitability of the new product are the following:

- Having a unique, superior product—one that is differentiated from those of competitors, offers unique benefits, and provides superior value to the customer
- Targeting an attractive market—one that is growing, is large, and has good margins, weak competition, and low competitive resistance
- Leveraging internal company strengths—products and projects that build from company strengths, competencies, and experience in both marketing and technology.

Note that all these characteristics are known relatively early in the project. Further, according to one major study, the correlations between some of these success factors and ultimate profitability are far stronger than the correlation between the NPV calculated prior to development and the product's eventual profits.[12]

So, why not use some of these known and strong predictors of success as tools for selecting projects? As one executive put it, "If you can explain success, then you can predict success!" Many companies have developed scoring model systems that incorporate qualitative factors and success proxies to help them rate and rank proposed new product projects. Although not the most popular tool, users indicate that scoring models work. According to our large sample study of firms' portfolio practice and performance (chapter 1), those companies relying heavily on scoring models as their portfolio management method achieved a superior portfolio of projects on several important performance dimensions. The theoretical justification—the fact that many qualitative factors are strongly linked to success, and therefore can be used as predictors, coupled with the superior results in practice—means that the scoring model should be considered one of your portfolio tools.

In a scoring model system, a list of criteria is developed to rate projects—criteria that are thought, or known, to discriminate between high-profit, high-success-rate projects and poorer projects. Projects are then rated on each criterion, typically on 1–5 or 0–10 scales with anchor phrases. Next, these rating scores are often multiplied by weightings and summed across all criteria to yield attractiveness scores for each project. Scoring models can be used at gate decision points to make Go/Kill decisions on individual projects (by comparing the project attractiveness score to a cutoff criterion); or they can be used at portfolio reviews and in portfolio management to help prioritize projects (for example, ranking by the project attractiveness score until there are no more resources).

Although many firms we interviewed claimed to be using such scoring models, either they were poorly crafted (e.g., inappropriate criteria) or there were serious problems in the actual use of the model at management decision meetings. The result was that such models often fell into disuse. The key seems to be in the construction of an appropriate list of scoring criteria—ones that really do separate winners from losers—and a procedure to seek management input and effectively employ the model at a management meeting.

We saw a number of firms with excellently constructed scoring models. In this chapter, we present several first-rate scoring models for you to consider:

- Celanese-U.S. Corporate Research & Technology constructed one of the best scoring models we have seen: It took several years of refinement, but the eventual model is so well conceived that we report it here. In addition, it has been validated by the company; that is, scores from the model were compared to eventual results in projects. It is a model that is best applied to larger, advanced-technology projects and even platform developments.
- We also present a scoring system used at DuPont. It relies on familiar and proven screening criteria and is used for new product projects.
- Smaller and more entrepreneurial firms also employ scoring models. We present a sample model from EXFO Engineering, a Product Development Management Association (PDMA)–award-winning company.
- The scoring model used at the Royal Bank of Canada (RBC) is reported later in the chapter, as it provides a solid example of a shorter scoring model and an example of one appropriate for the service sector.
- Finally we provide a composite "best in class" scoring model—one based on the models used in a number of firms such as Exxon, Guinness, International Paper,

Kodak, Bayer, Dainippon Ink & Chemical, and other leading companies. This model is best used for new physical products and seems to have applicability across a broad range of industries.

The Celanese (formerly Hoechst) Scoring Model

The particular unit within Celanese AG was the U.S. Corporate Research & Technology group whose special mandate is to develop and commercialize new products that lie outside the scope of the traditional business units. It tends to focus on larger, higher-risk, more step-out, and longer-term major projects (as opposed to projects designed to maintain and renew a business unit's existing product line). This group also uses a five-stage Stage-Gate™ new product process.

The scoring portfolio model comprises a list of 19 questions in five categories. Each question or criterion had been carefully selected and worded, operationally defined, and tested for validity and reliability over several years. We offer their model in Exhibit 3.8 as an example to other companies.

The five major factors Celanese considers in prioritizing projects are these:

1. business strategy fit
2. strategic leverage
3. probability of technical success
4. probability of commercial success
5. reward to the company.

Within each of these five factors are a number of specific characteristics or measures (19 in total), which are scored by management. These 19 scales are anchored (scale points 1, 4, 7, and 10 are defined) to facilitate discussion (see Exhibit 3.8 for the questions and their operational definitions).

Simple addition of the items within each factor yields the five factor scores. Then the five factor scores are added together in a weighted fashion to yield an overall score for the project; namely, the program attractiveness score. This final score is used for two purposes:

1. *Go/Kill decisions at gates:* Embedded within Celanese's new product process are predefined decision points or gates. These gates are staffed by a group of senior managers and executives, who review the projects under consideration and make Go/Kill decisions. The program attractiveness score is one input into the Go/Kill decision at each gate: A score of 50 percent is the cutoff or hurdle. But the decision is not quite as simple as a "yea/nay" based on this score. There are animated discussions at each gate, where opinions and the experience of managers surface and where other issues and qualitative factors not captured in the 19 measures are dealt with. These gate meetings take place about once a month and are facilitated by an outside referee, who walks the gatekeepers through the scoring model and also computes and records the scores.

Factor 1: Business Strategy Fit

Key Factors	Rating Scale				Rating	Comments
	1	4	7	10		
Congruence	Only peripheral fit with business strategies	Modest fit, but not with a key element of the strategy	Good fit with a key element of strategy	Strong fit with several key elements of strategy		
Impact	Minimal impact; no noticeable harm if program dropped	Moderate competitive, financial impact	Significant impact; difficult to recover if program unsuccessful or dropped.	Business unit future depends on this program		

Factor 2: Strategic Leverage

Key Factors	Rating Scale				Rating	Comments
	1	4	7	10		
Proprietary Position	Easily copied	Protected, but not a deterrent	Solidly protected with trade secrets, patents; serves captive customer	Position protected (upstream and downstream) through a combination of patents, trade secrets, raw material access, etc.		
Platform for Growth	Dead end/ one-of-a kind	Other opportunities for business extension	Potential for diversification	Opens up new technical and commercial fields		
Durability (Technical and Market)	No distinctive advantage; quickly "leapfrogged"	May get a few good years	Moderate life cycle (4-6 years) but little opportunity for incremental improvement	Long life cycle with opportunity for incremental improvements		
Synergy with Other Operations within Corporation	Limited to single business unit	With work, could be applied to another SBU	Could be adopted or have application among several SBUs	Could be applied widely across the company		

Factor 3: Probability of Technical Success

Key Factors	Rating Scale				Rating	Comments
	1	4	7	10		
Technical "Gap"	Large gulf between current practice and objective; must invent new science	"Order of magnitude" change proposed	Step change short of "order of magnitude"	Incremental improvement; more engineering in focus		
Program Complexity	Difficult to define; many hurdles	Easy to define; many hurdles	A challenge; but "do-able"	Straight-forward		
Technology Skill Base	Technology new to the company; (almost) no skills	Some R&D experience but probably insufficient	Selectively practiced in company	Widely practiced in company		
Availability of People and Facilities	No appropriate people/facilities; must hire/build	Acknowledged shortage in key areas	Resources are available; but in demand; must plan in advance	People/facilities immediately available		

EXHIBIT 3.8   Celanese Scoring Model

Factor 1: Business Strategy Fit

Factor 2: Strategic Leverage

Factor 3: Probability of Technical Success

Factor 4: Probability of Commercial Success

Key Factors	Rating Scale				Rating	Comments
	1	4	7	10		
Market Need	Extensive market development required: no apparent need	Need must be highlighted for customers; product tailoring required	Clear relationship between product and need; one-for-one substitution of competitors' product	Product immediately responsive to customer need; direct substitute for existing company product		
Market Maturity	Declining	Mature/Embryonic	Modest growth	Rapid Growth		
Competitive Intensity	High	Moderate/High	Moderate/Low	Low		
Commercial Applications Development Skills	Must develop: New to company	Must develop beyond current limited use	Need to tailor to proposed program	Already in place		
Commercial Assumptions	Low probability/low impact	Low predictability/ low impact	High probability/ high impact	High predictability/ high impact		
Regulatory/Social Political Impact	Negative	Neutral	Somewhat favorable (e.g. waste minimization, reduce hazardous materials in process)	Positive impact on high profile issues (e.g. plastics recycle)		

Factor 5: Reward

Key Factors	Rating Scale				Rating	Comments
	1	4	7	10		
Absolute Contribution to Profitability (5 year cumulative cashflow from commercial start-up)	<$10MM	$50MM	$150 MM	>$250 MM		
Technology Payback	>10 years	7 years	5 years	<3 years		
Time to Commercial Start-up	>7 years	5 years	3 years	<1 year		

Payback = Number of years needed for cumulative cashflow to equal to all cash costs expended prior to start-up plus capital invested after start-up.

Program Attractiveness Score: Summary of Scores on Five Factors
Abbreviated Form

Key Factors	Rating Scale				Rating	Comments
	1	4	7	10		
Probability of Technical Success	<20% probability	40% probability	70% probability	>90% probability		
Probability of Commercial Success	< 25% probability	50% probability	75% probability	>90% probability		
Reward	Small/breakeven	Payback > 7 years	Payback = 5 years	Payback < 3 years		
Business Strategy Fit	R&D program is independent of business strategy; also low SBU impact	Somewhat supports SBU strategy; moderate impact	Supports SBU strategy; moderate impact	Strongly supports SBU strategies; high impact		
Strategic Leverage	One-of-a-kind/ dead end	Several opportunities for business extensions	Opportunities to transfer to another SBU	Vast array of propriety opportunities		

EXHIBIT 3.8   Celanese Scoring Model (continued)

Factor 4: Probability of Commercial Success

Factor 5: Reward

Program Attractiveness Score: Summary of Scores on Five Factors

2. *Prioritization:* Immediately after the gate meeting, the portfolio of projects is reviewed. This is where the prioritization of "go" projects from the gate takes place and where resources are allocated to the approved projects. Here, the program attractiveness scores for the new projects (versus scores for already-resourced projects) determine how the new projects are prioritized in the larger list and whether these new ones receive resources or are placed on hold. Other considerations, besides the computed attractiveness score, are:

- Appropriate balance of projects
- Resource needs (people, money)
- Resource availability.

The DuPont Scoring Model

A number of business units at DuPont use a tried and proven scoring system for their stage-and-gate new product process. The criteria are familiar ones and, most important, seem to discriminate between excellent and poor new product projects.

There are seven criteria in the DuPont model:[13]

1. Strategy alignment
2. Value
3. Competitive advantage
4. Market attractiveness
5. Fit to existing supply chain
6. Time to break-even
7. NPV.

The details of these criteria are shown in Exhibit 3.9. You may wish to have a closer look at the items and the scorecard and then build them into your own portfolio management process. Also note that while Celanese's scoring criteria in Exhibit 3.8 are for advanced technology and platform projects, Dupont's list in Exhibit 3.9 is tailored to more traditional product development, which explains some of the differences between the criteria used in these two large firms.

A Scoring Model from a Smaller, Hi-Tech Firm

Not every firm we investigated uses a long list of screening criteria. EXFO Engineering is a midsized manufacturer of instruments in the field of fiber optics. We include EXFO, in part, because the company won the PDMA Outstanding Corporate Innovator award for the best-managed innovating company in the year 2000.

EXFO's senior management is intimately involved with both the Stage-Gate™ process and portfolio management meetings. Because so many projects must be reviewed at the same time and every quarter, the goal is to keep the criteria and scoring system simple. EXFO has boiled the scoring criteria down to these major questions:[14]

Rating Scale	15	5	1
STRATEGY ALIGNMENT	Fits Strategy	Supports	Neutral
VALUE	Significant Differentiation	Moderate	Slight
COMPETITIVE ADVANTAGE	Strong	Moderate	Slight
MARKET ATTRACTIVENESS	Highly Profitable	Moderately Profitable	Low Profitability
FIT TO EXISTING SUPPLY CHAIN	Fits Current Channels	Some Change, Not Significant	Significant Change
TIME TO BREAK EVEN	< 4 Years	4-6 Years	> 6 Years
NPV	>$20 MM	$4-$20 MM	< $5MM

EXHIBIT 3.9   DuPont's Attractiveness Scorecard

SOURCE: Adapted from Robin Karol, "Integrating the Selection Process to Stage Gates," paper presented at the IIR and PDMA Conference, Ft. Lauderdale, FL, 2001.

- Does the project fit the company's strategy? How well?
- What is the market potential? How large is the market?
- Are the financial estimates positive?
- Do we have the R&D know-how? Can we do the project?

Projects are scored on these criteria at gate meetings, and these criteria are used to help rank projects against each other at portfolio review meetings. Note that the company uses a relatively simple financial index that avoids the complexities of NPV:

$$\text{Financial index} = S \times P_{cs} / [D \times (1 - P_{ts})]$$

Where

S = expected annual sales for the product ($000)
D = development costs ($000)
P_{cs} = probability of commercial success
P_{ts} = probability of technical success.

The minimum cutoff for this index is 8.0. The company's average today is about 15.0, up from 5.0–6.0 several years ago. According to EXFO's vice

Key Items	Rating Scale				Rating
	0	4	7	10	
1. Strategic Alignment & Importance ✓ **strategic fit and importance** ✓ **fits our strategy** ✓ **important to do** ✓ **high impact on our business**	Product not in alignment with or important to our business strategy; low impact: KILL	Somewhat supports business strategy; not too important; modest impact	Supports business strategy; important; good impact	Product aligns well with our business strategy; product very important to strategy; high impact	
2. Product &Competitive Advantage ✓ **unique customer benefits** ✓ **value for money** ✓ **customer feedback in Stage 2**	None; negative or neutral customer feedback; poor value	Limited; marginally superior; fairly neutral feedback; OK value	Some new benefits; somewhat superior, good value; positive feedback	Major new benefits; very positive customer feedback; great value	
3. Market Attractiveness ✓ **market size & growth** ✓ **margins** ✓ **competitive situation**	Small or non-existent market; low growth & low margins; tough competition: KILL	Modest market; limited growth; fair margins; competitive	Significant market; good growth; good margins; modest competition	Large, growing, attractive market; good margins; weaker competition	
4. Leverages Core Competencies ✓ **technology** ✓ **production** ✓ **marketing & distribution/sales**	No opportunities to leverage competencies; required skills/experience/resources strengths are weak: KILL	Some opportunities to leverage our competencies; our skills/experience/resources are modest	Considerable leverage possible; skills/experience needed for projects are within Company	Excellent leverage of our strengths & competencies; excellent fit between project needs, our skills, experience, resources	
5. Technical Feasibility ✓ **small technical gap** ✓ **not too complex technically** ✓ **uses our in-house technology** ✓ **demonstrated technical feasibility**	Low; big gap; new science; technology new to Company; have not been able to demonstrate technical feasibility: KILL	Modest; fairly large gap; quite a few hurdles but do-able; technology fairly new to Company; limited evidence to support technical feasibility	Good; small gap; some hurdles, but attainable; have some evidence of technical feasibility	Straight-forward; largely engineering repackage; we have technology in house; have demonstrated technical feasibility	
6. Financial Reward vs. Risk ✓ **sizeable, excellent opportunity** ✓ **Payback, NPV & IRR OK** ✓ **certainty of estimates** ✓ **not too risky & difficult to do**	Poor, limited opportunity; NPV negative, payback > 5 yrs; difficult to make money here; risky & tough to do: KILL	Modest opportunity; NPV positive; payback = 4 yrs; fairly difficult to make money; fairly risky & tough to do	Fairly good opportunity; NPV positive & good; payback = 2 yrs; probably can make money; modest risk & difficulty	Excellent Opportunity; NPV positive & high; payback < 1 yr; not too risky & difficult to do	

EXHIBIT 3.10   Composite Best-Practices Criteria Scorecard (for use at Gate 3—See Appendix A)

president of R&D, the increase in the financial attractiveness of projects is attributed to both EXFO's Stage-Gate™ approach and its portfolio management system.[15]

The Composite, Best Practices Scoring Model

The Celanese model is designed for major technology projects, and the Dupont and EXFO models are designed for new product selection in their own respective industries. Here is a generic scoring system we developed for rating and ranking new product projects, taken from our standard Stage-Gate™ e-manual.* It has the advantage of being a composite model with items and facets taken from a large number of leading firms. It is also based, in part, on extensive research into the critical success factors for new products.

There are six major factors, and each factor has a number of subitems:

1. *Strategic alignment and importance*: Is the project aligned with strategy, and is it strategically important?
2. *Product and competitive advantage*: Does the product offer unique customer benefits? meet customer needs better than competitors? provide good value for money?
3. *Market attractiveness*: Is the target market an attractive one—size, growth, margins, competition?
4. *Leverage core competencies*: Does the project build on strengths, experiences, and competencies in marketing, technology, and operations?
5. *Technical feasibility*: What is the likelihood of technical feasibility—size of gap? complexity? uncertainty?
6. *Financial reward*: Can this project make money? How sure are we? Is it worth the risk?

These factors are shown in more detail in Exhibit 3.10 along with useful scoring scales. As in the Celanese system, management meets with the project team to discuss the project. Management then rates the project on each of the scaled questions (usually rated from 0 to 10). Some firms ask management to score only the six major factors above and only to discuss the checked items listed below each factor in Exhibit 3.10. A scorecard, not unlike Exhibit 3.10, is used. Other firms seek more detail and require that management score the project on all the subitems, a total of 21 questions in this model. (Appendix B shows a scorecard for a full 21-question model.) As shown in Exhibit 3.10, a zero score on some questions is an automatic kill or knockout.

The project attractiveness score is simply the weighted addition of the six factor scores, appropriately adjusted to make the value a percent out of 100. If the project clears a certain minimum—usually 60 out of 100—it is deemed a "pass"

---

* The e-guide is an electronic new product process e-manual, based on the Stage-Gate™ approach. It is a best-in-class new product process, based on many leading firms' processes, and is available from the Product Development Institute: www.prod-dev.com.

and resources are sought for the project. Alternatively, the project attractiveness
score is used to rank projects.

Developing and Using Scoring Models

Scoring models are not quite as easy to develop and implement as one might
imagine. One of the key issues is what questions, factors, and items the scoring
model should include. Exhibits 3.8 to 3.12, along with Appendix B, provide
some guidance and wording for these questions or factors. One important tip
here: Keep the list of questions short, especially if you plan to use the scoring
model at gate meetings with senior people answering the questions. The key is
to develop a model that the decision makers will use, and not necessarily to arrive at the most comprehensive scoring model in the world! Most firms find that
six to ten scored questions are about right. More than that and fatigue and confusion set in. For portfolio reviews, where scoring might be done on multiple
projects at the review meeting, the number of scoring questions per project must
be even less.

Here now are answers to some other vital questions that will arise as you attempt to design and install a scoring model approach.

What Weights to Use in Scoring Models

An often-asked question is, What weights should be placed on the various factors
in a scoring model? and, How does one determine the weights? We have found
that many companies simply use equal weights on all questions. The issue of
which is the most important factor proved too difficult to resolve, and so all are
given equal importance. As one manager put it, "We argued more about the
weights on the questions than the merits of the project!"

Still other firms argue that some factors are, indeed, more important than others and ought to have weights. At minimum, some factors are knockouts: for example, a zero score on strategic alignment in either the Celanese or generic scoring models in Exhibits 3.8 and 3.10 is enough to kill a project.

Finally, some firms use variable weights; that is, the weights depend on the
type of project. For example, one business within Hewlett-Packard has three
classes of development projects:[16]

- Sustaining projects
- New business project
- Must-do projects.

The Go/Kill and prioritization criteria used by the business unit depend on the
project class. As Exhibit 3.11 shows, some of the criteria are common across all
project classes; but the set of criteria employed for each project class is unique.
For example, for "must-do" projects there are only four criteria, and all four per-
tain to ability to execute.

	Sustaining Projects	New Business Projects	Must Do Projects
Percent of portfolio resources	**50%**	**35%**	**15%**
Strategic Fit/ Productivity/ Competency:			
Supports the business strategy of the business	X	X	
Importance as a core competency (strategic leverage)	X	X	
Worldwide or multinational benefit	X	X	
Market attractiveness		X	
Workload reduction/ productivity improvement	X		
Time and breadth	X		
Ability to Execute:			
Time to complete	X	X	X
Resources required (people)	X	X	X
Right resources available	X	X	X
Geographic dispersion of resources	X	X	X
Full time availability (vs. part-time)	X		
Competitive Offering:			
Builds competitive advantage (attracts new customers)	X	X	
Customer loyalty (keeps existing customers)	X	X	

EXHIBIT 3.11   Hewlett-Packard Differential Application of Criteria by Project Type

For this Hewlett-Packard business unit, there are three classes of projects (three columns). The X's in the columns indicate the criteria used to rate that class of project. For example, must-do projects rely on only four criteria that capture "ability to execute."

SOURCE: R.L. Englund, "Implementing a Prioritization Process That Links Projects to Strategy," *Proceedings, Portfolio Management for New Product Development*, Jan. 2001.

Example: A major U.S. consumer food products company uses the same criteria across all classes of projects, from line extensions and flankers through to new platforms, but the weights on the criteria change with project type. For example, there is more weight on strategic criteria for platform projects.

A word of caution regarding the use of variable weights: If you do elect to use them, recognize that you cannot then compare all projects against each other. By changing the weights, you have changed the scoring model, and the project attractiveness scores are not directly comparable.

Here are some ways to determine the weights for scoring models (other than by pure guesses):

- *Use a modified Delphi approach:* Assemble a group of knowledge people (ideally the decision makers) and discuss each of the criteria (factors) under consideration. Then ask each person to privately rate the importance of each factor on a 0-to-10 scale. Collect the scores, tally them, and display them anonymously on a projection screen. Single out those factors where major differences of opinion exist and discuss them. Repeat the voting process. Usually by the second or third round you will have reached consensus. The method is simple and has the added advantage of allowing potential users of the system to input their own views on what is really important.

Example: A division of Exxon Chemicals took this approach. The portfolio management team and members of various gatekeeping groups met. The seven factors under discussion were each displayed on flipchart pages on the meeting room walls (criteria very similar to the list in Exhibit 3.10). After intense discussion, a vote was taken to identify which factor was most important. Consensus was reached and that factor was given an importance value of 10. This process helped to define what a 10 really meant. Then each person indicated his or her importance score by writing a number from 0 to 10 for each of the remaining six factors on the sheets on the wall. A review of all six sheets revealed more or less agreement on four factors, but major differences of opinion on two factors. These two were discussed again, and the process repeated. The result was agreement: Not only had management arrived at a fairly good weighting scheme, but most important, there was buy-in: They had developed it, and they then agreed to use it!

- *Polling*: A similar but more streamlined approach is to use a simple opinion poll. Identify a group of knowledgeable people, again, ideally including the decision makers. Use a questionnaire to ask each to rate the importance of each factor, again on 0-to-10 scales. The importance weights across any one factor are the average of the responses. This process is faster and does not require a meeting (it can be done by e-mail). But the valuable discussion is missing, and so the results are not as good.

Example: A medical division of Procter & Gamble used this approach. P&G's standard scoring model for consumer goods was clearly inappropriate for ethical drugs; hence, a new list of criteria was needed. Once this list was developed, it was circulated broadly within the business. Each recipient was asked to rate the various questions—from "not too important" to "of critical importance" on a 0–10 scale. The average score for each factor was then used as the weight for that factor.

- *Use research results*: Countless studies have probed success factors in product innovation. Many have even reported correlations between these factors and the new product's eventual profits. Use these studies as a guide. For example, here are correlation coefficients* for the three important factors that we mentioned above, as reported in one study:[17]

  having a unique, superior product: R = 0.530
  targeting an attractive market: R = .315
  leveraging internal strengths: R = .365

  These and other correlations are a guide to the relative importance of the various factors in the success equation, and hence to your scoring model weights.
- *Use commercially available models*: The *NewProd™ 3000* model is an example of an empirically derived model that can be used to score, rate, and rank projects. It also finds use as a strengths/weaknesses diagnostic tool. The model's 30 questions were derived from research that compared new product winners to losers. The result was a fairly sophisticated statistical model, complete with weights, that purports to predict success. *NewProd 3000* has been independently validated by various researchers, and its predictive abilities are in the 73–84 percent range. See more on *NewProd 3000* later in this chapter.

Seeking Management Input for Scoring Models

Scoring models may use many criteria (witness the 19 criteria used by Celanese), and most of these are subjective. This means the decision makers themselves must provide much of the data in the form of subjective opinion at review meetings. As a result, a frequently mentioned problem with scoring models is that the model can become cumbersome at gate or portfolio meetings. Requiring decision makers to rate and score projects at a meeting is time-consuming (and something many senior people are loath to do). As well, collecting data in a time-efficient manner during the meeting is difficult.

---

*Correlation coefficient: a 0 to 1.0 statistic giving the degree of correlation or connection between two variables. Here the correlation was measured between each of the three factors and the new product's profitability.

Several companies have solved part of this data-collection problem by passing out a scorecard to the evaluators during the meeting. A facilitator walks the decision makers through the criteria one at a time. After some discussion, the facilitator calls for each evaluator to independently score the project on that criterion, and the meeting moves to the next criterion. The scorecards are collected after all criteria are evaluated. Then they are quickly tallied on an overhead transparency (or via computer and video projector) for display and discussion. Consensus or alignment is reached, and a decision on the project is made. While not the tidiest meeting format, the procedure does seem to work. (Appendix B provides a sample scorecard).

An Example of Effective Management Input

The Royal Bank of Canada (RBC) is one of the largest financial institutions in North America. It has branches around the world, 58,000 employees, and assets of $294 billion (U.S.$). Although much of its business is retail (consumer), its Business Banking division is where significant advances have been made in new product and portfolio management.

The bank's method involves the use of both a sorting technique and a scoring model. All the new and existing projects from the various product lines (product groups) are considered—together and against each other—since they all compete for the same resource pie.

The portfolio analysis is a critical all-day meeting to which the product group heads and other knowledgeable managers are invited. RBC is a heavy user of technology in meeting rooms, and the portfolio meeting is no exception. When issues arise, participants can type notes that appear on the computer screens of others in the room. The facilitator can also call for votes on issues. For example, "Now that we've discussed the revenue potential of this project, I'd like you to vote on this, scoring it from 1 to 9, where . . . ." Attendees then key in their scores. The results are tallied and displayed on the computer screens, including various statistics (means and deviations) or rank-ordered lists. Some discussion takes place and then the meeting moves to the next issue or vote.

This electronically based procedure has proven very effective in soliciting and integrating views from a diverse group of people (everyone gets a chance to be heard) and also for gaining closure on each issue in a time-efficient manner (via the electronic vote). Note that these are quite senior people, yet even they have adapted to the new meeting technology.

In the RBC's process, almost 200 projects competing for the same pool of resources are under consideration. Almost half of these are relatively small but nondiscretionary projects—vital maintenance work, or necessary systems changes and upgrades. These are automatically "in the budget." The remaining budget must then be allocated across discretionary projects, both new and existing. Prior to the portfolio meeting, each product group meets informally to discuss its own list of priorities.

The main portfolio meeting begins with a brief description of each of the roughly 100 discretionary projects (participants have received a listing of these and some description prior to the meeting). Voting begins with a sorting tech-

Decision Criteria in Portfolio Scoring:
Operational Definitions of Voting Criteria

Project Importance:
1. **Strategic Importance**
   How well does the project fit the overall strategic direction? This is relative to the
   context, since certain goals and critical success factors have higher organizational impact.

   9 = High   5 = Medium   1 = Low

2. **Magnitude of Impact**
   Evaluate the project in terms of its impact on the organization. Major areas are customer,
   profitability, revenue, productivity.

   9 = High   5 = Medium   1 = Low

3. **Economic Benefits**
   Assess a subjective rating based on total project cost to completion and perceived benefit
   such as dollar savings, revenue growth, business effectiveness.

   9 = High   5 = Medium   1 = Low

Ease of Doing:
1. **Cost of Doing**
   Evaluate the relative difficulty of funding the project in the current period.

   9 = High (over $2MM)   5 = Medium ($250M - $2MM)   1 = Low (under $250M)

2. **Project Complexity**
   Assess the degree of difficulty for design, development, implementation and roll out.

   9 = High   5 = Medium   1 = Low

3. **Resource Availability**
   Skilled resources are critical to successful project implementation.

   9 = None   5 = Partial   1 = Available

EXHIBIT 3.12   Royal Bank of Canada's Portfolio-Scoring Criteria with Operational Definitions

nique. The facilitator requests that each attendee select his or her top and bottom
15 projects (all votes are keyed in via attendees' computers). The results are displayed. The usual pattern is this:

- A subset of the more obvious projects, including many that are well underway, receive quite a few positive votes each—there is general concurrence on these.
- Similarly, a subset receives a number of negative votes each—these are the obvious "kill" projects.
- A group of projects are in the middle—few votes and mixed positive and negative votes. These are flagged for discussion.

Rank Order	Project Name	Project Score (%)	Development Cost (S&T[1] dollars 000) (annual)	Cumulative Development Cost (000)
1	RBCash	83	2,400	2,400
2	CashCore	76	1,920	4,320
3	EBX	76	1,800	6,120
4	EBY	73	500	6,620
5	BuyAct	73	6,000	12,620
6	CorpPay	70	2,000	14,620
7	Project A- PC	70	1,600	16,220
8	PC-MD	68	7,500	23,720
.	.	.	.	.
.	.	.	.	.
.	.	.	.	.
_26_	**Tiered/Interest Accounts**	**55**	**930**	_90,1502_
27	Tiered	52	1,000	
28	Trade-AP	52	1,200	
29	ATM-Y	50	500	
.	.	.	.	.
.	.	.	.	.
.	.	.	.	.

Note: The numbers and names of projects have been disguised.

EXHIBIT 3.13   Prioritized List of Projects at Royal Bank of Canada

1. S&T: Systems and technology (analogous to R&D).
Budget is $90 million; project #26 takes the portfolio slightly over budget. A line is drawn after project # 26.

At this point, anyone is allowed to lobby for any project in the middle group. Note that the very positive and very negative projects are not discussed because there was general concurrence on these. Only the uncertain ones (the exceptions) are debated.

Next, the facilitator calls for a scoring vote (between 1 and 9) for each project on each of two major factors, each of which contains three criteria:

Factor 1: project importance, consisting of
- strategic importance
- magnitude of impact on the bank
- economic benefits to the bank

Factor 2: ease of doing, consisting of
- cost of doing (negative scale)

- complexity of project (negative scale)
- resource availability.

Exhibit 3.12 provides detailed definitions for these six criteria.

Rating scores, averaged across the evaluators, are now added for each project to yield the two factor scores: importance and ease. A total project score is also computed (the sum of these two factors), which is then converted to a percentage. (At one time, RBC applied weights to its scoring criteria, but the choice of weights caused much debate. More recent scoring sessions have simply assigned equal weights to all criteria.)

After this sorting and scoring session, a prioritized list of projects is generated and rank-ordered according to the project scores. In this respect, the model so far is somewhat similar to the scoring approach used by Celanese. Also shown on the list are the expected annual expenditures for projects, as well as cumulative spending for all projects. (See the sample using disguised projects in Exhibit 3.13.) The list goes on for several pages, with the cumulative amount becoming larger and larger; when the cumulative amount equals the annual budget, a line is drawn under that project. For this first pass, projects above the line are tentatively "go"; those below the line are not and are tentatively placed on hold.

Projects are also displayed on an x–y bubble diagram, where the two axes are ease and importance. Which of the four quadrants a project is located in forms the basis for decisions and routings. (See more on bubble charts in Chapter 4.)

A second meeting takes place, at which managers reconsider the list of projects, particularly those close to the line or those that fall below the line yet might be important. Management judgment and experience can cause marginal and other projects to be shifted one way or the other. Also available at this meeting is a breakdown of the funded projects by product group, along with the total expected expenditure per group. This breakdown, together with the strategic role and mission of each group, is used to spot inconsistencies in resource allocation. For example, if a small business, whose mission is to "maintain and defend," was to receive a high proportion of funded projects and a significant percentage of the total development resources on this first pass, a flag is raised. This product group's projects are then reassessed. Ultimately, and after considerable discussion, the final and prioritized list of projects is agreed to.

Alternative Approaches to Obtaining Input Scores

The problem of getting a good scoring procedure in place remains a difficult one, however. The major obstacle is securing the decision makers' time: time for them to prepare for review meetings and finding mutually convenient meeting times. As a result, some companies have developed ways to streamline the project review process.

Electronic Gatekeeping.   Many companies with a systematic new product process are moving to electronic processes to guide users.* These e-processes offer the opportunity to streamline the rating and ranking of projects; thus, portfolio selection processes have become incorporated into electronic support systems.

Example: International Paper (IP), the largest paper company in the world, iron-ically has developed a world class *paperless* new product process. Part of the process involves electronic gate decision making by senior people—IP's portfo-lio process. Because many major projects cut across so many business units, it became next to impossible to assemble the right decision makers for timely re-view meetings. The electronic gate system was, thus, designed to allow for "vir-tual gate meetings."

The company uses a scoring model very similar to Celanese's, with the same five main factors and 18 questions—see Exhibit 3.8. Note that, like Celanese, the IP system and scoring model is for major projects and platform develop-ments. Here is how the electronic gate process works:

- Information on the projects under review is available electronically in stan-dard format and fields. The format of these deliverables corresponds to five main scoring criteria: business strategy fit, strategic leverage, probability of technical success, probability of commercial success, and reward. These summaries provide the decision makers with the current background on each project on-line.
- Decision makers review the deliverables and score the projects on-line. The 18 scoring questions are displayed along with anchor scales (much like Ex-hibit 3.8), and each person clicks their 0–10 scores for all 18 questions.
- Once all decision makers have scored the project, each at his or her own convenience and time, a gate meeting is held via video or telephone confer-ence. The results of the electronic scoring are available for display on par-ticipants' computers to discuss and debate. When consensus is reached, a decision is made.

The IP method is relatively new, but it promises a solution to a problem that plagues many companies: finding the time to get the decision makers or gate-keepers together.

Pre-scoring by Gatekeepers.   In a similar but nonelectronic process, project scores are generated before the project review meeting begins by management at National Sea Products, a major producer and marketer of branded seafood

---

* These e-processes are now commercially available. For example, *Accolade* is a very compre-hensive software package, which provides not only an e-manual but a complete automation of the product development process. Available from Product Development Institute (www.prod-dev.com) or from Sopheon (www.sopheon.com).

products. National Sea has a Stage-Gate™ new product process. At each gate or Go/Kill decision point, senior management (the gatekeepers) receive the deliverables on a given project several days before a gate meeting. Each gatekeeper reviews the facts and independently scores the project on 30 criteria several days before the meeting. The criteria cover topics such as competitive advantage, market attractiveness, and leveraging core competencies, and all are scored on 0–10 scales. Each question or criterion also calls for a confidence estimate to indicate (0–10) how sure evaluators are about their scores on each question.

The scorecards are then fed to the new product process manager, who uses a software package to integrate and analyze them. By the time the gatekeepers arrive at the gate review meeting, a summary table of all their scores, confidences, and areas of disagreement is on the table awaiting discussion.

One executive at National Sea expressed some concerns about the technique, however: "The method is extremely efficient and cuts to the chase—we don't waste a lot of time discussing things we already agree on. The trouble is, it's almost too efficient ... the decision is almost made before the meeting starts. We miss the benefit of walking through each criterion, discussing it, and reaching a consensus based on that discussion."

Note that unlike RBC, but like Celanese, National Sea uses these gate scores not only to make Go/Kill decisions, but to rate and rank projects against each other in periodic portfolio review meetings. This is a positive feature.

POINTS FOR MANAGEMENT TO PONDER

How are opinions of senior people and key decision makers in your business captured in order to make project decisions? Is there any rigor to the way you solicit these data and incorporate them into a Go/Kill or prioritization decision? Or is the project review just a meeting of senior people with a rambling agenda?

If you adopt a scoring model approach, we recommend the following:

The gatekeepers, or senior people, must do the scoring. Having the project team do the scoring introduces significant biases into the evaluation. The exception is self-managed gates (for less critical gates and lower-risk projects).

The scoring should be done at the gate review meeting. A major payoff from using a scoring model is the process itself, namely, that senior managers review the project together, discuss each criterion, score the project on each, and reach a consensus.

Use a scorecard at the meeting, where the decision makers can record their scores for each question. Two companies we encountered—one in North America, the other in Sweden—use electronic voting machines in the meeting room: Each decision maker has a numerical keypad. His or her answers are recorded instantly and fed into a computer. The results are projected onto a large screen. You can also use web-based electronic scoring and virtual gates, as does International Paper.

Pre-scoring by the Project Team.   In yet another approach, a project team is asked to score their project in advance of the project review meeting. The team then presents their scores to senior management at the gate review, who either accepts or refutes the scores. Only a minority of firms have adopted this approach, their argument being that the project team is in a much better position to do the scoring than are senior people, and that the gate decision process is more time-efficient. The counterargument (and majority view) is that the project team is not sufficiently objective to undertake the scoring (the "fox in the hen house" syndrome); that they have a vested interest in seeing the project move ahead; and that senior management is not afforded the opportunity to walk through each criterion in depth. Discussion and debate are shut down. A compromise between these two themes is applied in a division of NCR. This division uses the pre-scoring by the project teams but limits its use to straightforward projects only.

Nonetheless, the concept of "self-managed gates" is growing in popularity, especially for lower-risk projects and for certain noncritical gates. For example, Kraft Foods uses self-managed gates—where the team rates their own project and, in effect, makes the Go/Kill decision themselves—for lower-risk projects and for some less critical gates. Pre-scoring projects by the team and then presenting the scores and the decision to management—almost as a "done deal"—is a logical extension of self-managed gates.

Using the Outputs of Scoring Models

Scoring models provide a great amount of data, which can be displayed and used in various ways. The electronic gate meeting display at IP is one example. Here are some others:

- *At gate meetings:* Scoring models have been used for years at project gate review meetings to make Go/Kill decisions on individual projects. Here, the project attractiveness score is compared to a cutoff criterion. This is an *absolute process* during which projects are judged against some absolute standard. This is one way that Celanese uses its scoring model (Exhibit 3.8); the procedure at RBC is another illustration.
- *At portfolio reviews:* Here the scoring model outputs are used to rank projects against each other—this is a *relative process*. There are two approaches here:
  1. The project attractiveness scores generated by the scoring model can be used to rank projects in much the same way that projects were ranked using the NPV (see Exhibit 3.2). Celanese and others use their scoring models this way as well.
  2. Management ranks the projects *against each other* on *each* of the scoring model criteria. This is a forced ranking technique. Only a handful of major criteria are used, such as those used by Kodak at its portfolio reviews:[18]

     - Strategic fit
     - Product leadership (product advantage)
     - Probability of technical success

- Market attractiveness (growth, margins)
- Value to the company (profitability based on NPV).

Note that a project attractiveness score is not determined for each project. Rankings rather than ratings are generated on each criterion, and the final ranking is simply the average across all criteria.* So if Project A were #2 on strategic fit, #1 on product leadership, #3 on probability of technical success, and so on, chances are that it has a high overall ranking. Based on this forced ranking, projects are designated as "active" or "on hold."

- *As diagnostic tools:* One of the strengths of a scoring model is the process that people go through as they discuss the project, score it on scales, and then debate the scores. Indeed, more than one executive commented, "It's not so much the score that matters, it's the process that my colleagues and I walk through."

Scoring models provide an excellent list of questions for discussion—much like an agenda for a meeting. Each person has a chance to voice his or her opinion, and consequently much learning takes place. Scoring models help to identify critical areas of ignorance as well—things the review team simply does not know or disagrees on. The profile of the project can be displayed using software—for example, how the project fares on the six major factors in Exhibit 3.10. Thus the project's strengths and weaknesses are identified—for example, low scores on some vital factors—and discussion follows over how to correct these deficiencies.

So powerful is this diagnostic aspect of scoring models that in some firms, project teams are asked to score their own projects on the company's scoring model. This is encouraged not so much to rate or rank the project, but for the diagnostic capability—to identify critical information gaps, project strengths and weaknesses, and actions needed. The NewProd model (next) provides displays that facilitate this diagnostic process.

Computer-Based Scoring Model: NewProd™ 3000

NewProd™ 3000 is a computer-based scoring model based on the profiles and outcomes of hundreds of past new product projects.[19] It serves as both a diagnostic tool and a predictive model.** It is premised on the fact that the profile of a new product project is a reasonable predictor of success. Profile characteristics include such measures as competitive and product advantage, leverage of core competencies, market attractiveness, competitive situation, project innovativeness, and so on.

This model helps project teams understand their projects much better by examining strengths, weaknesses, risks, critical areas of ignorance, and what needs

---

* This forced ranking method is not a scoring model in the true sense: Projects are ranked on criteria (1 to N) and not rated on these criteria (0–10). But the process and criteria used are so similar to those in a scoring model that we include it here.

** *NewProd™* is a registered trademark of R.G. Cooper and Associates Consultants, Inc., a member firm of the Product Development Institute, Inc. For further information, see www.prod-dev.com.

fixing. It leads to a common understanding of the project and helps the project team to develop an action plan. *NewProd™ 3000* also predicts the likelihood of commercial success, which makes it valuable as an input to the Go/Kill and portfolio management decision. (For example, P&G uses NewProd's likelihood of commercial success score as one axis in their three-dimensional portfolio bubble diagram—Figure 4.3 in Chapter 4.)

NewProd™ 3000 works like this: Up to twelve evaluators assess the project on each of thirty key questions, which are proven discriminators between winners and losers. The profile of the project, based on these ratings, is compared with the profiles of hundreds of projects in the database that have known commercial outcomes. In this way, a likelihood of success and the project's strengths and weaknesses are determined.

Although originally developed for DuPont and Procter & Gamble, *NewProd™ 3000* is now commercially available and has been adopted as a selection and diagnostic tool in companies in Europe and North America. It has been successfully validated in Holland, Scandinavia, and North America and yields predictive abilities in the 73 to 84 percent range. This is not perfect, but it is considerably better than the typical manager's ability to pick winners![20] See Appendix C for more information.

Assessment of Scoring Models

Are scoring model methods effective as portfolio management models? They are only moderately popular, with a minority of firms using them as portfolio decision tools. There are still some concerns voiced by senior people at Celanese, Royal Bank, and other firms, and all confess that some "rough edges" have yet to be smoothed out. Overall, though, users appear satisfied with the scoring processes and the apparent rigor of their decisions.

Scoring models' major strengths are:

- They do not place too heavy an emphasis on financial criteria, whose reliability is doubtful at the early stages of a project. Note that in Celanese's model, only two questions deal with financial issues (see Exhibit 3.8).
- They capture multiple goals, such as strategic importance, competitive advantage, and market attractiveness. Some organizations recognize that some questions are more important than others and apply weights.
- They reduce the complex problem of making Go/Kill and prioritization decisions to a manageable number of specific questions.
- They subject each project to assessment on a complete set of criteria, ensuring that critical issues are not overlooked (as so often happens in unstructured meetings).
- They force managers to consider projects in greater depth and provide a forum for discussion.
- They are an excellent facilitation vehicle for a diagnostic assessment of a project's strengths and weaknesses.
- They yield a single score, which is a useful input into a project prioritization exercise.

Exhibit 3.14: A Typical Checklist of Must Meet Criteria (from Milltronics Inc.)

The following items are Yes/No. A No is a kill:

Strategic Fit: The proposed project is aligned with the Company's strategy and vision.
Technical Feasibility: There exists a reasonable likelihood of technical feasibility — that we can develop and manufacture the product — in light of the magnitude of the pay-offs (no obvious reasons why it cannot be done).
Competitive Rationale: A competitive reason exists to undertake the project: either it is necessary defensive or strategic product; or the product likely has significant competitive advantage (e.g., is a unique, superior product; better value-for-money; etc.).
Market Attractiveness: The market is large and growing; the need for the product is significant; competition is vulnerable.
Sustainable Competitive Advantage: The product has a protectable advantage; or raises barriers to entry to competitors.
Synergies: The project leverages (or builds from) our core competencies or strengths (marketing, technical, manufacturing).
Commercial Attractiveness: Given the market size, units and price projections, there is a strong likelihood that we could make adequate profits here.
Show-stoppers: There are no evident show-stoppers or potential "killer variables" at this point.

EXHIBIT 3.14   Typical Checklist of "Must-Meet" Criteria

Perhaps most important, scoring models seem to work: that is, they yield good decisions! Witness the 84 percent predicative ability claimed by P&G using their computer-based *NewProd* scoring model, and note the Dutch study's results.[21] Further, an investigation of 26 project selection techniques, including scoring models and financial approaches, revealed that scoring models were rated best by managers in terms of cost and ease of use, and that they were deemed "highly suitable for preliminary decisions" in the earlier phases of projects—namely, where key selection and portfolio decisions are made.[22]

Finally, our research into project selection methods reveals that of all methods, scoring models have much to recommend them and they fare remarkably well, in spite of their limited popularity and usage (chapter 6).[23] They yield a strategically aligned portfolio and one that reflects the business's spending priorities; they produce effective and efficient decisions; and they result in portfolios of high-value projects, more so than the other project evaluation tools!

Managers do express some major concerns about using scoring models as prioritization methods, however:

1. *Imaginary precision:* While useful, a scoring model should not be overused, nor its results automatically believed. Certain senior people suggest that scoring models impute a degree of precision that simply does not exist. As one executive at Celanese exclaimed: "They're trying to measure a [soft] banana with a micrometer!" Within the gate meetings themselves, there is evidence of this imaginary precision. For example, one project with a score of 49.7 percent (a fraction below the hurdle of 50 percent) was allowed to pass while another with a score of 48.3 percent was killed. Missing the hurdle by 1.7 percent was enough to do the project in.

2. *Halo effect:* The Royal Bank of Canada over the years has reduced the list of scoring criteria to six (see Exhibit 3.12). Why? Management argues that if a project scores high on one criterion, it tends to score high on many of the rest—a halo effect. Statistical analysis showed that the 15 criteria on RBC's original list* could be boiled down to a handful of key factors. Management in other firms do not share this view, however. Numerous firms use scoring models, and the scores across criteria for the most part are thought to capture quite different facets of a project (no halo effect). Our recommendation is to try to avoid overlap or duplication of factors and to keep the list of scoring factors as short as possible.

3. *Efficiency in allocation of scarce resources:* A final concern is that scoring models cannot ensure that the resulting list of "Go" projects indeed achieves the highest possible scores for a given total R&D expenditure. Recall that in the NPV, bang-for-buck method, the PI method, and the ECV method, the parameter to be maximized (the project's NPV or ECV) was divided by the constraining resource in order to maximize "bang for buck." The scoring models shown here fail to do this. For example, one artifact of some firms' scoring methods is that much larger projects tend to rise to the top of the list; however, if the ranking criterion had been "project score/R&D spend" instead of just "project score," then some smaller but efficient projects, requiring much fewer R&D resources, would have risen to the top.

Checklists As Portfolio Tools

Some firms use checklists instead of scoring models at their gate review or Go/Kill meetings. A good example of a checklist is shown in Exhibit 3.14 (from Milltronics, Inc., a midsized and leading-edge producer of level-measuring instruments in the process industries). The main difference between scoring models and checklists is that, while the questions are similar, the scoring procedure and end result are quite different. In a checklist method, the answers are yes/no. A single "no" answer is a knockout: It kills the project.

Checklists prove most effective at project review meetings as a culling tool to weed out poor projects, but they are not useful for project prioritization, since there is no 0–100 total project score that facilitates rank-ordering projects.

POINTS FOR MANAGEMENT TO PONDER

Do you use a checklist to make Go/Kill decisions on projects? If so, that's fine. Many companies do. It won't be of value in project prioritization, however.

Suggestion: Use a checklist method as a culling tool at project review or gate meetings—to discard the obvious misfit projects, then a scoring model to rank and prioritize projects.

---

*RBC used correlation and factor analysis on historical data (scores from scoring models used at gate meetings) to reveal that the many scoring criteria that they initially used were highly intercorrelated, which implied that only a subset of scoring factors were necessary.

Paired Comparisons

One project evaluation method encountered infrequently is the paired comparison approach. This method might be useful, particularly at the very beginning of projects (idea stage), when almost no information is available.

In this approach, managers compare project ideas against each other, one pair at a time. Here the question is, "If you had a choice, which of the two projects would you do?" There is discussion, and a consensus vote is reached on each pair. Projects are then rank-ordered according to the number of times they receive a "yes" vote in each paired comparison.

Example: One SBU within Telenor employed this method with mixed results. The business team regularly reviewed project ideas using paired comparisons, ranked the projects, and made Go/Kill decisions. While the method may have given good choices and yielded management consensus, it was criticized by those outside the team as being "soft, unstructured, political, emotional, and lacking rigorous criteria."

Paired comparison approaches have been expanded and facilitated in recent decades by mathematical models and decision support software. For example, today paired comparison can be greatly enhanced and streamlined using Analytic Hierarchy Processes (AHP), as described in Chapter 2.

In spite of these advances, we saw almost no use of computer-assisted paired comparison methods, even for early gate decisions. This is partly due to most managers' innate fear, or lack of understanding, of such mathematical models, even though today certain models and software are very user-friendly. But the method can also require considerable time. For example, if 10 ideas are considered, then a total of 45 paired comparison choices must be made. More sophisticated software packages make the decision process more efficient, however.

Value Maximization Methods: Summing Up

Six very useful value maximization methods have been outlined in this chapter:

1. NPV and bang-for-buck: a financial model that uses NPV to rank projects and incorporates resource constraints
2. Expected commercial value (ECV): a financial method based on a decision tree, incorporating probabilities and resource constraints
3. Productivity Index: a financial ranking approach using expected commercial value, technical risk, and R&D expenditures
4. Options Pricing Theory (OPT or Real Options): another financial method that recognizes project risk and the risk-reducing nature of the incremental decision process

5. Dynamic Rank-Ordered List: a ranking technique that combines several criteria—NPV, IRR, and strategic importance—and ranks projects concurrently on each
6. Scoring Model: a scoring technique that considers multiple criteria and combines ratings on these in a weighted fashion to yield an overall or project score.

Two other methods—checklists and paired comparisons—were also outlined, but they have limited use as portfolio tools.

The six main models have much to commend them. Specific weaknesses and problems with some of the models—quantity of data required, reliability of data, dealing with multiple objectives, imaginary precision, and halo effects—have been outlined throughout the chapter. As a group, their greatest weakness is that they fail to ensure that the portfolio is strategically aligned* or that it is even reasonably balanced. For example, the resulting list of projects from any of the methods in this chapter could maximize profits or some project score but still be a very unbalanced list of projects (for example, too many short-term ones), or it could fail to mirror the strategic direction of the business. These goals—balance and strategic alignment—are highlighted in the next two chapters.

In spite of these weaknesses, maximization of the portfolio's value is still a very worthwhile objective. We can argue about balance all we want and philosophize about the strategic direction of a portfolio, but if the projects in the portfolio rate poorly on profitability, have low likelihoods of success, or are simply unattractive, then the rest of the portfolio exercise is academic. First and foremost, the portfolio must contain good projects, and that is where the maximization methods outlined in this chapter come in. You should not ignore these methods. They ought to be part of your repertoire of portfolio models.

---

* Although scoring models deal in part with this issue, and as noted in Chapter 6, in practice some firms achieved strategically aligned portfolios using scoring models.

CHAPTER 4

Portfolio Management Methods: Seeking the Right Balance of Projects

Goal 2: Achieving a Balanced Portfolio

Most companies' new product portfolios are unbalanced; they feature the wrong mix of projects. This was one of the provocative findings of our large sample survey of portfolio practices and performance (Chapter 1). In fact, next to "too many projects," portfolio balance was the weakest portfolio performance element of all six metrics considered. Typically there are too many small projects in a portfolio—tweaks, modifications, updates, and fixes—and a dearth of major breakthroughs needed to sustain the growth of the company. Often the portfolio is far too heavily weighted toward the short-term, with a noticeable lack of visionary projects. And frequently an assessment of the spending breakdowns reveals that certain markets or business arenas of the company are receiving a disproportionate amount of the resources, far greater than seems sensible in light of the business opportunities. These are all issues of portfolio balance.

Portfolio balance is also important in order to manage risk. The financial expert understands well that diversity is the essence of risk management—we don't put all our eggs in one basket. So if attaining the correct *risk profile* in your portfolio is an objective, then the balance of projects in terms of risk and reward is an important dimension of portfolio balance.

Thus, the second major goal of many firms is the desire to obtain a balanced portfolio of new product projects. The means to achieving balance vary widely from company to company. As a result, many ingenious approaches were witnessed. In this chapter we explore several methods that can be used to reach the goal of a balanced portfolio of new product projects, and we provide some insights into the pros and cons of these methods.

What is a balanced portfolio? It is a set of development projects balanced in terms of a number of key parameters. Consider an investment fund, where the fund manager seeks balance in terms of high-risk versus blue-chip stocks, domestic versus foreign investments, and across industries in order to arrive at an optimally diversified investment portfolio. One way of managing risk is through diversity of investments. This is as true in new product development as it is in the stock market.

Charts are the most popular way to display balance in new product portfolios. Charts are favored for their ability to visually display the balance of projects in the portfolio, something that the rank-ordered lists, financial methods, and scoring models in Chapter 3 fail to do. Visual representations include the popular portfolio maps or *bubble diagrams*, which are adaptations of the four-quadrant BCG and GE/McKinsey business strategy models. We call these portfolio maps bubble diagrams—the description that most people are familiar with—simply because projects are shown as balloons or bubbles. Charts can also be traditional histograms, bar charts, and pie charts.

Our survey of best practices found that bubble diagrams are popular techniques. Hence, we devote considerable time to them in this book. A total of 41 percent of businesses use bubble diagrams. But note that hardly any companies use bubble diagrams as their dominant project selection method. Rather, bubble diagrams seem to be used more as a discussion tool to display the current portfolio breakdown, the "what is."

POINTS FOR MANAGEMENT TO PONDER

Have you considered what the right balance of projects for your new product portfolio is? Many managers in our study had not. In fact, they could not even tell us the current situation—the current breakdown of either projects or spending in their business. For example they did not know the percentage of funding going to new products versus maintenance work versus fundamental research; or the R&D spending breakdown across markets or technologies. Perhaps the place to begin is with an assessment of the current situation: Where is the money being spent now?

Bubble Diagrams

The typical bubble diagram shows development projects on a two-dimensional X–Y plot. The X and Y axes can be any dimension of interest, although some dimensions have proven particularly popular. A frequently used plot is risk versus reward, as shown in Exhibit 4.1. The circles or bubbles represent individual projects (or clusters of projects), and their size usually connotes some important third metric, such as the project's resource requirements. Some companies even use the shape of the bubbles, their colors, and their shading to represent key characteristics.

A casual review of portfolio bubble diagrams, such as the one in Exhibit 4.1, will lead some to observe that these new models are nothing more than the old strategy bubble diagrams of the 1970s. Not so. Recall that the BCG strategy model, and others like it (such as the GE and McKinsey models), plotted Business Units (BUs) on a market attractiveness versus business position grid. Note that the unit of analysis is the BU, an existing business—the "what is"—whose performance, strengths, and weaknesses are all known. By contrast, today's new product portfolio bubble diagrams, while they may appear similar, plot individual new product projects—future businesses or "what might be." As for the dimensions of the grid, the "market attractiveness versus business position" dimensions used for existing BUs may not be as appropriate for new product possibilities; so in our studies we saw other dimensions or axes extensively used.

Which Dimensions to Consider

What are some of the parameters that companies plot on these bubble diagrams to seek balance? Pundits recommend various parameters and lists, and even suggest the "best" plots to use. Here is a sample list of possible parameters to consider; any pair can be the X and Y axes for a bubble plot:

- fit with business or corporate strategy (low, medium, high)
- inventive merit
- strategic importance to the business (low, medium, high)
- durability of the competitive advantage (short, medium, long-term)
- reward based on financial expectations (modest to excellent)
- competitive impact of technologies (base, key, pacing, and embryonic technologies)
- probabilities of success (technical and commercial success as percentages)
- R&D costs to completion (dollars)
- time to completion (years)
- capital and marketing investment required to exploit (dollars).[1]

Other useful descriptors we found in bubble diagrams that help characterize the portfolio and portray balance are:

- markets or market segments (market A, market B, etc.)
- product categories or product lines (product line M, product line N, etc.)
- project types (new products; product improvements; extensions and enhancements; maintenance and fixes; cost reductions; and fundamental research)
- technology or platform types (technology X, technology Y, etc.).

About Risk-Reward Bubble Diagrams

The most popular bubble diagrams are variants of the risk-return diagram as shown in Exhibit 4.1. Two versions are proposed by two consulting firms. In both versions, one axis is some measure of the project's reward to the company, the other is the probability of success—thus, risk and reward.

Some firms use a *qualitative estimate of reward,* ranging from "modest" to "excellent." Management points out that too heavy an emphasis on financial analysis can do serious damage, notably in the early stages of a project. The other axis is the probability of overall success (probability of commercial success times probability of technical success).[2]

In contrast, other firms rely on quantitative and financial gauges of reward, namely, the risk-adjusted NPV* of the project. Here the probability of technical success is the vertical axis, since the probability of commercial success has already been built into the NPV calculation. Strategic Decision Group's method, for example, uses a quantitative, financial gauge of reward, namely, the shareholder value of the project.[3] **

A sample bubble diagram is shown in Exhibit 4.1 for a division of a major chemical company we label Company T. Note that NPV, adjusted for commercial risk, is the horizontal axis (reverse direction, from right to left) while the vertical axis is the probability of technical success. The size of each bubble shows the annual resources to be spent on each project. (In Company T's case, this is dollars per year. It could also be full-time equivalent people or work-months allocated to the project.)

The four quadrants of the bubble diagram model are as follows:

Pearls (upper left quadrant): These are the potential star products—projects with a high likelihood of success—which are expected to yield very high rewards. Most firms wish they had more of these. Company T has two such Pearl projects, and one of them has been allocated considerable resources (denoted by the sizes of the circles).

Oysters (lower left quadrant): These are the long-shot or highly speculative projects—projects with a high expected payoff, but with low likelihood of technical success. They are the projects where technical breakthroughs will pave the way for solid payoffs. Company T has three of these; none is receiving many resources.

Bread and Butter (upper right quadrant): These are small, simple projects with a high likelihood of success, but low reward. They include extensions, modifications, and updating of projects. Most companies have too many of these. Company T has a typical overabundance (note that the large circle here is actually a

---

*Risk-adjusted NPV: the net present value of the future stream of earnings (cash flow) from the project, less all remaining development, capital, and launch costs. The risk adjustment is carried out in one of several ways: by using a risk-adjusted discount rate; by applying probabilities to uncertain estimates in calculating the income stream; by weighting alternative scenario cash flows by their probabilities of occurring (as seen in the Productivity Index method in Chapter 3); or by using Monte Carlo simulation. Later in this chapter, we provide a comprehensive outline of the alternate methods for adjusting the NPV for risk.

**Shareholder value is the expected commercial value multiplied by the probability of technical success, less remaining R&D expenditures (see Productivity Index in Chapter 3). Uncertain commercial estimates—such as expected sales revenues—have probabilities built in; thus the commercial value has already been discounted for commercial uncertainty.

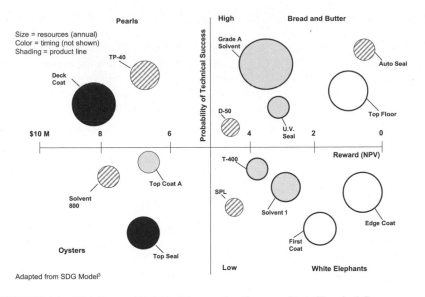

EXHIBIT 4.1   Risk-Reward Bubble Diagram for Company T: A Chemical Company

SOURCE: The basis of the diagram is the SDG Model described in note 3.

cluster of related product renewal projects). More than 50 percent of Company T's spending goes to these bread and butter projects.

White Elephants (lower right quadrant): These are the low-success and low-reward projects. Every business has a few white elephants, which are difficult to kill—projects that began life as good prospects but, over time, become less attractive. Company T has far too many. One-third of the projects and about 25 percent of Company T's spending fall in the white elephant quadrant.

An attractive feature of the bubble diagram model in Exhibit 4.1 is that it forces management to deal with the resource issue. The size of the circles denotes resource allocations per project so that, given finite resources (for example, a limited supply of people or money), the sum of the areas of the circles must be a constant. That is, if you add one project to the diagram, you must subtract another; alternatively, you can shrink the size of several circles. The elegance here is that the model forces management to consider the resource implications of adding one more project to the list—other projects must pay the price!

Also shown in this bubble diagram is the product line with which each project is associated (via the shading or cross-hatching). A final breakdown revealed by Company T via color is timing (although we could not show this in our black-and-white diagram). Hot red means "imminent launch" while blue is cold and means an early-stage project. Thus, this apparently simple risk-reward diagram shows much more than simply risk and profitability data. It also conveys resource allocation, timing, and allocations across product lines.

Using Risk-Reward Bubble Diagrams

How is the bubble diagram model used? Unlike the maximization models of Chapter 3, no prioritized list of projects is produced. Bubble diagrams are very much an information display and not so much a decision model per se. Nonetheless, certain quadrants have more preferred projects than others; and the balance across three of the better quadrants is also vital. From the example in Exhibit 4.1, management debates the appropriateness of the current portfolio and takes necessary action.

To deal with the overabundance of white elephants, Company T initiated immediate gate reviews of these five projects with the idea of pruning the list and reallocating resources to more deserving projects. There were a number of fairly good projects on hold awaiting resources (these are not shown on the bubble diagram, but several companies we interviewed also produced bubble diagrams of the projects on hold).

Management felt that the three oyster projects were about the right number, but they decided to increase resources to move them along more quickly. Two in particular were being starved for resources.

Projects in the upper right quadrant—the bread and butter ones, accounting for more than 50 percent of spending—were closely scrutinized. There was a general unease on the part of senior management about the high level of spending here (the business had been designated a "growth business"). There was also a concern about whether they were in danger of becoming "busy fools"—a lot of activity around a number of trivial projects. As a result, several projects were canceled or postponed.

Several projects in the hold vault were immediately activated (projects that had been placed on hold due to lack of resources or people to work on them). People were made available by cutting back on the white elephant and bread and butter projects.

Bubble diagrams find use in two settings. The first and most obvious is in portfolio review meetings, much like the situation described at Company T. Here the entire portfolio of projects is periodically reviewed (for example, semiannually or quarterly) and appropriate actions are taken, as described above.

The second use of bubble diagrams—and indeed all the visual charts in this chapter—is at gate or project review meetings. One method is as follows:

- The one project under consideration is shown on a bubble diagram as a dotted circle (yet to be approved).
- The same bubble diagram displays the other projects currently underway—the active projects and current resource allocations.
- A second bubble diagram (optional) displays projects on hold and awaiting resources.

In this way, the project under consideration is compared to others in the queue as well as to active projects. In addition, by showing the new project on the active bubble diagram, the impact that this new project has on the total portfolio (for example, what it would do to the balance or how it might fit into the portfolio) can be seen. Note that various software packages have been developed to assist in the construction of bubble diagrams, such as *Newport Max™*.*

Variants of Risk-Reward Bubble Diagrams

3M's Ellipses

3M's method is unique in that it visually portrays uncertainty and probabilities, which must be a key parameter in any portfolio decision. One problem with standard risk-reward bubble diagrams like the one shown in Exhibit 4.1 is that they require a point estimate of the reward, namely, the probable NPV. In reality, there is a distribution or range of probable rewards or NPVs for any project. Technical risks are captured by the vertical axis, namely, probability of technical success, but not so for the commercial risks. Even the estimate of technical success probabilities is problematic, because it may involve a range of estimates as well (for example, "the probability of technical success is in the 50 to 70 percent range").

Some business units at 3M use a variant of the bubble diagram that portrays uncertainties via the size and shape of the bubbles. In calculating the NPV, high and low estimates are made for uncertain variables. This leads to high- and low-case NPV estimates for each project. Similarly, high/low estimates are made for the probability of technical success. The result is shown in Exhibit 4.2. The size and shape of the bubbles or balloons on the portfolio map thus capture the uncertainty or fuzziness of projects. Here, very small bubbles mean highly certain—very tight—estimates on each dimension. In contrast, large bubbles or ellipses mean fuzzy or loose projects with considerable uncertainty—a high spread between the worst case and the best case for that project. Note: The size of the ellipse is such that there is an 80 percent probability that the value of the project falls within it.[4]

Procter & Gamble's Three-Dimensional Portfolio Model

Procter & Gamble is experimenting with a novel three-dimensional plot, made possible via computer-aided design (CAD) software. Exhibit 4.3, on two-dimensional paper, does not do the model justice. Here, time to market, NPV, and probability of commercial success are the three axes. The argument is that that three dimensions capture the key elements of any development portfolio:[5]

1. *NPV* is an obvious dimension—it captures the reward or payoff from the project.
2. *Time to market* serves two purposes. First, all other things being equal, faster projects are more desirable—the notion of "a bird in the hand" or that more distant economic returns are less desirable. Second, and perhaps subtler, is the idea that lengthy projects are invariably fraught with development and execution risk. The longer something is planned to take, the higher the likelihood that something will go wrong.

NewPort Max™, a portfolio management software tool for development projects; available from Product Development Institute (www.prod-dev.com) and Sopheon (www.sopheon.com).

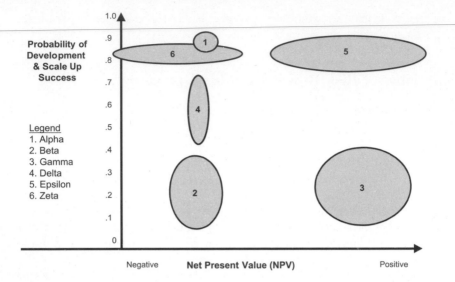

EXHIBIT 4.2   3M's Risk-Reward Bubble Diagram Showing Uncertainties

Note: Larger circles and ellipses denote more uncertain estimates.

SOURCE: Adapted from Gary L. Tritle, "New Product Investment Portfolio," internal 3M document.

3. *Probability of commercial success* is also an obvious dimension, but P&G uses a more rigorous method for estimating this value for projects than simply pulling a number out of the air (below).

Now the details of the model in Exhibit 4.3: The various shapes displayed represent development (new product) projects. Considerable information is displayed in this type of model:

- The horizontal or X-axis is the time to market, with long times being less favorable.
- The vertical or Y-axis is the NPV. This is calculated using a Monte Carlo probability model called "At Risk" (more on this later in the chapter). The I-beams in the vertical direction show the range of NPV values per project.
- The diagonal or Z-axis is the probability of commercial success. This is derived from the *NewProd* model, a 30-question scoring model, tailored for P&G's use (described in Chapter 3).
- There are four possible shapes to each project that capture the degree of fit the project has with the company's strengths: spheres are the best-fit projects; cubes are the worst-fit; cylinders and cones are somewhere in between.
- The model also shows the ROI of each project (by clicking one's mouse on each shape). The color of the shapes shows what stage the project is in according to P&G's SIMPL Stage-Gate process. Tracking of projects over time can be displayed via a "comet's tail" for each project (optional). Finally, because this is CAD soft-

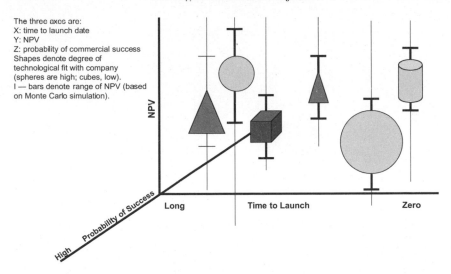

The three axes are:
X: time to launch date
Y: NPV
Z: probability of commercial success
Shapes denote degree of
technological fit with company
(spheres are high; cubes, low).
I — bars denote range of NPV (based
on Monte Carlo simulation).

NPV

Probability of Success

High

Long   Time to Launch   Zero

EXHIBIT 4.3   Procter & Gamble's Three-Dimensional Risk-Reward Bubble Diagram Using Nonfinancial Axes

SOURCE: Developed by Tom Chorman (formerly finance manager, CNV, P&G)

ware, any view from any direction, and zooming in or out are possible. For example, the model can be rotated in three-dimensional space to give the decision-making audience different perspectives of their portfolio.

From a visual standpoint, this is the most sophisticated bubble diagram we encountered. It was also relatively inexpensive to develop with off-the-shelf CAD software. P&G's model demonstrates what a creative mind can do in terms of the elegance of the visuals and the ability to display more than the usual amount of information in a user-friendly fashion.

Capturing Reward via Nonfinancial Metrics

Some pundits argue that strict reliance on financial estimates can do considerable damage to a new product portfolio. They maintain that low-risk, simple, "low-hanging fruit" projects will be favored while strategically important or potential breakthrough projects will fare less well. Sometimes strategic issues and the quest for significant projects must take precedence over strictly financial and short-term return. Moreover, financial data are very often highly unreliable, especially in the predevelopment stages, when the portfolio is being decided. And portfolio models, in which one axis is the NPV, assume a level of precision of financial data far beyond what most project teams can provide.

Arthur D. Little's proposed alternative is to use a nonfinancial measure of reward. This is a subjective estimate ranging from "modest" to "excellent" and depends not only on the financial prospects for the project, but on its strategic

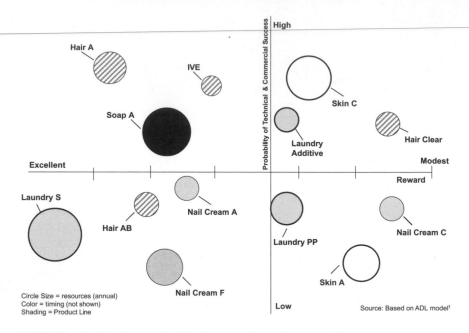

EXHIBIT 4.4 Risk-Reward Bubble Diagram Using Nonfinancial Axes

SOURCE: Based on P. Roussel, K. Saad, and T. Erickson, *Third Generation R&D, Managing the Link to Corporate Strategy* (Boston: Harvard Business School Press and Arthur D. Little, 1991).

importance and impact on the company. Conveniently, both probabilities—commercial success and technical success—are incorporated into the vertical axis, as shown in Exhibit 4.4.[6]

A Simpler Risk-Reward Portfolio Map

A somewhat simpler illustration of the risk-reward diagram is provided by Reckitt-Benckiser (formerly Reckitt & Colman) as one of the many visual charts that compose their portfolio model.

Reckitt-Benckiser is a multinational producer of frequently purchased household consumer goods and pharmaceutical products. Headquartered in London, England, the firm distributes its products in most countries worldwide under a variety of brand names. In North America, familiar brand names include Easy-Off oven cleaner, Air Wick air freshener, Lysol disinfectant cleaners, and Woolite fabric wash.

This company portrays its portfolio of projects on a less complex portfolio map diagram than Company T in Exhibit 4.1. Here the NPV is plotted against the overall probability of success, as shown in Exhibit 4.5. The various types of projects are also shown on the diagram: new business (new products in a new cate-

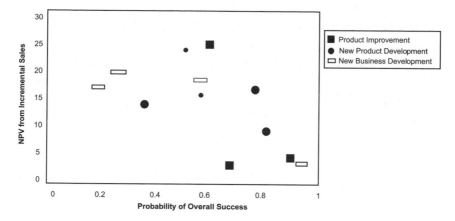

EXHIBIT 4.5   Reckitt-Benckiser Probability of Success versus NPV

Note: This chart is an illustration of the type of additional information available at portfolio review at R-B. Probability of overall success = probability of technical success x probability of commercial success.

gory), new products, and product improvements. Thus, two elements of balance are revealed in a single diagram: risk-reward and project type.

Here, the probability of overall success (horizontal axis) is simply the two probabilities—technical and commercial success—multiplied together. And the NPV considers only incremental sales (cannibalized sales are subtracted).

POINTS FOR MANAGEMENT TO PONDER

Do you consciously consider the risk profile of your business's new product portfolio via any of the popular bubble diagrams outlined above? If not, begin with one of the easier diagrams (Exhibit 4.1 or 4.5, for example). Or, if you are more comfortable with a less financially driven approach, try using a qualitative assessment of reward (Exhibit 4.4). Better yet, use a scoring approach (described below). The point is that these bubble diagrams are proving to be very useful, with the risk-reward diagram emerging as the most popular—and for good reason!

Portfolio Maps with Axes Derived from Scoring Models

Some companies combine the benefits of a scoring model with the visual appeal of a bubble diagram. Here the axes of the bubble diagram are computed or derived from scores on scaled questions. In some cases, the scoring results from gate meetings are used as direct input into the portfolio model. Three firms we encountered use variants of this approach: Reckitt-Benckiser (above); the Royal Bank of Canada (Chapter 3); and Specialty Minerals, a spinoff company from Pfizer.

Specialty Minerals' Risk-Reward Scoring Method

A combined scoring model and bubble diagram is used by Specialty Minerals. It merits attention because it solves several problems encountered in bubble diagrams. Management at Specialty Minerals is very aware that overuse of financial criteria (for example, using NPV as one of the axes of the bubble diagram as in Exhibit 4.1) is problematic. They argue that reliable financial data are simply not available at the very point in a project's life when prioritization decisions are required. Similarly, arriving at quantitative estimates of probabilities of success has also proven difficult. Finally, management seeks to link the portfolio model to gate decisions. Note that Specialty Minerals employs a Stage-Gate™ new product process, very similar to the model in Appendix A, which relies on a scoring model at gates.

The solution adopted is to combine the gate scoring model with the portfolio bubble diagram. Here's how. Specialty Minerals' gate scoring model considers seven factors:*

1. Management interest
2. Customer interest
3. Sustainability of competitive advantage
4. Technical feasibility
5. Business case strength
6. Fit with core competencies
7. Profitability and impact.

These factors are scored at gates on 1–5 scales in order to make Go/Kill decisions on individual projects. Five of the seven factors are also used to construct a bubble diagram, with probability of success and reward as the two axes (see Exhibit 4.6). Both axes are derived from the scores on the seven factors as follows:

1. Vertical axis: probability of success, consisting of a weighted (in parentheses) combination of

   - customer interest (0.25)
   - technical feasibility (0.50)
   - fit with core competencies (0.25)

2. Horizontal axis: value to the company, consisting of a weighted combination of

   - profitability (0.66)
   - competitive advantage (0.34).

This company's seven-factor scoring model thus does double duty. It is the basis for Go/Kill decisions at gate reviews, and it also provides five components (and data) to construct the two axes of the portfolio bubble diagram. The gate decisions are, thus, closely linked to portfolio reviews. In adopting this hybrid method, and by using the scores obtained at gate reviews to provide inputs to the

* The wording has been modified slightly from Specialty Minerals' list to provide greater clarity for the reader.

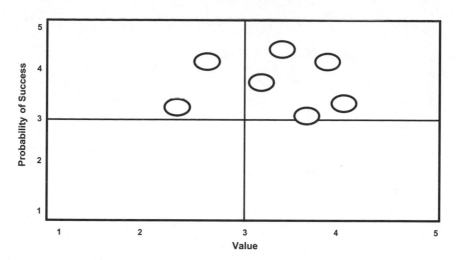

EXHIBIT 4.6   Specialty Minerals' Risk-Reward Bubble Diagram Using Scored Axes
Based on Gate 3 scoring results.
Value = .66 (profitability) + .34 (competitive advantage).
Probability of success = .25 (customer interest) + .5 (technical feasibility) + .25 (fit)

bubble diagram, Specialty Minerals achieves two goals of portfolio management in one approach: maximization of the portfolio (the gate scoring model) and appropriate balance in terms of risk and reward (the bubble diagram in Exhibit 4.6). The model has only recently been implemented, and time will tell whether it proves effective.

Ease versus Attractiveness

A very useful portfolio map at Reckitt-Benckiser (R-B), in management's view, is their ease-versus-attractiveness chart. As in Specialty Minerals' method, this bubble diagram also eliminates the heavy reliance on precise financial data, yet it incorporates factors that Reckitt-Benckiser management considers vital to project selection and portfolio balance.

Here the axes are market/concept attractiveness and ease of implementation (see Exhibit 4.7). Both axes are constructed from a scoring model; namely, multi-item 1–5 scales, which are added in a weighted fashion.

The concept attractiveness scale is made up of scores on six items, four of which are purchase intent, product advantage, sustainability of advantage, and international scope. Similarly, ease of implementation, the second axis, also comprises scored items, such as the firm's technological strengths and the expected absence of problems in development, registration, packaging, manufac-

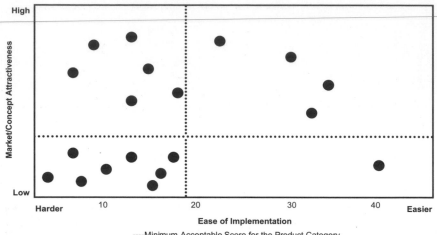

EXHIBIT 4.7   Reckitt-Benckiser's Market/Concept Attractiveness versus Ease of Implementation

Note: Both axes are based on a weighted addition of multiple items (much like a scoring model). See Exhibit 4.8. Each black circle represents a new product project.

turing, and distribution. (See Exhibit 4.8 for details of the scoring questions.) Thus, R-B uses a scoring model, but in this case to construct the axes of the two-dimensional portfolio bubble diagram.

A second and parallel bubble diagram plots market/concept attractiveness (defined in Exhibit 4.8) versus financial attractiveness (see bubble diagram in Exhibit 4.9). The latter axis is based on an NPV calculation.

Reckitt-Benckiser's portfolio maps are used much in the same way that Company T uses its bubble diagram. Managers look for projects in favorable quadrants (toward the upper right of the diagram in Exhibit 4.7), scrutinize those in the "unattractive and hard-to-do" quadrant, and look for balance between ease and attractiveness. For example, in Exhibit 4.7:

- There is a surprising shortage of easy-to-do projects. This is a departure from the plethora of "low-hanging fruit" projects the company typically focused on only a few years ago. Perhaps the pendulum has swung too far the other way and a better balance should be sought between easy and challenging projects. Therefore, management should be looking for ways to increase the number of easier projects.
- There are clearly too few projects in the desirable upper right quadrant. One outcome of this analysis is recognition of the need for increased focus on idea/concept generation and the need to move more concepts through the early phase screening. Further, while resource allocations are not shown on the diagram, clearly resource commitments for the four potential stars is an issue.

With 8 projects out of 19 in the lower left quadrant (more difficult and less attractive), management must ask some very tough questions: Why are there so

Items Comprising Market/Concept Attractiveness Score (Vertical Axis)		
Factor	Weighting	Scale (1-5)
Purchase Intent	5	1. Significantly below average. 2. Slightly below average. 3. Equal to average. 4. Slightly above average. 5. Significantly above average.
Advantage Over What's Available	5	1. Significantly below average. 2. Slightly below average. 3. Equal to average. 4. Slightly above average. 5. Significantly above average.
Performance in Use	5	1. Little prospect of performance advantage. 2. Uncertain prospect of performance advantage. 3. Some prospects for slight advantage. 4. Some prospects for important product advantage. 5. Good prospects for important product advantage.
Competitive Position Improvement	2.5	1. Helps to modernize brand, but doesn't enhance franchise long-term. 2. Contributes to brand's strategic plan & helps to make franchise contempary. 3. Contributes to brand's strategic plan & keeps franchise contempary. 4. Builds brand and franchise long term. 5. Significantly builds brand and franchise long term.
Sustainability of Competitive Advantage	2.5	1. <6 months 2. 6-12 months 3. 1-2 years 4. 2-5 years 5. >5 years
Geographic Scope[*]	2.5	1. Local project - developed market. 2. Local project - developing market. 3. Regional project - developed market. 4. Regional project - developing market. 5. Multi-regional project.

EXHIBIT 4.8   Definition of Factors Composing Market/Concept Attractiveness and Ease of Implementation for Reckitt-Benckiser

Note: The market attractiveness of a project is the weighted summation of scores on the items above.

*R-B divided the world into regions: Europe, North America, Central/South America, Pacific, and so on. A regional project accommodates multiple countries, e.g., Europe. A local project accommodates one country.

many projects here? Which ones should be canceled? What is the rationale for each? (Perhaps there are strategic, competitive, or defensive reasons for doing these.) How much are we spending this year on projects in this quadrant? (Perhaps management can postpone a few to reduce resource commitment here.) Can some of the better ones be made more attractive or easier to do by changing the definition, scope, resource commitment, or plan of action?

Items Comprising Ease of Implementation Score (Horizontal Axis)		
Factor	**Weighting**	**Scale (1-5)**
Technical Competitive Strength	4.5	1. Weak 2. Tenable 3. Favourable 4. Strong 5. Dominant
Technical Maturity	9	1. Embryonic 2. Growth 3. Mature 4. Aging
Registration/Clinical Trial	4.5	1. Major problems are anticipated in most markets. 2. Major problems are anticipated in some markets. 3. Minor problems are anticipated. 4. No problems are anticipated. 5. No registration or clinical trial required.
Packaging Components	3	1. Needs basic advances in packaging technology. 2. Several new components need development. 3. A new component needs development. 4. Needs modifications to existing components. 5. Uses existing components.
Manufacture	3	1. Needs basic advances in manufacturing technology. 2. Needs new manufacturing equipment (> 100,000). 3. Needs major modifications (< 100,000) or use of copacker. 4. Needs minor modifications (< 25,000) 5. Uses existing manufacturing equipment.
Sales & Distribution	3	1. New sales/buyer skills needed in new distribution channel. 2. Existing sales skills in new distribution channel. 3. New skills required by both salespeople & buyers. 4. Some new skills required. 5. No change necessary to existing sales effort.

EXHIBIT 4.8   (Continued) Definition of Factors Composing Market/Concept Attractiveness and Ease of Implementation for Reckitt-Benckiser

Note: The ease of implementation of a project is the weighted summation of scores on the items above.

Six projects are in the attractive but hard-to-do quadrant. Again, vital questions about these six must focus on ways to improve their ease of implementation. For example, by increasing resource commitments, can some of the technical, manufacturing, and packaging barriers be overcome?

Ease versus Importance

The Royal Bank of Canada uses a variation of the ease-versus-attractiveness bubble diagram used by Reckitt-Benckiser. Indeed, RBC's portfolio method has seen considerable evolution over the past few years as the bank has gained experience with it.

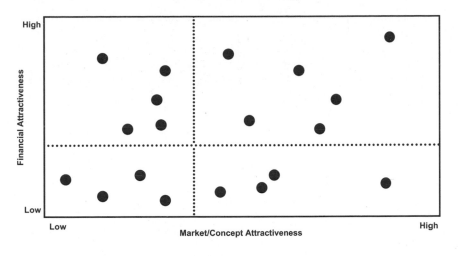

EXHIBIT 4.9   Reckitt-Benckiser Financial Attractiveness versus Market/Concept
Attractiveness

Initially, a standard financially based bubble diagram was used, on which
NPV and probability of success were plotted (much like Exhibit 4.1). Project
teams provided the data necessary to do the NPV calculation, and the probability
of commercial success was derived from a tailored version of the *NewProd*
model designed for financial institutions (Chapter 3), with the project teams
again providing the input data. Unfortunately, the method led to self-serving data
inputs from the teams. They soon realized what the data were being used for and
started to slant the input data to favor their own projects.

The current bubble diagram features two dimensions, or factors, which com-
prise six scored scales (see Exhibit 3.12). The resulting bubble diagram is very
similar to Reckitt-Benckiser's in Exhibit 4.7, except that circle sizes represent the
current year funding for each project (see Exhibit 4.10).

POINTS FOR MANAGEMENT TO PONDER

If too heavy a reliance on financial data and financial metrics is a concern, or if multiple objectives beyond strictly financial ones is the goal, consider building a risk-reward bubble diagram whose axes are based on scored criteria, as in the three companies above. If feasible, you might even use some of the same scoring criteria here
that you use in your gate scoring model. In fact, we'd suggest that you even use
project scores from gates directly as inputs to your risk-reward bubble diagram.

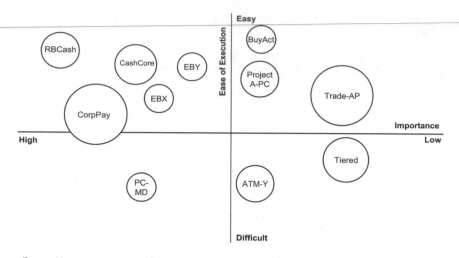

Ease and Importance are scored axes.
Circle sizes show current annual funding per project.

EXHIBIT 4.10   Royal Bank's Portfolio Map of Ease versus Project Importance

Note: Ease and importance are scored axes. Circle sizes show current annual funding per project.

Factoring Risk and Uncertainty into the Reward Calculation

Frequently, in the companies we studied, the reward of the project is captured on the portfolio map or bubble diagram by the NPV. In the examples above, P&G, Company T, 3M, and Reckitt-Benckiser all use NPV in their bubble diagrams, as was the case in many other firms we visited. But the issue of how to calculate the NPV, given uncertain estimates, is a common concern. Different models and different firms treat risk in a variety of ways in this NPV calculation:

- *Build probabilities into the NPV calculation:* Company G, which uses the dynamic rank-ordered list discussed in Chapter 3, also displays portfolio maps similar to those in this chapter. The company simply factors down all uncertain estimates in the NPV calculation by their probability of occurring. For example, if projected revenues are uncertain, the finance department multiplies these by a probability of 0.80, or perhaps 0.60, to account for that uncertainty. Mathematically, this procedure is not strictly correct, but it does serve to dramatically scale back wildly optimistic financial projections.
- *Use risk-adjusted discount rates:* Company T uses variable discount rates when it calculates the NPV. In effect, these are risk-adjusted discount rates. For example, new product projects whose commercial projections are highly uncertain use a discount rate of double the risk-free hurdle rate. Low-risk projects, such as product modifications and renewals or process improvements, use a discount rate of 1.5 times the risk-free hurdle rate, and so on. What this procedure does is penalize higher-risk projects—their NPV is scaled back accordingly.

- *Use probability-weighted cash flows:* This approach is used in determining the ECV in the Productivity Index method in Chapter 3. Here, develop different scenarios to represent possible outcomes of the project: for example, major success, good success, moderate success, break-even, failure. For each scenario, develop a cash-flow analysis and determine the respective NPVs. Then weight each scenario's cash flow by the probability of its happening (that is, multiply each scenario's NPV by its probability of occurring). Add up the probability-weighted cash flows and the result is the probability-adjusted NPV for the project.
- *Use Monte Carlo simulation:* Company M, a medical products firm, uses a portfolio model similar to Company T's in Exhibit 4.1. The probability of technical success is taken into account on the vertical axis, but the probability of commercial success is not. To account for commercial uncertainty, every variable requires three estimates: high, low, and likely.* As a result, revenue, costs, launch timing, and so on each have three estimates provided by the project team. From these three estimates, a probability distribution curve is determined for each variable. Next, random scenarios are generated for the project using these probability curves as variable inputs. Thousands of scenarios are computer-generated (hence the name Monte Carlo—thousands of spins of the wheel), and the result is a distribution of financial outcomes. From this, the expected NPV is determined—an NPV figure with all commercial outcomes and their probabilities figured in. This is an interesting technique, and a mathematically elegant one. Management at Company M strongly endorses the rigorous method, but it is proving to be a significant burden to the project teams, who are asked to supply an endless stream of data! Moreover, private conversations with team members revealed that they simply did not have the data required, and that they were providing the "model owner" with nonsense data—largely invented numbers. Even with this fault, however, a number of other companies find the Monte Carlo approach useful (one example is Procter & Gamble, which employs a version of Monte Carlo simulation called "At Risk"; other companies using a Monte Carlo approach include Foamex and Nova Chemicals).
- *Build a decision tree:* The expected commercial value (ECV) method, used by ECC, and the options pricing approach are both based on simple decision trees (see Chapter 3). They appropriately incorporate the future stream of earnings, various capital and development costs incurred throughout the project, and the probabilities of technical and commercial success. The computation is relatively straightforward, and the ECV certainly can be used here in various bubble diagrams. Based on its success at ECC, we recommend considering the ECV method as one way to build risk into the NPV calculation.
- *Use high case/low case:* This method, used at 3M and described earlier in this chapter, captures uncertainties on both risk and reward dimensions of the bubble diagram by using "high" and "low" case scenarios (or "best case" and "worst case"). The size and shape of the bubbles or ellipses denote the uncertainty associated with each project (see Exhibit 4.2).
- *Employ nonfinancial measures of reward:* Recall that the bubble diagram model (shown in Exhibit 4.4) relies on a nonfinancial measure of reward and hence does not use an NPV calculation per se. Realistically, however, the NPV is hard to ignore when assessing a project's potential reward to the company. Using nonfinancial measures has one major advantage: The approach eliminates the need to build probabilities or uncertainties into the NPV reward calculation. The metric here is a simple

* The 10, 50, and 90 percent points on the probability distribution curve.

"modest" to "excellent" scale. Note that both probabilities (commercial and technical success) are captured outside the reward metric: They are conveniently combined into an overall probability of success on the vertical axis of the bubble diagram.

- *Use the scales in scoring models as a proxy for reward:* Using a scoring model to determine the reward metric also eliminates the need to handle uncertainty and probabilities in a financial calculation. Specialty Minerals' approach to deriving a reward measure from their gate scoring model was outlined earlier in this chapter. This method is that firm's way of coping with the uncertainty of financial estimates. You might also wish to review Celanese's scoring method and our best practices scoring model, both discussed in Chapter 3. Recall that both models use multiple scales as proxies for reward.

POINTS FOR MANAGEMENT TO PONDER

How are uncertainty and probabilities built into your financial analysis calculations? Perhaps you've chosen to use a nonfinancial metric to capture project reward. Whether you're determining an NPV or a reward estimate for use in a bubble diagram, or in a value maximization method (previous chapter), or simply calculating an NPV, EBIT, IRR, or ROI for a project gate review, probabilities, uncertainty and risk must be considered. Chapter 8 shows how to apply rigor to the estimates of probabilities of success. In the section above, various options were presented on how to incorporate these probabilities into your financial analysis. The point is that you cannot ignore the uncertainty aspect in the calculation of the expected reward. Review the methods cited above and decide on the one approach that you like best!

Other Bubble Diagrams

There are numerous parameters, dimensions, or variables across which one might wish to seek a balance of projects. As a result, an endless variety of X–Y plots or bubble diagrams is possible. Here are some others to consider:

Market and Technical Newness

Various dimensions of project newness have been popular ways to characterize new product projects over the years. The original newness or familiarity matrix, proposed by Ed Roberts, has seen many variants.[7] And this thinking has crept into bubble diagram design. Thus a fairly popular version of a bubble diagram is to plot various measures of newness as the X and Y axes.

Example: Bayer is a major pharmaceutical and chemical company. One of its U.S. divisions has moved ahead to implement portfolio management. Among other charts, its newness bubble diagram is thought to be very helpful in characterizing projects (Exhibit 4.11). Here, two dimensions of newness are used:

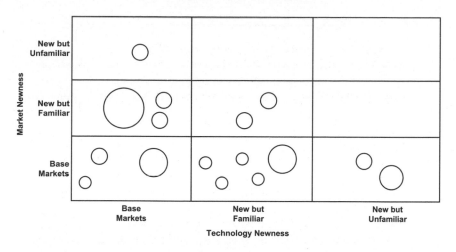

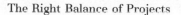

EXHIBIT 4.11   Example of Bayer's Market by Technology Newness Matrix

Note: Bubble size represents resource requirements. Bubble location and data are disguised.

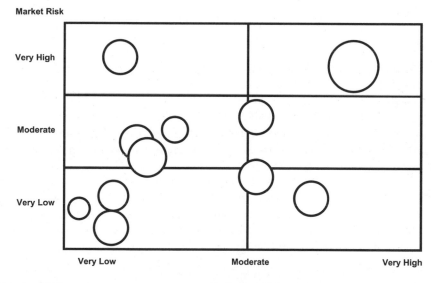

EXHIBIT 4.12a   Market and Technology Risk Bubble Diagram

Note: Circle size represents R&D resources.

1. Market newness—three categories:

- Base markets: markets already served by the company
- New but familiar markets: markets that are new to the company, but close enough to existing markets to be familiar ones
- New but unfamiliar markets: markets that are both new to the company and unfamiliar

2. Technology newness—also three categories:

- Base technologies: already in place or practiced within the company
- New but familiar technologies: new technologies to the company but ones that are sufficiently close to base technologies that they are familiar
- New but unfamiliar technologies: new technologies to the company that are quite unfamiliar as well; may be totally new technologies to the world

Development projects are put into the three categories on each of the two dimensions and then plotted on the newness bubble diagram (Exhibit 4.11). The size of the bubble represents the resource requirements for the project.

This newness diagram enables management to see in a glance the risk profile of the portfolio (newness is a proxy for risk), and to see the relative allocation of resources across quadrants.

Market and Technology Risk

Should all projects be low-risk? Exhibit 4.12a portrays projects in terms of both technology risk and market risk (used at Reckitt-Benckiser). Once again, a balance is sought. A similar risk bubble chart is used at Rohm and Haas. Here the probability of technical success is plotted against the commercial probability (chart not shown). The bubble sizes denote the total cost of projects, so that resource allocation can be seen. Rohm and Haas uses a matrix approach to determining probabilities of success (see Chapter 8).

At Unilever, technology risk is classified by the type of "enabling technology"; the types they use are base, incremental, next-generation, and radical. The market risk is viewed by degree of change in the product and the perception of value to the consumer (see Exhibit 4.12b). Management at Unilever then seeks to optimize the balance between the types of risk.

Market Segment versus Strategic Intent

One attempt to view the portfolio balance in terms of strategy was witnessed at Rohm and Haas. The next chapter deals with the strategic link in detail, but because this chart is in the form of a bubble diagram, we show it here.

Projects are displayed on a bubble diagram (Exhibit 4.13) that has as its two dimensions:

   1. *Strategic intent*: the purpose and type of project (defend, grow, new application, new business, fundamental research)
   2. *Market segment* served.

The bubble size is the total cost of the project.

Rohm and Haas worked over time to develop custom software for portfolio management (today such portfolio management software is available off the shelf). Each business has a portfolio manager, who is also the manager of the business's new product Stage-Gate™ process. Using the specialized software, these portfolio managers are able to display virtually any plot of any variable they wish in bubble diagram format.

Strategic Impact Matrix

Yet another chart displays the strategic impact of the portfolio of active projects.[8] This is displayed by C.R. Bard, Inc., a medical products firm, via two axes in Exhibit 4.14:

   1. *External impact*: from "me too" to "leapfrog product"
   2. *Internal impact*: from "support" to "breakthrough development."

The idea here is that the strategic impact of a project can be either internal or external or both. And this chart captures the distribution of projects in terms of their strategic impacts.

Bubble Diagram Recap

Which types of bubble diagrams are prevalent in industry? Earlier in this chapter we provided several lists of dimensions that can be used as the X and Y axes. In practice, however, management seems to prefer a handful of popular diagrams. Exhibit 4.15 shows the breakdown of industry usage of different types of bubble diagrams. By far, the risk-reward diagram (Exhibit 4.1), or variants of it, is the most popular, with 44 percent of bubble diagram users employing this one. Other moderately popular bubble diagrams show newness (as in Exhibit 4.11), ease versus attractiveness (as in Exhibit 4.7), and variants of the business strength and market attractiveness dimensions from the original BCG portfolio model.

Other Charts for Portfolio Management

Our investigation also uncovered an array of countless histograms, bar charts, and pie charts that help portray portfolio balance. Indeed, there are many parameters and characteristics across which you might wish to consider portfolio balance. Some examples follow.

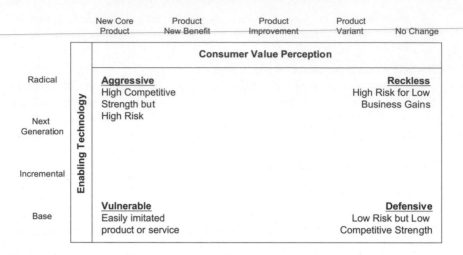

EXHIBIT 4.12b   Unilever's Managing Risk in Innovation

SOURCE: Adapted from a presentation by Adrian Dale, Creatifica Associates, formerly senior manager at Unilever, 2001.

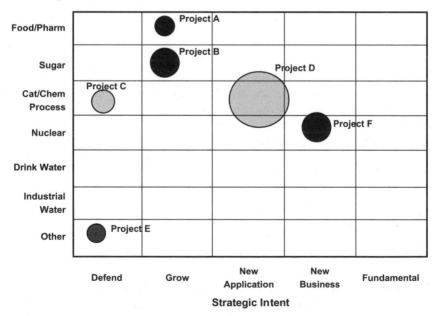

EXHIBIT 4.13   Strategic Intent Bubble Diagram at Rohm and Haas

Note: Circle size = total cost; different circle colors represent different product lines.

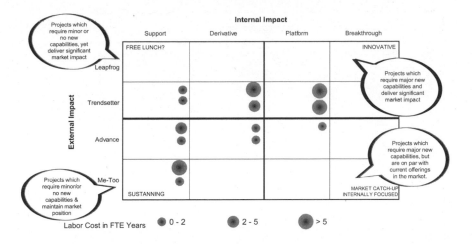

EXHIBIT 4.14   C.R. Bard's Strategic Risk Impact Matrix

SOURCE: H. Weintraub and C.M. Berke, "Make Portfolio Planning a Sustainable Business Process, in *Proceedings, Portfolio Management for New Product Development*, (Ft. Lauderdale, FL: Institute for International Research and Product Development & Management Association, 2001), p. 6.

Capacity Utilization

What proportion of allocated or budgeted resources are projects actually using? Often there are gaps between actual and proposed spending. The bar chart in Exhibit 4.16 shows an example. This is a useful chart when discussing the resource allocation issue in a portfolio review.

Project Timing

Timing is a key issue in the quest for portfolio balance. One does not wish to invest strictly in short-term or long-term projects. Another timing goal is for a steady stream of new product launches spread out over the years—constant "news" with no sudden logjam of product launches all in one year. The histogram in Exhibit 4.17 captures timing and portrays the distribution of resources to specific projects according to years of launch. For example, for Company T, 35 percent of resources are allocated to four projects—all due to be launched within the year (year 1). Another 30 percent of resources are being spent on four projects whose projected launch date is the following year, and so on.

Another timing issue is cash flow. Here the desire is to balance projects in such a way that cash inflows are reasonably balanced with cash outflows. For example, one might wish to avoid large cash outflows in one year and huge cash inflows several years later. Reckitt-Benckiser, thus, produces a histogram that

Rank	Type of Chart	Axis		Axis	%
1	Risk Vs. Reward	Reward: NPV, IRR, benefits after years of launch; market value	By	Probability of success (technical, commercial)	44.4
2	Newness	Technical newness	By	Market Newness	11.1
3	Ease Vs. Attractiveness	Technical feasibility	By	Market attractiveness (growth potential, consumer appeal, general, attractiveness, life cycle)	11.1
4	Strength Vs. Attractiveness	Competitive position (strengths)	By	Attractiveness (market growth, technical maturity, years to implementation	11.1
5	Cost Vs. Timing	Cost to implement	By	Time to impact	9.7
6	Strategic Vs. Benefit	Strategic focus or fit	By	Business intent, NPV, financial fit, attractiveness	8.9
7	Cost Vs. Benefit	Cumulative reward	By	Cumulative development costs	5.6

EXHIBIT 4.15   Popular Bubble Diagram Dimensions

Note: Rank-ordered in descending order of popularity; last column shows percentage breakdown of bubble diagram usage (as a percentage of business using bubble diagrams).

SOURCE: *Research-Technology Management* 41, 4 (1998).

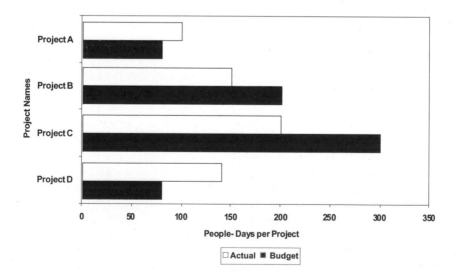

EXHIBIT 4.16   Bar Graph to Represent Capacity Utilization

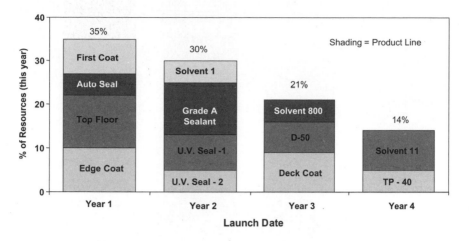

EXHIBIT 4.17   Bar Graph Showing Timing of Product Launches

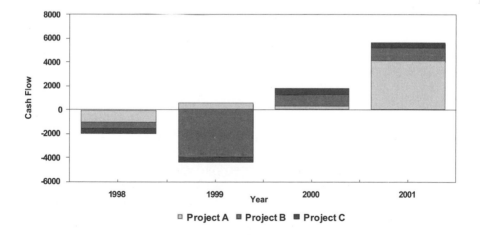

EXHIBIT 4.18   Cash Flow versus Time at Reckitt-Benckiser

Note: This chart is an illustration of the type of additional information available. Numbers have been disguised for each year.

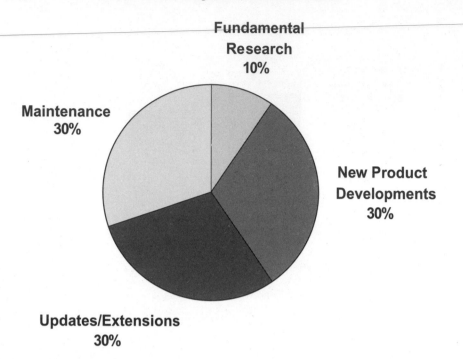

EXHIBIT 4.19   Pie Chart of Spending Allocation Across Project Types

captures the total cash flow per year for all projects in the portfolio (Exhibit 4.18). This histogram also reveals cash flows by project type.

Project Types

It is also vital in portfolio management to consider project types. What is the spending on genuine new products, on updates, on fundamental research? And what should it be? Pie or similar types of charts, which capture the spending split across project types, were found in just about every company we studied. Exhibit 4.19 provides an illustration. This is perhaps the most popular of all pie chart displays.

Markets, Products, and Technologies

Another set of dimensions across which managers seek balance is product, market, and technology type. Exhibit 4.20 provides a sample visual breakdown using pie charts that demonstrates how a specialty chemical company allocates funding across product lines and markets. The question is, Do you have the appropriate split in R&D spending across your various product lines? Or across

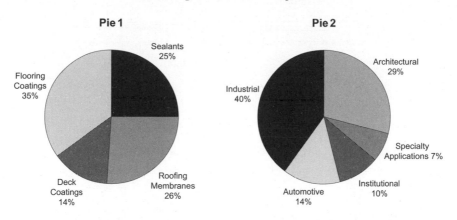

EXHIBIT 4.20   Pie Charts for Breakdown of Resources by Product Lines and Markets

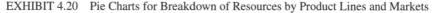

the markets or market segments in which you compete? Or across the technologies you possess? Pie charts are an excellent approach for capturing and displaying this type of data.

Customer Needs Profile

Customer needs are an important way to display a company's portfolio of projects. Although, for many businesses, products and projects change over time, customer needs are relatively stable. Listing these needs can provide the basis for a robust management tool.

Example: For a business in the hair care field, market research has identified five major long-term consumer needs: improved cleaning, improved hair quality, protection from damage, more convenience, and improved sensory cues. Importance weights are placed on each of the needs. Corresponding to each need may be a number of new products or technology solutions, which can be shown on a "needs tree" (Exhibit 4.21).

Mapping the development portfolio shows where the resources are being spent and whether the portfolio of projects is meeting the needs that are most important to the customer. From the data in the needs tree in Exhibit 4.21, the resources being spent to address each of the five needs can be computed and the portfolio chart of Exhibit 4.22 created. Exhibit 4.22 shows a poorly balanced portfolio of projects: Despite being the strongest customer need, "improved cleaning" accounts for the lowest proportion of spending. Management should redress the balance.

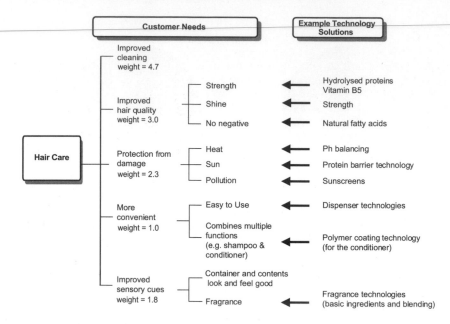

EXHIBIT 4.21   Customer Needs Tree for Hair Care Products

SOURCE: Adapted from J. Brook and P. Brewster, "Putting the C in R&D—Customer Focus for Technologists," *International Journal of Technology Management* 17, 6 (1999): pp. 639–40.

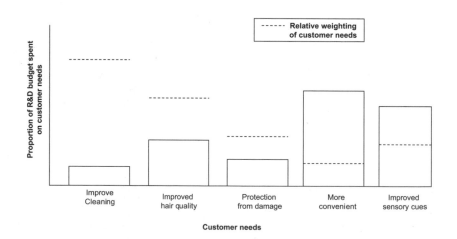

EXHIBIT 4.22   Graph of Customer Needs versus Portfolio Spending

SOURCE: Adapted from J. Brook and P. Brewster, "Putting the C in R&D—Customer Focus for Technologists," *International Journal of Technology Management* 17, 6 (1999): pp. 639–40.

Balance: Some Critical Comments

There is more to life than simply striving for a high-value portfolio; balance is also a critical issue. The trouble is that achieving balance—or selecting an appropriate tool to help achieve balance—is easier conceptually than in practice.

What impressed us, however, was the many intricate and ingenious charts and graphs companies had invented to deal with the balance issue. We could have filled an entire book with the maps, bubble diagrams, and pie charts we discovered in our studies. However, there remain problems with the quest for balance:

1. Some of the more popular bubble diagrams suffer the same fate as the maximization models outlined in Chapter 3: They rely on substantial financial data, which are often unavailable or, at best, highly uncertain. Witness the popular risk-reward bubble diagrams (Exhibits 4.1, 4.2, 4.3, and 4.5) where NPV is one of the axes.
2. There is the issue of information overload. "Maps, endless maps!" was the complaint of one exasperated executive, as he leafed through more than a dozen maps plotting everything versus everything in his firm's portfolio model. Note that very few companies had even attempted to use all the maps and charts recommended by the various pundits. Further, many firms had begun portfolio management with a number of maps, which over the months had been whittled down to the two or three deemed most important.
3. These visual and balance models are information display, not decision models per se. Unlike the value maximization methods of Chapter 3, the result is not a convenient rank-ordered list of preferred projects. Rather, these charts and maps are a starting point for discussion only. Management still has to translate these data into actionable decisions. This was the point at which some had failed. Too many maps, or the wrong maps, may have contributed.
4. It wasn't clear in all cases how the charts and maps should be used. At Milltronics, a mid-sized instrument company, the first time the R&D VP displayed a set of pie charts and bubble diagrams at a senior management meeting, there was hushed silence. After some moments, he asked, "What do you think?" The tentative reply: "We're not sure . . . is this good news or bad news?" Management had no idea how

they should interpret the charts—what they really meant! At Reckitt-Benckiser the initial inclination was to make these charts part of gate meetings. After a few attempts, the practice was halted because it added to the confusion. The company has since worked out a better method of integrating portfolio and gate decisions. At the Royal Bank of Canada, electronic portfolio maps were also used at gate meetings, but only a few times before they, too, gave up. Company G used the maps as an after-the-fact course correction, "to make sure we have the right balance." But it was never clear what would happen if the "wrong balance" ever occurred: would management immediately start canceling projects and approving others in the hold tank?

5. Finally, the "right balance" of projects was rarely defined. Management could stare all they wanted at various charts, but unless a portfolio is obviously and extremely out of balance (as in Company T's Exhibit 4.1), how does a manager know whether the right balance is there if he/she has no idea of what the right balance should be in the first place? What is the existing balance being compared to? A portfolio manager at Hewlett-Packard wondered whether there might be any "rules of thumb" about the best split in long-term versus short-term projects, high-risk versus low-risk, and so on—much like rules of thumb for stock market investment portfolios.

The fact that portfolio balance methods are far from perfect does not mean they should be dismissed outright. Certainly not! But these methods should be used with care. The choice of maps (which axes to use in the plots, for example) and charts (which parameters to show) must be well thought out. Avoid the temptation to portray too many maps and charts, and be sure to test the maps in portfolio or gate meetings before adopting them.

One added benefit of the various balancing charts and maps is that they connect very well with the methods used to achieve the other two goals in portfolio management. Portfolio maps, for example, provide inputs into maximizing the portfolio value against goals (Chapter 3). In one firm, projects that scored high on the risk and reward matrix were flagged for priority. These projects, if successful, would help the company achieve its goals of increasing the average margin of its portfolio of products on the market.

Portfolio maps can also be used as an effective tool for monitoring to ensure that the portfolio is in line with the strategy. Course corrections can be made periodically during the year. The next chapter explores this third goal of portfolio management—the strategy link—in more depth.

CHAPTER 5

Portfolio Management Methods: A Strong Link to Strategy

Goal 3: The Need to Build Strategy into the Portfolio

It all boils down to strategy. From your business's new product innovation and technology strategy, all else flows. The goal to maximize the value of the portfolio discussed in Chapter 3 is meaningless unless value is measured in terms of a company goal—and that goal is articulated as part of your strategy. Similarly, the desired risk-reward profile, the quest for the appropriate balance discussed in Chapter 4, ultimately comes down to strategy. The balance models in Chapter 4 are hollow unless senior management has a solid notion of what the ideal balance of projects should be. And that's decided by strategy. Thus your company's business strategy—and embedded within it, your new product and technology strategy—must drive your portfolio management process and the projects in which you ultimately invest.

Strategy and resource allocation must be intimately connected. Strategy becomes real when you start spending money! Until you begin allocating resources to specific activities that advance individual development projects, strategy is just words on paper. These are the views shared by enlightened management of the companies we investigated.

The prime goals of the leading firms we investigated are that:

- all active projects are aligned with the business strategy
- all active projects contribute to achieving the goals and objectives set out in the strategy
- resource allocations—across business areas, markets, and project types—truly reflect the desired strategic direction of the business.

The mission, vision, and strategy of the business must be operationalized in terms of where the business spends money and which development projects it undertakes. For example, if a business's strategic mission is to "grow via leading-edge product development," then this mission must be reflected in the number of new product projects underway. This means they must be projects that will lead to growth rather than simply defending the status quo, and they must be projects that really are innovative. Similarly, if the strategy is to focus on certain markets, products, or technologies, then the majority of R&D spending must be focused on these markets, products, or technologies. After all, isn't this what strategy is all about: to guide the actions and efforts of the business?

Not every company we studied has achieved proficiency here. For example, a mid-sized company's dedication to product development was stated in its annual report as "growth through industry leadership in product development." The magnitude of the effort did not quite match this strategic intent, however, with this firm's R&D spending at half its industry's average as a percentage of sales! In another company, the business strategy was to move into a new market aggressively—one thought to offer many opportunities for the corporation. Yet an analysis of the company's portfolio of active projects revealed very few projects and little spending targeted at the designated strategic market. Apparently the folks who made the Go/Kill decisions on projects were either not aware of or not heeding the strategy. Finally, in yet another firm, one business unit's senior executive claimed that "My BU's strategy is to achieve rapid growth through aggressive new product development." Yet when we examined his BU's breakdown of R&D spending, the great majority of resources was going to maintenance projects, product modifications, and extensions—not very aggressive at all! Clearly, these examples are cases of serious disconnects between stated strategy and where the money is spent. And these companies are not alone!

POINTS FOR MANAGEMENT TO PONDER

Have you given serious thought to how you link portfolio selection to your business's strategy? Do you have a business and new product strategy—one that is clearly articulated and well understood by management and other decision makers? If not, the place to begin is with the development of a product innovation and technology strategy. You cannot talk about "strategic alignment" and "strategic direction" to your portfolio unless you have such a strategy clearly defined for your business.

Linking Strategy to the Portfolio: Approaches

Three broad objectives arise in the desire to build in strategy and to achieve strategic alignment in portfolio management:

- *Strategic fit* is the first and easiest to envision. It addresses this question: Are all your projects consistent with your articulated strategy? For example, if you have defined certain technologies or markets as key areas on which to focus, do your projects fit into these areas—are they "in bounds" or "out of bounds"?

- *Strategic contribution* is more complex and subtler and asks this question: What projects must you do if you want your business strategy to be realized and your goals achieved? For example, if your business decides to target a new market segment, then what projects must or should you do to be successful in this new segment? What will it take to win here?

- *Strategic priorities* is also more difficult. It addresses this question: Does the breakdown of your spending reflect your strategic priorities? If you say you are a growth business, then the majority of your R&D spending ought to be in projects that are designed to grow the business. In short, when you add up the areas where you are spending money, are these totals consistent with your stated strategy? Often the answer is no.

The companies we studied use three general approaches to deal with strategic alignment.

1. Top-Down Approaches

Top-Down approaches begin with the business's vision, goals, and strategy, and from this, new product initiatives and/or resource allocations are decided. There are two general approaches, and the two can be used together or separately.

Product Roadmap: Here the development of your business and new product strategy helps to define what major initiatives or platform developments you should undertake. It answers the question "If this is our strategy, then what projects must we or should we do?" By identifying the major initiatives and platform developments, this strategic exercise goes a long way toward shaping your eventual development portfolio. The ultimate result is a product roadmap—a series of product or platform developments and their extensions on a time scale.

Strategic Buckets Model: Here the focus is more on resource allocation. It answers the question "If this is our strategy, then how should we be spending our development funds? What splits across various markets, technologies, or project types should our investment be?" The method begins with vision, goals, and strategy and then moves to setting aside funds—envelopes or buckets of money—destined for different types of projects. We label this the Strategic Buckets Model.

Both Top-Down Approaches begin with the business strategy and attempt to translate it into the right set of projects and timing (product roadmap) and the right resource allocation (strategic buckets).

2. Bottom-Up Approach

This approach begins with a set of opportunities in the form of new product proposals. These proposals or ideas "bubble up" from anywhere in the organization but must be screened so that the good ones rise to the surface and are funded. The Bottom-Up Approach, thus, focuses on project selection—on building in a solid review of specific projects and on selecting the best in light of the business's strategy and goals. Strategic criteria are built into the project selection tools; thus, strategic fit is achieved simply by incorporating numerous strategic criteria into the Go/Kill and prioritization methods.

The point here is that the Bottom-Up Approach starts first with individual projects, and by building in tough screens, ends up with a portfolio of strategically aligned projects.

3. Top-Down, Bottom-Up Approach

This combination of the two approaches above has merit because it overcomes deficiencies in both. It begins at the top, with strategy development, a product roadmap, and strategic buckets of money. It also proceeds from the bottom with a review and selection of the best projects. The two sets of decisions—Top-Down and Bottom-Up—are reconciled via multiple iterations.

Note that the Top-Down and Bottom-Up approaches are fundamentally different in philosophy, in how they are operationalized, and finally in terms of the list of projects that results.

Developing a New Product Strategy for Your Business—A Quick Guide

The Top-Down Approach is specifically designed to ensure that the list of projects— at least the major ones—is essential for the realization of the business's strategy and goals. Let's use a military analogy. After all, the term *strategy* was first used in a military context, and much of what we know about strategy comes from the military. You are a five-star general and are at war. You have certain clearly specified goals— presumably to win the war or to achieve certain ends. You have identified key strategic arenas—fronts or major battlefields where you plan to attack and win. But as you chart your strategy, you see that there are some key assaults or initiatives along the way—individual battles that you must fight in order to see your strategy succeed.

Now let us translate this into a new product context:

The goals translate directly: These are specific new product goals for your business. For example, what percentage of your business's growth over the next three years will come from new products? Or to what percentage of your business's sales will new products contribute?

Arenas, fronts, and major battlefields: these are the strategic arenas defined in your business and new product strategy. That is, which markets, technologies, and product types you plan to attack. Where will you focus?

Assaults and initiatives: These are the major developments you must undertake in order to implement your strategy—the major new product, technology, or platform developments. They evolve or flow logically from your strategy development.

The details of how to develop your business strategy and even new product strategy are beyond the scope of this book. But there are other excellent sources.[1] In the meantime, here is a quick guide (along with some examples and illustrations) to approaches we observed in our investigations of best practices.

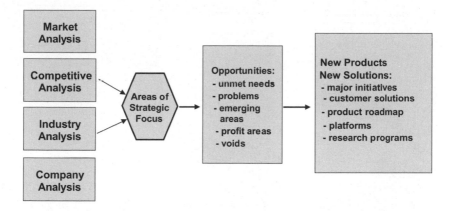

EXHIBIT 5.1   The Major Steps in Developing a New Product Strategy

SOURCE: Adapted and modified somewhat from the Discover stage of the *Thomson Solutions Process* of the Thomson Corporation.

Set New Product Goals

Begin with your new product goals. These should evolve from (or be part of) your business goals and its strategy. New product goals are often expressed in terms of:

- Percentage of revenue derived from new products launched in the last X years (this is the most frequently used form of new product goal, popularized by 3M)
- Percentage of profits to come from new products (this is, perhaps, a more appropriate goal but is often harder to measure precisely)
- Percentage of business growth—in either revenue or profits—to come from new products.

Analyze the Market and the Competition

Next comes the situation assessment, or SWOT analysis (strengths, weaknesses, opportunities, threats), with a specific emphasis on your marketplace (refer to Exhibit 5.1).[2] Conduct a thorough market analysis. Consider market size and trends over time. Be sure to consider market segmentation and the size and trends of segments over time. Exhibit 5.2 shows typical charts from a market analysis for a manufacturer of mobile phones.[3] And take a look at your own market share, both current and projected, in these segments and overall.

Next, undertake a complete competitive analysis. Identify competitors' strengths and weaknesses, core competencies, and competitive advantages (for example, the value proposition they bring to the marketplace and to the cus-

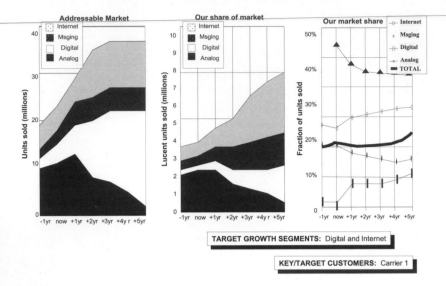

EXHIBIT 5.2   Market Share and Growth

SOURCE: R.E. Albright, "Roadmaps and Roadmapping: Linking Business Strategy and Technology Planning," *Proceedings, Portfolio Management for New Product Development* (Ft. Lauderdale, FL: Institute for International Research and Product Development & Management Association, 2001).

tomer). Try to impute their strategic goals from what you know. Exhibit 5.3 shows a typical competitive analysis chart. And while undertaking your market and competitive analyses, try to gain insights into the key customer drivers—the important criteria by which customers chose one supplier or product over another (the purchase motivators). That is, the relative importance of the purchase criteria shown in Exhibit 5.3 (bottom half) are identified (along with how well each competitor is doing compared to your company and other competitors for each key attribute).[4]

Assess Your Customers' Industry (Your Marketplace)

Here, the industry and market analysis shifts to a specific focus on new opportunities, new products, and possible new solutions. Begin by assessing your customers' industry, which is your marketplace. Unmet or unarticulated needs are often the result of changes and shifts in a user industry. An understanding of this is essential to determining where to focus—what changes are taking place and what new needs may be emerging that help you identify possible solutions opportunities. This approach is built into the *Thomson Solutions Process*, a Stage-Gate™ process that has an extensive, strategically oriented front end designed to uncover major opportunities (similar to Exhibit 5.1).

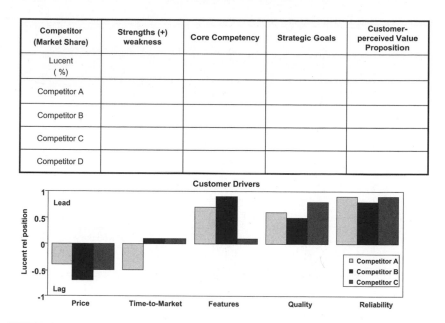

Competitor (Market Share)	Strengths (+) weakness	Core Competency	Strategic Goals	Customer-perceived Value Proposition
Lucent (%)				
Competitor A				
Competitor B				
Competitor C				
Competitor D				

EXHIBIT 5.3   Competitive Strategy and Differentiation

SOURCE: R.E. Albright, "Roadmaps and Roadmapping: Linking Business Strategy and Technology Planning," *Proceedings, Portfolio Management for New Product Development* (Ft. Lauderdale, FL: Institute for International Research and Product Development & Management Association, 2001).

Example: The Thomson Corporation is a major player in the financial, medical, and legal information business headquartered in Stamford, Connecticut. Among its many businesses are Thomson Financial Services, a number of textbook publishing companies, the well-known Thomson medical directories, Thomson business publications, West legal directories, and the (Toronto) *Globe and Mail* newspaper in Canada. Because of major changes taking place in the information and publications business, Thompson has been rapidly repositioning itself as a major e-business information provider. Thus, new product, new service, and new solutions development is front and center in this firm's overall strategy.

Here are the questions Thomson management asks when assessing customer industries:[5]

1. What arenas in the customer industry (e.g., segments, value chain, activities) are the most attractive for us?
2. What changes are occurring in customer needs or value chains? How will they affect the industry and its key players?

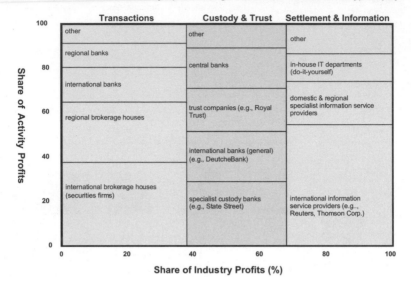

EXHIBIT 5.4   Example of a Market Map—Custody, Trust, and Settlements (Financial Institutions)

Reveals the distribution of an industry's profits along two dimensions—activities and type of player

SOURCE: From a major bank (disguised); method based on O. Gadiesh and J.L. Gilbert, "How to map your industry's profit pool," *Harvard Business Review* May–June 1998: 3–11.

---

3. What new opportunities could emerge from these changes—from new value chains and workflows to help make our customers more successful?
4. Are there opportunities to better meet customer needs and/or capitalize on a changing environment?

These are good questions, but it involves legwork to get answers to them. This is not just a desk exercise! Start by developing a map of the value chain and identifying the various types of players. Next, assess their futures: changing roles, who will gain, and who might be disintermediated (cut out).

Then identify customers' industry drivers and potential shifts in these drivers. That is, try to assess what factors make them (or their competitors) profitable and successful. Is it costs of materials or low-cost production? Or response time to customer requests? And how are these changing, especially in ways that might open up opportunities for you? And finally, can *you* provide solutions here to help your customers?

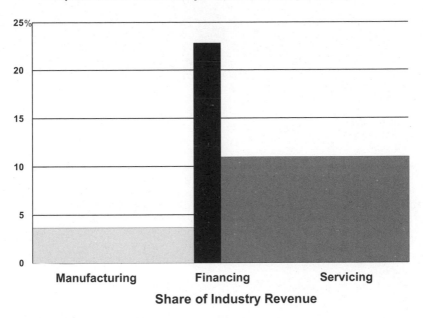

Compares a value chain activity's revenues with its profitability

EXHIBIT 5.5   Profit Pool Maps—U.S. Auto Industry

Source: O. Gadiesh and J.L. Gilbert, "How to map your industry's profit pool," *Harvard Business Review* May–June 1998: 3–11.

Then identify customers' industry drivers and potential shifts in these drivers. That is, try to assess what factors make them (or their competitors) profitable and successful. Is it costs of materials or low-cost production? Or response time to customer requests? And how are these changing, especially in ways that might open up opportunities for you? And finally, can *you* provide solutions here to help your customers?

Analyze historical trends and estimate future trends. Spell out a scenario (or alternate scenarios) of where your customer's industry is heading. Thomson management also uses Porter's Five Forces model to assess the industry, its attractiveness, and potential changes in it.[6]

The Thomson process also uses some new tools. For example, Market Maps are prepared. These are simply charts that show which types of players have what piece of the revenue in the industry—see Exhibit 5.4. A similar useful tool is the profit pool map: This map identifies activities in an industry, percentage of revenue by each, and profit margins in each (see Exhibit 5.5).[7]

Another useful insight may be gained from identifying potentially disruptive technologies.[8] A disruptive technology is a new technology that emerges and

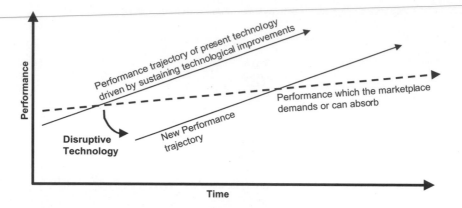

EXHIBIT 5.6 Disruptive Technology Framework That Helps to Eliminate Strategic Blind Spots

The disruptive technologies framework is

- An approach for *deconstructing a market* to frame areas of opportunity and vulnerability
- A methodology for *identifying* the set of *new strategic options* to be managed going forward
- A set of *principles* to guide companies in the exploration and protection against vulnerabilities.

SOURCE: G. Getz, "Looking Ahead at the Front End," *Proceedings, Portfolio Management for New Product Development* (Ft. Lauderdale, FL: Institute for International Research and Product Development & Management Association, 2001).

showing the original technology and then the disruptive technology, is a useful way to portray the effects and threats.[10]

The result of assessing your customers' industry should be an understanding of the changes taking place, potential opportunities for major new products and new solutions, and identification of the more attractive arenas where you could focus your new product efforts.

Assess Your Own Company's Strengths and Weaknesses

In parallel with the assessment of your customers' industry, conduct an internal assessment of your own business—strengths, weaknesses, and core competencies (refer to Exhibit 5.1). This assessment establishes a baseline of performance (how well your business is doing). It also determines your competitive position. This gives senior management a place to start when discussing a strategic vision and in deciding which areas or arenas they wish to focus on for innovative new products and solutions.

The old adage "attack from a position of strength" is especially true in product development. Witness all the research results over the years that repeat the message: leveraging your strengths and competencies increases new product success rates and new product profitability. So take a hard look at your business and undertake a core competencies analysis. This means looking at strengths and weaknesses in all facets of your business, for example:

- Marketing and sales:
  - customer relationships and loyalty of key customer groups
  - brand name or franchise in the marketplace
  - product reputation in terms of quality, reliability, and value
  - distribution and channels (i.e., access to key customer groups)
  - sales force (e.g., coverage, skills, reputation)
  - advertising, communications, and public relations
  - service, support, and technical service
  - market shares, presence in certain markets or segments
  - reputation overall

- Product technology:
  - areas of product leadership, technologically (e.g., product features, functionality, performance)
  - technological capabilities
  - access to new technologies
  - unique technologies or technological skills
  - intellectual property and proprietary positions
  - in-house technology skill base

- Operations or production capabilities and technology:
  - production or operations resources, facilities, and capacities
  - unique skills or abilities
  - technological capabilities in production or operations
  - unique production technologies, intellectual property and protection
  - access to raw materials
  - skills, knowledge, availability of work force.

Assess your business on each of these points, paying particular attention to how your company performs relative to direct and indirect competitors. Then identify areas where your company performs better than the rest—core or distinctive competencies. These are your strengths. Now look for arenas in which you can leverage these competencies to advantage.

Example: Imagine that you are in the competitive world of airline reservations systems. You currently sell a reservation system aimed at travel agents. You conduct an industry analysis as described above, and the results are provocative. Increasingly, travelers are using the Internet to book their flights, especially on major carriers with easy-to-use web pages. A profit pool map reveals that for airline travel, travel agents' margins have been squeezed by the major carriers. The travel agent, your principal customer, is in danger of becoming disintermediated and is quickly becoming the least profitable link in the value chain. This disruption threatens your business, but it also opens up new possibilities. A core competency assessment reveals that you have world-class technical skills in IT and in the development and operation of travel reservations systems.

End-user market research reveals that not all travelers are satisfied with booking flights on the web. They must search through home pages of multiple airlines to get the best schedules, and often they end up with a fare higher than an experienced travel agent could obtain. This voice-of-the-customer research reveals new opportunities for an IT product aimed directly at the end user: a single booking system that searches all airlines and hunts for the best deal. So you conceive, develop, and launch your new product.

Take note how *Travelocity* fares in the electronic reservations market. This travel booking service promises best prices and best schedules across multiple carriers. *Travelocity* was launched by Saber, one of the largest airline reservations systems currently aimed at travel agents.

POINTS FOR MANAGEMENT TO PONDER

Define a product innovation and technology strategy for your business. Begin with your new product goals. Then move to a market and competitive analysis. Prepare profit pool maps and market maps and use Porter's Five Forces Model to assess where you want to operate in this industry. Outline alternative scenarios for the future and look for disruptive technologies and their potential impact.

Then, as the Thomson Corporation does, take a close look at your own strengths and core competencies to determine where you have strategic leverage. Search for opportunities in your marketplace. Analyze the value chain, identify the industry drivers, review historical trends, and develop scenarios of the future. Look for gaps, emerging needs, and disruptions in your market or your customer's industry. These gaps and problems may signal major new product opportunities.

Analyze the Output

This in-depth industry, competitive, market, and internal analysis effort provides two major sets of insights:

- *The arenas:* An understanding of the potential arenas where your business may wish to operate—the attractiveness and viability of the current arena in which you operate, as well information on other potential arenas or business areas you may wish to consider (e.g., new markets, new technologies, or new product categories for you).

- *Specific opportunities:* Insights into some of the new product, new service, and new solutions opportunities. These provide the basis for potential new product projects for or offerings from your business.

Let us move first to a closer look at the strategic arenas.

Define Strategic Arenas

The next step is to identify and select your strategic arenas (refer to Exhibit 5.1). These are the product, market, industry sector, or technology areas where you will focus your new product efforts.

Example: One major European telephone company uses a product-market matrix to help management visualize the strategic options it has in various arenas (Exhibit 5.7). Across the top of the chart are existing and potential products and services: voice, data, Internet, etc. Down the side are the various market segments: SoHo (small office, home office), medium-sized business, residential, etc. Each cell in the diagram represents a potential strategic arena or "battlefield" where the company may choose to focus and attack (or choose not to). Each cell has multiple new product opportunities.

After identifying a number of potential arenas, the task is now to assess and choose the right ones. Many firms use a variant of the strategic map shown in Exhibit 5.8 in which the various arenas, or battlefields, are rated in terms of two familiar dimensions:

Products

	Voice	Data	Internet	Wireless	Long Distance
SoHo			★	★	★
Medium Business		★		★	
Large Business		★		★	
Multinationals		★		★	★
Residential	★			★	

(*Markets* along the left axis)

EXHIBIT 5.7   Ways to Define Arenas: A Product/Market Matrix

The axes of the diagram are products and markets. Each cell represents a potential strategic arena. Arenas are assessed for their potential and the company's business position. Stars designate top-priority arenas—where new product efforts will be focused

Adapted from a major European Telco.

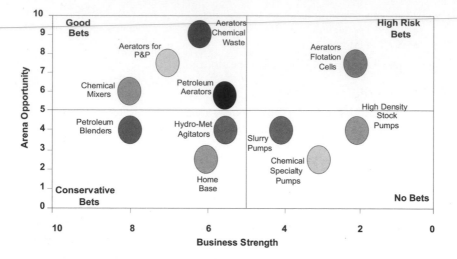

EXHIBIT 5.8   Strategic Map—Arenas Plotted

Adapted from a process equipment manufacturer.

1. *Arena opportunity* (or attractiveness): This is an external measure that captures how attractive this arena or battlefield is. Will you find a rich oasis here, or is it desert territory? This external measure is a composite dimension consisting of:

   - *market attractiveness:* the size, growth, and potential of market opportunities within the arena
   - *technological opportunities:* the degree to which technological and new product opportunities exist within the arena (for example, where the arena is on the technology S-curve).

2. *Business strength* (or business position): This is an internal measure that focuses on your company and asks, What do you bring to the table that suggests that you could win in this strategic arena? Business strength, thus, centers on the business's ability to successfully exploit the arena. The ability to leverage the organization's resources and skills to advantage is a key concept here. This is also a composite dimension, typically consisting of three factors:

   - ability to leverage the technological competencies
   - ability to leverage marketing competencies
   - strategic leverage—the potential to gain product advantage and differentiation.

The strategic map guides in the selection of the target arenas—the areas that you wish to focus on. These define what is "in bounds" and, perhaps more important, what is "out of bounds"—they are your "hunting grounds." They guide your new product selection and help provide focus for your new product portfolio. Without such arenas delineated, a scattergun effort is the result. Further, the definition and prioritization of arenas helps to decide resource allocation—which arena should receive the most funding—part of the next section to follow.

Example: A general manager in the modified plastics business of a major corporation faced many problems with his new product efforts. One problem was a lack of strategic focus and direction to projects in the pipeline. A more thorough analysis revealed that there was not really much of a new product strategy in the business at all! The first task for the leadership team of the business was to develop a new product strategy. Here is how they progressed over a three-day strategy retreat:

First, a set of new product goals was discussed and developed—a fairly tentative list initially. Next, possible strategic arenas were identified. At first, it was difficult to define these. After discussion, however, strategic arenas were defined and listed on a two-dimensional matrix by market segments and product performance characteristics (similar to Exhibit 5.7). About 20 cells in this market segment/product performance matrix in which there might be opportunities were delineated (possible strategic arenas).

Next, a set of criteria was developed so that management could rate and prioritize the various arenas. These criteria captured elements of segment attractiveness to the business's relative technological and marketing strengths in each arena (similar to the strategic map in Exhibit 5.8). Considerable homework had been done in advance, so that data were available for at least some of the segments and product performance categories. At this point, management began to discuss and rate the various arenas on the defined criteria.

At the end of the exercise, five key arenas had been defined: stiff/tough materials for automotive; stiff/tough materials for agricultural equipment; high throughput for packaging; fire-resistant materials for construction; and stiff/tough materials for construction. These arenas were next prioritized: number 1, number 2, and so on. Then resource splits were made across the five areas of focus in terms of percentage split in R&D funding.

By this point, the leadership team had gone a long way toward defining a new product strategy: They had defined goals; they had identified possible strategic arenas; they had made decisions on arenas of focus and had prioritized them; and they even had decided on an allocation of resources across arenas. The only task they failed to address was how to attack each arena (no product roadmap had been developed). All the same, much progress had been made on their new product strategy, which eventually led to more effective portfolio management.

Moving to the Attack Plan

Assessing your customer's industry, your market, and a competitive analysis, along with voice-of-the-customer research and working with lead users,[11] leads to the identification of emerging or unmet customer needs and new opportunities for new products and solutions. The opportunities can best be categorized as:[12]

- *Sustaining opportunities*, both in current businesses and in established markets that may be new to you. These are opportunities for incremental new products. These types of developments are obviously the most prevalent in most companies' portfolios, and so they should be. They are important in order to keep the firm's product line fresh and up to date; and they are the source of competitive advantage in the great majority of markets and for most businesses.
- *Disruptors of existing markets*, including disruptive threats in your current markets as well as others' markets. These happen less often, but when they do, can provide significant opportunities (or pose major threats, if ignored). The opportunity may take the form of serving only the needs of a specific segment with specific needs and demands, followed by a migration to serve the mainstream market. For example, the advent of the 3.5-inch floppy disk drive on PCs was a new technology that threatened makers of the then-dominant $5\frac{1}{4}$-inch drive in the late 1980s. The new drive was actually more expensive, but its small size offered a performance advantage valued by some PC makers and users. The new technology eventually replaced the dominant one.[13]
- *New markets* are both new to you and new to the world. The opportunity here is to build a new market space, as did Netscape and Yahoo in the early 1990s.

The next step is to develop your attack plans or roadmap. This usually consists of setting out the major assaults or initiatives that are needed in order to be successful in a given arena: *specific new products, platforms, and projects and their timing*. For example, once a product category is designated priority 1, what new products do you need in order to succeed in that category? Or, given that you want to grow in a specific industry sector, what new platforms do you need in order to win? Thus the attack plan may boil down to the *portfolio of proposed projects* aimed at that arena—in effect, a cluster of assaults or tactical moves.

The decisions to move ahead on some developments are self-evident: If the goal is to attack and win in a given arena (or perhaps defend an arena), then certain projects become "must do" projects—strategic imperatives. Others are less obvious, so they enter the new product process and are screened and developed to the point at which a fact-based Go/Kill decision can be made.

The Platform—A Base from Which to Operate

Many businesses now look to platforms as a way to think about strategic thrusts in product development. The original notion of a platform was very much *product-based*. For example, the PDMA handbook defines a platform product to be "design and components that are shared by a set of products in a product family. From this platform, numerous derivatives can be designed."[14] Thus, Chrysler's engine-transmission assembly from the K-car was a platform that spawned other vehicles, including the famous Chrysler minivan.

The notion of platforms has since been broadened to include *technological capabilities*. For example, Exxon's metallocene platform is simply a catalyst that has spawned an entirely new generation of polymers. A platform is like an oil drilling platform in the ocean in which you invest heavily. From this platform, you can drill many holes, relatively quickly and at low cost. The platform, thus, leads to many related new product projects in a timely and cost-effective manner.

The definition of platforms has also been broadened to include *marketing or branding concepts* as well as technological capabilities. For example, some consider 3M's *Post-It Notes*™ to be a platform that has created many individual products, and Nabisco's *Snack Well*™ products—indulgent but low-fat dessert food items—are another example of a marketing platform.

Product and Technology Roadmaps

A product roadmap is an effective way to map out a series of assaults in an attack plan and is one of the two Top-Down Approaches recommended. What is a roadmap? It is simply a management group's view of how to get where they want to go or to achieve their desired objective.[15] The roadmap is a useful tool that helps the group make sure that the capabilities to achieve their objective are in place when needed. Note that there are different types of roadmaps: Two useful types are the product roadmap and the technology roadmap.

- The *product roadmap* defines the product and product releases along a timeline—how the product line will evolve over time, and what the next generations will be. It

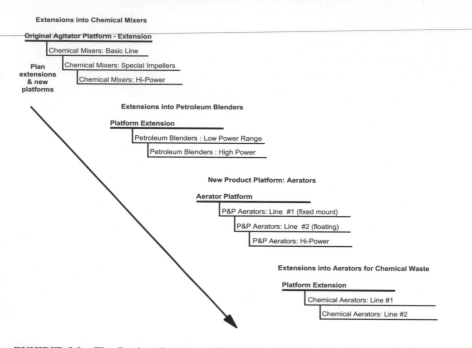

EXHIBIT 5.9   The Product Roadmap: The Major Initiatives in a Process Equipment Manufacturer

SOURCE: Based on models presented by: M. Meyer and A. Lehnerd, *The Power of Product Platforms* (New York: Free Press, 1997).

answers the question, what products? An example is shown in Exhibit 5.9. Here the product roadmap for a process equipment manufacturer not only defines the platforms and platform extensions needed, it also maps out the various product releases, specifies features or functionality that will be built into each new release, and indicates timing (launch date).

- The *technology roadmap* is derived from the product roadmap (Exhibit 5.10), but also specifies how you will get there. That is, it lays out the technologies and tech-

---

POINTS FOR MANAGEMENT TO PONDER

Do you have a product and/or technology roadmap constructed for your business? Is your business facing rapid technology change and short product life cycles? To maximize revenue opportunities, do you have to develop and release a series of new product launches all leveraging the same technology? If so, why not consider developing a product or technology roadmap? Going through the exercise is an excellent way to begin developing your new product strategy. Roadmapping forces you to think through both the present and future opportunities and the directions for your business or technology. Roadmaps also provide you with an excellent tool to help you communicate within your organization the opportunities that exist and the potential path forward.

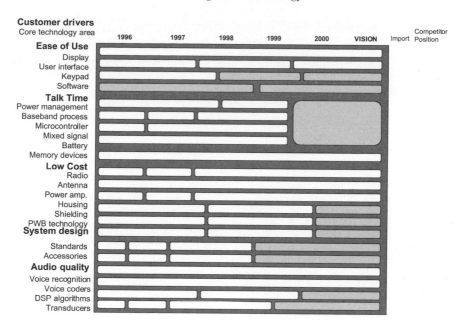

EXHIBIT 5.10   Technology Roadmap: Hardware/Software/Architecture

Note: Requirements and availability feed the product roadmap and needs/supply maps (supplier, manufacturing, development, and forward cost plans), which, in turn, all leads to an attack strategy.

SOURCE: R.E. Albright, "Roadmaps and Roadmapping: Linking Business Strategy and Technology Planning," *Proceedings, Portfolio Management for New Product Development* (Ft. Lauderdale, FL: Institute for International Research and Product Development & Management Association, 2001).

nological competencies that are needed in order to implement (develop and source) the products in the product roadmap. The technology roadmap is a logical extension of the product roadmap and is closely linked to it. Indeed, at Lucent Technologies, the two are combined into a product-technology roadmap as a tool to help teams link business strategy, product plans, and technology development.

Strategic Buckets: A Powerful Top-Down Approach

This second Top-Down Approach is designed to ensure that where the money is spent mirrors the business strategy and strategic priorities. This approach operates from the simple principle that implementing strategy equates to spending money on specific projects (or, put another way, "strategy is not real until it translates into spending money on specific activities or projects"). Thus, setting portfolio requirements really means setting spending targets. A number of firms we studied use parts or all of this approach. What we describe below is a composite of several companies' methods.

The Strategic Buckets Model operates this way:

1. The vision and strategy for the business are developed first, which in turn lead to a new product strategy.
2. Then decisions are made about where management wishes to spend its R&D and new product resources: which types of projects, across which markets and product lines, and so on.
3. Envelopes of money—buckets with ideal spending levels—are defined; for example, X percent to be spent on platform developments, Y percent on new products, Z percent on product enhancements and improvements.
4. Projects are then prioritized within buckets (via the maximization approaches presented in Chapter 3).

The results:

• There are multiple prioritized lists of projects and one portfolio per bucket.
• Dissimilar projects do not compete against each other (for example, product extensions do not compete with genuine new products for priority or resources).
• Resource spending at the end of the year is consistent with the desired or target breakdown; new product spending reflects the business's strategy!

Strategic Buckets: The Details

First comes the development of the business strategy and the new product strategy. Like military generals, the business leadership team must have clear business and new product goals—but that's not enough! They must also make decisions about which battlefields, or strategic arenas, they wish to attack; that is, the markets, product types, platforms, or technology arenas on which they wish to focus. As well they need to know how they will attack these arenas, and how much they will spend in each arena. The role of the Strategic Buckets Model is to translate the business strategy into clearly defined arenas (buckets) and to decide resource allocation to each.

Here are the key steps in more detail:

1. *Develop a vision and strategy for the business.* This includes defining strategic goals and the general plan of attack to achieve these goals—a fairly standard business strategy exercise (outlined earlier in this chapter).
2. *Make forced resource allocation choices across key strategic dimensions.* That is, based on this strategy, management allocates R&D and other resources (either in dollars or percentages) across categories on each dimension. In some businesses, this allocation is for R&D funds only; in others, it includes R&D, capital, and marketing resources for new products. Seven important dimensions that companies consider include:

- *Strategic goals:* Management splits resources across the specified strategic goals. For example, what percentage (or how many dollars) should be spent on defending the base? on diversifying? on extending the base?
- *Product lines:* Resources are split across product lines. For example, how much to spend on product line A? on product line B? on product line C? The stage of the product life cycle of each line's market should influence this split. Other factors include the product line's strength in the market, the importance of the product line to the business, and the product line's technological strength.
- *Market segments:* The business may operate in several market segments that have different degrees of attractiveness and potential. Thus, management splits resources across market segments.
- *Technology types:* The business may rely on several types of technologies or technology platforms. Technologies might be categorized as base, key, pacing, and embryonic. Management may wish to split resources across technologies, technology types, or platforms.
- *Project types:* What percentage of resources should go to new product development? to platform development? to fundamental research? to maintenance-type projects? to process improvements?

Example: One business within Exxon Chemical uses the product/market newness diagram illustrated in Exhibit 5.11 to visualize the split across project types. Here, each of the six types of projects receives a certain percentage of the total budget.

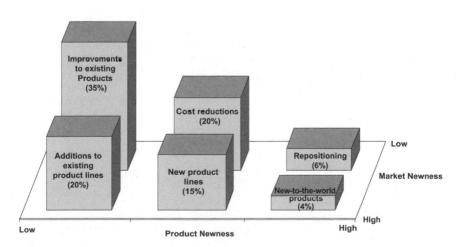

EXHIBIT 5.11   Six Project Categories (Used in an SBU in Exxon Chemical)

Note: Each type of project is represented by a box on the chart.

Example: A somewhat simpler breakdown is used at AlliedSignal-Honeywell, Engineered Materials Division. The chief technology officer explains: "We have our 'Mercedes-Benz star' method of allocating resources. We [the leadership team of the business] begin with the business's strategy and use the Mercedes star emblem [a three-point star] to help divide up the resources. There are three categories: fundamental research and platform development projects which promise to yield major breakthroughs and new technology platforms; new product development; and maintenance—technical support, product improvements and enhancements, and so on (Exhibit 5.12). We divide up the R&D funds into these three categories, and then rate and rank projects against each other within a category. This way, we ensure that we end up spending money according to our strategy."

- *Familiarity matrix*: What should be the split of resources to different types of markets and to different technology types in terms of their familiarity to the business? Some firms use the familiarity matrix or newness matrix proposed by Roberts,[16] where both markets and technologies are categorized into three types (see Exhibit 5.13):*
  - existing markets (or technologies) for the company
  - extensions of current markets (or technologies) for the company.
  - new markets (or technologies) for the company

  Eastman Chemical uses a four-cell version of this matrix to allocate resources into buckets. Dow Corning uses a nine-cell matrix.
- *Geography*: What proportion of resources should be spent on projects aimed largely at North America? at Latin America? at Europe? at the Pacific? globally?

3. *Define strategic buckets.* Here, the various strategic dimensions discussed above are collapsed into a convenient handful of buckets (see Exhibit 5.14). For example:

- product development projects for product lines A and B
- cost reduction projects for all products
- product renewal projects for product lines C and D.

The number of buckets varies, but it typically ranges from four to a dozen. Exhibit 5.14 shows only four buckets or columns (due to space constraints), but there were actually ten buckets in the case we investigated.

4. *Determine current spending.* This is a relatively simple accounting exercise of categorizing current or existing projects by bucket and adding up annual spending on each project within a given bucket.

---

* Note that the Roberts familiarity matrix (Exhibit 5.13) is somewhat different from the one used by Exxon Chemical (Exhibit 5.11). In the Roberts matrix, both dimensions are "newness to the company," whereas in the categories of new products matrix, originally proposed by Booz-Allen & Hamilton, one dimension captures newness to the company but the other is newness to the market. These are subtle but very important differences, and they can lead to quite different definitions of projects within each cell.

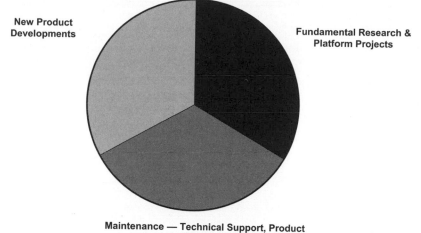

**New Product
Developments**

**Fundamental Research &
Platform Projects**

**Maintenance — Technical Support, Product
Improvements & Enhancements, etc.**

EXHIBIT 5.12   The Mercedes-Benz Star Method of Allocating Resources Across Project Types

Technology Newness	Market Newness	
	Existing/Base	**New**
New Step-Out	Step-Out Product Development	New Business and New Ventures
New But Familiar	New Items (existing lines)	Market Development
Base	Defend or Penetrate	Market Expansion (customer application projects)

EXHIBIT 5.13   Familiarity Matrix—Technology and Market Newness

5. *Determine desired spending*. This involves a consolidation of the "what is" information from current spending with the "what should be" from the strategic allocation exercise in items 2 and 3 above.
6. *Identify gaps*. This step compares the actual spending per bucket with the desired spending. Differences between the two levels are identified as gaps.
7. *Rank projects by bucket*. Companies use either scoring models or financial criteria to rank-order projects (see Exhibit 5.14). It is possible to use different criteria for each bucket. For example, in Exhibit 5.14, the cost reduction projects in the far right column might be rated on a simple cost-benefit ratio, whereas the new product projects in column 1 might be prioritized via a scoring model that takes into account a number of qualitative and strategic criteria. The result in Exhibit 5.14 is four distinct portfolios of projects—four lists. Note that the projects in column 1, the first bucket,

New Products: Product Line A Target Spend: $8.7M	New Products: Product Line B Target Spend: $18.5M	Maintenance of Business: Product Lines A & B Target Spend: $10.8M	Cost Reductions: All Products Target Spend: $7.8M
Project A 4.1	Project B 2.2	Project E 1.2	Project I 1.9
Project C 2.1	Project D 4.5	Project G 0.8	Project M 2.4
Project F 1.7	Project K 2.3	Project H 0.7	Project N 0.7
Project L 0.5	Project T 3.7	Project J 1.5	Project P 1.4
Project X 1.7	**Gap = 5.8**	Project Q 4.8	Project S 1.6
Project Y 2.9		Project R 1.5	Project U 1.0
Project Z 4.5		Project V 2.5	Project AA 1.2
Project BB 2.6		Project W 2.1	

EXHIBIT 5.14   Projects Prioritized Within Strategic Buckets

are not ranked against the projects—they do not compete for resources—in other buckets. Projects compete against each other only within the same column!

8. *Make necessary adjustments.* Where overspending occurs within a bucket—for example, too many maintenance projects—projects can be pruned; or, as most companies do, management gives proportionately fewer approvals for upcoming projects of that type. In the contrary case, where underspending is occurring—for example, not enough genuine new product projects for product line B in Exhibit 5.14—then management encourages more such projects and may even relax some of their Go/Kill gating criteria.

Over time, the portfolio of projects, and the actual spending across buckets, will eventually equal management's desired spending levels across buckets. At that point, the portfolio of projects truly mirrors the business's strategy.

How to Make the Forced Choices on Each Dimension

How does management make forced choices in resource splits across goals, across product lines, or across markets? The Strategic Buckets Model requires that such choices be made, but often firms were unclear about the management decision process. Here are four resource-splitting approaches that we saw:

1. *Discussion and consensus:* Each member of the leadership team proposes a resource split, views are discussed, and consensus is reached. Usually the meeting begins with a review of the business's vision, goals, and strategy, followed by a review of the current breakdown of resource allocation—the "what is." Inconsistencies between strategy and current spending splits are identified, and directional decisions—spend more here, less there—are decided.

2. *Scoring method:* Criteria are developed for scoring a market, product line, or strategic arena; managers then rate each product line, market, or arena on these criteria and prioritize accordingly.

3. *Strategic exercise*: The strategic map in Exhibit 5.8 is useful for deciding the split in resources among various businesses areas or strategic arenas. A similar exercise for product groups is illustrated later in the chapter (Exhibit 5.16).

4. *Directional decision rules:* Some companies have developed powerful rules to guide the breakdown of resources across product lines, product categories, or even businesses.

Example: One major U.S. consumer goods firm relies on a very simple three-part rule to allocate new product R&D and marketing resources to different product categories: feed the strong, focus the weak, and build the new. In practice, this means that product managers who are successful at new products receive proportionately more resources each year; those who are less successful are instructed to do less product development and to focus their business (for example, on a certain market segment or fewer products). And a certain proportion of resources is set aside for new businesses and opportunities. This decision rule is thus a heuristic that, over time, directs more resources to more fertile areas where there are more opportunities for winning new products, or where management is more successful at developing winners.

Strengths and Weaknesses of Top-Down Approaches

Of all the attempts to build strategy into the portfolio selection process, Top-Down Approaches, such as the Strategic Buckets Model and the product roadmap, are perhaps the most impressive and comprehensive and the most holistic. They extend from top to bottom of the organization and across all possible types of projects. They begin with the strategic goals of the business and end with a list of projects to be undertaken. The process, thus, scores top marks for trying to link projects undertaken (where the money is spent) to the goals of the business (where the money should be spent).

This comprehensiveness, however, may also be the Achilles' heel of these strategic approaches. They both require huge models and frameworks to implement and use:

- They require a business strategy and a new product strategy.
- They require management to make very tough choices about how it wants to operationalize that strategy. (Vague statements about strategic direction, which are found in so many firms, are not good enough!)
- The Strategic Buckets Model requires management to be very specific about where it wants to spend money—again, more tough choices.
- The product roadmap approach requires management to be decisive about which products and platforms it wishes to fund over the long term—still more tough choices.

The Top-Down Approaches described here are also sophisticated and some-what difficult to fully comprehend. They require much data and have many steps, each involving hard work (especially from senior management of the business). Whether management will stay the course is an issue with these approaches. By contrast, the Bottom-Up Approaches—which build strategic criteria into project selection methods and are described next in this chapter—are much simpler and less ambitious in scope. Implementation is straightforward by comparison.

One specific complaint about the Strategic Buckets Model is that there are just too many dimensions and too many resource splits required. One firm we inter-viewed is using five of the seven splits we outlined above. The leadership team breaks down resources by strategic goals, by markets, by product lines, by proj-ect types, and via the familiarity matrix. Assuming four choices on each of these five dimensions, that works out to 5^4, or 625 buckets! This is unworkable. We still are not sure how they are able to reduce this number of buckets to a more man-ageable size. One way to avoid this problem is to focus on only a few of the most relevant dimensions, as defined by your strategy (and these will vary by business, even within the same corporation).

Example: The view expressed by the head of strategic planning for R&D at Rohm and Haas is not to split spending along every possible dimension, as expressed in the Strategic Buckets Model; rather, the secret is selective breakdowns. "The key is to define the areas of strategic thrust for the business. That is, a business must have its strategy clearly defined, whether it be in terms of markets, or product lines, or technology areas. For example, if an area of strategic thrust is to 'grow via develop-ment of products aimed at China,' then that's the definition of areas of strategic thrust. Then the leadership team must define how much effort [or money] it wishes to spend against each area of strategic thrust. That's the essence of portfolio manage-ment!"

Other than the physical challenge of implementing Top-Down Approaches, we hear three specific complaints about the product roadmap method:

1. Strategy should not always drive the portfolio in a Top-Down fashion. There are times when new product projects should create the strategy! That is, getting into a specific new product project that might even be "off strategy" could open up all kinds of windows of opportunity, and thereby change the strategy of the business. A strictly Top-Down Approach prevents such opportunities and strategic changes from occurring.

   Was 3M's decision to enter the Post-it Notes™ business a strategic decision? Or was this a serendipitous discovery, which caused the company to change strategic direction? Most companies have their Post-it Notes™ examples.

2. Product roadmaps are stultifying and rigid—they thwart creativity and entrepre-neurship. It's as though the entire future is laid out in some pre-ordained fashion. There seems to be little room for opportunistic management and spontaneity. If

projects bubble up that do not fit onto the roadmap, they are dismissed, even though they might be excellent business opportunities.

3. The environment is fluid, so things change. How can one lay out a roadmap of product offerings years in advance in such a fluid environment? Within months, claim some managers, the roadmap is obsolete. The long-term strategy for the business may be fairly stable over time, but the product roadmap must constantly change.

In spite of these concerns, the product roadmap possesses many positive features. The obvious one is that it links strategy and strategic priorities very clearly to the choice, prioritization, and timing of projects. It also engages senior management in the portfolio management process by forcing them to address the question, If our strategy is X, then what major projects must we undertake in order to realize our strategy?

The second Top-Down Approach, Strategic Buckets, also has some detractors and weak points. In particular, the splitting exercise raises a number of concerns:

1. How can one split resources across buckets—for example, by project types—without first considering the projects within each bucket and how good they are? Some managers claim that this Top-Down dividing of resources into buckets is a theoretical exercise that is impossible to do without first looking at the relative attractiveness of potential projects in each bucket—more of a Bottom-Up Approach. As one executive said, "Surely the choice of buckets, and how much to spend in each, depends in part on what opportunities are available in each—on what projects are underway. You can't do this splitting exercise without looking inside each bucket!"

2. A parallel concern focuses on sub-optimization. Note that in Exhibit 5.14, the first bucket or column has too many projects, with projects X, Y, Z, and BB as excess. The Strategic Buckets Model suggests that they should be cut and that resources should be diverted to the second bucket, where there is a gap. But suppose projects X, Y, Z, and BB—the four bottom projects in Bucket 1—are better projects than the top four in Bucket 2? Would you still divert resources away from Bucket 1?
The quick rebuttal, of course, is that the strategic allocation of resources was wrong in the first place—that Bucket 2 should never have received so much money given the limited opportunities there, and that Bucket 1 should have received more money. Be careful of this knee-jerk conclusion, however. Another reasoned argument is that one should not let a shortage of good projects (or good opportunities) thwart an otherwise well-founded strategy. The problem might not be that the targeted heavy allocation to Bucket 2 is wrong; rather, the lack of effort (and people) to identify the good opportunities within Bucket 2 may be the problem. Thus, the solution may be to devote more effort—people and energy—in this arena so that Bucket 2 will be filled with excellent projects. As one general manager of a division put it: "If we decide to enter a totally new arena—say, a new market for us—we might also decide to allocate a certain percentage of our R&D budget there. The fact that we have no active projects or identified opportunities should not be the reason to say no to this arena!"

3. Another concern is what action should be taken. For example, faced with the situation outlined in Exhibit 5.14, would you really kill projects X, Y, Z, and BB simply because there are too many in Bucket 1? Suppose you know that all four are excellent projects, and that they are three-quarters completed! Of course you wouldn't kill them. That wouldn't make sense. So what action does the model suggest now? Pundits claim that, while immediate action to kill projects would not be taken, sig-

nals would be sent that no more Bucket 1 projects should be approved for the fore-seeable future; in addition, there would be a great initiative to generate high-quality projects for Bucket 2. Another possible action is to simply to change the strategy and deprioritize Bucket 2 in the future, allocating fewer resources to it.

4. The final complaint is that the Strategic Buckets Model seems just too complex and difficult for management to understand and walk through. The number of steps and splits required is overwhelming to some.

Viewed from another perspective, however, the Strategic Buckets Model is not as complex as it first appears. It really boils down to two major elements:

*   a strategic exercise wherein desired spending levels are established for each project type (the buckets that specify levels of spending)
*   rank-ordering of projects within each bucket, using one of the traditional maximization methods (for example, via a scoring model or a financial criterion such as NPV, PI, or ECV—see Chapter 3).

We witnessed examples of firms using only some elements of the Strategic Buckets Model rather than the full model and achieving positive results. For example, AlliedSignal-Honeywell does not consider all seven dimensions we outlined above, but only "project types" in its three-sector Mercedes star method (Exhibit 5.12); and the Exxon Chemical business unit cited above does much the same thing (project types, as in Exhibit 5.11).

Another positive facet of the Strategic Buckets Model is the recognition that all development projects that compete for the same resources can and should be considered in the portfolio approach. Conceptually, this is correct. For example, product development projects must be considered along with cost reduction projects, because both utilize R&D resources. Note that, while various types of projects are considered, they do not directly compete with each other. Separate buckets are established, and separate project portfolios—one portfolio per bucket—are developed.

Example: The analogous situation is that of running an investment portfolio. The portfolio manager makes strategic choices about how she wishes to split her investments: what percentage to bonds, what percentage to blue chip stocks, what percentage to more speculative stocks. Next, from the amount allocated to bonds, she prioritizes the available bonds and picks the best ones. She does the same with blue chip stocks, and so on. Note, however, that specific bonds are not compared to specific stocks.

A positive feature of the Strategic Buckets Model is that different criteria can be used for different types of projects. Therefore one is not faced with comparing and ranking very different projects against each other, an apples-versus-oranges situation. Because this is a two-step approach (first allocate money to buckets, then prioritize like projects within a bucket), it is not necessary to arrive at a universal list of scoring or ranking criteria that fits all projects. Similar projects are compared only against each other. So, one is comparing all apples against each other within one bucket, and all oranges against each other in another bucket.

Example: One company, which divides resources according to strategic buckets, uses somewhat different criteria for trying to rank-order projects within buckets. For example, for the bucket "product developments," one set of scoring model criteria is used—criteria that emphasize strategic fit, market attractiveness, and competitive advantage. For other buckets—namely, cost reductions and process improvements—the ranking criteria change to cost-benefit and financial ones.*

In this way the company is able to handle all projects competing for the same resources yet recognize the differences between projects and the fact that selection criteria for different types of projects ought to be different.

The Special Case of Platform Projects

The Strategic Buckets Model is particularly suitable for handling platform projects. Consider the Mercedes Star diagram used by AlliedSignal-Honeywell in Exhibit 5.12. It is a simpler Strategic Buckets Model, but it is worth taking a closer look at. Many senior people expressed interest in the approach when we shared Exhibit 5.12 with them.

At AlliedSignal-Honeywell, management within each business unit first meets to agree on goals and strategy. Then they translate their strategy into resource allocations across three categories of projects (Exhibits 5.12). Note that the upper right pie is for Fundamental Research and Platform Projects—these are defined as projects *that will change the basis of competition.* Thus, management makes a strategic and deliberate decision to allocate a certain proportion of resources to these longer-term platform developments. That has been a major step forward for the corporation, as increasingly the smaller projects in the bottom part of the diagram—product improvements enhancements and technical support—were consuming a larger and larger proportion of resources each year. This approach "protects" platform and major developments—it sets aside money or resources for these longer-term projects in a deliberate fashion. Note that once allocated, these resources cannot be spent on projects outside a bucket.

---

* The argument here is that the characteristics of a successful new product project are somewhat different from those for a successful process improvement; hence, different selection criteria ought to be used. Further, since cost reductions or process improvements are internal projects, usually the financial projection (or cost-benefit analysis) is much more predictable. Hence, cost-benefit ought to be emphasized more for such cost-reduction projects. By contrast, the financial projection is often a highly uncertain number, leading some experts to downplay it as the leading selection criterion for more innovative products (see scoring models in Chapter 3).

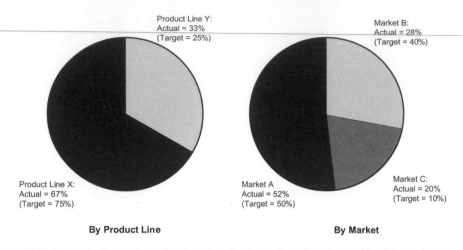

By Product Line   **By Market**

EXHIBIT 5.15   Target Spending Levels—Guides to Spending Across Key Dimensions

A second positive feature of Strategic Buckets is that three separate portfolios are established. There is a separate bucket and separate portfolio for platform projects; similarly there is a bucket and portfolio of new product projects (Exhibit 5.12). Projects in different buckets do not compete against each other. For example, neither product improvements nor new product projects are ranked against platform projects. What this means is that different criteria can be used to rate and rank the different types of projects, as noted above and also in Chapter 3, Exhibit 3.11. This is critical for the approvals of platform developments. If platform projects were subjected to the same criteria as new product projects—for example, NPV and certain product-related scoring criteria seen in Chapter 3—it is doubtful that any would survive. The financial prospects for platforms are simply too uncertain early on. As to scoring criteria such as product advantage and market attractiveness, the potential products from the platform may be so vaguely defined at this point that such ratings are almost impossible to do.

POINTS FOR MANAGEMENT TO PONDER

If your business is like many—the link to strategy is missing and there are too many of the wrong types of projects in your portfolio—then consider the Strategic Buckets Model. Even if you only consider a few simple splits (for example, by project type or by product line or market area), at least you will be bringing your portfolio closer to the strategic direction of your business. And Strategic Buckets are a must if platform projects are part of your portfolio: Strategic Buckets set aside protected funding for longer-term or larger projects and enable the use of individualized criteria to evaluate them.

A Variant on Strategic Buckets:
Target Spending Levels

Some companies use an approach similar to Strategic Buckets but arrive at a re-source allocation to target spending levels instead of to buckets. After developing the business strategy, spending splits are agreed across relevant dimensions. For example: "Our target spending split for R&D is 40 percent for market A and 60 percent for market B." Thus far, the method is identical to the Strategic Buckets Model.

The major difference is that there is only a single portfolio of projects, a list that covers all markets, product lines, project types, and so on (unlike Strategic Buckets, which has multiple portfolios, one portfolio list per bucket). A running tally of the spending breakdown is kept during the year, so that actual spending along dimensions (for example, by product line or project type) can be compared to the target spending level, and adjustments can be made as the year progresses. The pie charts in the previous chapter, which portray balance along various di-mensions, are useful display methods here (see Exhibits 4.19 and 4.20), but they should also include spending targets—the "what should be" versus the "what is" (Exhibit 5.15).

Example: One SBU in Exxon Chemical uses a similar but after-the-fact strategic check. Management begins with a good understanding of the SBU's strategy and strategic priorities. Tentative spending splits or target spending are then de-cided according to a project newness matrix (Exhibit 5.11). As the year pro-gresses, all projects are prioritized using a scoring model, both at gate decision points and during periodic portfolio review meetings. The split in actual spending is then displayed using the same newness matrix. Imbalances become evident, and adjustments are made for the upcoming year—decisions to emphasize cer-tain types of projects or to rethink the target spending splits.

Although seemingly similar, the two methods—Strategic Buckets and Target Spending—are somewhat different in operation. Here's how:

- In Strategic Buckets, the walls of each bucket are quite firm. Money and projects do not slide between buckets. By contrast, the Target Spending Method yields just that: guides or targets, which are somewhat flexible (porous walls).
- With Strategic Buckets, the result is multiple portfolios or multiple lists of projects, one for each bucket. With a Target Spending Method, there is only one portfolio or one prioritized list of projects.
- With Target Spending, all types of projects compete against each other; using the Strategic Buckets Model, only projects within one bucket compete.
- Target Spending Method means the same criteria must be used to rate all projects. With the Strategic Buckets Model, different criteria and different ranking methods can be used to rank projects for each bucket.

- The Target Spending Method enables splits across many dimensions—markets, product lines, project types, technologies, and so on—without encountering the problem of too many individual cells or too many separate buckets. It is not necessary to create buckets, only desired splits.

A viable compromise is to use Strategic Buckets for key business dimensions (as does AlliedSignal-Honeywell with buckets across project types) and then a series of target spending levels—guides, not buckets—on other dimensions, such as markets, technologies, product lines, and so on.

Bottom-Up Approach: Strategic Criteria Built into Project Selection Tools

"If you pick good projects, and build strategic criteria into your project selection method, then the portfolio will take care of itself!" This is the view expressed by a senior executive in a major firm with considerable experience in the portfolio management field. His point is that the emphasis ought to be on project selection—namely, at the bottom—and that in the process of selecting excellent projects, the portfolio will evolve and spending breakdowns will emerge. He is also quick to point out that strategic criteria ought to be built into the project selection tool so that the resulting portfolio of projects will be both on strategy and strategically important. We witnessed other businesses adhering to the same philosophy, either explicitly or implicitly.

The most popular and appropriate project selection method to achieve these multiple goals is the scoring model (introduced in Chapter 3). Scoring models can help achieve two key portfolio goals: ensuring the strategic fit and importance of projects and maximizing the value of the portfolio. One of the multiple objectives considered in a scoring model—along with profitability or likelihood of success—can be maximization of strategic fit and importance. The way to achieve this is to build into the scoring model a number of strategic questions.

Example: Celanese has adopted this Bottom-Up Approach. In Celanese's scoring model (Exhibit 3.8), 40 percent of the major factors—two major factors out of five—are strategic. Of the 19 criteria used to prioritize projects, six (or almost one-third) deal with strategic issues. Thus, projects that fit the firm's strategy and boast strategic leverage are likely to rise to the top of the list. Indeed, it is inconceivable how off-strategy projects could make the active list at all; the scoring model naturally weeds them out.

Note that the use of a Bottom-Up Approach at Celanese does not suggest that the business lacks a business or new product strategy; quite the contrary. For without a clearly defined new product strategy, there are no answers to the strategic fit questions in Celanese's scoring model!

Example: Reckitt-Benckiser subjects all projects to must-meet criteria at gates before any prioritization consideration is given. At the top of this list is strategic fit. Projects that fail to meet this criterion are knocked out immediately. Next a set of should-meet criteria is used via a scoring model. Unless the project scores a certain minimum point count, again it is knocked out. Embedded within this scoring model are several strategic direction criteria. For example, Reckitt-Benckiser's strategy calls for more international products and fewer domestically oriented developments; hence, this international criterion is one of the scoring criteria, so that projects that are international receive more points. In this way, the portfolio over time will be deliberately biased toward international projects. Finally, in Reckitt-Benckiser's bubble diagram (where attractiveness is plotted versus ease—see Exhibit 4.7), of the six parameters that make up attractiveness, two capture important strategic directions:

- competitive position improvement (ability to build the brand and franchise in the long term)
- geographic scope (international projects are favored).

Thus, Reckitt-Benckiser builds in strategic fit and direction throughout its scoring and bubble diagram portfolio approaches.

Note that in both companies the result is a single portfolio or rank-ordered list of projects, with all projects competing against each other (unlike the Strategic Buckets Model, which yields multiple buckets and lists).

The scoring model approach is recommended for three reasons:

1. It is simple to use and understand.
2. It kills two birds with one stone. Scoring models are appropriate techniques to achieve maximization of key variables (including financial) and at the same time can be used to ensure strategic fit.
3. Finally, scoring models are suitable for both gate project review meetings as well as portfolio review meetings. Recall that in Chapter 3, we saw that Celanese uses its scoring model at gates (Exhibit 3.8) and that Royal Bank uses its scoring model at the portfolio review, where all projects are considered (Exhibit 3.12).

This Bottom-Up Approach—using project selection methods that build in strategic criteria—overcomes a critical concern with Top-Down Approaches. Remember that one very tough criticism aimed at the Strategic Buckets Model is that undertaking the resource split based only on a Top-Down strategic view, without first considering what projects are available, is theoretical and difficult to do. Indeed, it may even be conceptually wrong. By contrast, the Bottom-Up Approach begins with projects and their relative attractiveness and by incorporating strategic criteria attempts to yield a "strategically correct" portfolio.

The weakness is that only one-half of the strategic goal is achieved; namely, ensuring that all projects are on-strategy. What scoring models do not do is ensure

---

POINTS FOR MANAGEMENT TO PONDER

Regardless of the approach you are considering, the Bottom-Up Approach might be a good exercise to try. It will provide you with a view of what is in your pipeline, where resources are committed, and the value of your current portfolio. Once you have this information, ask some critical questions, such as

- Are we satisfied with the profile of our portfolio?
- Should changes be made to it?
- Is a Bottom-Up Approach a good approach for our projects?
- Are the project selection criteria used at the gate meetings providing the rigor we need to rank projects?

---

that the spending breakdown in the portfolio reflects the strategic priorities of the business. In short, all projects may be on-strategy, but the balance or split of resource spending may be wrong. This shortfall leads logically to the third strategic method, which combines Strategic Buckets with this Bottom-Up Approach.

Top-Down, Bottom-Up Approach

In an attempt to overcome the deficiencies of the two methods outlined above, some firms adopt a hybrid approach, a Top-Down, Bottom-Up Approach, which:

- ensures strategic alignment, most notably that spending breakdowns mirror the strategic priorities of the business—a strength of the Strategic Buckets Model, but a weakness of the Bottom-Up Approach
- considers the specific opportunities—active and potential projects—as a key input to the spending and prioritization decision—a strength of the Bottom-Up Approach, but a weakness of both Top-Down Approaches.

The Top-Down, Bottom-Up Approach is similar to the Target Spending Method variation on the Strategic Buckets Model. It begins with the business strategy: mission, strategic arenas, and priorities. Next, flowing from this strategy, tentative target breakdowns of spending across categories are developed (for example, tentative splits across product lines, or markets, or technologies, or project types, or across some or all of these).

So far the approach closely resembles a Top-Down Approach. Now the approach moves to a Bottom-Up Approach. All existing or active projects and all projects on hold are rated and ranked. This ranking is achieved via a maximization method; for example, a scoring model or some other criterion or method outlined in Chapter 3. Some firms use the scores, ratings, or data from most recent gate meetings to do this; others rescore all projects. In this respect, the approach is similar to that employed by Celanese. This exercise yields a single prioritized list: a ranking of all projects and potential projects that are in the pipeline. Projects near the top of the list are obvious "Go" projects; those near the bottom (or below the cutoff line) are obvious kills—at least on this first iteration.

The final step is to merge Top-Down and Bottom-Up outcomes. Note that frequently the list of projects generated by the Bottom-Up ranking yields splits in resources that are inconsistent with the Top-Down tentative spending splits—the two approaches do not coincide on the first iteration. To bring the two approaches together, the breakdown of proposed spending on projects is computed, using the rank-ordered list of projects above (Bottom-Up exercise). This breakdown is done along the same dimensions as the Top-Down Approach (across product lines, markets, technologies, or project types).

Then, Bottom-Up spending breakdowns are checked against the desired tentative spending splits derived from the Top-Down Approach. Where gaps are identified, action may be taken; for example, reprioritizing some active projects (fewer resources) or activating projects on hold.

Several iterations may be required to reconcile the Top-Down and Bottom-Up decisions. The prioritized list of projects may be shuffled somewhat, with projects from over-represented categories removed from the active list. Here, the strategic priorities of the business are revisited, and tentative spending splits might be modified in light of available project opportunities. After several of these iterations, the Top-Down and Bottom-Up decisions are synchronized.

The Top-Down, Bottom-Up Approach, thus, checks that the resulting list of projects (and their spending breakdowns) is indeed consistent with the business's strategy and with the desired spending breakdowns. At the same time, the approach fully considers what projects—active and on-hold—are available and weighs their relative attractiveness.

In some respects, one might argue that the approach tends to be more of an "after-the-fact" model, a check or correction method designed to bring the portfolio closer to the strategic ideal. Instead of deliberately setting up firm buckets of resources, as in the Strategic Buckets Model, tentative spending targets per bucket are agreed to (more like the Target Spending Method). But these splits are modified as a result of the project prioritization exercise; that is, according to projects available in each bucket.

Example of a Top-Down, Bottom-Up Approach in Action

The strategic planning exercise used at the Royal Bank of Canada is fairly typical. It resembles the Strategic Buckets Model (or the Target Spending Method) in that desired spending levels per strategic arena are decided (in this example, by product group). Then projects are rated and ranked, spending per category is determined, gaps are identified, and adjustments are made. Either the portfolio of projects is adjusted as needed or desired spending splits are modified.

Recall that the Royal Bank uses a scoring model to rate and rank projects (see Exhibit 3.12). This is the bank's Bottom-Up Approach. The end result is a listing of projects, rank-ordered, with tentative "Go" projects above the line.

The strategic mapping exercise is one check that the business has built into its portfolio method to ensure that project spending is linked to strategy. It is Royal Bank's way of tentatively allocating resources across product lines. This is a strategic planning exercise wherein the 12 product groups in Royal

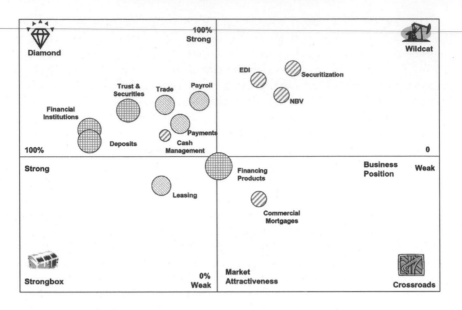

EXHIBIT 5.16   Royal Bank of Canada Strategic Map

Bank are analyzed via a high-level portfolio exercise. (Product groups are major product lines.)

This strategic allocation decision results in missions and macro-strategies for each of the product groups, as well a rough idea (directional) of what each product group ought to receive in R&D funding. In this example, the tentative buckets are product lines. However, as in the Strategic Buckets Model, buckets could just as easily have been market segments, product/market arenas, or even project types. This macro-strategic exercise is a fairly traditional one, but it is worth mentioning because of the way it is tied to new product spending and Royal Bank's scoring model.

First, the 12 product groups (product lines) are scored on each of 18 rating scales (0–10 ratings) that capture three main factors: market attractiveness, business position, and strategic importance. The evaluators are from the product groups as well as other units and functions (operations, sales, systems, and so on). Scoring takes place in an electronic meeting room, using a computer-based scoring technique along with a large-screen computer display of results. Several rounds of scoring are necessary to arrive at consensus. The computer display highlights areas of inconsistencies and uncertainties requiring further discussion. Animated exchanges are usually part of this meeting. Note that evaluators, invited from other units and functions (outside the product line), keep the discussion and scoring objective and "honest."

Three product line portfolio maps or bubble diagrams are constructed from the scores, showing the locations of the 12 product groups on all three factors or axes: market attractiveness, business position, and strategic importance (Exhibit 5.16).

RBC's First-Cut Prioritized List of Projects

Rank Order	Project Name	Product Group	Score (%)	Development Cost (S&T dollars $000)	Cumulative Development Cost ($000)
1	RBCash	Cash Management	83	2,400	2,400
2	CashCore	Cash Management	76	1,920	4,320
3	EBX	EDI	76	1,800	6,120
4	EBY	EDI	73	500	6,620
5	BuyAct	Deposits	73	6,000	12,620
6	CorpPay	Payroll	70	2,000	14,620
7	Project A-PC	Loans	70	1,600	16,220
8	PC-MD	Loans	68	7,500	23,720
-	-	-	-	-	-
26	Tiered/Interest Accounts	Deposits	55	930	90,150
27	Tiered	Loans	52	1,000	
28	Trade-AP	Trade	52	1,200	
29	ATM-Y	Deposits	50	500	
-	-	-	-	-	-

Split in Total Expenditure by Product Group

Target	Actual	Product Group
10%	18%	Cash Management
25%	30%	Deposits
5%	4%	Payroll
25%	15%	Loans
20%	13%	Disbursements
10%	11%	EDI
-	-	

EXHIBIT 5.17   Royal Bank of Canada—Prioritized List of Projects by Product Group

Note: All figures have been disguised.

Based on their respective locations, each of the 12 groups is, then, classed as a diamond (star product lines), strongbox (cash generator), wildcat, or crossroads product line. A mission and vision contingent on this classification are developed, along with a strategy for each product group. Virtually all groups are either diamonds (which means a "growth" mission) or strongboxes (which translates into a "hold and maintain the course" mission and strategy). A few newer and smaller ones are wildcats. Rarely is a product line classed as a crossroads (these product groups have either been weeded out or merged with a unit in another part of the corporation).

Next, spending breakdowns (very tentative and directional) are decided across product groups. Development spending is determined as a percentage of sales or revenue for each group. For example, diamond product lines receive a higher percentage of revenue for product development than would strongbox product lines. In contrast, crossroads product groups receive a fairly low percentage of revenue for product development (less than 1 percent of their revenues).

So far, the exercise resembles the fairly standard top-down strategic planning portfolio exercises we saw earlier in this chapter, except for the use of electronic scoring. It is the use of the classifications as an input to the new product portfolio exercise that is noteworthy. Recall that Royal Bank uses a scoring model that yields a single prioritized list of projects from all 12 product groups (see Exhibit 3.12)—a Bottom-Up Approach. But this list is only the first cut. The list of projects "above the line" (that is, judged as "Go") is quickly broken down by product group, and the total expenditures by group are determined. Exhibit 5.17 shows the outcome of this process: a rank-ordered list of projects, with expenditure breakdowns by product line.

These totals by group, as a percentage of revenue, are then compared across groups for inconsistencies. As noted above, the normal rule is that diamond product groups should receive far more than their fair share of project spending—as much as double the norm. In contrast, strongbox product groups receive proportionately less. Gaps are identified among actual spending levels per business versus the desired spending, based on the first-cut list.

A second round of project prioritization ensues, with some projects that were originally above the cutoff line being removed, while some below the line move up. This usually moves the project portfolio closer to desired spending splits dictated by the Strategic Planning exercise. Several rounds are required before the final list of projects above the line is agreed to. At this point, the prioritized list contains very good projects, according to the scoring model, and the spending allocations correctly reflect the strategies and missions of each product group.

The Top-Down, Bottom-Up Approach is one attempt to overcome the weaknesses of a strictly Top-Down Approach; namely, artificially splitting resources into buckets without considering specific projects and opportunities. It also deals with the major deficiency of the Bottom-Up Approach; namely, the failure to provide for strategic alignment and the right spending breakdowns. As in all hybrid or combined approaches, the end result—in this case, the portfolio management method—is not simple and tidy. The model becomes complex and cumbersome.

The main advantage of the Top-Down, Bottom-Up Approach over a strictly Bottom-Up Approach is that spending priorities are decided strategically, and these splits then direct the choice of projects. By contrast, in the Bottom-Up Approach, project choices dictate the spending splits and priorities. The Top-Down, Bottom-Up Approach's principal advantage over strictly Top-Down Approaches (for example, the Strategic Buckets Model or the Target Spending Method) is that it incorporates project attractiveness into decisions on spending splits (projects are concurrently prioritized, and spending breakdowns subsequently checked for consistency with strategy).

But How Much Should We Spend?

One issue that all strategic portfolio methods largely avoid is magnitude of spending. They have much to say about how the resource pie should be allocated across projects and project categories but are silent on the size of the pie in the first place. That is, what is the optimal spending level on development for our

---

POINTS FOR MANAGEMENT TO PONDER

We have now considered a number of methods for linking new product projects to strategy. A useful exercise would be to try out the various approaches. Once you have collected the project data, run the analysis from different perspectives. Weigh the pros and cons of each approach for your company. Then discuss seriously with key decision makers what you are trying to achieve and how well each approach meets your objectives. Does one approach deliver markedly more of the results you are looking for?

---

business? The assumption always seems to be that the resources available are always a given, and that portfolio management is about allocation of these given resources. Yet magnitude of spending on development is clearly a strategic issue, and the size of the portfolio is surely one element of portfolio management.

Some methods businesses use to decide how much to spend on development (R&D, marketing and capital expenditures) are:

- *Competitive parity*: Spend on your business roughly what the rest of the industry does (usually this means R&D spending as a percentage of sales).
- *Objectives and task*: Begin with your objectives (for example, sales from new products, next five years). Translate these into numbers of successful launches per year, and then break these into numbers of projects at each stage of the process. Assign an approximate dollar cost (or person-days) to do each stage; and multiply numbers of projects per stage times the cost per stage. This yields the total expenditure (dollars or full-time equivalent people) required to achieve the objectives.
- *Historical*: Take last year's budgeted amount and add or subtract a little.
- *Opportunistic rules*: Spend enough to finance the solid projects—those that clear a minimum financial hurdle. (Don't operate with a preconceived upper spending limit each year; many "good" projects will be put on hold, thereby reducing the total return of the company.)[17] An added rule we saw was: Never spend more than the cash inflow to the business (that is, do not borrow to finance projects). A counter-argument is that if the environment is turbulent, then the assumption that development funds will be internally generated (e.g., from cash cow products) may not hold; other funds outside the business must be found to support the new opportunities.[18]
- *Based on results*: Recall the "feed the strong, focus the weak" rule. This also applies across businesses. Each year, pour more development money into businesses that are successful at product development and take away from those that are less successful.
- *Corporate planning models*: Classify businesses according to the quadrants in the BCG or GE/McKinsey models (stars, cash cows, dogs, and oysters) and allocate money accordingly (more about these in Chapter 9). For example, Rhode & Schwarz* has developed scoring criteria against which each business is rated. Criteria include technological strength, market growth, and business strength. R&D funds are allocated across businesses according to their overall scores.

---

* Rhode & Schwarz is an electronics company located in Germany.

Summary

This chapter concludes our discussion on the three portfolio management goals: maximization of value, balance, and strategic alignment. From this point on, the book shifts to recommendations as we begin to look at the actual design and implementation of a portfolio management process for your company. For example, the next chapter begins the quest by focusing on benchmarking results that profile various portfolio methods in use and the performance results achieved. Chapter 7 highlights our conclusions about portfolio methods in practice and then identifies the various problems and pitfalls that other companies have experienced. This will permit you to preempt much of the learning curve that other organizations have undergone the hard way. Chapter 8 deals with an issue that plagues all portfolio approaches seen in this and the previous two chapters: integrity of the data. Finally, Chapters 9, 10, and 11 outline how to design and implement a portfolio management process tailored to the needs of your own organization.

CHAPTER 6

Portfolio Management Methods Used and Performance Results Achieved

How well is portfolio management working?[1] This is both a fundamental and a vital question. In Chapter 1, we provided a glimpse into the effectiveness of portfolio management by looking at the quality of portfolios on six key metrics (Exhibit 1.3). In the current chapter, we probe more deeply into portfolio management results, shedding light on which methods seem to yield the best results, and on what metrics. We also look at which methods are the most popular and how they are used. Note that popularity does not necessarily equate to performance. Indeed, one of the most popular approaches yielded the worst portfolio results! This chapter is based on an extensive investigation into industry best practices and portfolio performance (Phase 2 of the study referred to in Chapter 1).

Portfolio performance is a multifaceted concept, so six metrics were constructed to capture how well the business's portfolio performs. These metrics include decision effectiveness and efficiency, having the right balance of projects, high-value projects, and a strategically aligned portfolio. All are metrics that emerged as goals in an exploratory study.[2] Exhibit 6.1 lists the six metrics.

The Average Business

Portfolio management appears to be working in a *moderately satisfactory fashion* in our sample of businesses, as seen in Chapter 1. Mean scores across the six performance metrics are typically midrange—not stellar, but not disastrous either—although there are some differences across metrics (see Exhibit 6.2).

Some Details on the Best Practices
and Portfolio Performance Investigation

The purpose of the research reported in this chapter (Phase 2 of an ongoing study) is to determine the popularity and nature of portfolio management methods used by industry, and then to link performance to practice in order to identify best practice methods (see endnotes 1,3,5). The investigation was conducted with the help of the Industrial Research Institute (IRI), Washington, D.C., which represents most significant U.S. firms engaged in R&D. A detailed survey questionnaire was developed, which dealt with a number of topics, including the importance of portfolio management, the general nature of the portfolio management method used, the performance of the business's portfolio management method, and general demographics (industry, business size, etc.). The questionnaire itself was carefully structured, exhaustively reviewed by a committee of industry experts from the IRI, pretested on eight businesses via personal interviews, and finalized.

A listing of businesses known to be active in product development in North America was prepared, including the IRI membership list (largely CTOs of larger firms in the U.S.) as well as other private lists compiled by the authors. The eventual sample was a respectable 205 businesses, with no noticeable biases in the responding businesses versus those in the original population. The breakdown of respondents by industry is:

High technology	17.6%
Processed materials	8.3
Industrial products	8.3
Chemicals and advanced materials	26.3
Health-care products	6.3
Others	19.0

The mean size of corporations in the study is $6.4 billion in annual sales, while the mean size of the business unit studied is $1.9 billion in annual sales.

Average values do not tell the entire story, however. The distribution of performance results between the best and the worst businesses is very broad, with some firms achieving excellent performances, and others reporting dismal scores:

	Percentage of Businesses	
Performance metric	No or Poor*	Yes or Good
Projects are aligned with business's objectives	8.7%	74.4%
Portfolio contains very high value projects	9.7	55.1
Spending reflects the business's strategy	15.9	57.4
Projects are done on time (no gridlock)	30.2	29.7
Portfolio has good balance of projects	35.9	30.8
Portfolio has right number of projects	43.5	24.1

* No or poor score is 1 or 2 on the 5-point scale; yes or good score is 4 or 5.

Alignment   -   Projects are aligned with business objectives

Value   -   Portfolio contains very high value projects

Strategic   -   Spending reflects the businesss strategy

Timing   -   Projects are done on time (no gridlocks)

Balance   -   Portfolio has good balance of projects

Right Number   -   Portfolio has right number of projects

EXHIBIT 6.1   Portfolio Metrics Used in the Study

These substantial differences in portfolio performance between the best and worst performers, together with the moderate-to-poor mean performance scores on some metrics, are provocative. They send two messages:

1. Many firms are performing substantially below par. For example, almost half the firms report that they have far too many projects in their portfolios, while more than one-third admit to very poorly balanced portfolios. The fact that *many businesses have substandard performance suggests that much improvement is needed* in the way many companies' portfolios are managed. So the mean performance ratings shown as bar charts in Exhibit 6.2 should be used with caution, simply because only a minority of businesses are average.
2. The best performers show the way: They prove that effective portfolio management is not just a theory or a dream but is indeed possible. We will look more closely at the best performers for guidance later in the chapter.

The Best and Worst Performers

The large performance spread between the best and the worst begs the question: What is it that the better performers are doing differently from the poor performers? To answer this question, a single, composite portfolio performance metric was developed, based on the six individual metrics in Exhibit 6.1. The best performers (defined as the top 20 percent of businesses, measured by their portfolio performance on this single metric) were singled out. Then their results and practices were contrasted with those of the bottom 20 percent.

As might be expected, the top 20 percent achieve dramatically better portfolio performance results across all six metrics (Exhibit 6.2, shaded bars). However, the two areas where the best really excel compared to the poor performers are:

- portfolio balance—achieving the right balance of projects
- the right number of projects for the resources available.

Both are areas where the average business performs weakly.

Satisfaction with Portfolio Management Methods

How do managers view their portfolio management methods in terms of key parameters such as effectiveness, efficiency, realism, and ease of use? And would they recommend their approaches to other businesses?

The Average Business

Management in the average business is *not particularly satisfied* with their portfolio management approaches. Note the middle-of-the-road scores in Exhibit 6.3. The most positive facet of portfolio management is that the portfolio management approach used fits the business's management style.

The remainder of Exhibit 6.3 reveals lower scores. On average, the portfolio method:

- is perceived as effective (i.e., it leads to the right decisions)
- is used to make Go/Kill decisions—but only somewhat
- is not particularly efficient (somewhat laborious and inefficient)
- is not especially realistic in capturing key facets of the portfolio problem
- is not particularly user-friendly
- is not well understood by senior management.

The two lowest scoring items in Exhibit 6.3 are noteworthy. On average, businesses do not rate their portfolio methods as excellent (rather, a midrange score); nor do they strongly recommend their portfolio approaches to others.

Once again, there is a large spread in responses among businesses. The range in responses underscores the substantial differences in performance and satisfaction. Ten percent or fewer businesses and their managements are very happy with their portfolio management approach, but *the great majority are not*. For exam-

---

POINTS FOR MANAGEMENT TO PONDER

How does your business's portfolio rate on the six metrics in Exhibit 6.1? These are solid metrics against which to measure your portfolio performance. Are you among the best—with the top 20 percent of firms? Or are you closer to the worst performers—the bottom 20 percent? If you are typical, there is opportunity for much improvement in your portfolio management practices and the performance results you achieve, so read on.

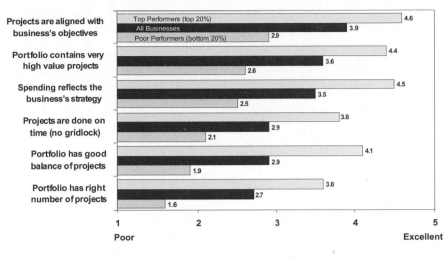

EXHIBIT 6.2   Portfolio Performance Results on Six Key Metrics

Notes: All differences between top and poor performers are significant at the 0.001 level. Performance metrics are rank-ordered by mean scores (best at top of exhibit).

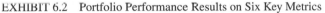

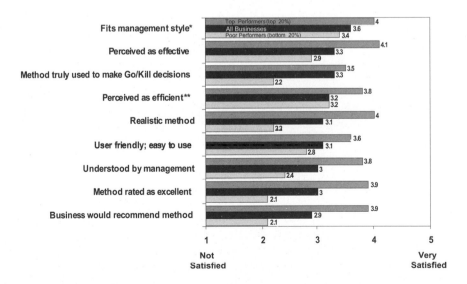

EXHIBIT 6.3   Satisfaction with Portfolio Management Methods

Notes: *Significant at the 0.01 level; **significant at the 0.005 level; all others significant at the 0.001 level.

ple, almost one-third of businesses surveyed rate their portfolio management approach as far from excellent (the bottom two boxes on this five-point scale). More than one-third would not recommend their approach to others! Repairs are clearly needed in the case of most businesses.

The Best Performers

As might be expected, management in the best-performing businesses are much more satisfied with their portfolio management methods than those in the poorer performers. Consider the differences between the top 20 percent and the bottom 20 percent in Exhibit 6.3. The three strongest discriminators between top and poor performers are that the best firms:

- boast *more realistic* portfolio methods that capture key facets of the portfolio problem
- rate their methods as *excellent*
- would highly *recommend their methods* to others.

In addition, the portfolio methods used by the top 20 percent tend to be understood well by senior management, are perceived to be effective, and are indeed used to make Go/Kill decisions.

POINTS FOR MANAGEMENT TO PONDER

The satisfaction metrics in Exhibit 6.3 become useful goals for your own portfolio management method, particularly if you plan to redesign your approach. Your method must be realistic, understood by management, and easy to use. It must be a useful tool for making Go/Kill decisions (not just information display); and it must be both effective—yielding the right decisions—and efficient (not waste time). Sadly, many in management view their portfolio approaches as failing on some or all of these metrics. How do you rate your own organization?

The Nature of Portfolio Methods Employed

Is portfolio management really done via an explicit, well-defined method with clear procedures encompassing all projects? Or is it a more unconscious or informal decision process with no defined method and no rules of the game? More important, does it really matter which is true? Should businesses be relying on more systematic portfolio methods, or are the pundits all wrong? Here, we explore the *formality* and *explicitness* of portfolio management methods in use, along with their impact on performance.

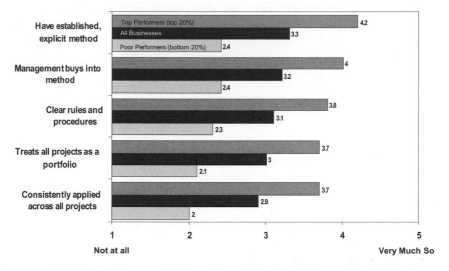

EXHIBIT 6.4 Explicitness and Formality of Portfolio Management by Business Performance

Note: All differences between top and poor performers are significant at the 0.001 level. Performance metrics are rank-ordered by mean scores (best at top of exhibit).

The Average Business

The typical business performs in a fairly mediocre fashion when it comes to the explicitness of the portfolio management process (see Exhibit 6.4). For example, on average,

- businesses use a somewhat established, somewhat explicit method for portfolio management and project selection (a midrange score here)
- management somewhat buys into the portfolio management method—their actions support its use
- the rules and procedures for portfolio management are somewhat defined.

But portfolio management methods score lower in terms of

- treating all projects as a portfolio (considering all projects together and comparing them against each other)
- consistently applying the method across all appropriate* projects.

* *Not all projects should be included* in the portfolio (for example, very minor projects or maintenance-type projects); thus we specify "appropriate" projects here.

Note that the range and spread of practices and scores is quite high in Exhibit 6.4. This suggests major differences in practices across the sample of businesses. The frequency count of businesses along each measure reveals the magnitude of the spread. Some businesses are, indeed, using explicit, consistently applied methods; others are not. Note the disparity here:

	Percentage of Businesses	
	No or Low*	Yes or High
Have an established, explicit portfolio method	28.2%	46.3%
Management buys into the method— supports its use	27.2	43.6
Rules and procedures are very clear	30.6	35.0
Treat all projects as a portfolio (compares them)	34.2	37.1
Portfolio method consistently applied (all projects)	36.5	32.5

The Best Performers

Having a consistently applied, explicit portfolio management process strongly affects performance. Consider the major and significant differences between the top 20 percent performers and poorer performers in Exhibit 6.4. The best, when compared to poorer performers, have the following characteristics:

- an explicit, established method for portfolio management
- a management that buys into the method and supports it through action
- a method with clear rules and procedures
- a method that treats projects as a portfolio (considers all projects together)
- a method that is consistently applied across all appropriate projects.

These differences between top and poor performers are major. The conclusion is that businesses with positive portfolio results—a balanced, strategically aligned, high-value portfolio, with the right numbers of projects and good times-to-market (no gridlock)—boast a clearly defined, explicit, all-project, consistently applied portfolio management process that management endorses. Poor performers lack all this!

Formal Versus Informal Portfolio Management

The majority of businesses studied claim to use *a formal system* for portfolio management (56.5 percent in Exhibit 6.5). The rest use an informal system or no system at all. The best performers clearly have a preference, however, for a formal system. This is illustrated by the fact that 77.5 percent of the best performers have a formal portfolio management system. By contrast, only 41.5 percent of poor performers have a formal system.

* No or low score = 1 or 2 on the 5-point scale; yes or high score = 4 or 5.

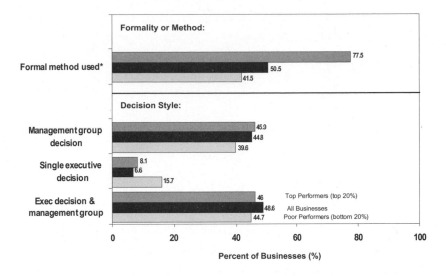

EXHIBIT 6.5   Portfolio Management Characteristics—Formality and Decision Style
*All differences between top and poor performers are significant at the 0.05 level.

POINTS FOR MANAGEMENT TO PONDER
Does your business employ an explicit portfolio management approach that is consistently applied across all appropriate projects, where the rules are clear and understood? If not, take note that the best performers in the study do. Is your portfolio management process a formal one? Is decision making done by a management team? If the answers to these questions make you feel uncomfortable, perhaps it is time to take action: Move toward a formal, systematic, and explicit portfolio management process—one in which the rules are clear and one that management buys into. Set up a portfolio management team or gatekeeping group—a senior team that is accountable for making the Go/Kill and prioritization decisions on projects.

Autocratic Versus Management Group Decision Making

Group decision making appears to be the dominant mode in portfolio management: 44.8 percent of businesses handle Go/Kill and investment decisions on projects in a management meeting. Here, managers discuss projects as a group, use their best judgment and make decisions (see bottom half of Exhibit 6.5). In another 6.6 percent of businesses, a senior manager or executive makes the portfolio or Go/Kill decisions. Finally, both decision processes occur in 48.6 percent of businesses.

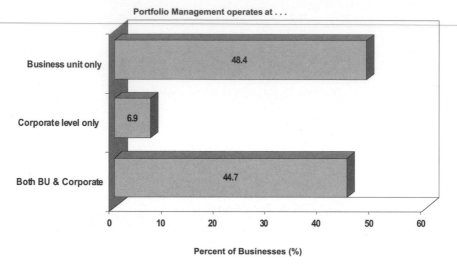

EXHIBIT 6.6   Portfolio Management Characteristics—Level in Corporation

The group decision approach appears to work better. At least it is the choice of the top-performing businesses. The best performers put more emphasis on the management group decision-making approach (45.9 percent of top businesses versus 39.5 percent for poor performers). Poor performers rely more heavily on a senior executive making the decision (15.7 percent of poor performers versus only 8.1 percent for the best—see Exhibit 6.5). These differences are tendencies only.

Business Unit Versus Corporation Decision Making

Almost half the businesses use portfolio management only at the business unit level. That is, funds or resources are somehow allocated to the business unit (for example, via a corporate planning and allocation process), and then the business unit operates and manages its own portfolio of projects. A total of 48.4 percent of businesses indicate that this is their mode of operation (see Exhibit 6.6).

A very small minority undertake portfolio management at the corporate level only (6.9 percent of respondents). That is, all projects from all businesses are considered together and centrally; projects are prioritized or selected, and re-sources are allocated across BUs. In effect, the project portfolio model becomes part of (or supersedes) the corporate planning and resource allocation method.

A significant number of businesses do both; that is, they operate portfolio management within the business unit; and they have a centralized portfolio man-agement method (44.7 percent of respondents).

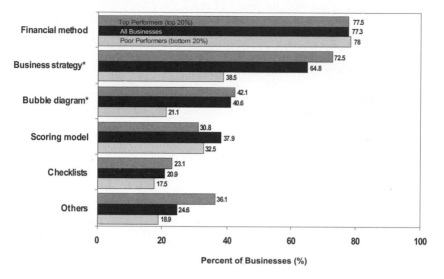

EXHIBIT 6.7   Popularity of Portfolio Methods Employed

*All differences between top and poor performers are significant at the 0.05 level.

Popularity and Use of the Various Portfolio Methods

Which are the most popular portfolio methods in use? And which portfolio methods dominate the portfolio decision process? Here, we explore the frequency of use of the various methods, and whether each method is the dominant decision tool. Note, however, that the mere fact that a method proves popular is not a reason for assuming it is the correct method or that it yields better performance. As we see later, quite the reverse is true: The most popular method yields the worst results! Nevertheless, there are merits in each approach discussed here. It is up to you to determine the combination that best suits your business. Exhibit 6.7 shows the most popular decision tools. Exhibit 6.8 shows which of these are the dominant means for making portfolio decisions.

Financial Methods

Financial methods dominate portfolio management and project selection approaches in terms of popularity. Financial methods include various profitability and return metrics, such as NPV, EBIT, RONA, ROI, or payback period. A total of 77.3 percent of businesses use this type of approach in portfolio management and project selection; for 40.4 percent of the businesses, this is the dominant method (see Exhibits 6.7 and 6.8).

Most often, the financial method is used to rank projects *against each other*. That is, each project's expected financial results, or *economic value,* is determined, and that value is used to rank-order projects against each other in order to

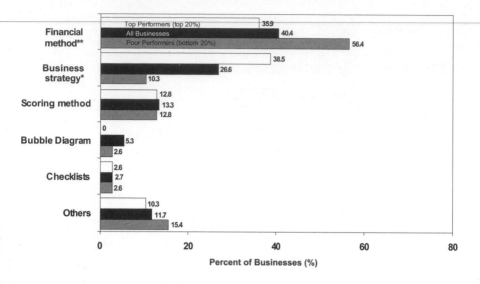

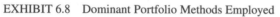

EXHIBIT 6.8   Dominant Portfolio Methods Employed

NOTE: Dominant methods employed add to 100%.
**All differences between top and poor performers are significant at the 0.001 level.

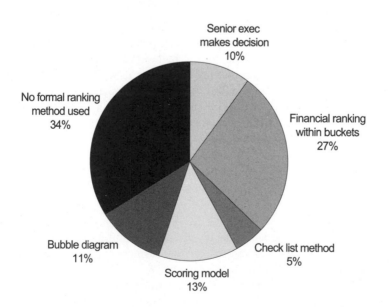

EXHIBIT 6.9   Strategic Buckets Method—How Projects Are Ranked Within Buckets

decide the portfolio (38.1 percent of all businesses employ this financial ranking approach).

A slightly less popular method is the use of a financial measure compared against a hurdle rate in order to make Go/Kill decisions on individual projects. This, in turn, determines the list of active projects; hence, the portfolio (28.4 percent of businesses do this). Some businesses do both: The project's financial value is used to rank projects against each other, and it is also compared to a hurdle to make Go/Kill decisions (10.2 percent of businesses).

Strategic Approaches

Here the business strategy is the basis for allocating money across different types of projects, or for selecting a set of projects. A total of 64.8 percent of businesses use a strategic approach; for 26.6 percent of businesses, this is the dominant method.

One such approach is Strategic Buckets Method (refer to Chapter 5); having decided the business's strategy, money is allocated across different types of projects and into different envelopes, or buckets. Projects are then ranked or rated within buckets. The dimensions of these buckets vary greatly by business, but the most popular splits according to the study are:

- by market
- by development type (maintenance, exploratory, systems, frontier research, line extensions, and so on)
- by product line
- by project magnitude (major or minor)
- by technology area
- by technology platform types
- by area of strategic thrust
- by competitive need.

The next question is, Now that buckets are defined, each with its allocated resources, how are projects prioritized within a bucket? Exhibit 6.9 shows the prioritization approach within buckets. Note that the majority of businesses use *no formal ranking method*, but financial value and scoring models are the most frequently cited formal ranking techniques. The fact that no formal method is used by the majority suggests that strategic issues drive the portfolio selection (i.e., strategy determines allocations by bucket and also heavily influences the choice or ranking of projects within buckets).

Bubble Diagrams or Portfolio Maps

In bubble diagrams and portfolio maps projects are mapped on X-Y plots and are represented as circles or ellipses. Projects are categorized according to the zone or quadrant they are in (e.g., pearls, oysters, white elephants, and bread and butter projects). See Exhibits 4.1 to 4.4 in Chapter 4 for examples.

Bubble diagrams are also a fairly popular portfolio tool, with 41 percent of businesses using them. But bubble diagrams appear more to be a *supporting tool*, with relatively few businesses relying on them as their dominant portfolio method (only 8 percent).

Numerous bubble diagram plots are possible. Exhibit 4.15 in Chapter 4 lists the more popular plots identified in the current study, with the common risk/reward plot at the top of the list by a considerable margin.

Scoring Models

In scoring models, projects are rated or scored on a number of criteria (for example, low-medium-high, or 1–5, or 0–10 scales). The ratings on each scale are added to yield a total or Project Attractiveness Score, which becomes the criterion used to make project selection and ranking decisions. A total of 37.9 percent of businesses use scoring models; in 18.3 percent, this is the dominant decision method.

Scoring models, when used, tend to be overwhelmingly employed as a ranking or prioritization tool; that is, the *project score* is used to rank projects against each other. Relatively few businesses, by contrast, use scoring models to make Go/Kill decisions per se (where the score is compared to some cutoff criterion or hurdle).

Checklists

In a checklist, projects are evaluated on a set of yes/no questions. Each project must achieve either all yes answers or a certain number of yes answers to proceed. The number of yeses is used to make Go/Kill and prioritization (ranking) decisions. Only 17.5 percent of businesses use checklists; and in only 2.7 percent is it the dominant method.

Checklists, unlike scoring models, tend to be employed mostly as Go/Kill decision tools and hardly ever for ranking projects. As a result, the roles of these two similar models are quite different: checklists see most duty as a Go/Kill decision tool, with a focus on individual projects; in contrast, scoring models are most popular as a ranking tool and for comparing a number of projects against one another.

Others

Twenty-four percent of businesses indicate that they use some method other than the ones described above. A closer scrutiny of these methods reveals that most are variants or hybrids of the above models and methods.

Which Methods the Best Performers Use

Top-performing businesses have decided preferences for which portfolio model or method dominates their decision process (see Exhibit 6.8):

- The best-performing businesses *rely much less on financial models* as the dominant portfolio tool than the average business. By contrast, poor performers place much more emphasis on financial tools. For example, only 35.9 percent of the top performers rely on financial models as their dominant method, whereas 56.4 percent of poor performers use this as their dominant portfolio method.

- The best performers rely on the business strategy to allocate resources and decide the portfolio much more than do poor performers. Only 10.3 percent of poor performers use the business's strategy as the dominant method, compared to 38.5 percent of the top 20 percent. Indeed, business strategy methods are the number-one method for the best.

The use of other methods—scoring models, checklists, and bubble diagrams—as the dominant approach is too infrequent to allow meaningful comparison of top and poor performers (Exhibit 6.8). Similarly, use of these other methods does not correlate with performance, simply because there is such overlap of methods used.

The best performers tend to rely on multiple methods for portfolio management; that is, they appear to acknowledge that *no one method gives the correct results.*[3] For example, the best on average use 2.43 portfolio management techniques per business to select projects and manage their portfolios, while almost half of the best (47.5 percent) use three or more methods! Even the average business uses multiple methods (2.34 per business). By contrast, the poorest 20 percent of performers tend to rely on far fewer (1.83 methods per business), with almost half the worst focusing on a single method only (46.3 percent of the worst use only one portfolio approach).

POINTS FOR MANAGEMENT TO PONDER

Is your business among the best performers, using a strategic approach to allocate resources and select projects? Or are you with the majority, relying heavily on financial models to select your portfolio of projects? If you rely heavily on financial techniques, then chances are you are disappointed with the results. Of course, no one method provides the total solution to project selection and prioritization. But, perhaps, you should be considering two or more approaches operating in conjunction, as do the best performers.

Specific Project Selection Criteria Employed

The specific selection criteria used to choose projects were also investigated. Often these were incorporated into formal scoring models, but sometimes they were just used as selection criteria in a decision meeting. Exhibit 6.10 reveals the proportion of businesses that use the various criteria for selecting and prioritizing projects against each other. Note that because businesses use multiple criteria, the percentages add up to well over 100 percent.

It is hardly surprising that the top two criteria parallel the popularity of portfolio methods used:

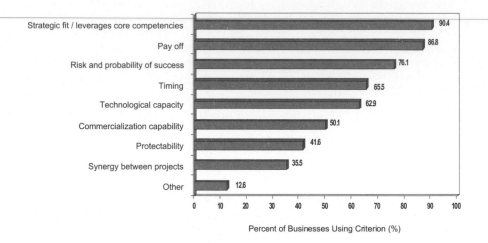

Percent of Businesses Using Criterion (%)

EXHIBIT 6.10   Criteria Used to Rank Projects Against One Another
Note: Percentages add to more than 100% due to multiple mentions.

- strategic fit and ability to leverage core competencies
- payoff (financial and reward).

Approximately 90 percent of businesses use both criteria to select and compare projects, with the strategic criterion used slightly more often. Other vital criteria, although used somewhat less frequently, are:

- project risk and probability of success
- timing
- technological capability of the business to undertake the project.

Commercialization capability, protectability of the venture (e.g., the ability to achieve sustainable competitive advantage via patents or proprietary knowledge), and synergy between projects are relied upon to a much lesser extent, even though numerous studies suggest that all three are strongly predictive of success and profitability.[4]

Note that most businesses use multiple criteria for project selection and prioritization. For example, the percentages in Exhibit 6.10 add to 523 percent, the conclusion being that the average business uses about 5.2 criteria to select projects. This result is reassuring. The evidence suggests that some firms are too quick to rely on a single criterion—namely financial—to select projects. In so doing, they are making naïve selection decisions. Moreover, using more criteria seems to be connected to better performance: The best performers, on average, rely on 6.2 criteria for project selection, whereas the poor performers use only 4.4 criteria on average.

Criteria	Important in First Round	Important in Second Round
Strategic fit/leverages core competencies	78.3%	22.2% [8]
Pay-off	69.5%	30.0 [5]
Risk & probability of success	54.7%	39.4% [4]
Technological capability	48.3%	31.0% [6]
Timing	34.0%	42.9% [1]
Commercialization capability	33.5%	40.9% [2]
Synergy between projects	15.3%	26.6% [7]
Protectability	14.2%	39.9% [3]
Other	40.3%	-

EXHIBIT 6.11   Selection Criteria in First- and Second-Round Tradeoffs (Percentage of Businesses Citing)

First-round criteria are rank-ordered (by usage). Second-round rankings are shown in brackets.

Selecting Projects in Rounds

A hierarchical approach is proposed as one method of using selection and ranking criteria for project selection. This approach uses rounds during which projects are rated and ranked, and then the best are selected. The first round may use several criteria, such as strategic fit and payoff, to weed out the poorer projects. The second round uses other criteria, such as timing and risk/probability of success to narrow down the field. The result after several rounds is a short list of the top-ranked projects. The method is a familiar one and likely captures what many people do, whether intuitively or formally. The method is similar to a scoring model in that a list of criteria is used; but instead of weights to give certain criteria more importance (as in scoring models), rounds are used, with the more important criteria applied in the earlier rounds. The use of must-meet criteria (or knockout questions) followed by should-meet criteria is an example.

Specific criteria used in each selection round are shown in Exhibit 6.11. Not surprisingly, the same list of criteria as noted above, with approximately the same rank-order, appears (compare Exhibits 6.11 with 6.10). For the first-round decision, the two most important criteria are, once again,

- strategic fit and ability to leverage core competencies
- payoff (financial and reward).

The rest of the first-round criteria are much as they are in Exhibit 6.10: risk, technological capability, and timing. Once again, note that most businesses use multiple criteria for the first round, with the average business relying on 3.9 criteria.

What is interesting is to observe the second-round criteria. Given that the project meets the payoff or strategic fit criteria, what separates the good projects from the poor in the next round? The most important thing is timing, followed by commercialization capability and protectability. The distribution of responses for round two is much more diverse than for round one, however. The top three criteria are mentioned only somewhat more frequently than the next three (risk and probability of success, payoff, and technological capability).

How Specific Portfolio Methods Perform

This is the money question: Which portfolio methods perform the best? The answer is not quite so simple and depends on which performance metric one elects. For example, some portfolio methods are better at delivering high-value projects, while others are better at achieving strategic alignment.

We saw earlier in this chapter that portfolio methods in general achieve only moderate to mediocre performance scores (Exhibit 6.2). In this section, we look again at performance scores, but this time for each specific portfolio method.

Only four portfolio models are dominant in enough businesses that conclusions about performance strengths and weaknesses can be drawn. These methods are strategic approaches, financial methods, scoring models, and bubble diagrams. Exhibit 6.12 shows the performance results on six metrics for businesses using each of these four methods as their dominant portfolio tool. The stars show the best methods for a given metric and the crosses show the worst. We also looked at management's satisfaction with each of the four methods to obtain greater insight into each method's strengths and weaknesses (Exhibit 6.13). Again, the stars and crosses indicate best and worst ratings per method.

Strategic Approaches

Overall, portfolio management based on strategic approaches fares well in terms of most performance metrics and many of the satisfaction measures. Reading down the columns in Exhibit 6.12, we see that:

- Strategic approaches yield a portfolio of projects that is *aligned with the business's strategic direction*—not surprisingly, the number two method here (very close behind bubble diagrams).
- The resulting portfolio of projects contains *excellent value projects*—the number two method here. Only scoring models do better.
- The resulting spending breakdown of projects in the portfolio reflects the business's strategic priorities—the best method here.
- Strategic methods appear to deliver portfolios with the right number of projects—no gridlock, and projects get done on time (the number one method on both metrics).

Performance Metric	Strategic Methods	Financial Methods	Scoring Model	Bubble Diagrams
Projects are aligned with businesss objectives	4.08 ★	3.76 ✗	3.95	4.11 ★
Portfolio contains very high value projects	3.77	3.37 ✗	3.82 ★	3.70
Spending reflects the businesss strategy	3.72 ★	3.50	3.59	3.00 ✗
Projects are done on time — no gridlock	3.22 ★	2.79 ✗	3.13	2.90
Portfolio has good balance of projects	3.08	2.80 ✗	3.20 ★	3.20 ★
Portfolio has right number of projects	2.93 ★	2.50	2.70	2.25

EXHIBIT 6.12   Strengths and Weaknesses for Each Portfolio Method

Notes: Ratings are 1–5 mean scores for each method when used as dominant portfolio method. Here 1 = poor and 5 = excellent.
★ = Best method on each performance criterion
✗ = Worst method on each performance criterion

In summary, besides the obvious strengths of strategic approaches in the areas of strategic alignment and strategic priorities, they also yield a portfolio with the right number of projects and projects of excellent value.

Strategic approaches are also viewed positively in terms of the following (Exhibit 6.13):

- They fit management's style of decision making—the number one method here, along with scoring models.
- They are well understood by senior management—number one here.
- They are very realistic and capture many facets of the decision situation—the number two method here, next to bubble diagrams.
- They are user-friendly—the number two method, again second to bubble diagrams.

Strategic approaches are thought to be about average in terms of both effectiveness and efficiency, yielding the right decisions in a time-efficient manner.

The only weakness of strategic approaches is that such methods are not really used to make Go/Kill decisions on projects (although all methods suffer here; but strategic approaches fare worse than average). Neither do strategic methods yield the best balance of projects in the portfolio (again, all methods suffer here).

Performance Metric	Strategic Methods	Financial Methods	Scoring Model	Bubble Diagrams
Methods truly used to make Go/Kill decisions	2.87 ✗	2.87 ✗	2.95	3.00 ★
Fits management style	3.72 ★	3.52	3.73 ★	3.40 ✗
Understood by management	3.25 ★	2.83 ✗	3.13	3.00
User friendly easy to use	3.14	3.10	3.04 ✗	3.40 ★
Realistic method	3.16	3.06 ✗	3.13	3.30 ★
Perceived as efficient	3.23	3.09	3.47 ★	2.90 ✗
Perceived as effective	3.29	3.08 ✗	3.47 ★	3.70 ★
Method rated as excellent	3.06	2.91 ✗	3.04	3.20
Business would recommend method	3.06	2.80 ✗	2.82	3.50 ★

EXHIBIT 6.13   Satisfaction with Project Selection Methods

Notes: Ratings are 1–5 mean scores for each method when used as dominant portfolio method. Here 1 = poor and 5 = excellent.
★ = Best method on each performance criterion
✗ = Worst method on each performance criterion

Financial Methods

Financial models, in spite of their apparent rigor and theoretical soundness, fare the worst of all as portfolio tools. They do poorly in terms of the six portfolio performance metrics and are negatively rated in terms of management satisfaction. Although they are the most popular portfolio tools, financial methods are rated as having *many more weaknesses than strengths.* Note the number of crosses and absence of stars in the Financial Methods columns of both Exhibits 6.12 and 6.13.

Financial methods have a number of performance weaknesses (Exhibit 6.12):

- Financial methods yield a portfolio of projects that are not well aligned with business objectives, the worst of all four methods.
- A portfolio containing lower-value projects is the result of applying financial models as the dominant selection tool—again the worst of all methods.
- Financial methods fail to deal with the portfolio gridlock issue (many projects are late to market)—the weakest of all methods.
- Financial methods fail to yield a properly balanced portfolio—balance between high-risk and low-risk, between long- and short-term, etc. Financial methods are the weakest of all methods here, producing the most unbalanced portfolios.

Financial methods do not fare much better in terms of management satisfaction (Exhibit 6.13):

- They are not really used to make Go/Kill decisions (although all methods are weak here).
- They and their results are not totally understood by management—the weakest of all methods on this measure.
- They are not particularly realistic methods, because they fail to capture key elements of the situation and decision—again, the worst of all methods.
- Finally, they are not thought to be effective decision tools. They yield the wrong decisions, the worst of all methods shown here.

No particular distinctive strengths are evident for financial methods. For these reasons, financial portfolio tools receive the lowest recommendations. Management does not view these tools as excellent, nor do they recommend these tools to others.

Scoring Models

Scoring models, although used by a minority of businesses as their dominant portfolio method, appear to have *a number of very positive features*, particularly with respect to selecting high-value projects and suiting management's decision-making style. A surprising finding was that scoring models also fare well in strategic terms. In terms of performance (Exhibit 6.12):

- They yield portfolios with high-value projects—the best of any method.
- They result in well-balanced portfolios—tied with bubble diagrams for number one.
- They also yield a portfolio whose spending breakdown reflects the business's strategic priorities—number two after strategic methods.

Managers also appear very satisfied with scoring models because

- They fit management's decision-making style—the best of all methods.
- They are time efficient—number one here.
- They are also perceived as effective, yielding the right decisions—number two here, after bubble diagrams.

Scoring models tend to be weak on user-friendliness and on producing the right number of projects in the portfolio for the resources available.

Bubble Diagrams or Portfolio Maps

Bubble diagrams see less frequent use as the dominant method. Therefore the strengths/weaknesses accorded them are based on a much smaller sample of businesses. Particular strengths are that:

- They are the best method for yielding a portfolio of projects aligned with the business's strategic direction (tied with strategic methods).

- They yield a balanced portfolio—the right balance of projects, tied for the best of all methods with scoring models.
- They also yield a high-value portfolio of projects (second to scoring models here).

Management in firms that rely on bubble diagrams as the dominant technique give the method top marks across a number of satisfaction metrics:

- They really are used to make Go/Kill decisions.
- They are easy to use—the number one of all methods.
- They are a realistic method, capturing many facets of the decision situation—number one here as well.
- Management believes that bubble diagrams are effective decision tools, yielding the right decisions—the number one rating here.

Bubble diagrams do have a few weaknesses, however. They are weakest when it comes to yielding a portfolio whose spending breakdown reflects the strategic priorities of the business. They are not particularly time-efficient models; they are rated the most laborious of all methods; and they do not fit management's decision-making style—the poorest of all methods. In spite of these drawbacks, management highly recommends these models—the number one rating here.

POINTS FOR MANAGEMENT TO PONDER

None of the methods discussed in this chapter scores top marks on all the satisfaction and performance metrics—there is no one best portfolio method! There is a loser, however: financial approaches score poorly on many metrics, and well on none. All the same, we are not suggesting that you stop using financial tools as selection models. Of course not; that would be foolish. There is much to be learned from applying financial tools to development projects. What we are recommending, based on these study results, is that you *don't bet the bank* based on financial models. Use them with care, be fully aware of their weaknesses, and use them in conjunction with scoring models, strategic methods, and bubble diagrams.

The Benchmark Businesses

In order to gain even more insights into best practices, we grouped the businesses in our investigation into clusters and then took a much closer look at each cluster. We identified four distinct types of businesses—in terms of their approaches to and use of portfolio management methods:[5]

- *Cowboy businesses:* Cowboy businesses shoot from the hip in selecting projects and managing their portfolios. They rely on a very poor quality portfolio model (or not much of a model or system at all!). For example, cowboy businesses indicate that their portfolio approach is the opposite of excellent; nor would they recommend their approach to others, again the lowest of all four businesses. Still, it is an approach that suits management very well. Cowboys are the smallest cluster of businesses, representing only 12.1 percent of the sample. We call these businesses "cowboys" simply because they have no real portfolio approach, they know it, and they like it that way! But cowboy businesses' portfolios perform poorly across the six metrics in Exhibit 6.1.

- *Crossroads businesses:* Crossroads businesses are the opposite of cowboy businesses. They employ a highly recommended, excellently rated, and very realistic portfolio method. But they are at a crossroads in the sense that management has yet to fully embrace the method—it does not fit management's style; it is not perceived by management to be particularly efficient or effective; nor is the method well understood by management. We call these businesses "crossroads" simply because they face choices. They employ an apparently proficient approach to portfolio management, yet there is some resistance on the part of management. This is a situation that must be corrected. An interesting note is that crossroads businesses perform well; that is, they fare second best, next to benchmark businesses (described below), but still significantly lower. Crossroads businesses account for 28.0 percent of the sample and thus are a fairly substantial group.

- *Duds:* Dud businesses are what the name implies: bad on all fronts. Of the four groups of businesses, they fare the worst in the perceived effectiveness of their method and its lack of fit with management's decision style. Moreover, their portfolio approach is perceived by management to be inefficient (it wastes time). These businesses rate their portfolio approach as unrealistic, not used by management, and not user-friendly. Finally, dud businesses do not recommend their approaches to others, and they rate it far from excellent. It is not surprising that dud businesses achieve very poor portfolio performance on the six metrics. Dud businesses are a relatively small group, representing only 18.1 percent of the sample.

- *Benchmarks:* Benchmarks are the good businesses—the ones we hold up as benchmarks or standards against which to compare oneself and to emulate. They fare remarkably well across the board. Their portfolio methods score the best in terms of quality and are rated the most realistic of those used in all businesses. Their methods come highly recommended and are rated excellent (the best of all businesses). They are, indeed, used by management to make Go/Kill decisions, and they are user-friendly. The business's method is perceived by its management to be very effective and is well understood. Benchmark businesses' portfolio approaches also fit management's style and are perceived to be efficient in use (they don't waste time). Benchmark businesses are also the largest cluster, representing 41.8 percent of the sample, thereby demonstrating that effective, high-quality portfolio approaches are not an elusive goal attained by a small minority of businesses. Note, however, that the sample of firms in our study is somewhat biased toward leading R&D firms in America, which may also partly explain the large size of the benchmark cluster.

What stands out in an analysis of the various characteristics of portfolio methods used is that benchmark businesses use much *more formal and explicit portfolio approaches* than do the other firms:

- Benchmark businesses have *established, explicit methods* of portfolio management, to a much greater degree than do other businesses. Cowboy and dud businesses rate very low here.
- Benchmark businesses use *much more formal approaches* to portfolio management; cowboy businesses use the least formal, indeed almost no process at all!
- Portfolio methods used by benchmarks feature *very clear and well-defined rules and procedures* for portfolio management. Cowboy businesses rate dismally here.
- Benchmarks *consistently apply their portfolio methods* to *all* appropriate projects; cowboys score also very low here, followed by dud businesses.
- The portfolio method used by benchmark businesses treats all projects as a portfolio—*considers all projects together* and compares them against each other.
- Finally, management at benchmark businesses *buys into* the portfolio methods used much more than management in the other three business types.

Earlier in this chapter, we reported on which portfolio methods deliver the best portfolio results. We also noted that most firms use multiple methods in combination. It is, therefore, interesting to note which combinations of methods are adopted by the better performers. Here are some results:

- The majority of both benchmark businesses (56.6 percent) and crossroads firms (54.9 percent) use both a *strategic* and a *financial approach* for portfolio management (significantly more often than the other two).
- By contrast, only 36.4 percent of cowboy businesses use these two methods together.
- A *strategic approach* combined with a *bubble diagram* is the portfolio combination relied on by more benchmark and crossroads businesses (28.9 percent and 33.3 percent respectively).
- More benchmark businesses rely on *three portfolio methods in conjunction* with each other: a financial method, a strategic approach, and a scoring model (21.1 percent of benchmarks). The other three clusters of businesses do so much less frequently.

Conclusions and Advice from Our Practices and Performance Study

1. Formal Portfolio Management Methods Work![6]

Businesses that have gone to the trouble of installing a systematic, explicit, and formal portfolio management system are clear winners. These are the businesses with clear rules and procedures, consistently applied across all appropriate projects. They treat all projects as a portfolio, and management buys into the process. Their portfolios outperform the rest on all six performance metrics: higher-value projects, better balance, the right number of projects, a strategically aligned portfolio, and so on. The message is clear: Step 1 is to make a commitment to installing a systematic, formal, and rigorous portfolio management process in your business.

2. There Is No One Right Portfolio Management Method—So Try a Hybrid Approach

Despite their weakness, financial models and methods are the most popular, with 77 percent of businesses using them, and 40 percent relying on them as the dominant portfolio decision tool. Still there is a great diversity of approaches as well: strategic approaches, scoring models, and bubble diagrams are also popular and can easily be used in conjunction with financial models, and in concert with each other. Indeed, the best businesses tend to use hybrid approaches—an average of 2.5 portfolio methods per business. And more benchmark businesses were concurrently using three portfolio tools, the most popular combination being strategic, financial, and scoring models together. Finally, no one method has a monopoly on strengths and positive performance. Rather, strengths and weaknesses were identified for all methods. While certain portfolio methods do yield superior results, the results are even better when used in conjunction with other methods.

3. Beware an Over-Reliance on Financial Methods and Models

Those businesses that use financial models as the dominant portfolio selection method end up with the poorest-performing portfolios! This is ironic, since these businesses adopted what appeared to be rigorous approaches to project evaluation in order to maximize returns and performance. Yet they achieved exactly the opposite outcomes. Why? One reason is that the sophistication of financial tools often *far exceed the quality of the data inputs.* (Financial tools can be quite elegant and include ECV, Productivity Index, and even probabilistic models such as *At Risk* and *Crystal Ball.* But the data inputs are often based on flimsy market and cost analyses.) A second reason is that the key Go/Kill and prioritization decisions must be made fairly early in the life of a project, precisely when the financial data are the least accurate! A final reason is that financial projections are fairly easy to "rig," consciously or unconsciously, especially by an overzealous project team.

4. Look More to Strategic Approaches As the Way to Manage Your Portfolio

Businesses that rely principally on strategic methods for portfolio management outperform the rest. Recall that 39 percent of the best businesses use strategic approaches as the dominant portfolio method, while only 10 percent of the worst do. Approaches like the Strategic Buckets Model can be used to allocate resources or funds. Look at the list of the popular bucket categories in this chapter: market, project type, product line, project size, and technology type. So first consider selecting one or more of these dimensions and splitting resources into buckets. Begin with your business's new product goals, vision, and strategy, and then move to resource splits and product roadmaps, as outlined in Chapter 5. Remember: strategy begins when you start spending money!

5. Consider a Scoring Model As an Effective Prioritization Tool

The users of scoring models have great praise for them and see them as effective and efficient decision tools for portfolio management. Scoring models have the advantage that they combine the popular financial criteria with the desirable strategic criteria. Use the sample scoring models displayed in Chapter 3, but also consider the often-used project evaluation criteria in Exhibits 6.10 and 6.11. Build these into a scoring model for your own use. Employ scoring models at gate meetings to make Go/Kill and to prioritize; and utilize the project scores (or rescore projects) to help decide priorities at periodic portfolio review meetings. A word of caution: do not use the project score mechanically. The real value is the process of decision makers walking through the criteria, discussing each, and gaining closure on each criterion, rather than dwelling on the score itself!

6. Bubble Diagrams Must Also Be Part of Your Repertoire of Portfolio Models

Bubble diagrams receive very high praise from management, who very strongly recommend their use to others. Moreover, they are thought to be an effective decision tool, yielding correct portfolio decisions. Bubble diagrams have the advantage that they portray the entire portfolio in visual format and are also able to display portfolio balance. Do look at the list of possible bubble diagrams: The majority of users plot the traditional risk-reward diagram (as in Exhibit 4.1), but Exhibit 4.15 shows some other axes that you should consider.

7. Just Do It!

Regardless of the portfolio method used, one thing is clear: Companies that employed a formal portfolio approach—any of the methods—outperformed those that did not. The message seems to be that moving ahead into formal portfolio management has significant payoffs. But don't be too worried about designing the perfect portfolio management system; rather, be more focused on just moving ahead on portfolio management. Any method seems to work better than no method at all!

POINTS FOR MANAGEMENT TO PONDER

Meeting the challenge of developing an effective portfolio approach for your company is no small task. In today's business environment, there is no question that portfolio management is a vital issue. The practices and performance investigation outlined in this chapter points to several fundamental truths, however. There is no single, magic solution. But a number of companies are developing, implementing, and achieving better results from formal portfolio management approaches. As this study has indicated, the top performers are, indeed, doing many things differently than the poorer-performing businesses.

Portfolio management processes can be successfully developed to help executives in their attempts to obtain better results from scarce R&D dollars, to achieve the balance needed between short-term and long-term pressures, and to ensure that R&D efforts are being directed toward helping the organization achieve its strategic objectives.

CHAPTER 7

Challenges and Unresolved Issues

Thirty years of development in portfolio management methods, and are we any further ahead? The answer is clearly yes! At worst, we've discovered what does not work in portfolio management. A more positive observation is that some companies are very close to solutions that work for them. And we now have concrete data on which methods seem to work better than others. But there remain many unresolved issues and barriers to overcome. This chapter highlights our major conclusions, identifies the problem areas, and leads up to our recommendations in the final three chapters.

In this chapter, we depart from our normal "points for management to ponder" because virtually every conclusion and challenge we present is food for thought.

General Conclusions

Portfolio Management Is a Vital Issue

If the amount of time and money that firms are spending is any indication, then portfolio management will likely be the number-one issue in new product development and technology management for the next decade. It may even be among the top three or four strategic issues faced by today's corporations.

Portfolio management is critical for at least four reasons, according to our research on best practices:

1. A successful new product effort is fundamental to corporate success in the decades ahead. And at the heart of a successful new product effort—a steady stream of new product winners—is the ability to select the right projects.
2. New product development is the manifestation of the business's strategy. That is, one important way a company operationalizes strategy is through the new products it develops. Portfolio management is the tool or mechanism that forges the link between the business strategy and its tactics, namely project selection. Portfolio management is also seen as vital to maintaining competitive position.

3. Portfolio management is about resource allocation. Today resources are scarcer than ever, as firms try to do more with less. At the same time, there is mounting pressure to launch more and more new products. Thus, effective resource allocation in product development is essential. The consequences of poor portfolio management are evident: Firms squander scarce resources on the wrong projects, and the truly deserving projects are starved.

4. Portfolio management helps to maximize the financial returns on R&D dollars spent. The ability to prioritize projects correctly and to select high-value projects for the corporation are basic to maximizing the financial return. The entire thrust of Chapter 3 was on portfolio techniques designed to maximize value, hence, financial return.

Many Methods but No Magic Solution

There is no magic answer or black box model to solve the portfolio management challenge. Indeed, the firms we studied—in spite of their expensive and extensive attempts to develop portfolio models—were quick to admit that there was no single "right answer." Management said they were still actively seeking solutions and making improvements to their own approaches. The fact that most firms were employing multiple portfolio models—an average of 2.5 methods per business for best-practice companies—suggests that no one has found the universal solution yet!

Not only is there no magic answer, there is not even a dominant approach! In spite of the fact that many of these executives had read the same reports, articles, and books, had benchmarked against the same firms, and had even hired many of the same consultants, the approaches they arrived at for their own companies were quite different from each other. There is no universal method, dominant theme, or generic model here; rather, the models and approaches employed are quite company-specific.

A great variety of concepts, tools, and approaches is employed in industry. The one that comes closest to being a dominant model is financial methods, used by about 40 percent of companies as the main project selection tool. But even these models varied greatly. Some were quite simple, such as payback period or NPV; others were very sophisticated and complex, such as probability adjusted cash flows, OPT (Options Pricing Theory), or Monte Carlo simulation. Further, financial methods yield poor results on average and are generally panned by users. Next in popularity are various strategic approaches (strategic buckets and product roadmapping). Less popular but still used by some are various portfolio mapping approaches (such as bubble diagrams) and scoring models. Best-practice firms employed a hybrid approach: a combination of models that looked at the issues of balancing the portfolio as well as maximizing its value against certain objectives.

There is no evidence at all of use of, or interest in, mathematical programming or optimization techniques, according to our study. Paradoxically, these models are very common in the literature, but they have rarely been implemented or tested in industry. Indeed, the notion of a "black box decision model" that would yield a prioritized list of projects was rejected by all firms studied. Instead they preferred a decision tool or decision support system.

Some Portfolio Methods Outperform the Rest

At least some performance metrics indicate that some portfolio methods perform better than others. And one thing is clear: The popular financial tools generally do more poorly than the rest on many of the performance metrics. They give poorer results than the other approaches in selecting high-value projects, attaining a strategically aligned portfolio, and achieving the right balance of projects. Management also rates financial tools as ineffective, unrealistic, and difficult to understand. Overall, they rated financial tools as the worst tools. Again, we stress that these poor performance scores are not because the financial tools are unsound, but because the data they demand are often not available or not reliable at the point in the project when financial tools are applied.

No one method scores top marks across the board. Strategic methods come closest: They yield a strategically aligned portfolio and a spending breakdown within the portfolio that reflects the business's strategic priorities (not surprising, as that is the intent of such models). But they also fare well in doing the right number of projects given the resource constraints and in avoiding pipeline gridlock.

Scoring models, although not nearly as popular as strategic and financial approaches, do best when it comes to selecting "good" projects. Their use results in a portfolio of high-value projects (which one might argue is the most important performance metric). They also yield the right balance of projects.

Finally, bubble diagrams yield a strategically aligned and balanced portfolio. They are also well rated by management, being perceived as effective, efficient, realistic, and user-friendly.

But no one model does it all! The implication is that a combination of models or approaches is best. Yes, employ a financial tool, because of what will be learned. But marry that to a strategic approach, along with a scoring model and bubble diagrams. This combined approach seems to make sense; it is also what the best performers do.

No "Flavor of the Month" Solutions

The portfolio management problem is far from solved. Many of the models we observed in companies, although elegant and comprehensive, are still relatively untested. For the most part they are new approaches only now being implemented in the firms we studied. No doubt it will be years before well-accepted portfolio models and methods are commonplace in industry.

Despite the lack of quick and easy solutions, virtually all the firms in our Phase I survey of leading firms had arrived at moderately satisfactory approaches. No solution was easy to come by, however. Developing a portfolio approach proved much more difficult, time-consuming, and expensive than initially expected. Nonetheless, the progress made by some companies is encouraging. In subsequent chapters, we offer a glimpse into the solutions to managing the portfolio of projects. These insights are based on the varied experiences of the firms in our study.

But first, let's have a closer look at specific conclusions from our study of firms' practices and at the challenges and issues that were encountered by the companies we investigated.

Specific Conclusions and Challenges Identified in Effective Portfolio Management

Our investigations revealed specific conclusions or findings in effective portfolio management, which are highlighted below. In addition, another twelve key issues and challenges were identified: questions, pitfalls, problems, and concerns that management must address if they are to develop effective portfolio management approaches. Our conclusions and challenges are summarized in Exhibit 7.1 and explained in more detail below.

1. Three Main Goals

Three goals provide the underpinnings of portfolio approaches:

- *Maximizing the value of the portfolio*: A prime goal is to maximize the value of the portfolio against objectives, such as profitability or strategic importance. Here financial methods (such as the NPV, ECV (expected commercial value), or the Productivity Index) and scoring models (which build the desired objectives into the criteria) are most effective.
- *Balance in the portfolio*: Portfolios can be balanced on numerous dimensions. The most popular are risk versus reward, ease versus attractiveness, and according to breakdowns by project type, market, and product line. Visual models, especially bubble diagrams, are thought to be most appropriate way to portray balance.
- *Link to strategy*: Strategic alignment—strategic fit, project selection, and resource allocation reflecting the business's strategy—are the issues here. Top-down methods (strategic buckets or product roadmaps), bottom-up methods (building strategic criteria into scoring models), and combinations of the two are appropriate techniques.

Of the three goals, no one goal seems to dominate; moreover, no one portfolio approach appears capable of delivering on all three goals.

2. Goal 1: Maximizing the Value of the Portfolio Against Objectives

Maximizing value is an obvious goal for portfolio management. Yet some of the techniques, notably the visual maps, are not particularly effective here. For example, mapping techniques do not logically lead to the highest-value portfolio of projects.

The maximization goal is more challenging when multiple objectives, such as NPV, IRR, and strategic importance, are sought concurrently. The six methods that work best for maximization of the portfolio's value are the following:

Specific Conclusions:
1. There are three main goals in portfolio management.
2. Goal 1: maximizing the value of the portfolio against objectives.
3. Goal 2: seeking the right balance or mix of projects.
4. Goal 3: the link to your business strategy.
5. Gate decisions must be integrated with portfolio decisions.
6. Portfolio management must consider all types of projects that compete for resources.
7. There is information overload in portfolio management.

Challenges and Issues:

1. Are there too many projects, not enough resources?
2. Once made, how firm are resource commitments?
3. Are there too many projects on hold?
4. Why have a prioritized or rank-ordered list at all?
5. Is there imaginary precision: is the quality of information of input data lacking?
6. How should needed information on projects be gathered?
7. Are project selection methods discriminating between projects?
8. Are there too many small projects, too few major hits?
9. Are the Portfolio Reviews monitoring reviews or project selection meetings?
10. When should the Portfolio Management Process kick in?
11. Should portfolio models provide information display or be decision models?
12. What problems do financial analysis methods pose?

EXHIBIT 7.1   Findings, Conclusions, Challenges, and Issues in Designing an Effective Portfolio Management Process

1. The bang-for-buck method, a financial model based on NPV, maximizes the value of the portfolio for a given resource constraint.
2. The ECV, a financial model based on a decision tree, incorporates probabilities and recognizes that total project costs are not incurred if the project is aborted.
3. The productivity index, a financial index, considers the ratio of payoffs (risk-adjusted NPV) to the R&D expenditures. Various methods for computing the risk-adjusted NPV have been proposed.
4. The Option Pricing Theory (OPT), or Real Options Approach, notes that the investor can opt out of a project, thereby reducing the overall risk of the project. This method can be approximated by a decision-tree approach, similar to the ECV method.
5. The dynamic rank-ordered list is again largely financial and has the advantage of considering several objectives concurrently, including nonfinancial criteria.
6. The scoring model, which is the least financial of the six and captures multiple objectives or desired characteristics of projects, is used by Celanese, the Royal Bank, Specialty Minerals, Reckitt-Benckiser, and many others.

3. Goal 2: Seeking Portfolio Balance

There is also a need to achieve the right balance of projects on a number of dimensions. For example, companies should look for the right mix of long-term versus short-term projects; or high-risk versus low-risk projects; or offensive versus defensive projects; or step-out versus close-to-home products; or across markets and product lines; and so on. For these dimensions, more is not necessarily better. Rather, the goal is to achieve the right mix, balance, or distribution of projects. The various mapping approaches are the most useful, such as bubble diagram risk-reward maps or pie charts and histograms, which portray the split in resources by timing or across project types, markets, and product lines. In particular, bubble diagrams or portfolio maps provide a visual portrayal of the portfolio, where balance or distribution of projects can be seen and debated.

Some visual maps also have the advantage of being able to hint at the appropriate portfolio. For example, in risk-reward maps, certain quadrants denote projects that are clearly better than others. So, even though mapping and chart models are information display methods and effectively portray balance, they are also important inputs to the maximization of the portfolio's value.

4. Goal 3: Link to Strategy

Portfolio management—the selection and prioritization of R&D projects—must be very closely tied to business strategy. Strategic alignment has three meanings, with subtle but important differences:

- First, portfolio management must ensure strategic fit—that all projects are on-strategy and consistent with the strategic direction of the business. For example, senior management defines the arenas of focus or areas of strategic thrust (products, markets, and technology areas) and then selects projects only within these boundaries.
- Second, the set of projects in the portfolio pipeline must be instrumental in helping the company implement its strategy and achieve its strategic goals. That is, if the strategy is "to attack market X," then logically there are certain products and releases that are required if one is to be successful in market X.
- Finally and most important, portfolio management must allocate spending across projects so as to mirror the strategy of the business. For example, if the business's strategy is very much a growth one, then the majority of spending on new product projects should be on business and market development projects rather than on "maintain the business" projects. Or if management has defined certain areas of strategic thrust—for example, a certain market or technology—then a heavy percentage of spending ought to be on projects in these areas.

Traditional portfolio models, such as mathematical programming, have failed to account for this strategic link. And many of the financial models, such as the Productivity Index and ECV, are weak here as well (although English China Clay was ingenious in building a strategic factor into their financial ECV calculations, as shown in Chapter 3). We found four methods in which the portfolio–strategy link is particularly well handled. These are described in detail in Chapter 5 and summarized here:

- Top-Down Approaches, such as the Strategic Buckets Model. This is a comprehensive method that begins with the business unit's strategy and culminates in the designation of envelopes, or buckets, of money for different types of projects. Within these buckets, projects are rank-ordered and prioritized. In this way, the spending allocation mirrors the strategic direction and desired spending patterns of the business. A variant of Strategic Buckets is the Target Spending Method, in which spending split guides are established and the breakdown of spending on projects is tallied against these guides.

- Top-Down Approaches such as the product roadmap. Here development of the business and new product strategy helps to define what major initiatives or platform developments you should undertake. It answers the question, "If this is our strategy, then what projects must we or should we do?" By identifying the major initiatives and platform developments, this strategic exercise goes a long way toward shaping your eventual development portfolio. The ultimate result is a product roadmap showing a series of product or platform developments along with their extensions, on a time scale.
- Bottom-Up Approaches like scoring models that build in strategic criteria. These are composed of multiple scoring scales, some of which capture strategic direction and importance, as illustrated by the Celanese method. By using a large number of scoring criteria that rate projects on strategic fit, strategic impact, and strategic leverage, Celanese ensures that the right projects—from a strategic perspective— rise to the top of the list.
- Top-Down, Bottom-Up Approaches, which combine the methods above. The process equipment manufacturer's and the major bank's strategic mapping exercises put into classes product/market arenas or product groups and define strategic missions for each. These, then, become major inputs to the allocation of resources in the portfolio selection exercise—this is the Top-Down part (see Exhibits 5.8 and 5.16). Concurrently, projects are prioritized using a scoring model—Bottom-Up. Results from the two methods are reconciled via several iterations. There are also simpler variants of this approach. For example, at Exxon Chemical, some BUs use rigorous scoring models (Bottom-Up, like Celanese) and also check for spending breakdowns after the fact (Exhibit 5.11), which leads to adjustments for the upcoming year.

5. Integration between Gate Decisions and Portfolio Decisions

Almost all the companies we studied rely on some type of new product process model, such as Stage-Gate™, to drive new product projects from idea to market. Embedded in these processes are gates or Go/Kill decision points. The gates are, in effect, resource allocation decisions. A potential for conflict exists between the gating decision process and portfolio reviews because:

- real-time decisions are made on individual projects at gates
- portfolio decisions are made periodically.

These are two different decision processes (and in some firms even involve different people and somewhat different criteria!), yet both purport to select projects and allocate resources—hence the potential for conflict. Consider some of the strengths and weaknesses of each decision process:

- Portfolio reviews consider all projects together—a comparison of one against another. This holistic view is healthy, but it does limit the amount of time decision makers can spend on any one project. Witness Royal Bank's portfolio meeting, at which 100 projects are scored in one day! At EXFO Engineering, senior management devotes three to four days to portfolio reviews every quarter just to get through the list of active and proposed projects! By contrast, gate meetings tend to focus on only one project. That single project receives a thorough management review—there is much debate and time to reflect on the project's merits—but the evaluation is done in relative isolation from the other projects.
- Gate decisions occur in real time as the project moves from one stage to the next. By contrast, portfolio review meetings are held in calendar time, perhaps annually, semiannually, or quarterly.

Given these two decision processes, the questions become Which process should dominate? And how should the two processes be integrated?

Some firms, particularly those whose portfolio methods have been in place for some time, have developed rules or conflict resolution methods. These rules tend to let one or the other decision model dominate.

- *The portfolio model dominates.* Royal Bank has developed a set of decision rules to integrate the portfolio model with gate decisions. Here, the annual portfolio meeting earmarks funds for certain projects for the next year. (There are quarterly updates, so the portfolio list is relatively current.) But merely being "in the portfolio" does not guarantee funding or "Go" decisions. Each project still has to pass through each gate. In short, the gate decisions can override the portfolio decisions. In practice, however, it is rare that a project, once approved at a portfolio meeting, is rejected at a gate meeting (unless the project is in serious trouble). In effect, the portfolio meeting takes precedence.
- *The gates dominate.* Celanese management is adamant that the gate decisions take precedence. Here, the portfolio review is viewed only as a course correction. The view is "Make sound decisions at the gates, and the portfolio will take care of itself." The argument is that one might not achieve the optimal balance or mix of projects, but if the gates have been rigorous, at least all the projects in the portfolio will be good ones.

We conclude that both decision approaches—gate decisions and portfolio reviews—have their merits:

As noted above, decisions made at gates focus on single projects. Gate reviews can last hours, they are in-depth, they utilize many criteria, and they have access to current information. As a result, the decision is likely to be a more thoughtful one for that particular project. But the decision is made in relative isolation (all projects are not considered together), and the project may not be prioritized against either all other active or on-hold projects (although many companies do build in project prioritization for the project under review right at the gate meeting).

Portfolio reviews are holistic. They consider all projects together and take into account the ideal balance of projects, strategic alignment, and the desire to maximize against an objective. But with all projects considered in one meeting, the discussion on any one project is likely to be limited and superficial, unless days are devoted to the portfolio review. Moreover, the data may not be the most current. For example, the data used to develop portfolio maps or lists are often retrieved from a databank whose input comes from the most recent gate meeting for each project, which may have been months ago for some projects.

Neither decision approach is robust enough to eliminate the need for the other; thus, both methods—gate decisions and portfolio reviews—must be married to yield the best portfolio and project selection decisions.

Further, letting one process make all the decisions is dangerous: for example, in some firms, the gating process is noticeably weak (no projects are ever killed at gates!), so that management is forced to rely totally on the portfolio reviews to make all the Go/Kill decisions. The problem here is that these reviews are often not timely ones; nor is enough time allowed for a thorough discussion on all projects. Equally, having excellent and tough gate meetings may yield a high-quality portfolio containing many high-value projects, but because a holistic portfolio review is missing, the mix of projects may be all wrong and the total portfolio may not support the business's strategic direction.

Example: Reckitt-Benckiser has developed a useful approach to link gate decisions with its portfolio model. Recall that this company's portfolio model features a number of maps: ease versus attractiveness; probability of success versus NPV; and so on. It also boasts a Stage-Gate™ new product process. Here's how the two are linked.

Reckitt-Benckiser's portfolio model kicks in at Gate 3, the "Go to Development" decision point. That is, before a project is considered in the portfolio analysis, it must first clear the Gate 3 Go/Kill criteria. Thus, at Gate 3, for Go/Kill decisions, individual new projects are not compared to the whole portfolio, but to hurdle scores that ensure that the minimum standards of the portfolio are met. These hurdles are adjusted periodically to favor certain types of projects desired in the portfolio. Exhibit 7.2 provides a flowchart to illustrate the decision process.

Quite separately, portfolio reviews are conducted periodically. Here management reviews the balance and mix of active projects. Reckitt-Benckiser utilizes a number of the bubble diagrams and charts displayed in Chapter 4 to check for balance and strategic alignment. If imbalances are spotted, or if there are gaps between target and actual spending in given arenas, then adjustments are made. For example, the minimum hurdles for the gate scoring model are adjusted accordingly—hurdles are raised for some types of projects and lowered for others—in order to correct portfolio imbalances.

Additional concerns regarding integrating gate decisions with portfolio reviews focus on the criteria used at each. In a handful of firms, we were surprised that management was using different sets of criteria at gate meetings than at portfolio reviews! For example, in one major consumer goods firm, projects were rated at gates on a comprehensive set of scoring criteria via a scoring model and then were rescored at portfolio reviews (also via a scoring model), but with fewer and even different criteria!

Suggestion: In order to minimize confusion and conflict between gate meetings and portfolio reviews, we suggest the following:

- Define clearly the role of each decision process and meeting: Gate meetings focus on Go/Kill decisions for individual projects; by contrast, portfolio reviews consider the entire set of projects and deal with issues such as portfolio value, balance, and strategic alignment.
- Use the same criteria at both the gate and the portfolio review (or at least an abbreviated version of the gate criteria at portfolio reviews).
- Finally, life is much simpler if the same people—the leadership team of the business, for example—are at both reviews (that is, they are the gatekeepers at the critical gate meetings, and they also conduct the portfolio reviews).

6. Portfolio Management Must Consider All Types of Projects

All projects that compete for the same resources ought to be considered in the portfolio approach! "All projects" includes new product projects as well as process improvements, cost reductions, fundamental research, platform developments, and perhaps even customer request projects, maintenance items, and infrastructure projects. Conceptually this is quite correct, but it does increase the magnitude of the portfolio problem. Rather than simply comparing one project to another, management must deal with a myriad of different types of projects—a much more complex decision situation.

The argument about which projects ought to be in the portfolio is often controversial. Logically, any project that competes for resources should be in the portfolio system. From a marketer's standpoint, this would encompass any project that utilizes marketing resources: These include new and improved products, but they might also include relaunches, repositionings, and even major merchandizing or marketing initiatives.

The R&D or engineering departments may have quite different views of which projects should be "in the portfolio system." Logical projects for such technical groups might include new and improved products, but also cost reductions and manufacturing or process improvements. Fundamental research and platform developments are other kinds of projects that use up considerable technical resources and are in the portfolio; but because these projects use no marketing resources, they are not even on that department's radar screen! Finally, if the company is in an IT or related business (e.g., software, banking, communications), then even infrastructure projects—developing a new sales reporting system, for example—are in the portfolio, since they too consume considerable technical (in this case, IT) resources.

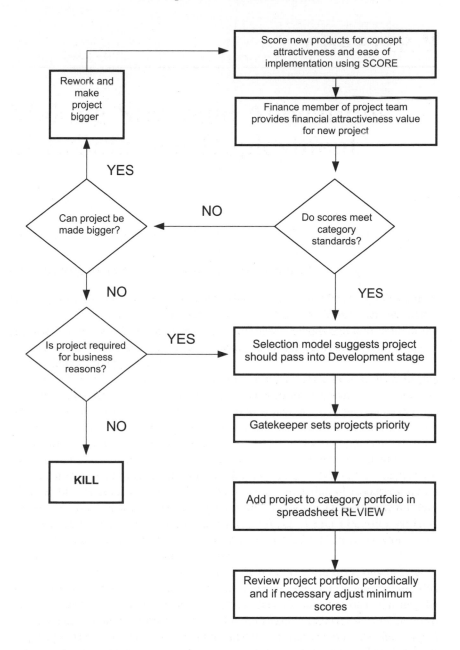

EXHIBIT 7.2   Reckitt-Benckiser's Logic Flowchart of Selection Model

Note: SCORE and REVIEW are spreadsheets provided for use with the selection model.

One class of projects that is often handled outside the normal portfolio is e-business projects. But e-business projects—for example, developing a web-based channel of distribution for your existing projects—also consume resources, both technical and marketing. What surprises us is how many firms handle e-business projects outside R&D (i.e., they are not part of the R&D portfolio) and outside the marketing department. E-business projects should be consciously included as part of your portfolio of projects.

If the portfolio is to consider a number of different types of projects, then how does one rank or prioritize them against each other? This issue of whether all projects should be compared against each other has proponents on both sides of the argument. Some firms studied simply set aside envelopes or buckets of money for different types of projects. Within each envelope, projects are rated and ranked against each other. The Strategic Buckets Model outlined in Chapter 5 is an example of this route; so is Honeywell's Mercedes star method. Using Strategic Buckets solves two problems:

1. First, the Strategic Buckets Model removes the task of comparing and ranking unlike projects against each other. Ranking dissimilar projects against each other is a very difficult task, for these reasons:

   - The nature and quality of information differ greatly between project types. For example, a process improvement project is likely to have fairly certain cost and benefit estimates, while a new product project does not, especially early in the project.
   - The criteria for comparison are likely different. The most important criterion for a cost reduction project may be cost-benefit; for a new product project, it may be strategic importance and sustainable competitive advantage.

   So how does one compare two projects when even the criteria for a good project differ? Via the Strategic Buckets Model, the task is simplified: One uses different rating or scoring models and quite different criteria for evaluating projects in different buckets.

2. Second, by setting aside buckets of money or resources, one is assured that spending and resource allocation across different types of projects mirror the business's strategy—that the right balance among project types is the result. Recall that this is the major strength of the Strategic Buckets Model: It forces resources to be allocated into buckets a priori.

The opposing viewpoint is the Darwinian theory of portfolio management: survival of the fittest. That is, all projects should compete against each other, and there should be no pool of money or resources set aside for any particular type of project. For example, if all the cost reduction projects are superior to all the product development projects, then all the resources ought to go to the cost reduction projects. This is survival of the fittest, where the merits of each project should decide the total split of resources, rather than having some artificial and a priori split in resources. The decision rule may be applauded by financial people as yielding an efficient allocation of resources and hence maximizing shareholder value, but the strategist might have problems with this lopsided portfolio that features no new product projects.

7. Information Overload in Portfolio Management

One deficiency with certain visual methods—maps, charts, and bubble diagrams—is the large number of possible displays and exhibits. Admittedly, portfolio selection is a complex problem, and one is tempted to plot everything against everything. As noted in Chapter 4, there are many possible parameters to consider. Indeed the possible permutations of X–Y plots, histograms, and pie charts are almost endless.

Are managers simply overwhelmed with all the information and plots? Experience in some firms suggests they are. In one company, the illness that management was suffering from was labeled "bubble-itis"—exposure to too many bubble diagrams. Further, when first conceived, Reckitt-Benckiser's portfolio approach contained far more maps and charts than the final version now in use. Managers quickly realized that they needed to simplify the problem and boil the decision down to a few key parameters and a few important charts.

In Chapter 4, we illustrated some of the more useful maps and charts from among the many we saw in use:

- The various risk-reward bubble diagrams
- Bubble diagrams based on scoring models (for example, concept attractiveness versus ease of implementation)
- The timing histogram (resources being spent and projects by year of launch)
- Various pie chart breakdowns: project types, markets, and product lines.

Exhibit 4.15 listed other popular bubble diagram dimensions.

Challenges and Issues

Many challenges, major problems, and issues remain to be resolved before effective portfolio management can be realized. Here are the more critical issues and unanswered questions we identified.

1. Too Many Projects, Not Enough Resources— The Number One Challenge

Pipeline gridlock plagues many business portfolios. A lack of resources (and related problems of resource allocation) is likely the most serious problem that firms face in implementing effective portfolio management. "Too many projects and not enough resources to do them" is a universal complaint within product development groups everywhere. And the performance results in the Chapter 6 underscored this problem: Having the right number of projects for the limited resources available was the weakest performance metric, with 43.5 percent of firms rating themselves as weak or poor here! The demand for more new products than ever coupled with corporate restructuring has helped to create this resource crunch.

One frustrated new product project leader at her company's technology conference exclaimed: "I don't deliberately set out to do a bad job. Yet, when you look at the job that the project leaders around here do, it's almost as though our goal is mediocrity. But that's not true . . . we're good project leaders, but we're being *set up for failure*. There simply isn't enough time and not enough people or the right people to do the job we'd like to do!" She went on to explain to senior management how insufficient resources and budget cuts coupled with too many projects were seriously compromising the way key projects were being executed. She was right! Resource commitment must be aligned with the business's new product objectives, strategy, and processes for positive results.[1]

The lack of resources is only part of the problem. The other side is the failure to allocate resources effectively. Here portfolio tools and methods are partly at fault, along with a lack of will on the part of senior management to cut back the number of active projects—to say "no" to some worthwhile initiatives.

The fact is that most project selection and portfolio management methods do a poor job of *resource balancing*. Projects are evaluated, go decisions are made, but resource implications are often not factored in.

Illustration: One of the most popular methods for evaluating projects and making Go/Kill decisions is the use of financial models, such as NPV.[2] More advanced versions introduce probabilities and uncertainties into the financial calculation. Management is presented with the NPV of the projects, along with probability distribution curves. These same models, while so elegant in their handling of financial estimates, revenues, costs, and profits, are notably lacking in their handling of the resource constraint problem: Resource availability is rarely part of the financial calculation. The exception is the bang-for-buck approach (Chapter 3).

The majority of project selection techniques are weak when it comes to making Go/Kill decisions or choosing the portfolio in light of constrained resources. There is really no way to check that the required resources are available when using most selection tools. Indeed most selection tools consider individual projects one at a time and on their own merits, with little regard for the impact that one project has on the next. Worse yet, human resources are assigned to projects, but only later is it discovered that the same people are committed to multiple projects, and that some people have 150 percent of their time committed.

Example: In one major beverage company, there were constant complaints that major bottlenecks were occurring in new product projects in the package development department. A resource demand analysis was undertaken on a project-by-project basis; only then was it discovered how heavily committed certain players were. When the packaging department's time commitments were totaled up across all active projects, it turned out that this three-person group had about 100 person-days committed each month. Figure it out: that is greater than a 150 percent commitment. No wonder there were logjams in the process!

The results of too many projects in the pipeline are serious. Here are some additional negative effects:

- Time to market starts to suffer as projects end up in a queue—waiting for people and resources to become available.
  Example: A senior technology manager in one Xerox division, concerned about project timelines, undertook a quick survey. He picked a day at random and sent an e-mail to every project leader in his division: "How much work got done on your project today?" The shocking news: More than three-quarters of the projects had no work done on them at all! Subsequent follow-up revealed that a minority had legitimate reasons for inaction—waiting for equipment to be delivered or waiting for tests to be completed. But the great majority were simply in a queue, waiting for people to get around to doing something on them. His best guess was that he could have halved time to market for most projects simply by having fewer active projects underway, thereby avoiding queues.
- People are spread very thinly across projects. With so many "balls in the air," people start to cut corners and execute in haste. Key activities may be left out in the interest of saving time. Thus, quality of execution starts to suffer. The end result is higher failure rates and an inability to achieve the full potential of would-be winners.
  Example: One major chemical company undertook an audit of its new product practices and performance across its many businesses. One common conclusion, regardless of business unit, revealed a lack of good market knowledge and customer input in the typical new product project. A task force was set up to study why. Their conclusions: Marketing people were so thinly spread across so many new product projects that they barely had time to oversee the launch of new products, let alone even think about doing market studies and solid market research.
- Quality of information on projects is deficient. When the project team lacks the time to do a decent market study or a solid technical assessment, management is often forced to make continued investment decisions in the absence of solid information. And so projects are approved that should be killed. The portfolio suffers.
- Finally, with people spread so thinly across projects and trying to cope with their "real jobs" too, stress levels go up and morale suffers. And the team concept starts to break down.[3]

The resource crunch issue spawns other resource-related issues—items 2, 3, and 4 below.

2. Once Made, How Firm Are Resource Commitments?

Should viable and active projects be killed or put on hold, just because a better one comes along? Here, too, we encountered some controversy and very different philosophies:

View 1—Very Flexible. Resource commitments to projects are not firm. Resources may be moved at will from one active project to another. For example, even though one project has been given a go decision and resources have been committed—and even if it remains a positive one—when a better project comes along, resources can be stripped from the first project to feed the second (Rhode & Schwarz's new portfolio approach uses an adaptation of this method). The argument here is that management must have the flexibility to allocate resources optimally, regardless of commitments previously made to project teams.

One implication is that the portfolio is a very dynamic one, constantly changing (no project has a firm go commitment); and the portfolio of projects must constantly be reviewed. A dynamic portfolio management method is essential here.

View 2—Fairly Firm Commitments. Resource commitments made to project teams must be kept—for the sake of continuity and team morale—even if a more attractive project comes along. While it may be desirable to have resource flexibility to allocate resources optimally, team morale and the negative implications of "jerking around" project teams and leaders are more important. Further, if projects are "on again, off again," there is a great waste of resources and time. Shifting resources from one project to the next is not seamless—project startups and shutdowns cost time and money. Finally, newer projects always look better than projects that are partway through development (warts always seem to appear as time passes!), so that the inevitable outcome is that resources are stripped from projects in their later phases to support new ones. Taken to an extreme, no project ever is completed!

One implication of this second philosophy is that the portfolio of projects has some stability. As a consequence, the portfolio of projects does not need to be reviewed so frequently, nor does the portfolio management method need to be quite so dynamic.

Generally companies with a longer-term perspective and considerable experience in major new product projects embrace the more stable view that resource commitments are firm (for example, some of the chemical companies we interviewed). Firms in shorter-term projects and in very dynamic markets lean more toward the flexible resource model (for example, some of the IT and high-technology firms in the study).

Even among companies that embraced the "committed resources" approach, there are differences in just how long or firm the commitment is. All agreed that if the project "shot itself"—that is, runs into serious problems such as delays, negative changes in the business case, or technical barriers—it must be reviewed immediately. This review or immediate gate meeting could change the resource commitment and even kill the project. Some companies had even developed a list of red flags that signaled problems and required the project leader to call for an immediate project review. Exhibit 7.3 provides a sample

New product projects sometimes encounter problems. Often original estimates are revised that render the project less attractive. When a flag situation occurs, the project leader must inform immediately gatekeepers, who may call for an immediate gate review. Here are some red flags:

Project Schedule: if the project falls behind schedule by more than 30 days, according to the agreed-on time line.

Project Budget: if the project goes over budget by more than 5% at a point defined in the plan approved at the previous gate (for example, versus milestone projections).

Resources: if any major functional area is unable to meet ongoing resource commitments according to the agreed-on time line.

Product Cost: if any change in the expected product cost occurs (for example, manufacturing cost) that is greater than 5% above cost estimates provided at the previous gate.

Sales Forecast: if any change greater than 10% occurs in the number of forecast sales units; or if any change occurs in the configuration ratios (product mix) that affects margin by more than 3%.

Business Case: if any change occurs that impacts significantly on the business case and financial outlook for the project (more than 5% impact).

Product Specs: whenever the product design or product requirements are revised and affect negatively meeting a customer need or the product specs.

Service: whenever a change in the service and support planned for the product occurs, which impacts negatively on a customer need or requirement.

Quality: if product quality metrics fall outside 0.3 sigma value.

EXHIBIT 7.3   Red Flags for Projects

list of red flags from Company G; one business within Motorola uses a similar flagging approach.

Assuming the project avoids red flags and remains in good shape—meets milestones, continues to look financially attractive, and so on—then how firm is the commitment?

At Exxon Chemical, the commitment is firm until the next gate. That is, "once resources are committed, they are not expected to be changed until the next gate review, barring an extraordinary development in the project."[4] In short, at each gate in Exxon's process, the project "is up for grabs." The implication is that the project can be reprioritized at each gate. The portfolio model is applied at each gate decision point, and the portfolio of projects—including where this project fits in—is discussed at each gate meeting.

Rohm and Haas management suggests that they cannot guarantee resource commitments once they are approved and that project leaders must recognize the realities of business: Circumstances change—better opportunities do come along—and the corporation must be able to respond. At one BU within Mobil Oil, management makes the commitment to project teams that resources are firm between gates (much like Exxon Chemical above), but that if circumstances do change, management will call an "emergency gate meeting" to re-review an active project and possibly strip away committed resources.

At other firms, the commitment is made right through the end of the project. That is, barring negative results or red flags, commitments made at the "Go to Development" decision point are firm through to launch. The project still has to pass all gates and reviews and could still be killed in the event of negative information. Royal Bank employs this practice; so does EXFO Engineering. EXFO goes as far as calling their process "a funnel leading to a tunnel." The inference is that for the early stages of the project, resources are not firm—the project could be killed (a funnel); but once the project is past Gate 3, resources are almost 100 percent committed (a tunnel).

The implication of the latter commitment model—the "funnel leading to a tunnel"—is that there is only one major decision point in the new product process, and as long as the project remains in good shape, it continues to obtain needed resources. Thus, the role of gates is to provide a critical review to ensure that the project remains sound. The portfolio model applies to one key decision point only, where the proposed project is compared to all ongoing active projects and to those in the queue (on hold).

3. Too Many Projects Are on Hold

When more projects pass the gate criteria than there are resources to fund them, even greater pressure is placed on the prioritization process. In some firms interviewed, the list of projects on hold was far longer than the list of active projects!

The problem here is that no one—especially senior executives—wants to kill potentially good projects. The fear expressed by one CTO was that "many excellent projects are left on the cutting room floor." This fear of "drowning puppies" is pervasive, even when it is recognized that:

- there are likely to be a number of other projects better than this one
- prioritization decisions are essential to achieving focus—this means killing projects.

So it becomes much more convenient to start a "hold tank" and to dump good projects into this tank. The implicit argument is this: A kill decision is averted and no one's feelings are hurt. Besides, someday there may be resources available to do some of the projects in the "hold tank" (often wishful thinking on the part of the senior gatekeepers).

When it first implemented its Stage-Gate™ new product process, ECC encountered this hold problem. Quickly, a logjam of projects awaiting entry to development occurred. By the time the hold list exceeded the active project list by a factor of two, managers knew they were in difficulty. A new decision rule was instituted: A project can remain on hold for no longer than three months. After that, it's "up or out"—either it becomes an active and resourced project, or it's killed. A tough rule perhaps, but at least it forces the gate decision makers (gatekeepers) to be more discriminating and to make the needed decisions. Further, it has encouraged gatekeepers to search for additional funding and resources for meritorious projects that are in danger of being killed (for example, new people, joint ventures, partnering arrangements, or outside help).

4. Why Have a Prioritized or Rank-Ordered List at All?

This is a philosophical question. According to management in one leading firm, there are only three classes of projects:

- funded and active projects with assigned people
- good projects with no one working on them (currently unfunded)—these are the on-hold projects
- dead projects.

If there are only three types of projects, why the need for rank-ordered lists? In this instance, management believed there was no great need for a prioritization or scoring model or any other model that led to a rank-ordered list. All that was needed was a triage approach: active, hold, or dead!

A contrary opinion expressed at many other firms is that a rank-ordered list is not only important, it is necessary. For example, even though a project is a go, there are varying degrees of go, according to the project's importance, payoffs, and priority. For example, management at Celanese regularly selects a subset of active projects and performs a full court press on these; that is, they resource these chosen projects to the maximum, ensuring that they are done as quickly as possible. Given that different levels of resource commitments can be made to any project, logic dictates that not only must projects be separated into go and hold categories, but that go projects themselves must be prioritized. These top-priority projects receive maximum resources for a timely completion.

5. Imaginary Precision: The Quality of Information of Input Data Is Lacking

A universal weakness is that virtually every model we studied implies a degree of precision far beyond people's ability to provide reliable data. And next to a lack of resources, the issue of poor quality of information is the next most serious problem facing portfolio managers.

The reality is that the sophistication of portfolio tools far exceeds the quality of the data. Recall the criticism that using a scoring model imputed a degree of precision that simply did not exist: "They're trying to measure a [soft] banana with a micrometer!" The same concern was voiced for other models as well. And we saw this time and again: portfolio task forces designing and trying to implement very exotic portfolio methods, only to be thwarted by the very poor quality of the data inputs.

Example: A major tool manufacturer has dozens of development projects underway at any one time. In order to help prioritize projects and make better Go/Kill decisions, management has implemented a "Go to Development" gate decision point. The project team is required to submit a business case, which includes estimates of market size, expected revenue, and profits. These data are key inputs to the prioritization decision. The trouble is, these numbers are best guesses, often based on numbers pulled out of the air. Hence management is lulled into believing that they are making rigorous Go/Kill decisions based on objective criteria. In reality, the numbers they are using to make these decisions are *pure fiction.*[5]

Early in the life of a project, management must make some important Go/Kill and resource commitment decisions on specific projects.[6] The dilemma is that the upfront homework is not done well enough to provide the quality of information that management needs to make sound decisions. For example, a study of over 500 projects in 300 firms revealed major weaknesses in the front end of projects: weak preliminary market assessments, barely adequate technical assessments, dismal market studies and marketing inputs, and deficient business analyses.[7] These are critical homework activities, yet in study after study, they are found wanting: the upfront homework simply does not get done well.[8] Even worse is that these activities are strongly linked to ultimate project outcomes: The greatest differences between winning products and losers is in the quality of execution of the homework activities for the project.

Poor market information—including estimates of market size, expected revenue, and pricing—plagues many projects. Not only are inadequate market analysis and poor market research cited as major reasons for new product failure, but they are major causes of difficulties in portfolio management and project selection. If revenue and pricing estimates are inaccurate, how can one believe portfolio models that rely heavily on NPVs?

The dilemma was summed up by one frustrated executive: "If we had spent as much money on improving the quality of market information in projects as we have on developing the perfect portfolio model, we'd be farther ahead!"

Why is quality of execution of these early stage activities so pivotal to new product success? There are two reasons we observe:

1. When the quality of this early stage work is better, an excellent foundation is laid for the project. Thus, subsequent activities are more proficiently executed: better product design, better testing, better launch and production startup; and so success rates rise.[9] As an example, better upfront homework usually results in sharper customer input, which in turn means earlier, more accurate, and more stable product definition. Note that unstable product specs is one of the major causes of long cycle times, while sharp, early product definition that is fact-based is strongly connected to product profitability.[10]

2. When the early work is done better, market and technical information on the project is superior. Thus, management has the information it needs to select the winning

projects (and to remove the dogs). The result is a much better portfolio of projects, and again higher success rates. For example, bad market information plagues many new product projects. Lacking good data on market size, expected revenue, and pricing makes it difficult to undertake a reliable financial analysis. Indeed, one company's analysis of the accuracy of its financial analyses undertaken just prior to Development revealed a 300 percent error in NPV estimates on average! Since so many firms rely on NPV numbers as the dominant decision criterion, such errors render the decision-making process a hit and-miss exercise. One might be better off tossing a coin!

The overriding message here is that doing projects right will ultimately lead to better project selection decisions, therefore higher odds of doing the right projects. "Right projects right" becomes the means to achieving the overall goal of a higher success rate.

A second overriding message is that, while useful, portfolio models should not be overused nor their results blindly accepted. Ironically, management sometimes confessed to being mesmerized by their models into believing that the data were accurate. The financial models, rank-ordered lists, or bubble diagrams appear so elegant that one sometimes forgets how imprecise the data are upon which these diagrams or charts are constructed.

Clearly, before one proceeds to develop even more sophisticated portfolio approaches, there is a great need to bring the quality of the data up to the levels required by the current models. We identified four key areas in which data are consistently weak, and which detract from the reliability of portfolio tools:

1. Technical success estimates (probabilities of technical success) prove elusive for many managers, especially in the predevelopment stages. Various consensus, Delphi, scoring model, and matrix scoring methods are employed (see Chapter 8), but the fact remains that predicting the probability of technical success remains problematic for some types of projects.
2. Market information including market size, market penetration (or expected sales), and pricing are often grossly in error. Many market research and market intelligence techniques are proposed to sharpen these estimates, but rarely are they employed effectively if at all.
3. Manufacturing and capital cost estimates are also difficult to obtain, especially during the earlier phases of a project. Note that many firms require a financial analysis prior to development, and these financial data (such as NPV) become inputs to the portfolio model. The problem is that the product is not even developed yet. Still, manufacturing (including material) costs and capital equipment needs must be estimated.
4. Resource estimates are plagued by inaccuracies; specifically, how long the project will take and how many person-days or dollars are required for its execution. Sometimes this is the result of an overzealous project team with a "can do" attitude, submitting an aggressive timetable. Other times, the problem is that senior management puts undue pressure on the project team to reduce timelines and reduce resources required; even worse, the team agrees to the reduced timeline! Finally, it is often difficult to forecast how long something will take: "Invention is difficult to predict," noted one technical executive in a high-tech, leading-edge company.

Much better information fairly early in the project—market, technical, and manufacturing—is essential if effective portfolio decisions are the goal. This means much better upfront homework is required. The effectiveness of the portfolio model is severely limited by the quality of the data in too many firms! So important is the topic of data integrity that all of Chapter 8 is devoted to methods designed to yield better project information.

6. How Should Project Information Be Gathered?

Sometimes the data is available somewhere in the company, but getting one's hands on the data becomes a much bigger challenge than expected. Often portfolio management must deal with dozens of projects, both new and existing.

Example: One division of Bayer in the United States embarked on portfolio management. The first task was to portray the existing portfolio on a series of pie charts and bubble diagrams. But to the portfolio manager's dismay, getting the data on existing projects was far more difficult than anticipated. Many projects had never had a business case prepared; hence, NPVs were missing. For others, project leaders literally guessed at probabilities of technical and commercial success. The exercise was valuable in that it revealed how deficient the basic information on many projects was.

Example: In one health-care products company, project leaders claimed they were being "driven to distraction" by the amount and detail of information required by the portfolio manager and the consulting firm he had hired. Very detailed financial information, estimates of uncertainty, and resource requirement data were required for every project—data far beyond that normally required for regular gate meetings. Project leaders complained bitterly about how much time this "make work" task was taking, when often their projects were suffering from lack of time and attention. Others had simply given up and had resorted to providing nonsense data.

Portfolio models invariably require at least some data on all the projects in the pipeline. This means that a pipeline database must be established. It also means that methods for routinely collecting and inputting the vital data must be established.

Example: When Company T first implemented the bubble diagram approach to portfolio management, the data-collection task was thought to be relatively easy. "Data on NPV, likelihoods of success, resources being spent, and a few other pieces of information for every project seemed like a straightforward information request I made of each project leader," the portfolio manager explained. But it took more than three months to gather this "readily available" data, often only after considerable arm-twisting.

One solution is that only projects that have passed at least some gate reviews—for example, the "Go to Development" decision point—should be considered in the portfolio model. This greatly reduces the number of projects under consideration, with a corresponding decrease in the amount of data required. This approach also means that the results of the "Go to Development" gate review—for example, financial data, resource requirements, probabilities, and ratings from the scoring model—can be collected at the gate meeting and be used as input data to the database and the portfolio model.

7. Project Selection Methods Fail to Discriminate Between Projects

The inability to discriminate between projects is a serious problem with some portfolio approaches, which leads to a number of other problems. A failure to discriminate means that it's difficult to arrive at a reliable rank-ordered or prioritized list of projects—one that everyone accepts. Lacking such priorities in turn leads to difficulties in killing projects, so the list of active projects becomes too long. Suddenly there is a resource crunch. The problems multiply.

The discrimination problem is this: Most project selection tools used at gate meetings (for example scoring models and financial tools) consider the project against some hurdle or "minimum acceptable value." In the case of NPV, for example, it is calculated using a risk-adjusted cost of capital. If the NPV is positive, the acceptable hurdle rate is achieved, and the project is deemed a Pass.[11] The trouble is, lots of projects pass the hurdles. What these methods really fail to do is provide for a forced ranking of projects against each other. Projects are rated against objective criteria, but they are rarely force-ranked against each other. So there is little discrimination between projects: they are all go's!

Example: An international banking organization had established a well-oiled new product process, complete with rigorous Go/Kill decision points built in. These Go/Kill decisions were based in part on a scoring model and on traditional profitability criteria. The problem was that many projects passed the hurdles at the gates and kept getting added to the active project list. As the list got longer and longer, the resources became spread thinner and thinner! The gating method looked at projects, each on their own merits, but failed to distinguish the top priority ones from the rest.

Forced ranking of projects means making tough decisions. The result is a prioritized list of projects with the best ones at the top. Projects are listed until the business runs out of resources. Below that point, projects are put on hold or killed outright. But all too often these tough decisions are not made. As one executive put it, "No one likes to drown puppies in our business!"

This failure to discriminate among projects—where the best rise to the top of the list—is, in part, due to weaknesses in the particular selection tools used.

NPV was designed for one-off decisions; for example, the decision to buy a new piece of equipment. But NPV was never meant for portfolio decisions, where multiple projects compete for the same resources. And ranking projects according to their NPVs does not yield the right portfolio either—the method ignores resource constraints. Finally, NPV calculations are always suspect in the early stages of a new product project. As one senior manager remarked: "What number do you want to hear? The project team always delivers the right number to get their project approved!"

Scoring models are valuable decision aids for evaluating projects. But they too tend to rate projects against absolute criteria, rather than against each other. Admittedly, one might consider ranking projects according to their project scores, as some firms do. But, again, the issues of resource constraints and "bang for buck" are ignored.

Another complaint about scoring models is that often they fail to discriminate well. They tend to yield middle-of-the-road scores—60 out of 100—which makes it difficult to spot the stars among the dogs. This is especially true when a large number of scoring criteria are used: High scores on some criteria cancel out low scores on others, and the result regresses toward the mean—a project score of 50 or 60 out of 100.

Bubble diagrams have the advantage of looking at all projects together. And resource requirements are displayed by the size of the bubbles or shapes (Chapter 4, Exhibit 4.1). The problem is that bubble diagrams tend to be information displays only—a discussion tool—and do not generate a list of prioritized projects.

8. Too Many Small Projects, Too Few Major Hits

The shortage of major hits or big breakthroughs in the portfolio is a problem common to many firms. Anecdotal evidence from our research suggests that there are many reasons for this:[12]

- A preoccupation with financial results and overemphasis on shareholder value (Financial evaluation techniques inevitably favor small, well-defined, fast projects over long-term, less defined ones.)
- Management impatience and the desire for some quick hits (One executive called this the Nike theory of management: "Just do it!")
- A lack of discipline ("Urgent things always take precedence over important things!" exclaimed a frustrated manager, annoyed with his business's preoccupation with quick-hit projects.)
- The dynamic nature of markets and the competitive situation (which make it difficult to predict the long term and thus more difficult to predict and justify long-term projects)
- The difficulty in finding major revenue generators (Markets are mature, and the opportunities for major breakthroughs just are not there, according to some people in certain industries.)

Short-term projects—extensions, modifications, updates, and fixes—are clearly important projects if the business wishes to remain competitive and keep its product lines current. But if these projects consume almost all your development resources, the issue is one of balance. A certain proportion of your development resources must be committed to bolder projects that promise breakthroughs, or to change the basis of competition: genuine new products, platform developments, and even technology breakthroughs.

Part of the problem is a lack of a product innovation strategy that gives direction to the development efforts and spending priorities. With no strategy in place, tactics take over; and tactics favor the small, quick projects. Another root cause is the lack of deployment decisions in the business. Many companies we interviewed did not consciously address the deployment or resource allocation decision across project types. For example, there is no attempt to set aside envelopes or "buckets" of money for different project types—major projects, long-term projects, technology developments versus shorter projects, extensions, modifications, and fixes (as in the Strategic Buckets Model in Chapter 5). With no conscious envelopes or buckets in place, every would-be project is thrown into the same bucket, and the results are predicable: The quick, short-term, and well-defined extensions, modifications, and fixes win out in the competition for resources, often to the longer-run detriment of the business.

9. Portfolio Reviews: Are They Monitoring Reviews or Project Selection Meetings?

Some firms view portfolio reviews (and the portfolio models used at them) as monitoring meetings—a check on the portfolio and its mix. Others think that portfolio reviews are active project selection meetings. In chapter 10, we explain how both approaches can work, the choice depending upon your particular business requirements. For now, we will look at the general reasons for each point of view.

View 1—Monitoring. Some businesses view a portfolio review as enabling senior management to gain a better perspective on the current portfolio. The portfolio review is expected to provide minor course corrections only—5-degree course shifts—but not result in numerous Go/Kill decisions or a total realignment of resources—a 90-degree shift! Witness the Reckitt-Benckiser example cited earlier in which portfolio reviews signal shifts needed in gate hurdles. The argument here is that the gating process should be making fairly sound Go/Kill and allocation decisions on projects on an ongoing basis. Assuming this is true, the portfolio review should be largely a sanity check that the gating process is indeed working and that the resulting gate decisions are yielding the right balance of projects, high-value projects, and projects with strategic alignment.

Example: This monitoring view, in its extreme, was expressed by the manager of research planning for a major U.S. chemical firm, who had been implementing portfolio management across the corporation for the past five years: "The portfolio review should not look at individual projects (except for a few very large ones that dramatically impact the business strategy). Rather, at portfolio reviews, we look at projects in aggregate—at where we are spending our money, and where we should be; and that the portfolio of projects is consistent with the business's strategy. We don't confuse the portfolio review with project selection! Project selection takes place at gates."

View 2—Selection.   The position in other firms is that portfolio reviews are very much project selection meetings. Indeed, in one major firm, virtually all project selection is done at the portfolio reviews, with the gate meetings on individual projects reduced to progress reports—in effect, rubber stamps. We witnessed two sets of circumstances where the portfolio review involved numerous project selection decisions:

- First, where the business's gating process was broken. By default, project selection had to be done at the periodic portfolio review meetings.
- Second, where portfolio management began very early in the life of projects, even before Gate 1, the idea screen. That is, the portfolio review becomes a substitute for the first few gate decision points in the business's new product process.

Example: Telenor's business communications division had set up RATs (resource allocation teams) to undertake portfolio reviews. Projects considered at these reviews included new product ideas, which had not even entered their new product process (that is, had not even cleared Gate 1, the idea screen). In effect, this division is using portfolio reviews not only to monitor the portfolio's balance and composition, but also to make the first few gate decisions—project selection.

Other companies, such as some businesses at Rohm and Haas, have a definite policy: A project must go through at least one gate and be defined before it can be considered in the portfolio review.

Opinion: For some firms and in some circumstances, we favor view 1, the monitoring approach: ensure that the gating process is working and use the portfolio reviews to monitor the mix and composition of the portfolio, but not as the principal project selection venue.

The problem at those firms that are the strongest proponents of view 2—where portfolio reviews are where the real decisions are made—is that projects tend never to be killed once the initial go decision is made at the portfolio review. The result is tunnels, not funnels. In short, there is only one review point in the process, namely, the entrance gate. Thus, even as new and possibly negative information becomes available, the project continues along and gets a life of its own. Coincidentally many of these firms are in the services and IT sectors and are heavily reliant on software and electronics for their new products. We speculate that perhaps the risks of their projects are reasonably low (technical success is all but guaranteed, unlike pharmaceuticals, for example). In many of these cases, the belief was that the markets and industries were moving so quickly that merely getting a product to market all but guaranteed commercial success. Thus, subsequent rigorous reviews at later stages of the project were not thought to be required.

More on this issue of which decision process should be dominant—gates or portfolio reviews—later in Chapter 10.

10. When Should the Portfolio Management Process Kick In?

Again, there are widely differing views here. Some of them coincide with whether the portfolio review is a monitoring effort or a selection process.

View 1—Projects Enter Very Early.   Projects should enter the portfolio management process at the idea stage. That is, not only should the portfolio review consider projects already underway, but it should include brand-new proposals or ideas and make decisions based on those. More than one major firm took this position. Indeed, in some cases, the portfolio review meetings evolved to become substitutes for the idea screen (Gate 1), as well as the next two gates in the new product process. Ironically, once past Gate 3 (the "Go to Development" gate), projects are not reprioritized, they are simply "in the portfolio," unless they turn sour.

The arguments we heard for this approach are convincing:

* The initial decisions to start projects (the idea screen) are important ones and should involve the senior people. Therefore, ideas should be on the table at the portfolio review where the senior people are.
* Executives often argue that "Ideas are future projects. We want to see early on what the impact on the portfolio will be if certain ideas are approved. Why even begin a project if it's wrong for the portfolio?"
* "Our organization abhors risk. It will kill breakthrough projects unless senior people are there at the outset," claimed a senior technical officer at Lubrizol, the leading oil additives firm. Other senior technical people generally agree.

View 2—Projects Enter at Later Stages.   Projects should pass at least one or two gates in the new product process before they are seriously considered in the portfolio management process. The majority of firms took this position. The argument is pragmatic:

* For the first few stages, projects are too ill-defined to consider in the portfolio. For example, many of the portfolio models require financial estimates and probabilities of commercial or technical success. These types of data are simply not available at the idea stage.
* Resource commitments in the early stages of a project are minimal, and portfolio management is about resource allocation. If the resources committed are so small, then such projects should not be on the portfolio maps or on the rank-ordered lists.

- One should not confuse portfolio reviews with idea screening (Gate 1 decisions)! There still can be an effective idea-screening decision point quite separate from the portfolio review. Here, ideas are screened, and strategic issues—rather than financial and technical feasibility—are the main screening criteria.

Even an executive at one major financial institution, which embraced View 1, expressed concerns about entering projects early into the portfolio model: "Some of the projects we considered that day (at the portfolio review meeting) were little more than a gleam in people's eyes—it was very difficult to score and rate them against projects already underway."

There were some words of caution about not considering embryonic projects in the portfolio review (view 2), however. For example, at Rohm and Haas, although projects do not enter the portfolio model until they have passed a gate or two in their new product process, there is concern whether "there is the right number and balance of early-stage (pre-portfolio) projects coming down the pipeline." For that reason some businesses in Rohm and Haas do monitor these early-stage projects, but in aggregate, and they do not appear on the business's portfolio maps.

Example: Company G's portfolio management method kicks in at Gate 2 in their new product process, after some technical and market investigation has been undertaken. Recall that Company G uses the financially based dynamic rank-ordered list (Chapter 3); therefore management argues that it must have at least first-cut estimates of NPV and IRR in order to undertake a ranking of projects. And before Gate 2, these data are not available at all.

However, to ensure the right number and balance of projects in the early stages of their pipeline, management sets aside a bucket of money for all early-stage projects (projects prior to Gate 2). This bucket or fund of money—the VP of marketing calls it the "seed corn money"—is allocated to projects in Stage 1 (investigation) and Stage 0 (ideation). There is some attempt to look at the balance of projects in these early stages, and the senior people are informed of Gate 1 decisions (idea screening)—no surprises coming down the pipe. Thus, although the formal portfolio management process does not kick in until later in the process, there are techniques in place to oversee, at least informally, the portfolio of early-stage projects.

---

11. Should Portfolio Models Provide Information Display or Be Decision Models?

Should the portfolio method merely display information to managers in a useful way (as bubble diagrams do), or should it produce a prioritized list of projects (as a scoring model or dynamic rank-ordered list does)? The display approach means that management must review the various maps and charts, integrate and assess the information, and then arrive at prioritized lists themselves. By contrast, the prioritized list approach provides management with a first-cut list of projects, prioritized according to certain criteria. Management then reviews and adjusts the list as needed.

Managers interviewed were divided on this issue:

- A common view is that the portfolio model ought to be an input to the portfolio meeting, discussion, and decision. However, the ranking of projects into a final prioritized list must be a non-mechanical process. There are simply too many factors, many of them "soft," that are far beyond the capability of any decision-making model to capture. Managers, not a decision model, are the decision makers. This implies that the portfolio tools must be enablers or decision-support systems only— display the right kinds of information.
- An opposite view is that mangers do not necessarily make consistent and good decisions. If a model can be developed that captures most of the considerations that should enter the portfolio decision, then at least part of the managerial decision-making process can be replaced by this model. For example, if a solid scoring model can be developed, that captures all the important criteria and considerations, and then if management does the scoring on projects, why not use a software package to crank out rank-ordered list of projects, from best to worst? Moreover, these models (such as a financially based ranked list or a scoring model) provide only a first cut on the list of projects. Management retains the final say on the exact prioritization. They adjust the list to capture factors not considered by the portfolio model.

12. What Problems Do Financial Analysis Methods Pose?

For more than half the firms in our study, a strict reliance on financial methods and criteria in order to prioritize projects is considered inappropriate. Financial data are simply too unreliable during the course of a project, especially in the earlier phases when prioritization decisions are most needed. Postproject reviews suggested that estimates on key variables, such as expected revenues and profits at the "Go to Development" decision point, are highly inaccurate. Yet this is the point at which serious resource commitments are made and the project enters the portfolio model.

A second problem is that sophisticated financial models and spreadsheets often imply a level of reliability beyond the facts on which the data are based. Computer spreadsheets in some firms have become quite complex and produce best- and worst-case scenarios, sensitivity analyses, and so on. Managers are often mesmerized by these in a gate or portfolio meeting. They begin to believe the financial projections (due in part to the elegance of the financial model and the dazzling output it produces) and lose sight of the fact that the data inputs are highly unreliable.

A final problem is that, in practice, financial models do not yield the best portfolios. Indeed, as seen in the last chapter, financial models yielded the poorest results on a number of portfolio metrics, and they were generally rated poorly by their users.

Nonetheless, these methods remain popular, and some senior executives demand that financial analysis be employed as part of every project's business case development. And for good reason: While often inaccurate, a solid financial analysis will often provide directional information, and it will certainly pinpoint key uncertainties and risks along with critical areas of ignorance.

Even when valid financial data are available and reasonably reliable, there are still problems. Here are some examples:

- Traditional NPV (discounted cash flow) incorrectly penalizes some types of projects, because it does not consider the options facet of new product decisions. Recall from Chapter 3 that NPV assumes an all-or-nothing investment situation. Reality suggests that in most new product projects, companies invest a small amount, seek additional information, and, assuming positive information, invest more in the project. There are investment options along the way. NPV's failure to recognize these options portrays certain kinds of higher-risk projects—high-cost ones with low probability of success—much more negatively than they should be. A more appropriate route is to use a decision-tree approach (much like the OPT method in Chapter 3), which unfortunately can make the computation considerably more complex but yields the more accurate economic value of the project.

- How does one deal with the possible cannibalization of other products already in the product line? Often negative interrelationships among products—especially between new and existing ones—are complex. Hence quantitative estimates are difficult to arrive at. For example, a new product might be expected to cannibalize the sales of an old product in the company's lineup. But at how fast a rate? Reliable estimates are very difficult to make. And this argument was often heard: "If we don't cannibalize our own products, a competitor surely will; thus, no cannibalization cost effects should be borne by the new product." In contrast, other companies did count cannibalization as a cost that must be borne by the new product in its financial analysis. The issue is difficult to resolve.

- The treatment of capital cost requirements is another complex issue, especially in the case of shared or idle facilities. For example, one capital-intensive product developer always faces the problem of determining the cost of spare production capacity on capital equipment. How much of this cost should the new product bear? Some pundits in the company argue "none." They reason that, after all, the equipment is idle and that there is no opportunity or incremental capital cost. Others in that company make a case that the new product should bear a "fair share" of the equipment capital costs, even when equipment is otherwise idle. Finally, the argument often is that the equipment may be idle this year but may not be next year, and so there really is an opportunity cost.

- How does one deal with terminal values of projects? That is, what is the project "worth" at the end of the five- or ten-year projection considered in the cash flow analysis? An assumption that the project is worth nothing after, say, ten years could penalize a project severely, especially in the case of projects for which the IRR is relatively low and close to the hurdle rate.

    When the IRR or the discount rate is quite high in a 10-year discounted cash flow analysis, the value of the income earned in year 11 is almost negligible by the time it is discounted to the present. For example, suppose you undertook a 10-year cash flow analysis of a project that had profit of $1 million in year 10. One might logically argue that the project is still worth something in year 11, say 10 times the earnings in the previous year. So you value the project at $10 million in year 11—its terminal value. If this is discounted at 15 percent (a reasonable discount or hurdle rate), it adds $2.1 million to the NPV of the project. This sizable $2.1 million might make the difference between a go and a kill decision. If discounted at 35 percent, however, this $10 million amounts to only $0.37 million, likely a negligible amount to the total value of the project. So when the IRR is barely above the discount rate, the terminal value you elect can have a major impact on the project's financial analysis.

Example: One major financial institution developed a standardized compiled spreadsheet analysis for use in all business cases from their "Go to Development" gate on. This standard 10-year cash flow model provides three alternative assumptions, or treatments, of the terminal value:

- The project has no terminal value in year 11
- The project is worth 5 times year 10 earnings in year 11
- The project is worth 10 times year 10 earnings in year 11.

For each assumption, both the NPV and IRR are calculated. Management can then view the effects of the three alternative terminal value treatments and judge accordingly. Interestingly, the three treatments often yield quite different IRR or NPV results.

Summing Up

The list of findings, conclusions, issues, and challenges discussed here are the points that you and your leadership team must consider as you move toward effective portfolio management. Not all points may apply to you, but do read over the list in Exhibit 7.1 a second time and envision how you and your business might handle each problem or challenge. There is one final conclusion to consider: Don't rely too much on portfolio management for all the answers!

Portfolio Management Is Not the Complete Answer

Some managements we interviewed have taken the case for portfolio management to an extreme. The view seems to be that portfolio management will solve all that ails their new product efforts. Perhaps the fact that portfolio management appears, at first glance, to be such a tangible and immediate solution is attractive. The notion of optimizing resource allocation also has a certain theoretical appeal to some. Next, portfolio management has been pitched at senior management, and so senior people see this as an avenue for them to become more directly involved. Finally, the fact that a number of pundits are popularizing the topic and proposing elegant solutions has generated much interest.

Viewing portfolio management as a total solution, however, is a very dangerous and simplistic view. Portfolio management is a very important piece of the new product puzzle, but it is by no means the single answer.

Years of investigation into the critical success factors that underlie new product performance have revealed numerous performance drivers. Many of these drivers are directly connected to portfolio management and project selection, but others are not.[13] These important success factors are listed in Exhibit 7.4; two types of success factors are identified:

1. *Controllable*: First, there are some success factors that are readily controllable; action can be taken on them. Examples are:
   - developing a unique, superior product: one that is differentiated, offers unique benefits to users, and provides superior value for money to customers
   - quality of execution of key activities from idea to launch
   - building the voice of the customer into the new product process
   - undertaking solid upfront homework prior to moving ahead with a full project
   - achieving sharp, early product definition prior to development
   - utilizing a true cross-functional team, with empowerment, accountability, and a defined leader.

   An understanding of these critical success factors is important, because management and project teams can take immediate action to ensure that they are built into the new product process and into specific projects. For example, a well-designed Stage-Gate™ new product process incorporates these success factors into the game plan in a deliberate fashion.

2. *Givens*: Next, there are success factors that are more situationally defined, and not quite as controllable by the project team. These are characteristics that are more or less "givens" for a specific project. Examples are:

   - how large and growing the market is
   - how tough and entrenched the competition is
   - whether the product is unique and differentiated (this factor fits into both categories—partly controllable, partly not)
   - whether the project leverages the business's core competencies in marketing, technology, or production
   - how new the project is in terms of technology and its marketplace
   - whether the project fits the business's strategy
   - whether the competitive advantage is sustainable.

   Often these characteristics are difficult to control: for example, the project team cannot suddenly make the market grow, or wish the competition away, or develop instant core competencies that the project might leverage. Where these characteristics see their greatest benefit is in project selection. That is, an understanding of the profile of a winning new product helps define the selection criteria.

New Product Process Factors — Largely Controllable by Project Team:

- Product advantage (partly controllable)
- Proficiency of technological activities
- Proficiency of marketing activities
- Voice of the customer built in
- Proficiency of up-front (homework) activities
- Getting sharp, early product definition
- Speed to market
- Proficiency of financial/business analysis
- The new product's strategy
- Internal/external relations (of the team)
- How the project team was organized

Non Controllable Factors (Givens):

- Market potential and size
- Market growth rate
- Market competitiveness
- External environment (hostile/friendly)
- Product advantage (partly a given)
- Marketing synergy (ability to leverage competencies)
- Technological/manufacturing synergy (ability to leverage competencies)
- Project familiarity (familiar markets, technologies)
- Availability of resources

EXHIBIT 7.4   Factors That Drive New Product Success at the Project Level

A provocative question is: Which is more important in the success equation:
- doing the right projects? or
- doing projects right?

That is, are success factors under item 1, namely, controllable factors, the most important? Or are situational factors (under item 2) the most vital? An analysis of the various success factors and their impacts shows that success depends on both doing the right projects and doing projects right. Moreover, the relationships between the factors in Exhibit 7.4 and success have been quantified. The exact split between the two sets of factors is difficult to state accurately, but after a number of success/failure studies we have done over the years, we estimate that that about two-thirds of success (measured various ways) is attributable to the controllable factors (doing projects right), and one-third is accounted for by uncontrollable factors (factors useful in selecting the right projects).

Further, as noted previously in this chapter, doing projects right—the upfront homework and building in the voice of the customer—will lead to better data, which will in turn enable one to pick the right projects. The point is that there is more to new product success than project selection. Project selection and portfolio management are not panaceas—don't forget quality of execution, doing projects right! So if your new product process is broken—projects not being executed as well as they should be, upfront homework and voice of customer missing, cross-functional teams not performing well—fix these problems first! Then turn to effective portfolio management.

On the other hand, there are many positive outcomes of effective portfolio management that go beyond simply picking the right projects. And these outcomes, indeed, affect quality of execution and new product success:

- One outcome of effective portfolio management is picking the right *number* of projects. One reason that projects are so poorly executed is that there are too many projects in the pipeline, project team members are spread too thinly, and too many corners are cut. By having the right number and balance of projects, quality of execution decidedly improves.
- A second outcome is management commitment. That is, effective portfolio management leads to alignment among the functions in the company, together with senior management commitment to specific projects and common priorities across projects. This, too, positively affects quality of execution and, ultimately, new product success.

In spite of these latter arguments, we still urge senior management not to place too much emphasis on portfolio management as the total answer. Remember: quality of execution, having a solid new product process, building best practices into projects, and practicing discipline in projects still account for much new product success.

The Path Forward

Overcoming the challenge of developing an effective portfolio approach for your company is no small task. In today's business environment, there is no question that portfolio management is a vital issue. Our investigation points to several fundamental truths, however. Do not expect a "magic solution" here! And the "flavor of the month" solution probably will not work long-term. In this chapter we identified a number of key conclusions about effective portfolio management, and we uncovered numerous issues that still must be addressed by management (summarized in Exhibit 7.1). These seven conclusions and twelve issues and challenges naturally lead to the next question: Now that we know the various approaches and have identified a number of challenges, how do we carry out the process? In subsequent chapters we present our recommendations on how you can take steps to implement an effective portfolio management process for your company.

CHAPTER 8

Data Integrity: Obtaining Reliable Information

The devil is in the details! No matter how sound your portfolio tools, if the information you feed into them is inaccurate or unreliable, the resulting portfolio displays and decisions will be wrong. Integrity of data is absolutely vital for effective portfolio management. The quality of your new product information—forecasts of sales, costs and profitability, and assessments of the market environment and its future, as well as estimates of success probabilities—makes or breaks your well-thought-out portfolio management process.

There are major problems with data integrity, however. We saw in Chapter 3 how inaccurate financial estimates and forecasts can be (see "The Dark Side of the Financial Approaches to Project Evaluation"). There are huge errors, by orders of magnitude. Also recall that quantitative approaches to portfolio management, namely the financial methods, yielded the worst portfolio results in Chapter 6. Again, we note that this poor performance stems not so much from the fact that these models lack rigor (quite the contrary); rather, it results from very poor data and forecasting in new product projects.

Why are these data so often in error? A better understanding of the reasons may lead toward corrective action. Here are some common reasons (or excuses) for poor data:[1]

Excuse #1. "We simply skipped over the upfront homework: We failed to devote the time, money, and people to do the necessary upfront market, competitive, technical, and operations analysis on the project." Often the underlying reasons cited are no time, no people, or no money to do the work. One of the weakest areas is market information. Indeed, poor market information continues to be cited as a major cause of new product failures. Moreover, market studies are rated as the most poorly undertaken of all activities in the entire new product process. Seventy three percent of project teams confess to simply doing a poor job on the upfront market research and analysis.[2]

Be sure to build one or two upfront homework stages into your new product process. Upfront homework pays off in three ways. First, the product and its launch strategy are designed with the benefit of much better market and technical insights, which leads to higher success rates. Second, there is clear evidence that more homework done in the early stages results in less time wasted later in the project—times to market are shorter. Third, better upfront homework means better data so that project valuation and project selection decisions are likely to be better.

Excuse #2. "Predicting the future is difficult—invariably there will be errors, simply because it is the future." True enough, especially in very new market and technology situations. Nonetheless, for many new product projects, reasonably reliable methods exist to provide adequate data and sound projections. Look for more about these methods as we move through this chapter.

Excuse #3. "We wanted to do this work but lacked the skills, knowledge, and people needed." This is a more serious problem, but it is not a surprising one. There are some very specialized techniques for the analysis phases of a new product project, and they are not in everyone's knowledge base.

If your company lacks people with the skill sets required for the early phases of a project—people who know how to analyze markets, identify business opportunities, and build good business cases—then read on. We cannot magically cure your human resource deficiencies, but we can suggest activities in the homework phases that seem to work best; and we can give you some pointers on how to complete them. Armed with these insights, you can start to fill the void.

Types of Information Required

Four main types of project information are required for effective portfolio management:

1. Marketing, Revenue, and Pricing

Market, revenue, and pricing information are central to new product success, and they are vital to project selection decisions:

- market size
- market trends, growth, and potential (or market forecasts)
- expected market share and penetration
- pricing and expected revenue
- competitive analysis, including competitors' market shares and pricing
- marketing (advertising, selling) and distribution costs.

2. Manufacturing or Operations and Related Costs

Financial models all require estimates of project profitability—year 1, year 2, year 3, etc. Manufacturing or operations costs are important inputs to these calculations, along with expected sales and pricing. Relevant data include:

- manufacturing, operating, or delivered costs
- equipment and capital costs.

3. Estimating Probabilities of Success

Success probabilities figure prominently in many of the portfolio models. Generally, these are some combinations of technical success (can we do it?) and commercial success (can we win?). Among probabilities required for a typical portfolio model are:

- probability of technical success
- probability of commercial success.

4. Estimating Resource Requirements

Finally, resources required per project is a key input to many portfolio models. They are the basis for many of the costs factored into the financial and related models. But project resources also play an important role in other ways. For example, sizes of bubbles in bubble diagrams and the denominators in many of the portfolio value maximization methods (such as bang for buck) are based on resource requirements per project. Relevant resources can include:

- development resources
- testing resources
- upfront homework resources
- commercialization resources.

Each of the above can be expressed in terms of:

- elapsed or calendar time (months)
- person days, and
- dollars.

Obtaining totally accurate data for a typical project on all the items above may be next to impossible. The problem is made worse by the fact that project selection decisions must be made *fairly early in the life of a project*—precisely when the least is known about the project! But there are ways to increase the reliability of your estimates, and before the development stage begins. We discuss some of these methods in the sections that follow.

Marketing, Revenue, and Pricing Data

More new products fail because of a lack of market information than from any other single cause.[3] Not only does this deficiency lead to poor product decisions—for example the design specifications, positioning, or pricing is wrong—it also leads to difficulties in selecting the right projects.

Upfront homework before the project proceeds into the development stage is critical to success. Management must recognize the importance of the upfront steps and be prepared to devote the necessary resources—people, time, and money—to ensure they are done well. Many companies build two homework phases into their Stage-Gate™ new product processes (Exhibit 8.1): the Scoping stage and the Business Case stage (Stages 1 and 2).

Gathering Market Information for Stage 1

Scoping, the first homework stage, is a short and low-cost preliminary assessment of the market. The effort here is much like detective work and clearly does not involve primary research, either marketing or technical. In this first homework stage, data are collected through such techniques as desk research, examination of secondary sources, contact with selected potential users, and canvassing of outside sources. Stage 1 usually takes one calendar month or less and amounts to 5–20 person-days of work; but it is surprising how much information about a product's market prospects can be gleaned in this short period of solid sleuthing.

The object in Stage 1 is to do a "quick and dirty" assessment to:

- assess market attractiveness and potential
- gauge possible product acceptance
- size up the competitive situation
- conceptualize the product (help shape the idea into a tentative product design).

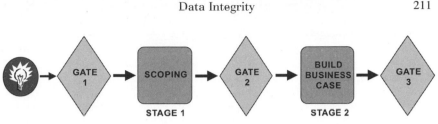

EXHIBIT 8.1   The Front End of the Process

Here are some sources of market information that can provide reliable data and be accessed relatively inexpensively for Stage 1:

- *Internet research:* There is a wealth of information out there, and much of it is available via the Internet. But you need someone who knows how to do an Internet-based market analysis. This person can hunt through trade magazines, journals, reports, and other on-line items with information on your market, the product type, and your competitors. For example, develop a customized search engine to seek out and filter information on your competitors.
- *The company library:* Corporate librarians can be worth their weight in gold in conducting preliminary market assessments. Often an experienced reference librarian will be able to track down impossible-to-find data or at least point you in the right direction.
- *Internal reports:* In larger firms, there are often numerous reports and surveys undertaken annually. Often the information you need is buried somewhere in one of these many studies, such as a customer satisfaction survey. So start with your own library or market research department.
- *Key customers:* Stage 1 is premature for detailed customer surveys and interviews. But face-to-face discussions with a reasonable number of key, trusted customers can prove very useful at this early stage. These can even be unstructured and exploratory interviews. For business-to-business markets, try to pick trusted yet representative or leading users. If budgets are tight and time is pressing, telephone interviews are acceptable.
- *Focus groups:* In spite of their limitations, focus groups remain a cost-effective and relatively quick way to gain insights into customer needs, wants, and preferences and reactions to your proposed new product concept. A handful of customers, either consumers or industrial users, will suffice. To keep the cost per project or concept low, try running several related concepts or projects at a time through the focus group.
- *Competitors' promotional material:* Study your competitors' advertisements, press releases, and trade literature. Find out what they are saying about the features and performance characteristics of their products. Note how your competitors are positioning their products.
- *Your sales force:* Interview your own sales force and service representatives. These people are your front-line troops—the eyes and ears of the company. Often they can provide you with superb information on customer habits, likes, dislikes, and product preferences. They can also provide insights into the order-winning criteria, on the competitive situation, and on pricing practices.

- *Consulting and research firms:* Some consulting and research firms publish multi-client or standardized reports that provide an overview of an industry. While not specific to your new product, these reports or studies can provide cost-effective information on market size, trends, competition, and other details.
- *Financial houses:* The research arms of many brokerage houses conduct industry and market analysis. Many also keep up-to-date files or can provide overviews of companies listed on the stock exchanges. Annual reports can be helpful, as are the 10K reports publicly listed firms must submit to the stock exchange.
- *Government agencies:* Governments collect all kinds of data. Finding it can be a problem, but don't give up before you begin. Often a phone call to a state, provincial, or federal government office will identify a department or division that just happens to have the report or the statistics that you are looking for.
- *Industry experts:* You can hire an industry expert for a day or two and pick his or her brain. Although the per diem may be high, the knowledge gained may save you weeks of work.
- *Editors:* Editors of trade magazines are not the normal source of market information, but on occasion they have proven very useful in tracking down reports, studies, and even informed people. A good editor usually has a good breadth of knowledge about what is going on in an industry.
- *Trade associations:* Some industries have trade associations that provide excellent market data. They can also provide advice about where to go for the other information.

When undertaking your preliminary market assessment, do not neglect the international dimension. Gather market information for multiple international markets, not just your domestic one. And engage international business units too. For example, Guinness, the brewer, builds an international alert into Stage 1 of its *Navigate* new product process. Through the alert, brand managers around the world are asked whether they are interested in participating in a given project, and if so, to provide market information from their respective countries.

Gathering Market Information for Stage 2

Building the business case (Stage 2 in Exhibit 8.1) is perhaps the most difficult and certainly the most expensive of the predevelopment steps; moreover, this is the *critical homework* stage—the one that makes or breaks the project. Coincidentally, this is the stage that is so often handled poorly. Actions for this stage are summarized in Exhibit 8.2.

Estimating Current Market Size. Market size estimates are important inputs to financial analysis. In the case of existing markets, one usually begins with the size of the current market. On occasion, market size data are published or readily available. But often the task of arriving at the size of the current market—either dollars or units—requires some digging:

- *Revisit the sources in Stage 1:* Stage 1 provided a cursory review of a variety of fruitful market data sources. But this time, drill down more deeply to get the information you need, spending much more time and effort on or at each source.

User needs-and-wants study	Voice of customer research to determine product requirements; face-to-face interviews (or camping out) — in-depth market research. Determines what is value and what is a customer benefit; seeks to define a winning product concept from customers perspective. Probes customer needs, wants and preferences, choice criteria, likes, dislikes and trade-offs regarding product requirements and design; also the customers use system and products value-in-use (economics); seeks insights into competitive product strengths and weaknesses.
Competitive analysis	A detailed look at the competition — both direct and indirect. Determines who they are, product strengths and weaknesses, anticipated future products, pricing, competitors other strengths and weaknesses, how they compete and their performance.
Market analysis	Pulls together all market information from the two studies above plus secondary sources. Determines market size, trends, segmentation and size, buyer behavior and competitive situation. Also relies on similar sources as in Stage 1, only much more in-depth.
Detailed technical assessment	Translates these market inputs into a technically feasible product design or concept (on paper). May involve some physical technical work (modeling or lab work) and also techniques such as Quality Function Deployment (QFD). Maps out the technical solution and technical route; highlights technical risks and solutions; reviews intellectual property issues and develops IP strategy; assesses possible technical partners and develops partnering strategy. Also looks in depth at manufacturability and source of supply: production route, costs and capital (equipment) requirements.
Concept testing	The final market test prior to full commitment to develop the product. Tests the proposed product concept with the customer (product concept, model, virtual prototype). Involves face-to-face interviews; gauges interest, liking, preference, purchase intent and price sensitivity.
Financial/business analysis	Looks at the business rationale for the project. Includes strategic assessment (fit and impact). Also a core competencies assessment and partnering (or out-sourcing) strategy is mapped out, along with the role of international units. Finally a detailed financial analysis is developed: NPV, EBIT, ECV, IRR and sensitivity analysis.
Plans of Action	Develops recommendation for project (Go/Kill) and a detailed Action Plan for Stage 3 (Development Plan), including resource requirements; also tentative plans for Stage 4, Testing, and Stage 5 (both preliminary Marketing and Operations Plans). A launch date is specified.

EXHIBIT 8.2   Summary of Stage 2 Actions: Building the Business Case

SOURCE: Adapted from R.G. Cooper, *Winning at New Products: Accelerating the Process from Idea to Launch,* 3d ed. (Cambridge, MA: Perseus Books, 2001), p. 185.

- Access published industry data—especially for consumer goods (e.g., Nielsen's) and pharmaceutical categories
- Undertake Internet research—search trade publications, look for reports, etc.
- Visit your the company library and describe your information quest to your reference librarian (or at your local business school library)
- Review internal company reports
- Call friendly customers

- Run focus groups—ask how much they buy and gauge their response to your proposed offering
- Secure and review competitors' promotional material
- Conduct internal interviews—your sales force and technical service people
- Buy reports from consulting and research firms
- Use reports on companies and markets prepared by financial and brokerage houses
- Contact government agencies serving this industry
- Hire an industry expert, especially in markets totally new to you
- Contact trade publication editors
- Get data from industry trade associations.

- *Extrapolate survey results*: Survey customers who use the type of product or service you plan to develop and determine how much they purchase each year. If obtained reliably, these results can be extrapolated to the general population to give you a better-than-guess estimate of your market's size.

Example: A major truck manufacturer was interested in developing a new truck body for fire trucks. To find out how large the fire truck market was, the company selected a representative sample of large and small city governments. Some of the questions asked were, Did you buy any new fire trucks in the last twelve months? how many? what size? How large is your fleet of fire trucks? Do you expect to purchase any trucks in the next year? And so on. Population data for each city was also sought in the survey. As one might expect, there was a fairly close link between city population and the number of trucks purchased or planned. This data was plotted on curves that enabled the manufacturer to predict the number of trucks a city of any size could be expected to purchase. Using existing data on the number of cities and towns in each size category across the country, researchers were able to estimate the past year's market, the next year's market, and the total number of fire trucks in the United States. This survey was a lot of work, but the data permitted the determination of market size and expected sales, and hence it was an important input to the prioritization of this project.

- *Aggregate data from the sales force (business to business):* Your sales force is your direct contact with the marketplace. Be sure to use them in product development, not only to identify product requirements and desired features, but also to make estimates of current market size. Ask each salesperson to make the following estimates for each of the accounts or clients in the target market for the new product:

  - How much are they buying currently—annual dollars or units?
  - Roughly what percentage of the market does this client represent?

  Often the salesperson with a solid relationship can engage in direct questioning of people in the buying firm to obtain fairly accurate estimates of these numbers. With these data in hand from each client in the target market, one can make a number of estimates and simply average the results to estimate market size.
- *Aggregate data from your competitive analysis:* Competitive analysis methods are outlined later in this chapter. Among other data, information from competitive

analysis often provides estimates of each competitor's sales and market share. For each competitor using these two estimates—sales and market share—an estimate of market size is computed. Done across many competitors, the calculation yields multiple estimates of market size. The probable market size is then determined by averaging these multiple estimates. Also, by adding the sales estimates for all competitors (and knowing their combined market shares), yet another calculation of market size is made.

- *Hire a research or information search firm:* Some firms are in the business of doing customized research.

Forecasting Future Market Size.

Forecasting expected market size is more difficult than coming up with an estimate of the current market size, because the future is always uncertain. Still, there are several ways to enhance the reliability of your forecast:

- *Purchased reports*: Many research houses and consulting firms sell industry reports in which analysts study the market, assess trends, and often employ sophisticated techniques to arrive at reliable market forecasts. For example, forecasts of various computer disk drive markets made by *Disk/Trend* have been almost dead on for existing markets and product types.[4]
- *Trend analysis*: For existing markets, it is often possible to acquire historical data on market size. Plotting these values versus time often reveals predictable long-term trends, which can be used as forecasting models.[5] There are different types of trend analysis or time-series techniques. The most common one is simple: fitting a line (straight or curved) to historical sales data. However, this line can be skewed by such things as cyclical or seasonal trends within the period, or by random events. Statistical methods such as moving averages, exponential smoothing, and auto-regressive time-series analysis can be used to remove these biases.*
- *Market size versus market drivers:* Instead of plotting market size against time, size is related to various market drivers using statistical techniques, such as multiple regression analysis. For example, a truck manufacturer attempted to develop a model to forecast the market for heavy-duty diesel trucks. Sales of new trucks depend on shipments of goods as well as on operators' abilities to pay. Ability to pay is partly determined by interest rates, especially in the case of large capital goods, such as heavy trucks, which are usually financed. Historical data coupled with statistical analysis (multiple regression) is used to the generate the coefficients (A, B, and C) in the equation below, thus yielding a market forecasting model:

Truck Market = A x (Manufacturing Output) + B x (Interest Rate) + C

More sophisticated regression models, along with the inclusion of additional market drivers, lead to a fairly accurate forecasting model for the diesel truck market. One challenge in using this type of analysis is to make sure that the market drivers you select are reasonably independent of each other.

---

* The Box-Jenkins technique can be used to refine forecasting approaches. A well-known approach for time-series analysis is the ARIMA model (autoregressive integrated moving average). For further details see Czinkota, Kotabe, and Mercer, *Marketing Management*, 181–87; and Bingham and Raffield, *Business to Business Marketing Management*, 223–25.

- *Scenario generation:*[6] This helps companies envision possible futures they otherwise might not have considered, and it helps them become alert to signals that foreshadow major changes in the marketplace.

Example: One of the most significant strategic decisions in recent decades was AT&T's decline on a free offer to take control of the Internet.[7] In the late 1980s, the U.S. National Science Foundation wanted to withdraw from administering the Internet and offered AT&T a free monopoly position. But AT&T envisioned a future in which their centrally switched technology would remain dominant. Technical experts at AT&T concluded that a packet-switched technology (which the Internet uses) would never work. These experts decided that the Internet was insignificant for telephony and had no commercial significance in any other context. The intervening years have proven the magnitude of that misjudgment.

Instead of risking a major forecasting mistake, AT&T could have generated alternate scenarios of the future. This technique includes developing a scenario of the expected future—in AT&T's case, a future in which centrally switched architecture remains dominant. But it also includes developing other scenarios as well. In this example, it would include a potential future in which new markets for Internet services and new kinds of telephony challenge the dominant AT&T architecture. At a minimum, this type of scenario generation would have given decision makers at AT&T a sense of the Internet's potential, and it might have led them to consider alternate courses of action.

Scenario generation appears to be an ideal strategic planning tool for emerging technologies in emerging markets.[8] AT&T executives, by defining another scenario, might have taken an option on the Internet in the 1980s; and then they might have been more alert when an increasing number of customers began to use the web, when web pages began to mushroom, and when PC sales to home users grew by leaps and bounds in the early 1990s.

Developing alternate scenarios takes time, involves senior people, and may employ PC-based simulations. Since your purpose is to identify new product opportunities, restrict discussion to scenarios that are relevant to the business and deal with the external (or extended market) environment. Typical questions to start discussion include:

- What is the best future scenario? Try to describe in as much detail as possible what the company's world will look like, given the best-case external environment assumptions.
- What is the worst future scenario?
- What are some relevant dimensions that characterize these scenarios? (For example, in AT&T's case, a relevant dimension was centralized versus decentralized switching.)

- Take each scenario in turn and imagine it is true. It is now possible to identify new product opportunities. Among questions to be answered at this point are, Should a new business or new product be launched? Should the company be investing in a new technology or technology platform? What types of new products should get serious consideration? Scenarios are utilized by imagining that one or another will be true, and assessing the consequences of making each decision, assuming each alternate future. Then probabilities that the various scenarios might occur are calculated.

Finally, markers or signals that either scenario may be occurring should be identified. This will give managers the tools to spot telltale signs through the next business period. For example, one banking scenario is that there will be no bank branches in the future—that bricks and mortar will be history. Telltale signals in the next decade may be the number of new e-banks launched, the proportion of users in various age groups moving to e-banking, the amount of customer traffic at bank branches, and the development of new Internet devices that can handle financial transactions. If momentum picks up in these areas, expect total branchless banking around the corner.

- *Modified Delphi method:* The Delphi method has been introduced in chapters 2 and 3. It is designed to assemble the collective wisdom of knowledgeable people into a well-informed conclusion (in the following example, a forecast of market size and trends). The method is subjective, but it has proven over the years to be an effective way of capturing both qualitative and quantitative views from groups of experts.

Example: A major aircraft engine manufacturer was trying to estimate the future market for a certain size of airframe targeted at commuter flights within North America. By estimating the airframe market, the engine market for a newly envisioned engine could also be forecast. A sophisticated computer model of the commuter airline network had been constructed, and simulations had yielded quantitative forecasts of future airline commuter traffic and hence aircraft sales.

Not satisfied with the computer-generated forecast, the marketing person on the engine project decided to obtain a second data point by using a modified Delphi method. He assembled some aircraft industry experts from both inside and outside the firm. The initial dialogue focused on the future of the commuter aircraft market—trends, direction, growth, and so on. The group was then asked for their estimates of commuter traffic—volume and routes. The forecast based on this method was considerably different and much more aggressive than the computer-generated forecast. The project team leaned toward the Delphi results and went with the higher forecast. Based on these sales projections, the project was approved, and the PT-6 turboprop engine went on to become a mainstay engine for United Technologies, powering many of the commuter aircraft used worldwide.

- Unlike the modified Delphi method just described, the true Delphi method does not require assembling experts together as a group at one location. Rather, 20–30 carefully selected experts are identified, and then are individually questioned (e.g., by e-mail). After this first round, each expert is provided with anonymous feedback information from the others in the group. These rounds of questions and feedback continue until there is a convergence of the total group's opinion. All the experts have access to the same information on which to base their opinions. This approach reduces the risk that biases might creep in due to such factors as specious persuasion, unwillingness to abandon publicly expressed opinions, and the bandwagon effect.[9]

Forecasting Markets for Disruptive Technologies

Disruptive technologies present difficult challenges for market forecasting.[10] The one thing that is certain in forecasting the size of these markets is: The forecast will be wrong, and often by orders of magnitude.

What is a disruptive technology? Most new technologies result in improved performance, which can come from incremental innovations or from those that are more radical in character. Most technological advances in industry are sustaining, but: "Occasionally disruptive technologies emerge: innovations that result in worse performance, at least in the near term."[11] These innovations may be inferior to the existing technology when measured on traditional performance metrics, but they bring a new performance dimension or a new value proposition to the market. For example, the first digital cameras actually produced a poorer picture (lower resolution) than traditional film cameras and were considered inferior products by most camera users. But for a handful of users—most notably those who wanted the picture in digital format so that they could modify or electronically transmit the photo—there was new value in the digital camera.

And so how does one estimate market size and potential in the case of a totally new market and a disruptive technology? There is no easy solution, but in addition to the sources and ways outlined above, here are some ways we have seen companies try to develop better quantitative estimates of totally new, emerging, or disruptive technology markets:

- *Do field work*: Send the entire project team into the field for face-to-face discussions with potential users. Let team members learn first-hand about the various potential applications of the product or new technology and users' potential for adoption. The better the entire project team understands potential applications, market segments, and exactly what features and performance each user seeks, the better the team can converge on the target market and make estimates of market size and growth.
- *Look beyond the mainstream:* Be aware that in the case of disruptive technologies, the initial application is not likely to be the mainstream market.[12] It pays to focus on market niches or applications that are often outside the mainstream, where the new product's particular strengths are appreciated (and its weaknesses can be tolerated).
- *Examine parallel markets:* There are very few totally new markets in the world. Usually there is something to benchmark. Even in the case of dramatic breakthroughs, such as the first jet engine or the introduction of xerographic copying, there was an "existing market." Potential users were "solving their problem" in some other way, albeit unsatisfactorily. In offices, people used carbon paper, Gestetner machines, and Kodak's wet photographic process for making copies. The military, the first target users of jet engines, was using piston engines at the time. The trick is to identify the handful of potential customers who stand to benefit the most from the new solution and to determine what proportion will convert to the new solution.
- *Make your assumptions clear:* As you develop market and sales estimates, be sure to state clearly the various assumptions you made along the way. When the project is reviewed by senior management or is compared to other projects, the underlying

assumptions that went into the market and sales estimates will then be known, and managers will be able to challenge them or test their criticality.

- *Apply sensitivity analysis*: Having identified your assumptions, test the impact of each assumption on the financial prospects of the project. For example, suppose you assume that users will adopt the new technology quickly. Test how critical this assumption is. That is, repeat the market size estimation and financial analysis, but this time assuming a slower rate of adoption. If the results of both analyses are positive, then you can declare that the adoption rate is not a critical assumption—that the project looks good under both sets of assumptions. (See more on sensitivity analysis later in this chapter.)
- *Try various scenarios:* Create various views of the future, much as in the scenario generation exercise described earlier. You might label the scenarios "best case" and "worst case"; or "fast adoption" and "slow adoption." Create quite a few scenarios, and for each one consider the decisions you would make if that scenario came true. For example, under the worst case scenario, would you still proceed with the project?
- *Apply untraditional project evaluation:* Perhaps the most important recommendation is to evaluate new market or disruptive technology projects differently from traditional or sustaining new product projects. Recall from Chapter 5 the Strategic Buckets Model—how resources are strategically allocated to buckets, and how different criteria for prioritizing projects should be applied to projects in the different buckets. The case of disruptive technologies is a good example of where strategic buckets and different criteria indeed apply. Exhibit 5.12 showed three buckets used at GE-AlliedSignal-Honeywell. One bucket had resources reserved for platform projects—projects that will change the basis of competition. Disruptive technology projects probably fit into this bucket. And the criteria for such projects are indeed different from criteria applied to normal new product projects.

We recommend applying the following evaluation criteria to disruptive technology and new market projects, because we have seen them work:

- *Strategic alignment and impact:* Determine whether the project fits the business strategy and the impact it will have on the business if it is successful.
- *Reward:* Use some measure of reward, including magnitude (the size of the prize) and timing—how long before investment is recovered. (In some firms, quantitative estimates are replaced with qualitative assessments, such as "modest" through to "very large".)
- *Strategic leverage:* Determine whether the project will spawn a number of new products (and be a platform for growth) and identify the competitive advantage to be gained—magnitude, longevity, and sustainability.
- *Probability of commercial success:* Determine the existence of an identified market need or market application and key commercialization resources within the business.
- *Probability of technical success:* Examine the size of the technical gap, project complexity, and existence of technological skill base within the corporation.

These are very similar criteria to those used by Celanese for its advanced technology programs. Note that financial projections and estimates of market size and share are not critical to this scoring model. There is a good reason for this: Since market size and profit estimates are likely to be very much in error, we recommend using other criteria to select these special projects.

Estimating Market Penetration and Making Sales Forecasts

Making precise estimates of a new product's expected market penetration, or its expected sales, is difficult. After all, one is dealing with the future and uncertain events. Further, the first estimates of market acceptance must be made before the product has even been developed! One rule we have, however, is that when dealing with unreliable measures, such as expected sales or market share, several attempts at pinning the number down are better than one. By using a variety of techniques, we triangulate on the final estimate. The multiple methods include:

- Undertake concept testing early in the project
- Include the sales force in your forecasts
- Analyze the competition
- Try a modified Delphi method.

Undertake Concept Testing.   Concept tests attempt to measure expected sales or probable market share before development begins by presenting a representation of the product to a prospective customer and then measuring interest, liking, and purchase intent. A "product representation" can be anything from a virtual product to a model or crude prototype, which means that concept testing can begin in Stage 2 in the Stage-Gate™ model of Exhibit 8.1. Properly undertaken, this is a particularly effective method for gauging expected sales, especially for product types that are familiar to the customer.

There are several keys to making a concept test work well:

- *Be clear:* The concept presented must be realistic and understandable. Try to get it as close to the final product as possible, without actually developing the product. Use models, CAD drawings on your laptop, PowerPoint presentations, and even virtual products to display the concept to the user.
- *Pick the right people*: In the case of a consumer product, selecting and interviewing prospects from the target segment is usually not a problem. But for industrial goods, where there may be a number of people within one firm influencing the buying decision, great care must be taken to cast the net broadly. All too often we see a concept presented to one person in a buying firm. The problem is that person does not speak for the entire company, so the result—yea or nay—is invalid.
- *Be structured:* To collect customer responses, use a structured research design, complete with a questionnaire, perhaps one that can be completed on the interviewer's laptop computer. But make sure that the customer indicates responses by pointing to the screen or by filling in a scorecard. A sample concept-testing questionnaire is shown in Exhibit 8.3.
- *Be cautious with the test results:* Use the results of a concept test with caution. They merely provide an indication of likely product acceptance. There are no guarantees. Nor should the results be used blindly. For most new products, particularly in categories familiar to the customer, concept tests are likely to overstate the market acceptance.[13] For example, a result of "30 percent of respondents definitely would buy" is not likely to translate into a market share of 30 percent for a number of reasons: an overly enthusiastic presentation, the natural tendency of people to say

1a. What is your **level of interest** in the proposed new product? You can answer using this five-point scale (show him/her the scale; let them indicate their response with a pencil or pointer):				
Not interested at all	Not too interested	Somewhat interested	Quite interested	Very interested
1b. Why so interested (or not interested?):				

2a. To what extent **do you like** the proposed product? Again, please answer on this five-point scale:				
Don't like at all	Don't like very much	Like somewhat	Like a lot	Like very much
2b. What things do you like most about the product?				
i.				
ii.				
iii.				
2c. What things do you like the least about it?				
i.				
ii.				
iii.				

3a. Compared to product X, which you are (now buying/familiar with), **how would you rate** the proposed new product?				
Much worse than	Somewhat worse	About the same	Somewhat better	Much better than

3b. What's better? What's worse?

Better	Worse

3. How much **would you expect to pay** for (new product). You can answer in dollars, or give a price relative to a product you are familiar with:

5a. Assuming that the new product was available at a price of $ _____ (or relative to another product), what is the likelihood that **you would buy it**?				
Definitely would not	Probably would not	Maybe	Probably would	Definitely would
5b. Why or why not?				

6. (If answers are negative): What would you like to see different or improved about the proposed new product?

EXHIBIT 8.3   Standard Concept Test Questionnaire

"yes," the fact that your launch effort may not reach the entire market, split purchasing behavior, and so on. So be sure to factor back considerably the "intent to purchase" figure you obtain from a concept test.

Testing a product that does not yet exist is tricky, but there are a number of good approaches.[14] Simple concept descriptions—written descriptions and some drawings or sketches—are a low-cost approach and best used when doing concept testing to reduce large numbers of new product ideas to those more promising (or for relatively simple product extensions) before any technical activities are carried out.[15] Technology makes it increasingly possible to test products that seem very much like the real thing but cost comparatively little to produce.

Online concept testing has become accepted in the last few years.[16] Visual depiction and animation (virtual prototyping) have proven comparable to concept tests with physical prototypes. Because virtual tests are less expensive than physical prototypes, more concepts can be developed and tested.[17] On-line concept testing permits access to a large number of possible customers otherwise difficult to access. An emerging feature of on-line testing is that respondents seem more outspoken and honest with their answers.[18] Speed and economy make this approach a powerful tool.

Here are some examples of effective methods for concept tests: A major UK firm, which produces air filtration equipment, has a "virtual prototyping" department. One of their tasks is to develop virtual products using CAD and other techniques. These product concepts are then presented to customers on a laptop computer as rotating three-dimensional images.

Fluke, a well known instrument company, used dummy brochure and dummy spec sheets to test a new line of calibration instruments. As one member of the project team said, "We developed the brochure, printed it on our color printer, and showed it to dozens of prospective users (instrument engineers) along with a dummy spec sheet and a presentation. Developing a dummy brochure is a lot cheaper than developing the full product!" By the end of the presentation, the instrument engineers had an accurate idea of the product. As a result, they were able to answer interest and purchase intent questions intelligently.

National Semiconductor has its entire product database on its website. By tracing customer searches, the company can identify performance metrics of particular importance. This information can then be used to develop new products.[19]

Conjoint analysis is becoming a commonly used tool in concept testing. Originally, this method was used for packaged consumer goods and more recently for industrial goods and services[20] to identify optimal product profiles (including price). This method has recently proven very useful for the following situations: where new products and services are relatively complex; where the final design features are not certain (including price/demand relationships); where substantial consumer learning may be involved; and where the item may involve high costs of being wrong for either the seller or the buyer.

Include the Sales Force in Your Sales Forecast. Salespeople should have extensive knowledge of their existing customers or clients, as well as of the industry and the competition. This knowledge can be complete, sensitive, and current.[21]

Salespeople can be asked to provide sales forecasts by customer for the new product or product type. The inevitable uncertainty in these figures can be reduced by asking for a single "best guess" figure plus an estimated range. Salespeople can also be asked to estimate the probability of each potential sale. Pooling of data may help to overcome individual biases.[22] The sales forecast then becomes the sum of all the potential responses, each weighted by the probability of occurring.

Even though a company's sales force possesses valuable information about existing and potential markets, there can be a number of problems associated with trying to access this wealth of knowledge: Salespeople often lack relevant information about customer companies' plans and overall industry trends; they may be overly optimistic or pessimistic in their forecasts; and salespeople may not see sales forecasting as part of their paid duties.

Try a Modified Delphi Method.   This approach is highlighted number of times in this chapter because of its flexibility and effectiveness. The modified Delphi method involves bringing a number of people together who are considered "experts." Through successive rounds of discussion and writing down of opinions, these experts come to a consensus on a particular issue. In this case, you may want to bring together people from a number of functions in your company who are able to make knowledgeable guesses about your new product's expected market penetration or to make sales forecasts. These "experts" might be from sales, marketing, manufacturing, and R&D, for example. Note that the aircraft engine example cited earlier resulted in an industry or market forecast for engines, not a sales forecast for that company's specific new product; but the approach is much the same.

Analyze the Competition.   Competitive analysis is important during the homework phases for making sales estimates (in Stages 1 and 2 of the Stage-Gate™ process, Exhibit 8.1) for four reasons:

1. Such analysis defines the unique benefits and relative advantage of your new product—its strengths and weaknesses versus competitors' products (including price); thus, your product or competitive advantage. This helps you assess whether you will likely fare better or worse—your probable relative market share—than the other players in the market.
2. Competitive analysis provides estimates of market shares of competitor's products. From these shares, along with a strengths/weaknesses and relative advantage assessment versus each competitor (above), you can often arrive at a ballpark estimate (or at least a range of estimates) of your probable market share.
3. Competitive analysis provides an assessment of competitors' possible reactions to your new product. These reactions may include aggressive defensive moves and even price cuts. The issues of "will they defend" and "how aggressively" must be factored into your sales estimates.
4. Finally, competitive analysis reveals competitors' sales and market shares so that it permits estimating market size (method described earlier), the starting point for estimating your new product's sales.

The most important sources of competitor analysis information in top-performing companies, according to an 85-firm study based on *Business Week's* "America's 1000 Most Valuable Companies," include (in this order)[23]:

* the company's own sales force
* customers

- competitors' annual reports
- business magazines
- professionally prepared reports
- 10 K reports
- distributors and dealers
- trade shows
- government publications.

In addition to relying on marketing and R&D, successful firms also involve their manufacturing people in competitive analysis, beginning as early as the pre-development activities.[24] Cross-functional competitive analysis leads to the examination of competitive aspects that can easily be overlooked in a single-department perspective.

An important facet of competitive analysis is defining who the competitors are. For any new product, three general classes of competitors can be identified:

- industry members, both domestic and international
- manufacturers of (potential) substitute products
- firms possessing emerging new technologies, which might pose a competitive threat.

The same study cited above (based on the *Business Week* listing) revealed commonly used methods that leading firms use to identify possible competitors. These methods include:

- internal brainstorming
- consideration set elicitation: Simply ask your customers and noncustomers whom they would consider as suppliers for this product type
- product deletion: Ask your customers to identify suppliers sequentially after their favorite products or suppliers would no longer be available
- substitution-in-use analysis: a two-step approach using two groups, perhaps experts in your company:

  a. the first group identifies situations in which the customer would use the product
  b. a new second group is presented with the situation and asked to identify products they would use

- international and market expansion assessment: Look abroad and see if there are new competitors in other countries
- assessment of new product expansion into your markets—recent product introductions
- an analysis of the industry structure—vertical integration by others
- assessment of alliance partners and their strategies—the threat that they will become competitors.

Not all direct and possible competitors require the same level of analysis, but in the long run, all should be assessed.[25] The difficulty of assessment is likely to increase with distant or potential competitors, but these are precisely the firms that may represent the greatest long-term threat.

> **POINTS FOR MANAGEMENT TO PONDER**
> How do your project teams go about estimating the current market size, forecasting the future market size, and determining expected sales revenue for their new product? Do they use a rigorous approach, such as one or more of the approaches suggested above? Or are the estimates typically a "best guess" and pulled out of thin air? If the latter, review the many approaches offered above to make better estimates of market size and revenues. Note that these approaches do work, certainly better than pure guesses. They require some effort and cost, but the cost is never prohibitive, and the impacts of this better information are so great—improved allocation of your R&D and marketing development resources. A final thought: recognize that none of the above methods promises total accuracy, so your teams might want to adopt several approaches and zero in on a composite estimate. When in doubt, multiple data points are better than single-point estimates!

Setting the Price

Pricing is vital to the homework stages. Without price estimates, no financial forecasts are possible. However, there are many challenges associated with setting prices for products that are yet to be developed. The customer's perceived value of the new product is elusive at this early stage, particularly for entirely new products or disruptive technologies. Typical questions faced include the following: Will the market perceive the value of the new product in the price? And what is the "value" of your new product for the customer? Pricing is further complicated in industries moving at Internet speed,[26] and by immediate market reaction to the product's introduction (e.g., a competitor reacts by introducing a similar product at a lower price).

Perceived Value to the Customer.   For products that are new to the company but not new to the market, the price band or range is dictated by the competitive situation. Indeed, if a new product is a copy of an established competitor, a lower price may be the only advantage it has. Still, low price alone does not guarantee success.[27] Other real product advantages have a much stronger impact.

At the heart of the price-setting process is the concept of perceived value to the customer. To define value, start by identifying the new product's competitive advantages and disadvantages. Quality functional deployment (QFD) modeling that became popular in the 1990s is an example of this approach. The procedure goes as follows:

- List all product and service attributes or characteristics that are relevant to the target segment's buying decisions
- Have potential customers rate the importance of these attributes
- Have customers evaluate how they perceive the performance of existing products on these same attributes.

Data collected this way can be used to calculate relative performance by comparing the new product's performance attribute by attribute versus the performance of its strongest competitor.

Value-in-Use Pricing (VIU).   Value-in-use is a logical extension of perceived value. VIU is defined as a product's economic value to the user relative to specific alternatives. It constitutes the price that would equalize the overall costs and benefits of using the new product rather than an alternative.

Example: A new type of sealing ring extends the time between changes from three months to six months. The cost to replace the existing sealing ring is $12.00 every three months. Assuming everything else stays constant (e.g., the labor to change the new ring is the same as for the old one), the new product's price can approach $24.00. Use of the new product results in identifiable economic savings over existing products and justifies a higher price.

To use value-in-use pricing correctly, you must understand the potential costs and benefits to the customer—the product's economics from the customer's point of view. Note that your costs of production are not relevant to product value or to VIU pricing. Where your production costs are important, however, is in determining whether you can operate profitably in this market and hence to the decision to move ahead with the project (see the section on "Manufacturing and Related Costs" later in this chapter).

Lifetime Cost or Value.   In complex products, buyers are often more interested in the total value or lifetime cost of the product or service than they are in the initial price. For example, customers focus more on how long the product lasts, availability of spare parts, length of the warranty, timeliness of delivery, and other operational or financial benefits. Customers also incur costs beyond the purchase price of the product. These costs may include order handling, freight, installation, and training. Then there are other "costs" such as the cost of late delivery, the potential for modification, or potential product failure (the product does not function as expected). For really new-to-the-world products, there may also be apprehension about the impact of the new product on existing ways of doing business and costs related to this impact.

Outside-In Versus Inside-Out Pricing.   Modern price setting for the majority of new products begins with the marketplace (as opposed to beginning with your production costs). *Outside-in* pricing (or market-based pricing) means determining the price on what customers are willing to pay rather than the *inside-out* approach (basing it on the cost of production, such as cost-plus-margin pricing).

Note that market-based pricing, such as VIU, is not as easy as it looks. It requires a much greater market understanding and insights about what customers want and what they see as having value. Thus, product functionality and quality must be defined early in the homework stages.[28] By contrast, when new product development is driven by technical considerations, features may be built in with little regard to whether they create real value in the eyes of the customer. And a cost-plus-margin approach may then be used to set the final selling price, very often as the product is getting ready to be launched.[29] Clearly this inside-out approach is not a formula for success in most cases.

The *outside-in* approach prices new products not according to what is technologically possible, but according to what the market wants and the price it will accept. The price customers are willing to pay for a product that fulfills their requirements is identified first.[30] With this information, a target cost can be determined. While this target cost can dictate the number of attributes, features, functionality, or performance offered to the consumer (i.e., some product features may have to be dropped), the goal here is to optimize the difference between value and target cost.

The earlier in the new product development process that specific targets are defined, the better—both for costs and product requirements and features—because modifications are easier and less expensive in the early stages. Best-practice businesses try to pin down their product definition—requirements and price point—before the Development stage, or by Gate 3 in the model in Exhibit 8.1. For example, these companies claim that up to 70 percent of target costs should be fixed at the concept stage. Others indicate that for some new products they are

---

POINTS FOR MANAGEMENT TO PONDER

How does your business go about determining the price for a new product? Is it done rigorously and based on solid market information and research? And when is it done—early in the project, prior to development? or much later? If the answers to these questions make you feel uneasy, then perhaps your new product-pricing practices leave a bit to be desired, which likely means that you're also leaving money on the table!

The marketplace ultimately determines your new product's price, so you should be focusing on *outside-in* pricing approaches. This means acquiring a much greater understanding of users' needs and wants, what they see as having "value," and what they perceive to be a real product benefit. Consider using value-in-use pricing, where the economic value of the product to the customer determines the upper limit on your price. Regardless of pricing approach, your product definition—target market, positioning, price point, and product requirements—should be pinned down early, during the conceptual phase of the project—"Building the Business" Case in Exhibit 8.1—and be a mandatory deliverable to the "Go to Development" decision point (Gate 3).

able to lock in more than 80 percent of the manufacturing cost by the end of the concept stage.[31]

Manufacturing or Operations and Related Costs

Pricing and revenue is one facet of the profit equation; the other is production costs. Until you have an accurate picture of what your new product will cost to produce and deliver, you cannot determine its economics and financial value to your company, a key input to most portfolio prioritization schemes.

The first step is to define the product. As mentioned above, this product definition is done during the Business Case stage and is a key deliverable to Gate 3 in Exhibit 8.1. The next step is to map out the manufacturing or source-of-supply process on paper—a rough outline in Stage 2, and the process in detail in Stage 3. With this product definition and production process map in hand, most firms are quite adept at defining production costs and equipment needs and providing capital cost estimates. Proficient companies usually have a fairly well defined cost-estimating procedure and also a rigorous CAPEX or capital appropriations process, which defines the key steps to specifying equipment needs and capital requirements. So we do not go into too much detail here. However, we make three important points in approaching the cost-estimation exercise:

1. An outline of the manufacturing, operations/delivery, or source-of-supply process—a "paper process"—is a key and mandatory deliverable as part of the Stage 2 Business Case in Exhibit 8.1. Make it a rule: There must be a preliminary operations or source-of-supply plan in place at Gate 3 before development begins!
2. Involve manufacturing or operations people early, making sure there is someone from the operations/delivery side of your business on the project team, even as early as Stage 2. All too often, we hear tales of woe from project teams who did not include manufacturing until the project was halfway through development, only to learn the hard truths—that the product could not be made with existing equipment, or that the plant through-put would be half what was anticipated!
3. Once the manufacturing or source of supply process is mapped out on paper, then rely heavily upon the experts in manufacturing and costing to define manufacturing costs, equipment needs, and capital costs.

Here are some ways you can work with costing and manufacturing people as you estimate manufacturing or operations and capital costs.

Activity-Based Costing (ABC). Activity-based costing allocates fixed costs and factory overheads to a new product according to the activity that drives the cost. Each activity (cost driver)—in marketing, manufacturing, development, purchasing, or experimental engineering—is assigned a separate overhead rate. The drivers themselves might be numbers of setups, numbers of components purchased, numbers of shipments, numbers of engineering design changes, and numbers of calls on customers. Other drivers could be labor hours, machine hours, floor space used, orders entered, warehousing size, and sales costs.[32] An ABC system recognizes that many costs are driven by product complexity. If these costs cannot be recovered in the new product's price, product complexity (features and functionality) is reduced, and this helps drive the costs down. Of course, this assumes that the less complex product still satisfies the customer and delivers customer value.

The basic argument for ABC is that it is more accurate and realistic than conventional costing. Proponents of ABC argue that methods such as contribution pricing—where only variable costs are considered—result in too low a cost and hence underpricing; or that full cost (cost-plus) pricing, which uses traditional overhead allocations, results in distorted product costs. Some words of caution on ABC, however: This type of costing is best applied in stable manufacturing environments, where the drivers of cost are known and where they can be easily tracked in the cost accounting system.

Target Costing.   Target costing aims to ensure that a new product will be profitable when it is launched. It achieves this by determining the price the consumer will bear, and then working backward to arrive at a production cost that is acceptable to the company.[33] Thus the method is consistent with *outside-in* or market-based pricing.

The approach to target costing is simple:

- establish the market price customers are willing to pay in the long run for a given new product with specific attributes
- identify the long-term profit margin the firm requires
- compute the cost target that must be met in order to produce the new product with the specified attributes, yet yield the desired profit margin.[34]

The target cost equation is expressed this way:

$$\text{target cost} = \text{target selling price} - \text{target profit margin}$$

Target cost calculations include material, parts, direct labor, special equipment, depreciation, and overhead over the expected lifetime of the new product. Overhead includes all specific support activities during development and launch and, after launch, all ongoing support activities for the life cycle of the product. A target costing system implies that manufacturing and cost accountants are early members in the product development team, and that cost accounting systems are in place to provide the required data.[35] Manufacturing should play a major role in the early stages to understand the impact of product attribute changes on customer value perception and to be intimately involved in the review of manufacturing processes that affect cost and "manufacturability" of the evolving concept and design.[36]

One cardinal rule must prevail to make target costing workable: The target cost must never be exceeded. This rule ensures that failure to achieve the target cost will trigger cancellation of the project.[37] The only time this rule should be violated is when getting to market on time is so critical that cost is a secondary consideration in the short term. In this case, two analyses are required: A thorough review of the design process to identify why the target cost was not achieved and an intensive cost-reduction effort immediately after launch so that the rule violation is as short-lived as possible (this is the approach used by SONY).[38]

Companies not using target costing in most cases apply estimated engineering costs developed from standard cost tables that are related neither to the firm's accounting data nor to experience in producing similar products with similar processes. The target costing concept presents an opportunity for management accountants to participate in product design through the provision of timely, firm-specific data on the cost of products and processes, including overhead activities or business processes.[39]

During Stage 2 of the new product process (Exhibit 8.1)—the key homework stage when customer demands are translated into a product concept—a method for meeting the cost target must be clearly established. This may include changes to product attributes together with assessment of the effect these changes could have on the market price and expected margin. It may also include reviews and possible changes in production processes. Strong emphasis should be placed on reducing product costs before manufacturing begins.[40]

Estimating Capital or Equipment Costs.   Capital cost estimates are a necessary input to the financial calculations. And this detailed financial calculation first occurs in some detail in Stage 2 of the typical new product process (Exhibit 8.1), Building the Business Case. Thus, not only is a product definition required at this point, but also a rough outline on paper of the manufacturing or operations/delivery process—a "paper process." Often this information is missing, the result being that manufacturing considerations—for example, equipment needs in the plant—are not factored in until far too late in the project. Once the manufacturing process is mapped out, then rely on your process engineering group and your CAPEX process to define the equipment needs and capital costs.

POINTS FOR MANAGEMENT TO PONDER

Estimating manufacturing and capital costs is usually less problematic than obtaining accurate sales estimates. And several useful approaches have been offered above. Regardless of the costing method, however, note that manufacturing and operations people must be involved in the project well before development begins. Their input is essential to mapping out the manufacturing process or source-of-supply process as part of Stage 2, Building the Business Case. Once mapped out, cost estimates can usually be made fairly accurately. But the key is to get manufacturing engaged early as members of the cross-functional project team!

Estimating Probabilities of Success

Four of the value maximization methods in Chapter 3—ECV, Productivity Index, Options Pricing Theory, and dynamic rank-ordered list—require quantitative estimates of probabilities of success (as a percentage). So do a number of the bubble diagrams: The popular risk-reward bubble diagram plots probability of success versus reward, for example. These probabilities of success are difficult numbers to estimate; moreover, small variations in the numbers can cause major changes in attractiveness scores of projects and strongly affect their relative ranking. For example, in the ECV method, two probabilities are, in effect, multiplied together: probability of technical success and probability of commercial success. If these two numbers are somewhat inaccurate, then the error is magnified in the final ECV number. This is one of the reasons some managers we interviewed were skeptical about using these financially based models with probabilities built in as part of their project selection and portfolio management process.

Here are techniques used by some companies to improve the reliability of their success probability estimates:

Modified Delphi Method

This is yet another application of the Delphi method described in previous sections. At the project review meeting, following an open discussion on the technical issues and risks, each senior person is asked to write down a number giving his or her best estimate of the probability of technical success. By the end of the third round of discussions, there is usually consensus. Psychological experiments suggest that this method not only yields consensus, it usually yields answers very close to the truth!

The same method can be used to estimate the probability of commercial or market success as well. An open discussion on the market and competitive situation, competitive advantage, and the launch strategy precedes the vote. Alternatively, participants can be asked to indicate different expected sales levels and their best estimate of the probabilities that each will occur (see previous section on "Estimating Market Penetration and Making Sales Forecasts"). This type of data—sales levels and their probabilities—are useful inputs to financial tools such as ECV and Monte Carlo simulation.

Matrix Approach

A number of companies have identified the drivers of success probabilities and portray these as dimensions in a matrix, with success probabilities shown in the various matrix cells. An excellent example is Rohm and Haas, a United States–based chemical company, which uses two matrices to portray probabilities of commercial and technical success. The commercial success probability is determined via a two-dimensional chart, whose axes are:

- market newness, ranging from "current market" to "new to world"
- degree of competitive advantage, ranging from "me-too product" to "enabling benefit that opens up significant business opportunities."

Market	Probability Scores			
Current	0.5	0.6	0.85	0.95
New to R&H	0.1	0.2	0.5	0.7
New To World	0.05	0.05	0.1	0.2
	Low	Moderate	High	Very High
	Competitive Advantage			

For example: A current market with a low competitive advantage would score 0.5, or 50% probability of commercial success.

Definitions for Competitive Advantage Scale

Low	Me-too or catch-up product; minor cost reduction; benefits cannot overcome significant switching costs.
Moderate	Benefit seen as marginally great enough to switch in absence of other factors.
High	Benefit perceived to justify switching costs in the context of all competing demands.
Very High	Enabling benefit that opens significant new business opportunities for the customer.

EXHIBIT 8.4   Rohm and Haas—Matrix for Commercial Success

The theory here is that the likelihood of commercial success decreases with increasing market newness and increases with competitive advantage. Different probabilities of commercial success have been developed for the 12 cells in the chart (see Exhibit 8.4).

The probability of technical success is also based on a two-dimensional matrix, which captures newness to the company of both product and process technology. The probability scale is defined this way:

- very high: "solution already demonstrated; need only final engineering; repackage"
- very low: "probably beyond current technology or don't know how to approach; need to import new technology."

Exhibit 8.5 shows how the second matrix works. The product of the commercial and technical probabilities provides an overall probability of success, which may change as the product moves through the development process.

Scoring Method

Celanese uses a similar approach in estimating the probability of technical success but considers different parameters and uses a scoring model format. The company employs a four-item method to determine a score for the probability of technical success (see next section and Exhibit 8.6). The 1–10 score on this factor can be translated into a probability of success from Celanese's summary table (Exhibit 3.8).

Process	Probability Scores				
Very High	0.2	0.5	0.75	0.9	0.95
High	0.15	0.4	0.65	0.8	0.9
Moderate	0.15	0.3	0.5	0.65	0.75
Low	0.1	0.2	0.3	0.4	0.5
Very Low	0.05	0.1	0.15	0.15	0.2
	Very Low	**Low**	**Moderate**	**High**	**Very High**
	Product				

Note: For example: Probability of technical success for process (very high) and product (very low) would be 0.2, or 20%.

Definitions for Technical Success

Very High	Solution already demonstrated; need only final engineering; repackage.
High	Prototype in hand demonstrating all necessary characteristics but need to optimize performance.
Moderate	Prototype not yet in hand, but good lead within current technology; experts believe this can be done.
Low	Technology route/lead not well established; scouting work to be done; experts think this probably can be done within available technology.
Very Low	Probably beyond current technology or don't know how to approach; need to import new technology

EXHIBIT 8.5   Rohm and Haas—Matrix for Technical Success

Probability of Technical Success

	Rating Scale					
Key Factors	1	4	7	10	**Rating**	**Comments**
Technical "Gap"	Large gulf between current practice and objective; must invent new science	"Order of magnitude" change proposed	Step change short of "order of magnitude"	Incremental improvement; more engineering in focus		
Program Complexity	Difficult to define; many hurdles	Easy to define; many hurdles	A challenge; but "do-able"	Straight-forward		
Technology Skill Base	Technology new to the company; (almost) no skills	Some R&D experience but probably insufficient	Selectively practiced in company	Widely practiced in company		
Availability of People and Facilities	No appropriate people/facilities; must hire/build	Acknowledged shortage in key areas	Resources are available; but in demand; must plan in advance	People/facilities immediately available		

EXHIBIT 8.6   Celanese—Technical Success Scoring Model

R&D (Product Fitness)	
Attribute (for yes answers score +0.1)	**Score**
Validated requirements definition available	
Supports NCRs solution approach by providing all, or some, of the components which comprise an offer	
Commitment of suitable development resources to meet objectives	
Experience already gained with complexity (scale or scope) of the offer	
Solution leverages proven / existing technology	
Combined Plan / Develop & Deploy cycle times will be under 33-45 weeks	
Experience in creating like offers	
Dependent external groups (partners, ISVs, suppliers, OEM providers, etc.) are strategically and operationally aligned	
Solution conforms to NCRs architecture	
Any tools and/or processes required to support offer development in place	
Total	

Market Readiness	
Attribute (for yes answers score +0.1)	**Score**
Validated value proposition	
Fit with NCR Strategy	
Commitment of suitable marketing resource available to support program	
Market / Sales plan readiness	
Market segmentation complete and reliable market research data used to validate opportunity	
Market builds on existing strengths / market leadership of NCR in other areas	
Market has progressed beyond the early adopter stage	
Low market entry barrier exists for NCR	
High market entry barriers to competition / competitive strategy defined	
Total	

Deployment Readiness (Sales & Delivery)	
Attribute (for yes answers score +0.1)	**Score**
Adequately defined targeted customer within market segment	
Availability of an associated business impact model	
No entrenched competition in market / key customer sites	
Channel readiness (& lack of conflict)	
Deployment collateral availability	
Support services committed and available	
Experience in the delivery and support of like offers	
GST and RST operational plans interlocked	
Suitable sales and professional services committed and available to support program	
Any tools and/or processes required to support offer deployment in place	
Total	

EXHIBIT 8.7   NCR's New Risk Model Employed for ECV Calculations

Example: NCR's Financial Solutions Group, with more than 5,000 employees and more than $3 billion in sales, is a major supplier in the ATM market, the checks management area, and in bank customer management solutions (data mining). In calculating financial outcomes of a new project, NCR uses an adjusted version of ECV with estimates for three probabilities:

- probability of technical success, which is called "product fitness"
- probability of "market readiness"
- probability of "deployment readiness" (sales and delivery).

The use of these three probabilities is different from most other approaches (usually estimating technical and commercial probabilities) in that the "commercial" dimension is split into market and deployment readiness. This reflects the complexity of services and software solutions.

Each of the three probability or risk areas has ten questions (called attributes) that are scored "yes" or "no." For each "yes," a value of 0.1 is assigned, so that if all ten questions are answered positively, the probability for that risk area is 1.0 (see Exhibit 8.7). Management has found that this approach identifies the key areas of risk while providing overall risk values that are considered intuitively accurate and reflect the current status of programs. This method was verified on more than 50 ongoing projects before being implemented within the organization.[41]

NewProd 3000

Procter & Gamble, Exxon Chemical, Hercules, and others use the *NewProd 3000* model to estimate probabilities of commercial success.[42] This model, described in Chapter 3, is an empirically based computer diagnostic tool that has been customized to each user firm or industry. For each project, knowledgeable people answer approximately 30 key questions, the answers are combined, and the resulting project profile is compared to profiles already in the NewProd database to predict whether it will be a winner.

The advantage of this model is that it is based on more than 2,000 past new product cases whose commercial outcomes are known. The probability of success is then linked via statistical analysis to a number of potential driver variables. Procter & Gamble claims an 84 percent predictive ability using this model,[43] while a Dutch study reports similar positive results in Europe.[44] The best experience has occurred when users have had the model customized to incorporate their own data and cases or have used industry-specific versions of the model.

None of the methods presented above is a perfect estimator of success probabilities. The best method will vary from company to company and project to project. Each of the approaches described here brings some degree of objectivity and validity to the estimates. By mixing and matching the above techniques, you can improve your ability to predict whether your new product will be a winner.

Estimating Resource Requirements

Estimating resource requirements is important for portfolio management for several reasons. First, the various financial models—NPV, ECV, Productivity Index, etc.—all require estimates of project costs and times in their calculation. And resource requirements are often the denominator in the bang-for-buck approaches, where the ratio of the project's economic value to the resources required is the ranking criterion. And virtually all methods that result in a prioritized or rank-ordered list of projects require that you list projects, rank-ordered, until you run out of resources. Thus the resource requirements of each project are often shown in one of the columns of this ranked list. Finally, many of the bubble diagrams and pie charts require resource needs as input variables:

- The size of the bubbles of bubble diagrams is usually the annual resources required for each project.
- Pie charts usually portray the breakdown of the portfolio by spending splits (or resource splits), not by numbers of projects.

So at every turn in portfolio management, you are faced with the dilemma of estimating resources required for projects.

Estimating Time: Execution Time and Person-Days

There are two types of time estimates required in any project:

1. execution time—the calendar or elapsed time that tasks in a project will take—the times shown in a typical project timeline.
2. resource requirements—the person-days or person-months that are required to execute each of the tasks in a project. From these times, project cost estimates are determined.

Both types of time estimates are usually problematic. Our experience suggests that, in general, project teams seem to be far too aggressive and unrealistic in setting timelines, so they most often underestimate and propose optimistic timelines and resource needs. These optimistic time-and-resource estimates stem from four major reasons:

- It is difficult to estimate how long some tasks will take, especially technical ones, and also to foresee all the possible obstacles along the way.
- An overzealous team often adopts a can-do attitude and becomes too enthusiastic about their ability to get things done quickly and efficiently, hence an unrealistic timeline.
- Similarly, a committed team is usually desirous of presenting their project in the best possible light, especially at gate reviews, so that their project will be approved. Optimistic estimates of time-to-market and resource requirements make the project look better and so get built into the project plan.
- Finally, management has an uncanny ability to shift priorities among projects. Hence resources that had been committed to one project are suddenly shifted to another project, throwing the carefully determined timelines out the window.

Reduction of cycle time or time-to-market is also an important issue, along with the accurate prediction of those times to begin with. (The two are connected, since long cycle times and inability to predict times seem often to occur together.) Some firms—such as Black & Decker, Motorola, and Chrysler—have made impressive, sustained time-to-market gains over the years in reducing product cycle times. For example, Motorola management stated that "we achieved rapid development the same way we achieved breakthroughs in quality—with old-fashioned hard work and constant management attention. . . . Fundamental changes in your development process require careful analysis, broad involvement, and extensive efforts." Motorola invested heavily in organizational changes for product development. Chrysler also spent generously for its enviable time-to-market success.[45]

Here are some tips and hints in forecasting both execution time and resource requirements (person-days) required to carry out project tasks.

Develop a Team-Based Timeline.   Too often an aggressive timeline is imposed on the project team, and frequently some team members were only peripherally involved in its development. Wrong idea! If timelines and resource requirements are to mean anything at all, the project plan must be developed by the entire project team. That is, the team meets and maps out their project—stage by stage and task by task. Then they try to make realistic estimates of both execution time and resource requirements (person-days) for each task on the timeline. A FMEA-style analysis* is next, where the team tries to imagine obstacles and speed bumps that could prolong the project or get in the way of their first-estimate timeline. Probabilities and impacts are assigned, and a more realistic estimate of time and resources is generated.

Experience suggests that the development of the project plan by the entire team is a great team-building exercise. And so we recommend this as an early team activity, right at the beginning of the project or at the start of each stage of the project. This project planning, team-building exercise is important for three reasons:

---

* FMEA: failure modes effects analysis, normally reserved for product design and process design. The method can also be used in project planning—to identify potential fail points of the project.

- Five heads are really better than one: A project plan or timeline developed by the entire project team is likely to be a lot more realistic than any one person's plan.
- There are cross-functional inputs: Too often we see key players left out of the project-planning exercise. For example, manufacturing or operations people often are involved far too late, yet they have valuable insights in to how long production trials or acquisition of production equipment might take. The same is true of the sales force—often the launch and rollout tasks are grossly underestimated simply because there was no one from Sales engaged in the project-planning exercise.
- The third reason is commitment: If you really want people to adhere to a proposed timeline and plan of action, then make sure they have helped to craft that plan. Accountability begins with the project-planning exercise!

Consider Project Priorities and Competing Projects.   Forecasting execution time can be done only within the context of the number of projects a company has underway at a given time (the portfolio of projects), together with available capacity to handle these project. A project team might look only at their specific project and fail to consider the totality of all new product projects, for example:

- the fact that other projects might be underway that require the same resources or skills desired for the team's specific project
- the fact that functional areas may have other initiatives underway, which will take resources away from the team's project
- the fact that senior management may not consider this project to have top priority; as a result, resources promised may not be forthcoming.

Planning in isolation is a major contributing cause to poor estimations of execution times.

Use Benchmark Studies As a Guide.   There are still very few benchmarks available to help estimate project execution time. But we have found a few. One recent study sheds much light on the subject.[46] Cycle times were identified in a broad sample of varied projects: 343 projects in 21 divisions of 11 companies in 5 industries. The key parameters or variables in predicting time to market (from the start of development to product introduction in the market) are:

- product newness—the percentage of change in the new product compared to the company's previous products
- product complexity—the number of new features or functions added to the product.

The results of this time-to-market study are shown in Exhibits 8.8 and 8.9. Here are some provocative conclusions and useful time-benchmarking information:

- The average product in the study had a 55 percent newness rating and three new functions; the project took 26 months from start of development to product introduction without a cross-functional team and without a new product development process, such as Stage-Gate™, in place.
- By contrast, companies with cross-functional teams and a new product process took only 15.3 months for similar projects.

- For a new-to-the-firm (100 percent newness) and complex project (six new functions), the cycle time was 42.6 months with no cross-functional team or process.
- With a team and a new product process, the time to market for 100 percent new projects dropped to 22.2 months.

The impact of relying on cross-functional teams coupled with an effective new product process is thus dramatic: Time to market is cut by almost half! More benchmarking results:

- Newness affects the front end of projects significantly, adding 1.5 to 1.6 months for every 10 percent increase in newness.
- Increasing newness adds to time to market—approximately 0.9 months for every 10 percent increase in newness. But this increase can be fully compensated for by the use of a truly cross-functional team.
- Complexity adds 3.7 to 4.2 months for each new function added to the product, but this can only be partially compensated for (45 percent) by having a new product development process.

Can these results in Exhibits 8.8 and 8.9 be used to estimate your cycle? As a first very rough approximation, this is good beginning, and at minimum, provides yet another data point in your time estimation exercise. However, don't forget that this analysis is based on only two descriptors of projects—newness and complexity—and two managerial elements: having a cross-functional team and a new product development process. Clearly there are many other factors that influence time to market.

Yet another study reveals some benchmark data across a broad array of technology industries and by project stage (Exhibit 8.10). Note that average times to market are shown in one column (right), and times to profit (from project initiation to cost recovery) are in the final columns. The cells show the percentage of the total time required at each stage. Note how similar these average times per stage are, regardless of industry. Finally, the mean time in weeks per stage across all industries and the mean effort as a percentage of the project are shown across the bottom two rows.

Keep a Record of Your Forecast and Actual Times and Resources. One way to improve the accuracy of your time and cost estimates is to apply a correction factor. A correction factor is developed over time from experience: by comparing what your forecast was versus what actually happened. How? Increasingly, companies are undertaking postlaunch reviews or PLRs (the final step in the Stage-Gate™ model of Exhibit 10.2). Here the actual versus forecast project results on a variety of parameters or metrics are assessed: How did the team fare versus how well they expected to?

As part of the PLR, have the team map out the project retrospectively—end to end, from idea to launch—on a large piece of paper. (We call this a "brown paper exercise" because we use a large roll of brown wrapping paper, stick about 12 feet or 4 meters worth on the wall, give the team members marking pens, and challenge them to map out their project in hindsight). It's much like analyzing the plays in a touchdown march in a football game on a Monday morning.

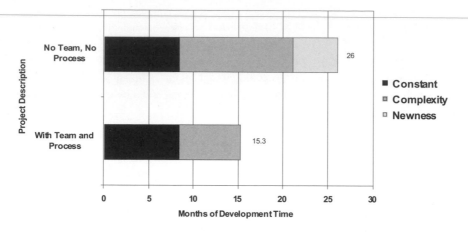

EXHIBIT 8.8   Expected Contributions to Development Time for the "Average" Project (55% New, 3 Functions)

SOURCE: A. Griffen, "The Effect of Project and Process Characteristics on Product Development Cycle Time," *Journal of Marketing Research* 34, 1 (1997): p. 32.

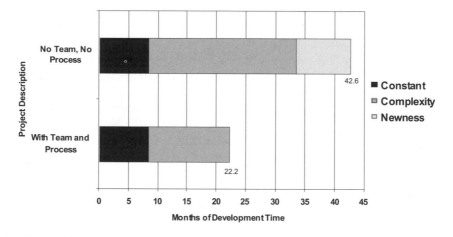

EXHIBIT 8.9   Expected Contributions to Development Time for a New-to-the-Company, Complex Project (100% New, 6 Functions)

SOURCE: A. Griffen, "The Effect of Project and Process Characteristics on Product Development Cycle Time," *Journal of Marketing Research* 34, 1 (1997): p. 32.

Industry	Concept	Specification & Planning	Detailed Design & Development	Testing & Evaluation	Launch & Ramp-Up	Average Total Time-to-Market	Average Total Time-to-Profit
Electronics & Systems	12.3%	13.7%	39.8%	20.4%	14.1%	93 weeks	142 weeks
Medical Devices	11.2%	13.4%	41.6%	20.4%	13.1%	126 weeks	195 weeks
Aerospace & Defense	7.2%	15.5%	45.3%	17.3%	14.6%	146 weeks	NA
Auto & Industrial	7.4%	9.5%	47.7%	20.7%	15.0%	107 weeks	148 weeks
Semi-Conductor	8.1%	9.4%	35.0%	28.1%	17.9%	110 weeks	150 weeks
Average Range	7-12%	9-16%	35-48%	17-28%	13-18%	93-146 weeks	142-195 weeks
Mean Time: Weeks	10.7	14.3	48.7	24.9	17.4	116.4	-
Mean Effort: Person-Days	6.4%	10.0%	46.3%	25.0%	12.3%	-	-

EXHIBIT 8.10   Average Time per Stage Across Various Industries

SOURCE: Adapted from Jim Hutchinson, "Journey to a World Class Time to Market Capability at Xerox Corporation," presentation delivered to Pennsylvania State University's Institute for the Study of Business Market Members Colloquium on New Products, Pittsburgh, PA, Fall 2000.

For each play or task shown on the map, we ask the team several questions:

- What did you do? (a description of the task in some detail)
- How well was it done? (a zero-to-ten proficiency score)
- How long did it take, and what did it cost? (days or weeks; and person-days or dollars)
- What was the forecast time in the approved project plan (teams usually present a project plan—for example, an MS-Project timeline complete with resource needs by task—at each gate review, so the forecast times and resources have been recorded and are available).
- How could you have done that task better?
- How could you have done the task faster?

This retrospective analysis provides valuable insights, not only into how the next project could be done better and faster, but also into the accuracy of time and resource requirements projections.

When you first begin this procedure, you will find some fairly inaccurate projections of task and stage times. But over time, you get better and also develop some good data. By taking the ratio of the actual-to-forecast times and resources for each type of task, you arrive at a set of correction factors to be applied to the next forecast. For example, suppose you find that the actual-to-forecast time to do customer trials is typically 1.40, then the correction factor 1.40 is applied to the next best-estimate forecast to arrive at a more realistic and adjusted forecast for customer trials.

A word of warning: Taken to an extreme, this method may begin to build too much of a cushion into the timeline—the timelines are not aggressive enough. Note however, in addition to developing correction factors, this same exercise helps you to discover ways to accelerate projects. Thus, checks and balances are built in: correction factors, which build some realism into an overly optimistic timelines forecast (based on past experience); and also an attempt to reduce the timeline by focusing on doing tasks better and faster (again from past experiences).

Don't Become a Speed Freak! Be careful that your zeal for cycle time reduction does not cloud your estimates of time and resource requirements. Overly aggressive timelines are often designed with the best of intentions—an attempt to accelerate the project to market—but later become very elusive goals and create frustration and morale problems for the project team. Remember that you must strike a balance between speed and quality of execution. Don't simply cut corners to achieve time reduction, particularly in a hostile competitive environment.[47] And be aware that cycle time or time to market is also related to the level of technology desired. If the goal is to build new or leading-edge technology or more complex technology into your new product, a longer development cycle is needed to ensure success.[48]

POINTS FOR MANAGEMENT TO PONDER

How many new product projects has your company completed on time and within budget in the past few years? Estimating resource and time requirements is almost as difficult as coming up with accurate sales and revenue forecasts. But the methods for improving resource estimates are not as well known and as proven as the methods designed to provide more solid market and sales estimates. So we offer these methods with some caution:

- Encourage your teams to develop a team-based timeline—the entire project team working together to develop a realistic project plan for their project, complete with cross-functional inputs.
- Consider project priorities and competing projects—do not plan timelines and resource requirements on one project in isolation from the rest.
- Use the benchmark studies as a guide—for example, the data in Exhibits 8.8, 8.9, and 8.10.
- Undertake a postlaunch review on every project and keep a record of your forecast and actual times and resources. And from this develop empirically based correction factors to adjust your time and resource estimates. Identify major reasons for delays and variances from forecasts. Learning why forecasts have been wrong in the past can help you make better ones in the future.
- Don't become a speed freak: Demand aggressive timelines and resource requirements, but not so aggressive that the team is doomed to failure.

Deal with Uncertainties: Sensitivity Analysis and Monte Carlo Simulation

Many uncertainties exist in product development, but one thing that is certain is: Your numbers, forecasts, and estimates are probably wrong! Yes, try your best to improve the integrity of your data using the many techniques offered in this chapter. Even then, you are still likely to have faulty data. But instead of ducking the issue of incorrect or uncertain data, deal with it. Various techniques exist that allow you to cope with uncertain estimates in key financial numbers such as revenues, margins, costs, and times.

We recommend two approaches:

1. Sensitivity analysis or estimation of possible ranges for data (e.g., upper and lower cost/revenue ranges and "what if" scenarios)
2. Monte Carlo simulation methods.[49]

Sensitivity Analysis

Sensitivity analysis tests how sensitive your projected financial outcome is to various assumptions you might have made. We highlighted this method earlier in the chapter as one way to deal with uncertain sales estimates, but it has much broader applicability, helping you cope with uncertain estimates in many parameters. You undertake this analysis by changing key estimates, forecasts, assumptions, or financial inputs in your spreadsheet model, one variable at a time, and holding the others constant.

For example, start with changing one input: Expected sales might be adjusted 5, 10, and 20 percent above and below the assumed, expected, or most likely value in the base case. A new discounted cash flow (DCF) is computed after each change. Then the DCF result, for example the NPV, is assessed for each "what if" scenario.

Varying each financial input, one at a time, and gauging the impact on the output (for example, on the NPV) reveals just how sensitive the output is to each input assumption. For example, if small changes in the assumed profit margin yield major changes in the NPV, then you conclude that the margin assumption is a critical assumption.

The technique can be expanded so that a number of variables or estimates are altered simultaneously. One can even generate the best-case and worst-case scenarios for the project—estimating a high/low range for each input parameter—and witness the spread in NPV values.

One problem with this approach is that it is very time-consuming: The inputs must be changed manually after each iteration of the model. Further, interpretation of the output becomes difficult after only a few iterations of the model, since there is a unique solution to each "what if" analysis. Because it is next to impossible to test the entire range of possible outputs, this approach becomes a hit-or-miss technique. But the hope is that the most critical combination of inputs has been identified and tested. Even then, this analysis is limited to showing envisioned outcomes rather than the most probable ones.

Monte Carlo Simulation

Sensitivity analysis and estimating ranges does not fully indicate how sensitive the results are to:

- poor estimates of cash flows and other input factors
- skewed distributions with large deviations (that generate greater uncertainty and higher risk)
- interactions and correlations between inputs
- how the results may be affected by the variable life of the project.

When these conditions are present, the more sophisticated Monte Carlo modeling technique, described in Chapter 4, can help. This method is better able to deal with inputs that have high uncertainty (often the case in higher-risk projects), and also with inputs that are correlated with each other. This technique may also show which inputs influence the project's DCF the most.

Monte Carlo simulation provides a structured approach to sensitivity analysis that explicitly incorporates uncertainty into financial models. Each input to the model is represented by a range of possible values, not just the single value that is most likely. Further, it is easy to model interrelationships between inputs. And unlike most other modeling techniques, Monte Carlo simulation does not require rigorous certainty or normality.

The Monte Carlo technique allows users to run thousands of iterations quickly, each iteration representing a separate what-if scenario. It then summarizes the entire range of possible outcomes efficiently, not simply giving what is probable or most likely. The output can be represented in various graphical and tabular formats. The dynamic response of the model can help practitioners understand the degree of risk associated with a given project. Thus, users gain a better grasp of a project's probability of success.

Recent technological developments in both software and hardware allow complex simulations on a PC platform using familiar spreadsheets. Numerous iterations of the Monte Carlo model can be run in a fraction of the time it took just a few years ago.

Uncertain inputs can be described in normal, uniform, lognormal, and triangular distributions. The location and shape of the distribution determine the chance that a single value will occur during each iteration of the model. Distributions may be "tight," with small standard deviations denoting relatively low risk, or "flat," with large standard deviations indicating greater uncertainty and higher risk.

Of all the possible ways that risk and uncertainty can be handled, we recommend the Monte Carlo technique, especially for large and costly projects. Numerous versions of this method are available in software form, which reduces the complex world of Monte Carlo analysis to a simple matter of inputting variables and obtaining results.*[50]

*Another type of sensitivity analysis is illustrated via the use of tornado diagrams. This approach simply has the user estimate upper and lower forecasts (or a range) for each factor in the model they created to develop the NPV forecast. The output is displayed via bar charts that illustrate the range of potential impact on the NPV for the project.

POINTS FOR MANAGEMENT TO PONDER

The nature of product development means that virtually every project entails risk. Charging ahead with financial calculations without factoring in uncertainty is naïve and usually leads to gross overestimation of the economic value of your projects, thus, often incorrect project prioritization. Don't duck the risk and uncertainty issue—deal with it. Use sensitivity analysis to identify the impacts of your uncertain estimates and key assumptions. Or for more complex and larger projects, move to Monte Carlo simulation described above and in Chapter 4. In-use results revealed in Chapter 6 showed that financial techniques tended to yield poor portfolios. True enough, but that is no reason to abandon the use of such techniques altogether. Rather, try to get better data using the methods outlined in this chapter and then employ techniques such as sensitivity analysis and Monte Carlo simulation that cope with less-than-perfect data.

Summary

In this chapter, we have outlined some of the methods designed to improve the reliability of the data that you should collect in the all-important homework stages of your projects. This chapter is by no means an exhaustive list, but we have tried to include the methods that we have seen work best. Note that we have provided only basic information on these techniques, enough to help you understand each and to evaluate which approaches are best for your company; but we have tried not to make this chapter a "how-to" guide. Our intent is that you will note the data-gathering procedures you deem appropriate for your use and then go to the original sources—to textbooks, articles, training courses, colleagues, or outside vendors—in order to obtain the specific expertise you need to implement these estimation and forecasting tools correctly. Many sources are listed in the chapter notes.

CHAPTER 9

Making Strategic Allocations of Resources: Deployment

In Search of the Right Portfolio Method

Which portfolio management method is right for you? In Chapters 3 through 5, we examined the portfolio approaches used by leading firms. Then we had a glimpse into the strengths and weaknesses of these methods and into some of the issues faced in their use. Now the key questions: Which approach is best? What is the recommended approach?

This is not an easy question, because there is no single best answer. In this chapter and the next, we map out the preferred portfolio approaches and indicate which ones are most appropriate for different situations. Our recommendations are based, in part, on what managers told us worked and what did not. They are also based on our own efforts inside numerous companies to implement portfolio management, as well as on the benchmarking studies outlined in Chapter 6.

Let's now provide a roadmap for this chapter and the next. In this chapter, we consider the top-level or macro decision making: allocation of resources across business areas or business units, namely resource deployment. Using the military analogy, having decided our arenas of strategic focus, the next question is: How many troops and tanks do we allocate to each battlefield? In other words, we begin to apply the Strategic Buckets Model.

Most senior managers are faced with difficult allocation decisions in how to split development resources across business areas. In some corporations, this means strategic allocation of resources across business units; in others, it may be allocation across business areas, product lines, market or industry sectors, or product groups. The terms may vary, but the challenge is the same: to allocate limited resources to competing, yet worthy, interests within your business. This allocation decision is a key part of portfolio management. It involves the allocation of development resources; it affects which projects are undertaken, especially the major ones; and it determines the split of resources across project types.

The portfolio decision across business areas and other relevant dimensions is what the Strategic Buckets Method is all about. Recall in Chapter 5 we introduced the concept of strategic buckets, whereby senior management makes strategic splits of resources. This is fine in theory. But the questions we are always asked are, How does one make these splits—they seem so arbitrary? Are there any guides or normative splits—what should the ideal split be? The answer to the second question is "unfortunately, no." But we can give you some guidance on the first question—how to make these splits.

In Chapter 10, we move away from macro allocation or strategic buckets decisions and look more at the prioritization of projects. That is, given that you have already decided to devote a certain percentage of your development resources to Business Area A, which specific projects within that area should you undertake? What should your portfolio of projects be? In Chapter 10, we outline specific project selection and portfolio management techniques for arriving at the right set of projects in order to achieve the three goals, namely, value maximization, balance, and strategic alignment.

Resource Allocation Across Business Units: The Methods

Resource allocation across business units (BUs) is a top-level issue. It deals with corporate strategy and corporate planning at the highest level. While methods vary by firm, Exhibit 9.1 provides a typical framework:

- Here, the corporation decides strategy and direction (top of Exhibit 9.1). Resources are then allocated to individual BUs (downward arrow in Exhibit 9.1).
- Concurrently, each BU develops its own business and new product strategy. In this way, opportunities and resource needs are identified and fed upward as input to the corporate strategy (upward arrow in Exhibit 9.1), which in turn affects the resource allocations.

The resource allocation exercise across BUs should be a fairly iterative process, with corporate strategy and goals helping to decide the allocations across business areas. At the same time, the performance, strengths, opportunities, and plans of the BU provide upward input into the decision. Some typical approaches to making this across-BU resource allocation decision were outlined in Chapter 6 and are summarized here.

- *Objectives and task*: Each BU begins with its business and new product objectives (e.g., annual growth and sales from new products for the next five years). Then it computes how many product launches, how many projects per stage, and hence amount of resources that will be required to achieve the objectives.
- *Competitive parity*: R&D resources are allocated across BUs so that each business spends roughly what the rest of its industry does (R&D spending as a percentage of sales).
- *History*: Some companies base the allocation on previous years' budgeted amounts, and add or subtract a little.

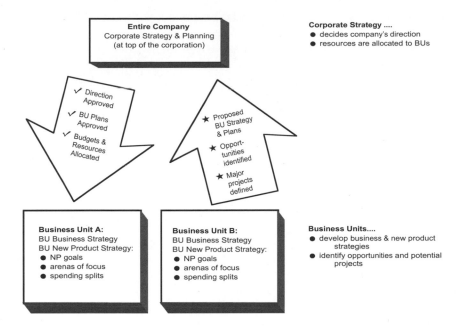

EXHIBIT 9.1   Linkage Between Corporate and Business Unit Strategy

- *Opportunistic*: Spend all you can afford in each business, as long as the projects are good ones (e.g., when profitability exceeds the risk-adjusted cost of capital).
- *Based on results*: This approach does not begin with either the corporate or the BU's strategy, but simply focuses on results. Allocate more development money to businesses that are successful at product development, and take away from those that are less successful; that is, feed the strong, focus the weak. Before you dismiss this method, recall that this decision rule tends to allocate money to those business units with excellent new product opportunities or to those with considerable product development expertise—which is exactly where the money should be allocated!
- *Corporate planning models*: Perhaps the best-known models for resource allocation across businesses are the traditional "stars, cash cows, dogs" models, the BCG and GE/McKinsey models.[1] In these models, each BU is scored or rated on various factors, which are then combined into a few major dimensions. Depending on the model, these dimensions usually boil down to market attractiveness and business position. A two-by-two or three-by-three matrix is constructed and BUs are located on this two-dimensional matrix (see Exhibit 9.2). Each BU develops a strategic mission, which depends in part on its location on the matrix. The location of the BU on the matrix, together with its strategic mission, helps determine how much funding the business unit receives (both R&D funds and people).

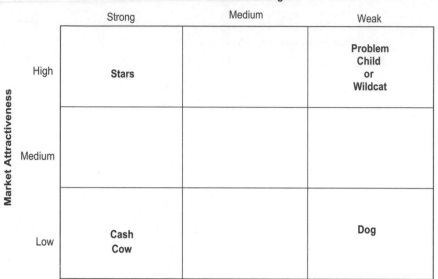

EXHIBIT 9.2   Typical Corporate Allocation Model

Note: Business Units are each classed into one of the nine cells. From the distribution, a mission and strategy are decided; resources are allocated.

SOURCE: Adaptation of the General Electric (GE) model.

> **POINTS FOR MANAGEMENT TO PONDER**
> How does your company make the development resource allocation decision across BUs? Is it a strategic approach, which recognizes that some BU areas are more attractive than others strategically? Or is it simply a matter of a percentage of sales applied universally across all BUs? If not a strategic approach, which looks at factors such as market/industry attractiveness and business position, then perhaps you should move to one of the corporate planning approaches or models, such as outlined in the last item above.

Deciding the Spending Splits: The Strategic Buckets Model

Almost every major company faces the issue of allocating development resources across business areas and project types. Sometimes this allocation occurs at several levels. For example, there is the top-level decision of how much development funding each BU receives, noted above. Moving one level down within Business Units, the same issue is faced again: allocating resources across markets, industry sectors, product groups, or project types. And this allocation decision across areas—deciding on strategic buckets and how many resources each bucket gets—is the topic of this section.

There are several points to note here:

- Do approach resource allocation across strategic buckets deliberately, systematically, and formally. An informal or ad hoc process or none at all is the default option. Lacking any systematic approach will probably result in allocating the resources in a way that is far from optimal.
- Next, whatever method you elect, make sure that is it both Top-Down and Bottom-Up (see Chapter 5 for more information). Here is what we mean:

    1. *Top-Down:* Allocating resources across business areas or buckets must be strategic. That is, from a strategic standpoint, some areas merit more than the normal allocation, other areas merit less. The goal is to allocate funds to each business area so as to maximize the returns to the last dollar spent in each. For example, some product lines are in mature, relatively unattractive markets and yet continue to have heavy R&D spending. Others are in a relatively weak business position, so one wonders: why continue to spend heavily?
    2. *Bottom-Up:* The resource allocation across business areas and buckets must be opportunistic. That is, it must consider the *specific projects and opportunities* that each business area has. For example, if one product group is working on (or can propose) a number of very attractive new product projects, and better projects than other product groups, then this group merits more funding and support. And it should get proportionately more funding regardless of what the Top-Down or strategic exercise suggests.

POINTS FOR MANAGEMENT TO PONDER

How does your business or BU allocate product development resources across business areas or buckets—for example, across product lines or market sectors? Is this a conscious decision, or does it "just happen"? What about project types? Do you "let the chips fall where they may," or is there strategic thinking in the amount of resources you devote to new products versus product improvements versus maintenance projects? Don't be disheartened by your answers, as these are difficult issues. We offer some guidance below.

Strategic Buckets: A Step-by-Step Guide

Here are the suggested steps in allocating funding across business areas—a method that we have used effectively. In this walk-through or illustration, we consider two types of buckets: allocating resources across business groups (industry sectors) and also allocation of resources across project types. You can modify the approach to suit the idiosyncrasies of your own business, defining business areas in any way that suits you.

AN ILLUSTRATION:
PORTFOLIO MANAGEMENT AT ABC CHEMICAL

ABC Chemical is a major multinational chemical firm with a number of large divisions. The L&P Division is almost a stand-alone company, with its own R&D labs, marketing department, and so on. Each of L&P's four business groups serves a separate industrial market: Sectors A, B, C, and D.

Traditionally, resources for the development of new products have been split across the four business groups based on their proposed projects and the funding they had received the previous year. This has become a political process, simply because there are no clear-cut procedures for making decisions. Managers at L&P are convinced that a strategic assessment of resource allocation would yield splits that are quite different from the current ones.

ABC Chemical classifies product development projects by type: fundamental research, new products, product improvements (including changes in response to customer requests), product maintenance, and process developments. However, there is no strategic effort to optimize the split across these five types. Moreover, L&P management believes that two categories, product improvements and product maintenance, are consuming too many of the division's limited resources.

L&P Division's senior managers realized that, before they undertook the portfolio allocation exercise, they must have a business strategy that specifies goals and how they will be achieved. Management in L&P had already been through a strategic exercise, which defined the role of new products in the business strategy and resulted in a product innovation and technology strategy for the division. This strategy specified the new product goals for the division and defined specific areas of strategic focus for the division's NPD efforts—the markets, product types, and technologies—and their relative priorities.

Step 1: Start with Current Portfolio Breakdown: The Status Quo

Senior management must first assess the current portfolio—a high-level or aggregate look at the current spending breakdowns, answering the question: Where is the money going? The key dimensions of this assessment typically include resource allocation across:

- Business areas (could be product groups, product lines, categories, market or industry sectors or segments, geographic regions of the world, and so on)
- Project types (could be product improvements, maintenance, or new products; or they could be based on other typologies, such as share maintenance projects, market development projects, and diversification projects).

Exhibit 9.3 provides some sample breakdowns taken from our illustration company.

The status quo is a good place to start for several reasons. First, it often comes as a great revelation to senior management just where the resources are currently being spent. For example, one division executive in a large corporation began the portfolio allocation meeting with a statement of frustration: "Every month, we [the executive committee] meet to approve major projects. We've approved more than $100 million for R&D projects so far this year. But I still don't have a clue where the money's going!" What he was seeking was some simple but often missing breakdowns depicting current allocations within the existing portfolio. Animated discussions often result from a simple display such as Exhibit 9.3.

A second reason to begin by assessing current spending is that it reminds decision makers of what the current situation is, and that the purpose of the decision exercise is to make better decisions than those under the status quo. The third reason is that you are never starting with a clean slate; there are already resources in place, with certain skills, and work on certain projects is occurring. People cannot be transferred seamlessly between business areas or project types; and many existing projects, to which firm commitments have already been made, will continue to consume resources into subsequent fiscal years. You can make directional shifts from the current situation (for example, deciding to spend more on Business Group D in Exhibit 9.3, or more on product developments as opposed to improvements), but the beginning point does limit somewhat your eventual decisions on spending breakdowns.

REVIEWING THE CURRENT BREAKDOWNS AT ABC CHEMICAL

At L&P, the senior people in the division as well as from the four business groups meet to begin their portfolio allocation initiative. They first review the charts in Figure 9.3. To no one's surprise, there is major concern that far too high a proportion of resources is going to "today's" projects (improvements and maintenance)—35 percent of the total—and not enough resources are being used to build the business. Although Business Group A is the largest business and receives the most development support, it is also in very mature markets with limited potential for growth and few new opportunities.

Step 2: Next, Move to a Top-Down or Strategic Allocation Process

The prerequisite to the portfolio allocation exercise is having a solid understanding of the business's strategy and, in particular, its product innovation and technology strategy. If this strategy is not yet in place in your business, that is where to begin (see Chapter 5 and the section entitled "Developing a New Product Strategy for Your Business—A Quick Guide").

For now, let us assume that these strategies are in place, for each business area or BU:

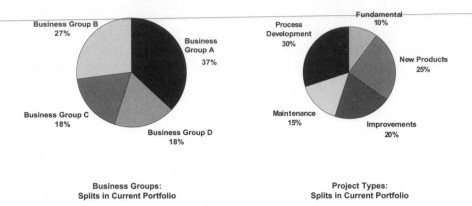

Business Group B
27%

Business
Group A
37%

Business Group C
18%

Business Group D
18%

Fundamental
10%

Process
Development
30%

New Products
25%

Maintenance
15%

Improvements
20%

Business Groups:
Splits in Current Portfolio

Project Types:
Splits in Current Portfolio

EXHIBIT 9.3   The Current Portfolio Breakdown: The Status Quo in L&P Division

---

POINTS FOR MANAGEMENT TO PONDER

Do you know where your development resources are being spent? Or are you like the exasperated executive who was pleading for some insight? A good place to begin your portfolio management exercise is by understanding the "what is." Assign someone to get a list of all the projects where R&D resources are spent in your various businesses or sectors. Start recording some key metrics or characteristics of each project: size, R&D spending this year, project type, market sector, latest NPV estimate, probability of success, and so on. Then start creating some useful portfolio diagrams to help management understand the current shape of its portfolio. Bubble diagrams and pie charts are the most common, and many of these were illustrated in Chapters 3 and 4.

- Mission
- Goals
- Objectives
- Strategy and tactics.

Concurrently, the results of a strategic mapping exercise should also be reviewed. Chapter 5 explained how a strategic mapping exercise is used to determine the relative attractiveness of various business areas or business units (the example of the major bank and its 12 product groups was cited in Chapter 5). The raw data for strategic mapping are obtained in questionnaire format from the business areas to capture key strategic metrics and characteristics for each. Concurrence is reached on these metrics.

In the strategic mapping exercise, each business area is rated on the two strategic dimensions shown in Exhibit 9.4:

1. Market/technology attractiveness and
2. Business strength.

This two-dimensional strategic mapping map is an adaptation of the GE-McKinsey strategic map.[2]

1. *Market/technology attractiveness* is an external metric that captures how attractive each business area's marketplace is, and what the opportunities are for new products or technical developments in that marketplace.
2. *Business strength* is an internal measure that captures how strong each business group is—can it exploit the opportunity?

A number of subquestions or strategic metrics are used to determine the dimensions:

Market/Technology Attractiveness

Market attractiveness:
- size of markets
- growth
- margins and pricing
- concentration of buying power
- competitive intensity.

Technological opportunity:
- technological elasticity (opportunity for developing new products in this arena—bang for buck?)
- location of the industry on the technology S-curve (mature versus new)
- technological activity in this market area.

Business Position

- market share
- product quality and integrity
- technology resources and skills
- manufacturing resources and skills
- marketing resources and customer relationships.

REVIEWING THE STRATEGIC MAPPING RESULTS AT ABC CHEMICAL

Management from each of the four business groups in L&P has already undertaken their strategic mapping exercise as part of strategy development, scoring their four business groups on a number of questions similar to the ones above. The questions capture each group's business position and relative market attractiveness. To ensure consistency and honesty in the scoring, a number of people independent of each of the business groups were also invited to rate the groups. The strategic map in Exhibit 9.4 is the result.

What becomes clear at the senior management portfolio allocation meeting is that Business Group A, the traditional heavy R&D spender because of its size, is

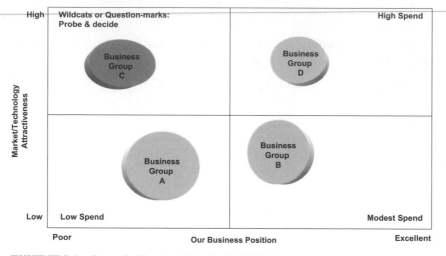

EXHIBIT 9.4   Strategic Planning Map for L&P Division

Note: Sizes of circles are proportional to revenue for each business group.

perhaps in the worst strategic position to be spending heavily on R&D (see the lower left quadrant of Exhibit 9.4). Business Group D is one of the smallest units and has low spending on R&D. But strategically this business group, located in the upper right quadrant of the strategic map, offers the most opportunities. In an ideal world, divisional management would like to increase spending for Business Group D. Business Group B is also large, like A, but spends less than A on R&D. It faces modest opportunities, so perhaps its spending level is about right.

Step 3: Do a First-Cut Allocation of Resources

Based on the strategic discussions and strategic map chart above (Exhibit 9.4), together with an understanding of the status review of current spending (Exhibit 9.3), management must make a first-cut allocation of resources across the business areas and project types (Exhibit 9.5). Note that this is still very much a Top-Down approach. Specific projects within each business area have not been considered yet. It is also fairly directional, beginning with the status quo or current splits, and debating whether each business area or project type should have more or less resources, based on the strategic mapping results and strategic assessments.

For this top-level, first-cut decision, we recommended using a modified Delphi approach (see Chapter 8 for an explanation of this method). Here, the issue—how to split resources—is discussed openly. Next, each member of the decision group writes down his or her proposed split in resources—privately and without duress. Next, these "votes" are collected and displayed anonymously on an overhead transparency or video projector:

- If the "votes" match closely, the decision is reached.
- If they are far apart, more discussion ensues, and a second round of voting takes place.

By the end of two or three rounds, a consensus and an informed decision is usually reached: the first cut at the "what should be" split.

The result of this first round of decisions is a matrix denoting desired resource splits across project types and across the business areas (as in Exhibit 9.6). Note that only one row and one column are completed in this chart.

MAKING THE FIRST-CUT SPLIT IN RESOURCES AT ABC CHEMICAL

Much heated discussion takes place at the L&P senior management portfolio allocation meeting, with the conclusion being that Business Group D ought to have more funding. On the other hand, Group D is a relatively small business in terms of sales. So spending levels per business group are also displayed as a percentage of their sales (charts not shown). Finally, management "votes" and the results are displayed. There is more debate and discussion, and the resulting Delphi outcome, after several rounds, is shown in Exhibits 9.5 and 9.6. Business Group D indeed should have a major increase in funding—more than a 50 percent hike from 18 percent to 30 percent of the pie. And Business Group A should not be spending nearly as much, dropping to 20 percent. Business Group B is left alone—its spending is just about right at 27 percent of the total—while Group C receives a small increase . . . at least in this first-cut exercise.

Note that management at L&P recognizes that this first-cut Delphi exercise has ignored the fact that some major projects are already underway, and the fact that major commitments had already been made to them. It also has ignored the relative attractiveness of the various proposed projects that each business group could do. At this point, it is merely a high level, first-cut—"strategically, here's where the money should go"—assessment.

To recap the exercise so far:

- First, we began with a look at the status quo with breakdowns by:

  1. business areas
  2. project types.

- Then we reviewed the strategies of the business areas using a strategic map.
- Using a modified Delphi approach, we made tentative, first-cut splits across business areas and project types in terms of both dollars and percentages.
- So far, everything has been "in aggregate" and top-level.
- Now it is time to lower the microscope and look at individual projects and specific opportunities—moving to a more Bottom-Up approach.

Each business area now submits its list of active and proposed projects, broken down by project type.

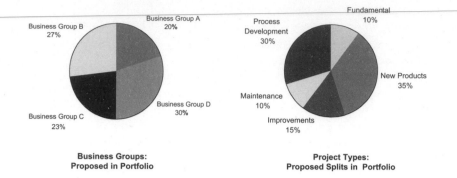

Business Groups:
Proposed in Portfolio

Project Types:
Proposed Splits in Portfolio

EXHIBIT 9.5   First-Cut Allocation of Resources Using a Delphi-like Approach

Notes: Provides a tentative split in resources on two key dimensions: business groups and project types.
All resource splits are noted as percentage split.

	PROJECT/ ACTIVITY TYPES	Fundamental	New Products	Improvements	Maintenance	Process Development
Groups		10%	35%	15%	10%	30%
Business Group A	20%					
Business Group B	27%					
Business Group C	23%					
Business Group D	30%					

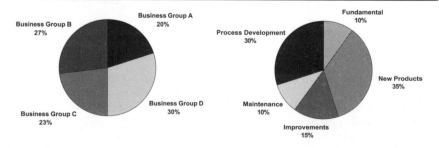

EXHIBIT 9.6   Result of First-Cut Allocation Decision

POINTS FOR MANAGEMENT TO PONDER

Does your business have a new product strategy that defines your new product goals, arenas of strategic focus, and how you plan to win in each arena? Has your innovation strategy been translated into spending decisions—across business areas, market sectors, or project types? And is this strategy readily available and widely communicated? If so, your company has taken a first, important step.

If not, then try the approach outlined in Chapter 5 to develop a product innovation and technology strategy for your business, and then to move toward spending allocations or strategic buckets as outlined above. By having the leadership team take the time to discuss and agree on what tentative spending splits might look like, you will have taken an important first step toward getting them to articulate how new product resources should be spent at the macro level.

Step 4: Move to a Bottom-Up Approach—Look at the Major Projects from Each Business Area

Resource allocation, while strategic in nature, also depends on the specific opportunities; namely, the projects themselves. Note that this portfolio exercise must not become a sterile strategic exercise driven from the top down. Rather, it must also be opportunistic—it must consider the specific opportunities within each business area as well. Thus, at this point, the focus of the exercise turns to the larger or more significant projects from each of the business areas.

Each business area brings a list of desired projects to the portfolio session. This list can be broken down into two types:

- *Must-do projects*: these are projects that each business area views as absolutely essential to include in their portfolio. These encompass strategically critical projects, as well as those that are already underway (previously approved and committed resources) and that remain good projects (i.e., the business case remains solid).
- *Should-do projects*: these projects are discretionary (i.e., may or may not be done), but they are attractive. If resources were available, the business areas would certainly like to see these projects included in the active portfolio.

How has each business area arrived at their list of desired projects? By undertaking portfolio analysis and project selection within that business area. This is more of a micro and project selection or project prioritization exercise. That's the topic of the next chapter. But for now, let's just assume that each business area comes with a fairly well defined and ranked list of must-do and should-do projects.

Note that for practical purposes, the complete list of all projects from all types—fundamental research through maintenance items—is usually not brought to this senior portfolio meeting. That would overwhelm the meeting. Besides, many projects are simply too small to be of interest to this level of management. Thus smaller projects should be lumped together into categories or clusters and presented that way. Thus, this senior portfolio meeting really only sees the major initiatives from each business area along with smaller projects in aggregate.

Step 5: Review Lists of Desired Projects Across the Business Areas and Roll-Up

Next management scrutinizes the lists of new product opportunities offered by each business area. Perhaps the most useful approach is to construct a rank-ordered list of the projects. This includes the must-do and should-do projects from each business area, but rolled up or combined. That is, projects from the various business areas are shown on one chart together, so that they can be compared against each other.

Don't try to compare apples with oranges, however—new products versus product improvements versus cost reductions. Instead, prepare one ranked list for each category of projects (see the example in Exhibits 9.7 and 9.8).

When ranking projects, be very careful about the choice of ranking criteria that you use to construct these lists. Note that within each column in your table, the projects are rank-ordered from most attractive to least attractive. We strongly recommend against using a universal or single set of criteria to rate and rank all types of projects. Instead, some suggestions are:

- *Fundamental research projects*: Use a simple scoring model with strategic criteria, impact on the corporation, and likelihood of technical feasibility as the key ranking criteria.
- *New product projects*: Again use a scoring model, but this time employing more traditional new product criteria, such as strategic fit, competitive advantage, likelihood of technical feasibility, ability to leverage in-house resources, and risk/reward (see Exhibit 3.10 for a complete list).
- *Product improvements, fixes, enhancements, tweaks, and maintenance items*: Use a financial metric such as NPV/R&D costs.
- *Cost reductions*: Again use a financial metric, either NPV or perhaps a simpler cost/benefit ratio.

At this point, management must make some choices and cuts. The obviously poor projects are killed outright. But this usually leaves a list of desirable projects that is considerably longer than the resources available. Then, management makes some tough choices, albeit tentative ones. This results in a tentative first-cut list of "will do" projects.

How? The procedure is to proceed down each ranked list of projects in Exhibit 9.7 until resources run out. Those projects above the resource limit line in Exhibit 9.7 are tentative go projects. The lower-value projects—those toward the bottom of the ranking lists in Exhibit 9.7—are tentatively put on hold. This procedure may not yet yield the best portfolio in terms of strategic importance or balance, but it moves you in the direction of a high-value portfolio.

How are the resource limits for each column decided? Simple: from the first-cut Delphi resource split exercise (Step 3 above and Exhibit 9.6).The percentages in the horizontal row in Exhibit 9.6 are translated into dollars (or person-days) and provide the first-cut resource limits for each column in Exhibit 9.7.

All Business Groups combined — $25 million R&D budget

Fundamental ($2.5)	New Products ($8.8)	Improvements ($3.7)	Maintenance ($2.5)	Process Improvements ($7.5)
✓ Project-D129 $0.4	✓ Project-C023 $0.9	✓ Project-C201 $0.3	✓ Bundle-A $0.7	✓ Project-B403 $1.1
✓ Project-B105 $0.6	✓ Project-A011 $0.6	✓ Project-C202 $0.2	✓ Bundle-B $0.2	✓ Project-A411 $1.1
Project-D112 $0.3	✓ Project-D009 $1.0	✓ Project-D211 $0.4	✓ Bundle-C $0.8	✓ Project-B409 $0.5
Project-A134 $0.5	✓ Project-D034 $0.3	✓ Project-D215 $0.1	✓ Bundle-D $0.7	Project-C413 $0.7
Project-C143 $0.5	✓ Project-B004 $0.2	✓ Project-A219 $0.2	Project-D331 $0.1	Project-D408 $0.6
Project-B116 $0.2	Project-C013 $0.6	✓ Project-C221 $0.1	Project-D310 $0.05	Project-D424 $1.0
Project-B121 $0.6	Project-D039 $0.6	✓ Project-B209 $0.5	**Project-C313 $0.05**	Project-C417 $0.3
Project-A119 $1.6	Project-B022 $0.7	Project-D214 $1.0	Project-A350 $0.02	Project-A420 $0.6
Project-D115 $0.9	Project-A027 $1.0	Project-B244 $0.8	Project-D321 $0.2	Project-B405 $1.3
Project-A106 $1.5	Project-C036 $1.2	**Project-A222 $0.3**	Project-B334 $0.5	Project-C407 $0.2
Project-B109 $2.0	Project-B007 $0.9	Project-D245 $0.4	Project-B335 $0.1	**Project-D418 $0.2**
	Project-D015 $0.3	Project-A233 $0.1	Project-C345 $0.3	Project-B422 $1.1
	Project-D028 $0.5	Project-D246 $1.5	Project-A341 $0.1	Project-D427 $0.9
	Project-D041 $0.9	Project-D237 $0.4		Project-A421 $0.1
	Project-A003 $0.4	Project-B236 $0.6		Project-A430 $0.4
	Project-B016 $0.7	Project-C239 $0.3		Project-C434 $0.9
	Project-B030 $1.1			Project-D431 $1.5
	Project-B031 $1.4			Project-B445 $0.7
	Project-D040 $0.4			
	Project-C010 $0.2			
	Project-C025 $0.5			
	Project-A024 $0.7			
	Project-D042 $0.9			
	Project-B043 $0.1			

EXHIBIT 9.7   Ranked List of Projects for L&P Division by Project Type

✓ Indicates a must-do project.

Bolded project with an underline indicates that the resources for that project type have all been allocated. Number in parentheses is the target spending level for the column; for example, "fundamental" has a target of $2.5 million.

DECIDING ON THE TENTATIVE LIST OF "WILL DO"
PROJECTS AT ABC CHEMICAL

The management team from L&P and the four business groups meet again, but this time to review lists of major projects. Each business group provides its desired list of projects, and these are combined into a single list for the whole division (see Exhibit 9.7). Note that the division list shows a ranked list of projects, but broken down into five columns: the five project types. Smaller projects are clustered rather than showing each project individually; this proves particularly helpful for collapsing the many maintenance projects and some improvement projects into a smaller set.

As recommended, management does not use the same criteria to do the ranking in all five columns. Rather,

- For fundamental research projects (column 1), L&P uses a four-question scoring model: strategic fit, strategic leverage, technical feasibility, and impact on the corporation.
- For new product projects, management employs a six-factor scoring model almost the same as our recommended model in Exhibit 3.10.
- For improvements and process developments, they use a criterion similar to the productivity index in Chapter 3, namely NPV/R&D.
- For maintenance projects, they also use the NPV/R&D index.

Data and updates on all projects have been previously provided to senior management—summaries of each project that coincide with the criteria used to rank it. Note that in L&P's case, each business group had already pre-ranked the projects before the combined four-group portfolio allocation meeting reconvened (how to do this ranking is the topic of Chapter 10); you may choose to do this right at the senior meeting as a team.

The resulting list for one business group is shown in Exhibit 9.8, along with the combined list for all four business groups in Exhibit 9.7. This latter table shows all the projects from the four business groups in a finalized format, and ranked using the criteria above.

Projects that are must-dos are first highlighted. These are usually ones that are well underway and are still solid investments. A few new strategically necessary projects are added to the must-do list as well. Note that the numbers in each cell in Exhibit 9.8 show the annual R&D resources required if the project is to be done. Clearly the must-do projects do not consume all the division's R&D resources; but when all the projects are considered, L&P is over the resource limit in all four project type categories.

After considerable discussion, the first-cut list of projects is agreed—the so-called "tentative list of will-do projects." Note that this is only a first cut.

Step 6: Display What the Portfolio Would Look Like Based on This Tentative Ranked List

Management next considers what the portfolio would look like in terms of the various portfolio charts, assuming this tentative list of will-do projects selected in

Business Group D — $7.5 million tentative R&D budget

Fundamental ($0.75)	New Products ($2.65)	Improvements ($1.1)	Maintenance ($0.75)	Process Improvements ($2.25)
✓Project-D129 $0.4	✓Project-D009 $1.0	✓Project-D211 $0.4	✓Bundle-D $0.7	Project-D408 $0.6
Project-D112 $0.3	✓Project-D034 $0.3	✓Project-D215 $0.1	**Project-D331 $0.1**	Project-D424 $1.0
Project-D115 $0.9	Project-D039 $0.6	**Project-D214 $0.8**	Project-D310 $0.05	**Project-D418 $0.2**
	Project-D015 $0.3	Project-D245 $0.4	Project-D321 $0.2	Project-D427 $0.9
	Project-D028 $0.5	Project-D246 $1.5		Project-D431 $1.5
	Project-D041 $0.9	Project-D237 $0.4		
	Project-D040 $0.4			
	Project-D042 $0.9			

EXHIBIT 9.8   Business Group D—Ranked List of Projects by Project Type

✓ Indicates a must-do project.

Bolded project with an underline indicates that the resources for that project type have all been allocated. Number in parentheses is the target spending level for the column; for example, "fundamental" has a target of $0.75 million.

Step 5 above. Here is where the various charts we saw in Chapters 3 to 5 are helpful. These charts can be drawn for each business area, and of course, for all business areas combined. Given the number of ways you may wish to view the projects, and the need for up-to-date information, it is advisable to acquire portfolio management software. Such software greatly facilitates the production of these alternate views or charts. Here are some examples:

- Construct bubble diagrams of the tentative list of will-do projects for each of the business areas (Exhibit 9.9) as well as for all business areas combined.
- Draw some pie charts (Exhibit 9.10) showing the breakdown of projects by business area and by project types, and by any other dimension that might be relevant.
- Create a breakdown table or resource matrix as in Exhibit 9.11. This is simply a different way of showing some of the pie chart data. It reveals the breakdown by business area and project type in the same matrix. Note that this time, the entire matrix can be filled in.

THE TENTATIVE WILL-DO PORTFOLIO IS REVIEWED AT ABC COMPANY

Exhibits 9.9, 9.10, and 9.11—bubble diagrams, pie charts by project type and business group, and the resource matrix—are created from the decisions revealed in Exhibit 9.7 and displayed. These can be shown for all the projects rolled up from the four business groups, as well as for each business group separately. From these, management can see the total divisional picture and the leadership teams from each business group can see their own groups' pictures.*

*The use of software greatly facilitates this effort. To learn more about NewPort Max™, see www.prod-dev.com.

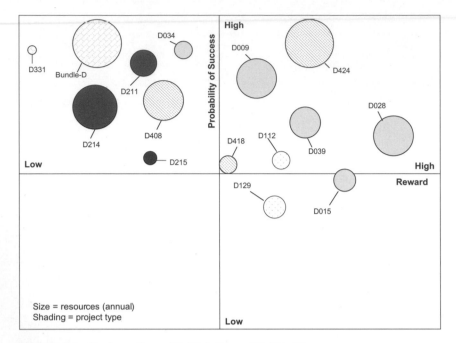

EXHIBIT 9.9   Business Group D's Risk-Reward Bubble Diagram

Step 7: Start the Next Iteration and Arrive at Next and Final Cut

There are usually some revelations when management sees the results of its first-cut strategic buckets exercise. Sometimes the splits are way off what they ought to be—too much going to one business area, not enough going to a given project type, and so on. So Step 5 is repeated. The rank-ordered lists of all projects are displayed again, and there is some arbitrary adjusting and sorting—perhaps removing some projects from a business area that received too many projects and resources, or bumping a project up the priority list. Even the first-cut Delphi splits—across business areas and project types in Exhibit 9.5—are questioned and adjustments are made as projects are added and deleted.

Again the bubble diagrams, pie charts, and resource matrix are displayed. After several rounds or iterations, there is usually agreement on the final list of projects and resource allocations. By now, the breakdown of resources across project types and business areas is fairly close to what it should be—a reasonable compromise that accommodates what projects ought to be done and is also consistent with the strategic or Top-Down view according to the strategic mapping and Delphi exercises. As well, the list of projects seems to make sense—the good ones are at the top of the list in each column in Exhibit 9.7, and the less attractive or less critical are below the line (on hold).

Several iterations might be required with management—back and forth among the rank-ordered list of projects (Step 5), looking at the resulting portfolio

(Steps 6 and 7), and even reconsidering the strategic-Delphi split (Step 3). The final iteration produces the strategic buckets both by business area and by project type. Management has decided:

- The final list of major go projects (and the clusters of smaller ones)
- Resource allocations across business areas required to do these projects
- Resource splits by project types.

The resource matrix is now finalized—one row per business area (as in Exhibit 9.11).

Note that this final round has had many inputs:

- The current situation or current portfolio—the status quo—Step 1
- The strategic considerations and the strategic map—Step 2
- The first round Delphi—Step 3
- A top level look at projects and opportunities within each business area—Steps 4 and 5
- And potentially several iterations through Steps 3, 5, and 6 where the ranked list of projects is adjusted and displayed, and then adjustments are made to both the list of projects and spending splits across business areas and project types.

This final portfolio resource allocation represents a comprehensive, strategic, and opportunistic view of what the spending splits or buckets should be, and which major projects should be undertaken.

THE ITERATIONS, ADJUSTMENTS, AND FINAL DECISION AT ABC CHEMICAL

After several iterations—making adjustments to the ranked list (Exhibit 9.7) and to the split in resources (Exhibit 9.6), then seeing the results in Exhibits 9.8–9.11, management settles on the final allocation:

- resource splits across the four business groups
- resource splits across the five project types
- major projects (and clusters of smaller projects) and their rankings.

The exercise is a tough one, but a very considered and rational way of allocating resources, making choices on strategic buckets, and ensuring that the portfolio really does reflect the strategic priorities of the business. A job well done—meeting adjourned!

Some Features of the Strategic Buckets Decision Process

There are several positive points to note in L&P's strategic exercise:

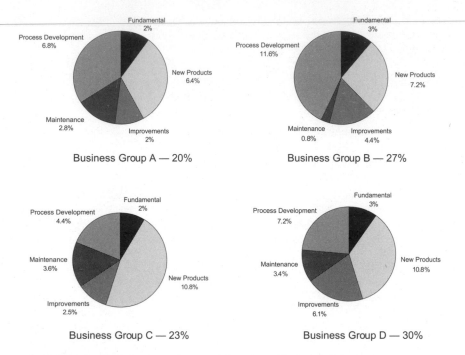

EXHIBIT 9.10   Each Business Group's Allocation of Total R&D Budget

For example: Business Group A is allocated 20 percent of the total R&D budget; 2 percent of the total R&D budget is allocated to fundamental spending in Group A.

	Project/ Activity Types	Fundamental	New Products	Improvements	Maintenance	Process Development
Groups		10%	35%	15%	10%	30%
Business Group A	20%	2.0	6.4	2.0	2.8	6.8
Business Group B	27%	3.2	7.2	5.2	0.1	11.6
Business Group C	23%	2.0	10.8	2.4	3.4	4.8
Business Group D	30%	2.8	10.8	5.2	3.4	7.2

EXHIBIT 9.11   Result of the Allocation Decision Process

1. Senior management leads the way: It was the senior people in the L&P business who took up the challenge and decided the business strategy before this portfolio allocation exercise even began.
2. The business strategy is translated into a new product strategy for the business, complete with arenas (markets, product lines, and project types). In management's eyes, the most important of these was project types; that's why buckets were created here.
3. The split in resources across arenas—in this case business groups and project types—although Top-Down and strategically driven, also considers opportunities within each arena. This is not a sterile strategic or accounting exercise, but rather an iterative one between a Top-Down, strategic approach and a Bottom-Up approach that takes into account active as well as proposed projects and opportunities.
4. Strategic buckets and spending targets—two slightly different techniques outlined in Chapter 5—can both be employed. L&P used strategic buckets for project types (five columns with spending limits in Exhibit 9.7), but spending targets across the business groups, at least for this decision process (no definite upper limit was set for spending in each group, only a guide from the Delphi split). Once the spending targets were agreed, then they became firm buckets for the four business groups.
5. Different criteria were used for ranking (or rating) different project types. L&P management did not make the mistake of trying to compare apples and oranges (dissimilar project types); nor did they rely simplistically on a single financial criterion for all project investments.
6. The process was a difficult and long one, but one that yielded very positive results. Not only was management convinced that the decisions they had made were better than those in previous years, but the process that management went through—the seven steps—was a real learning experience. It engaged them in the decision-making process as they had never been engaged before, and in a very positive way.

POINTS FOR MANAGEMENT TO PONDER

Consider whether the deliberate decision process outlined above could provide value to your organization. Note that once the tentative Delphi strategic splits have been made (for example, across business areas and project types, or on other dimensions that are relevant to your business), it is time to move to a Bottom-Up approach. That is, look at the project opportunities themselves. These projects are identified and pre-ranked by each business area but then rolled up onto a master list. Note that not all projects should be listed together; rather separate portfolio lists and buckets should be created for each project type (new products, improvements, platform or fundamental research projects, and so on).

In each bucket, rank-order the projects. It is wise to use different criteria for each project type. Then look at the resulting portfolio using various types of charts. Several iterations of this process should yield the right portfolio: the best projects—the high-value ones—are at the top of the list; and the portfolio has the right balance of projects as well as being aligned with the business's innovation strategy and its strategic priorities.

Summary

The place to begin portfolio management is with the strategy of your business—both your business strategy, and flowing from it, your new product strategy. Strategy development is the job of the leadership team of the business. The senior people must lead here. Indeed, this is how the senior people become involved in your portfolio management process—by charting the business's strategy.

First, define the new product goals for the business: what percentage of sales or profit or growth new products will contribute. Then map the battlefields. Identify arenas of strategic focus (markets, product lines, technologies, and platforms), and prioritize them. Next, develop spending splits across key dimensions (for example, these might be markets, product lines, or project types; or pick dimensions that represent strategic thrusts to you). Define strategic buckets across dimensions, much as L&P did in Exhibit 9.5.

Then move to individual projects and look at the specific opportunities within each business area or strategic bucket. The specific opportunities you see may cause you to rethink some of your initial decisions on allocations across buckets. That's normal—the process is iterative between strategic, Top-Down, and opportunistic, Bottom-Up.

Arrive at decisions on your strategic buckets—by business areas, market sectors, or product groups. And don't forget project types! If you are successful at this macro or strategic allocation phase of portfolio management—as L&P management was—you are now ready to move to the micro phase—selecting specific projects outlined in Chapter 10.

Making Portfolio Management Work for You: Portfolio Management and Project Selection

The question in this chapter is: Which development projects should the business undertake? And how should they be prioritized? As with the last chapter, the issue is still one of resource allocation. But in Chapter 9 we dealt with broad splits—across business units, across business groups, and across project types—a macro or strategic buckets decision. In this chapter, we move to the micro issue: Which specific projects should we be selecting?

How does one go about making project selection decisions? "That's easy," you might say. "Projects are chosen at gate meetings in our new product process!" But not so fast. If projects are selected one by one at gate meetings, then who is looking at the totality, the entire portfolio? Selecting the best projects is a complex process and, it should be no surprise, there is no single right way to do it. The "right project selection process" depends on the nature of your business, how dynamic your portfolio is, and on what decision processes you already have in place for charting your new product direction and project selection.

Three Key Components of the Portfolio Management Process

The key components of an effective portfolio management process (PMP) are outlined in Exhibit 10.1 and described in detail in the sections that follow. Recall that there are three important decision processes at work:

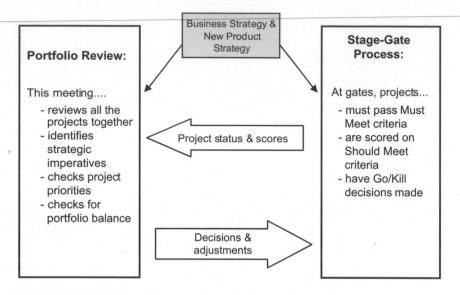

EXHIBIT 10.1 The Three-Part Decision Process in Portfolio Management

1. The development of the business and new product strategy
2. The new product process, consisting of a series of stages and gate decision points
3. The portfolio review process.

In this chapter:

- We begin in the shaded box at the top of Exhibit 10.1 with the role of new product strategy, how it must drive the portfolio, and how this is done in practice.
- We move to the right side of Exhibit 10.1, where we focus on the gates in the new product process and how the portfolio management process is operationalized at the gate decisions.
- We next move to the left side of Exhibit 10.1 and outline the portfolio review and various models/tools used here, how the portfolio is adjusted, and how the portfolio review provides directional inputs to the gating model in the new product process.
- We bring all three decision processes together to form an integrated decision system: the portfolio management process (PMP). Two fundamentally different approaches are outlined.

Strategy: The First Key Driver of the Portfolio Management Process (PMP)

The portfolio management process is driven by strategy. Why? Because strategy begins when you start spending money. Since portfolio choice is about allocating resources and making Go/Kill decisions on projects—in short, decisions on where the money is spent—the portfolio choice must begin with strategy. After all, strategy guides and directs a business. It defines what is in or out of bounds for development; and it defines arenas of focus as well as their relative emphasis. The manifestation of strategy is decisions about where you will spend your money—your portfolio decisions.

Strategy Is Vital to the PMP

A guide to developing a new product strategy for your business was outlined in Chapter 5. Recall that we moved from goals through to delineation of strategic arenas and areas of strategic focus, along with their relative priorities. Then, in Chapter 9, we translated your business's product innovation strategy into deployment decisions—spending splits or strategic buckets—the business areas and project types in which financial and human resources should be used.

To recap, in the PMP, strategy provides direction in three ways:

1. *Strategic fit and importance*: The BU's business and new product strategy is used as a criterion to ensure that all projects are on strategy. All projects must be within a product, market, or technology area defined as an arena of strategic focus, and selected projects must indeed be the strategically important ones. Note that one of the first questions in most checklist or scoring model schemes is, "Does the project fit our strategy?"

2. *Breakdown of spending*: Strategy should also be used to define spending breakdowns across markets, product types, technologies, and even project types (extensions versus new products, long-term versus short-term, and so on). In the section on strategy in Chapter 5, we saw how a defined new product strategy for the BU or business should not only define what is on strategy but should go as far as defining desired spending splits along key dimensions. In this way, strategic buckets of funds or target spending levels are pre-established, and the levels should mirror the business's new product strategy.

3. *Strategic imperatives:* Strategy may also define some must-do projects right away (that is, unless there are some other killer variables). Must-do projects are *strategic imperatives*. For example, if the business's strategy were to expand aggressively into one key market, and one new product project was identified as pivotal to this expansion, the decision here might be an immediate go. Alternatively, if an *existing* market segment were defined as a strategic priority, and a key product improvement was needed just to defend share in that market, once again a strategic imperative decision might be made: an immediate go!

Gating: The Second Key Driver of the Portfolio Management Process

The second vital decision-making system in the PMP is the new product process (the right side of Exhibit 10.1). Often called the Stage-Gate™ process, this is the game plan, or *modus operandi* for driving development projects from the idea stage through to launch (see Exhibit 10.2; also Appendix A for more detail).

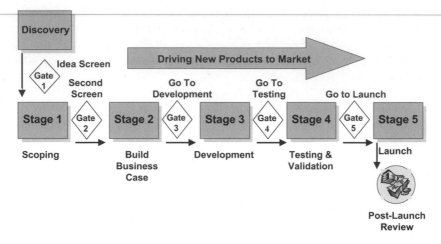

EXHIBIT 10.2   Overview of a Typical Stage-Gate™ Process

POINTS FOR MANAGEMENT TO PONDER

Does your business's new product strategy drive your portfolio management process? Review your PMP to determine whether your business strategy affects it in these three ways:

- by providing the key "strategic fit" and "strategic importance criteria" used to rate and rank projects via checklists and scoring models (at either gate meetings or portfolio reviews)
- by providing guides to spending breakdowns—either strategic buckets or target spending levels—so that spending mirrors the business's strategic priorities
- by identifying strategic imperatives—"must-do-now" projects.

If your business lacks a new product strategy, then you are missing a key element in the PMP. Revisit Chapters 5 and 9 for some guidance.

Example: Recall L&P Division, an example used in the last chapter. L&P relies on a new product process to drive product to market. It is a five-stage, five-gate model, very similar to the standard one in Exhibit 10.2. The gates are working effectively, according to management, culling out the poor projects and allocating resources to the designated go projects. Management is confident that good Go/Kill decisions are being made on individual projects via their stage-and-gate process. But what about the entire portfolio of projects?

Embedded within the Stage-Gate™ process are gate decision points, where regular Go/Kill decisions are made on individual projects. In an effective new product process, gates are the quality control checkpoints. Gates are where senior management puts its blessing on projects and where resources are allocated on a day-to-day basis throughout the year. Thus, the PMP is operationalized, at least in part, at gate meetings on individual projects. Note that these individual decisions on specific projects must be integrated into a greater whole, the portfolio. View the individual projects as the fingers and the portfolio of projects as the fist!

At some gate in the Stage-Gate™ process, resource commitments become sufficiently large that prioritization must take place. Prior to this gate, projects are reasonably small and ill-defined, so that putting them into the PMP—subjecting them to a formal portfolio prioritization—does not make much sense. Either the data on each project are still uncertain, resource commitments are too small, or both. In most firms, the PMP begins at about Gate 2 or Gate 3 in Exhibit 10.2. (See "When Does the PMP Kick In?")

When Does the PMP Kick In?

This is a tricky issue. One does not want to ignore early-stage projects in the portfolio management process; yet, most of these are ill-defined and lack the data needed for inclusion in a formal portfolio model. Recall the discussion in Chapter 7 (issue 10). Our suggestion:

- Design your formal PMP to begin at a gate in your Stage-Gate process where the project is sufficiently defined and where estimates of data needed to do portfolio analysis are available.
- In addition, design an early-stage portfolio of projects. This is a separate bucket of "seed corn money" for early-stage projects that are too ill-defined to subject to a formal portfolio review. Monitor this portfolio separately and informally (that is, less rigorously, less quantitatively).

Portfolio Reviews: The Third Key Driver of the PMP

Portfolio reviews are periodic meetings held throughout the year to consider the entire set of development projects together—the left side of Exhibit 10.1. Remember: The gates look at individual projects, the fingers; the portfolio review looks at all the projects—the fist! In many firms, portfolio reviews are little more than a twice-a-year meeting by senior management to gain a 50,000-foot view of all the projects—to make sure the right ones are active (versus on hold), that the priorities are right, and that the spending breakdowns of resources in the portfolio are consistent with spending targets, strategic buckets, and strategic priorities. This is where the various charts—the rank-ordered lists of Chapter 3 and the pie charts and bubble diagrams of Chapter 4—become useful to depict priorities and spending breakdowns. Many firms make few or no decisions at the portfolio reviews. They are viewed more as checks and minor course corrections. In some firms, individual projects are not even considered at the portfolio review; rather, management simply considers projects in aggregate as displayed by the various diagrams. By contrast, other firms treat portfolio reviews as much more proactive decision meetings, with individual projects very much under scrutiny. Regardless of the approach—and we will expand on the various approaches below—the role of the portfolio review is to consider all the projects together and look at them as an investment portfolio.

Who are the portfolio reviewers? Very often they are the same people who tend the more important gates, namely Gates 3, 4, and 5 in the new product process. In most businesses, this means the leadership team of the business.

Two Fundamentally Different Approaches to a Portfolio Management Process

There are two fundamentally different approaches to a portfolio management process: Each use the same tools, but in fundamentally different ways. Here's how.[1]

Approach 1: The Gates Dominate

Here, the philosophy is that if your gating process is working well, the portfolio will take care of itself. Therefore, make good decisions at the gates! The emphasis of this approach is on *sharpening gate decision making* on individual projects. If you make good individual project selection decisions at gates throughout the year, then at the end of the year you will indeed end up with a great portfolio of projects!

In Approach 1, senior management, or gatekeepers, make Go/Kill decisions at gates on projects one at a time. Also at gates, the project is prioritized and resources are allocated. Gates, thus, provide an in-depth review of projects, one project at a time, and project teams leave the gate meeting with committed resources—with a check in hand! This is a *real-time decision process,* with gates activated many times throughout the year. By contrast, the periodic portfolio review, held once or twice a year, serves largely as a check to ensure that real-time gate decisions are good ones—a look back at the sum total of these individual project selection decisions.

This "gates dominate" approach is often used by companies that already have Stage-Gate™ processes in place and working well. They then add portfolio management to their gating process, almost as a complementary decision process. Our research found this approach used most often in larger companies, in science-based industries, and where project development cycles are lengthy (such as the chemical industry).

Approach 2: The Portfolio Reviews Dominate

The philosophy of the second approach is that *every project must compete against all the others* at least several times per year. It is much like an auction with all projects and potential projects up for grabs. A single decision on all projects thus replaces one of the gates in the gating process.

Here, the leadership team makes Go/Kill and prioritization decisions at the Portfolio Reviews, where *all projects* are considered on the table together. This review occurs 2–4 times a year. The gates in the Stage-Gate™ process serve merely as checks on projects—ensuring that they remain financially sound and are proceeding on schedule.

The result of the portfolio review dominates approach is a more dynamic, constantly changing, portfolio of projects. The method may suit faster-paced companies, such as software, IT, and electronics firms, but it requires a much stronger commitment by senior management to the decision process. These people must commit the time to look at all projects together and in depth several times a year.

Approach 1: The Gates Dominate— An Overview of How It Works

Projects proceed through the Stage-Gate™ process as portrayed in Exhibit 10.2. They are rated and scored at gates, usually by senior management, especially at more critical gates (Gate 3 and beyond).

To introduce portfolio management, gates become two-part decisions (Exhibit 10.3). The first part of the gate is a pass-versus-kill decision, where projects are evaluated in isolation. They are assessed against an absolute set of hurdles or acceptable project scores.

The second half of the gate meeting involves *prioritization* of the project under discussion versus the other projects (Exhibit 10.3). This is a relative, not an absolute, evaluation. In practice, this means making a go-versus-hold decision; and if go, allocating resources to the project. A rank-ordered list of projects is displayed to compare the relative attractiveness of the project under discussion to

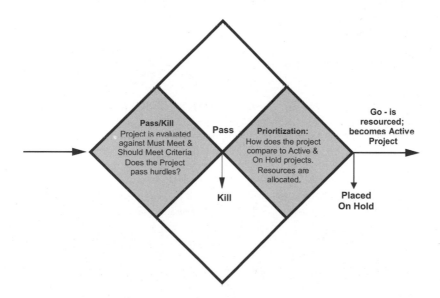

EXHIBIT 10.3   The Two-Part Decision Process at Gates

the other active and on-hold projects. Here, projects can be ranked on a financial criterion or on the project attractiveness score derived from the scoring model.

The impact of the proposed project on the total portfolio of projects is also assessed. The question is, Does the new product under discussion improve or detract from the balance of projects, and does the project improve the portfolio's strategic alignment? Bubble diagrams and pie charts are the tools commonly used for visualizing balance and alignment.

Note how the gates dominate the decision process in this approach: Go/Kill, prioritization decisions, and resource allocation decisions are made in real time, right at the gate meeting. But other projects are *not* discussed and reprioritized at the gate; only the project in question is given a relative priority level compared to the rest.

What about looking at all projects together in Approach 1? That is the role of portfolio reviews. In this approach, the portfolio reviews serve largely as *a check that the gates are working well.* Senior management meets perhaps once or twice a year to review the portfolio of all projects:

- Is there the right balance of projects?
- Is there the right mix?
- Are all projects strategically aligned? (Do they fit the business's strategy?)
- Are there the right priorities among projects?

If the gates are working, not too many decisions or major corrective actions should be required at the portfolio review.

Details of Approach 1: The Gates Dominate

Assume that the portfolio management process kicks in at the pivotal "Go to Development" decision point, or Gate 3 in the Stage-Gate™ model.* This means that

- Projects are prioritized beginning at this gate.
- From this gate onward, resource commitments are firm, either until the next gate or, possibly, through the end of the project.

Example: From Gate 3 onward, one rule might be that the project continues to receive resources as long as it does not shoot itself. If the project meets all deliverables, stays on its timeline, and continues to meet all successive gate criteria, it remains a go and the resource commitments remain in place.

Note that different businesses employ different rules regarding the firmness of resource commitments. We recommend one of two rules:

1. Once past a certain gate, resource commitments are firm, as long as the project remains a good one and continues to meet all criteria at successive gates.
2. Resources are firm between gates (unless a project turns sour), but reprioritization occurs at every gate.

* In some firms, the PMP kicks in at Gate 2. See box insert "When Does the PMP Kick In?"

Achieving the Three Goals of Effective Portfolio Management

The gate decision criteria must be deliberately constructed to achieve three portfolio goals. Recall from Chapters 3–5 what these goals are:

1. Maximization of value to the business
2. Proper balance of projects (for example, between high-risk and low-risk, between high-payoff and more modest projects)
3. Strategic alignment, where projects and spending breakdowns are consistent with the business's strategy.

How can these three potentially conflicting goals be realized in the same decision model? And how can projects be quantitatively rank-ordered from best to worst? Scoring models are a preferred tool here. Recall how well scoring models perform (Chapter 6), and how well they are rated by users. When multiple goals exist, scoring models are particularly suited to rating projects as well as ranking them in order to yield a prioritized list. Note that financial models are particularly limited in dealing with multiple goals.

In practice, we recommend that the gates should first use a checklist method (yes/no) to provide an initial culling, followed by a scoring model to deal with the multiple portfolio goals defined above:

- The checklist is used to weed out obvious misfit projects; for example, those that are way off-strategy or nonstarters for other reasons.
- The scoring model is, then, used to rate and rank projects against the three goals noted above.

Gate Criteria for Rating and Ranking New Product Projects

The checklist usually includes a handful of knockout or must-meet questions, designed to cull out the obvious misfits and dog projects. A single "no" answer means a project must be killed. Typical must-meet questions for new product projects are:

1. Does the project lie within strategic boundaries of your business (is it within your business mandate or definition)?
2. Does the project fit your values, policies, and ethics?
3. Is there a competitive reason to do the project—does it offer a competitive advantage or is it necessary to defend a position?
4. Are there no obvious show-stoppers or killer variables (factors that could devastate the project)?

Next, use a scoring model to gauge the relative attractiveness of the project. Scoring models include should-meet criteria. These highlight highly desirable characteristics of good projects, but failure to meet them does not mean a knockout. Thus we use a point-count scoring system. Chapter 3 described a number of scoring models and questions. The six criteria listed below are our f●orites, and they have been widely validated:

1. *Strategic alignment and importance*: Is the project aligned with your strategy, and is it strategically important to do?
2. *Product and competitive advantage*: Does the product offer unique customer benefits? meet customer needs better than competitors? provide good value for money for customers?
3. *Market attractiveness*: Is the target market an attractive one—size, growth, margins, competition?
4. *Leveraging of core competencies*: Does the project build on your strengths, experience, and competencies in marketing, technology, and operations?
5. *Technical feasibility*: What is the likelihood of technical feasibility—size of technical gap? complexity? uncertainty?
6. *Financial reward*: Can you make money here? How sure are you? Is it worth the risk?

New product projects are scored on each of these six questions using a 1–5 or 0–10 scale (usually a scorecard is used at the gate meeting), and the scale ratings are added (either weighted or unweighted) to yield the project attractiveness score out of 100. Appendix B shows the detailed scorecards for this six-factor scoring model.

Example: As seen in the last chapter, L&P Division uses different rating schemes for different types of projects:

- For fundamental research projects, they use a four-question scoring model: strategic fit, strategic leverage, technical feasibility likelihood, and impact on the corporation if successful.
- For new product projects, they employ a six-factor scoring model almost the same as our recommended model in Exhibit 3.10 and the six factors listed above.
- For improvements and process developments, L&P uses a criterion similar to the productivity index in Chapter 3, namely NPV/R&D.
- And for maintenance projects, they also use the NPV/R&D index to rank projects.

Management in Business Group D looks now at the "new product projects" category, but only for their own business. In L&P's Stage-Gate™ process, Gate 3 is the vital decision point at which the project goes to full-fledged development. The Gate 3 gatekeepers are senior management, and the meeting is chaired by the general manager of the business.

Consider a new product project at the Gate 3 decision point, Hydro-P (project D501). The project has had a two-person team working on it for the past four months. Market studies have been completed. Some preliminary technical (laboratory) work has been undertaken, enough to establish a reasonable likelihood of technical feasibility. The business case has been built. The product has been defined (target market, product benefits, price point, technical requirements, and high-level specs); the project has been justified (in the financial analysis and business rationale); and the action plan has been mapped out for the next stages of the project.

At Gate 3, senior management reviews Hydro-P against a set of must-meet criteria (similar to the four listed above). Hydro-P passes all of them: There are no negative votes here. Next, the project is scored on the should-meet items. Here a 0–10 scoring model is used. Factors are averaged to yield a project attractiveness score. Exhibit 10.4 shows the scoring model results accorded Hydro-P. The project scores 75 out of 100 (a pass is 60/100). The project, thus, scores fairly well and clears all the Gate 3 hurdles, including the 60 percent hurdle on the total project score. It looks like a go—but is it?

Must Meet Criteria (must yield Yes answers):
- Within Strategic Boundary for BU
- Existence of a Competitive Need
- Meets SHEL Policies of Company (safety, health, environmental, legal)
- No Show-Stoppers (absence of killer variables)

Hydro-P passes all Must Meet items

Should Meet (scored 0-10):

	Hydro-P Scores *out of 10*	
Strategic		
degree to which project aligns with BU s strategy	8	
strategic importance	7	Strategic = 7.5
Product/Competitive Advantage		
unique customer benefits	9	
meets customer needs better	8	
good value for money	7	Product Advantage = 8.0
Market Attractiveness		
market size	9	
margins in this market	7	
market growth	7	
competitive situation	5	Market Attractiveness = 7.0
Synergies (Leverages Core Competencies)		
marketing synergies	6	
technological synergies	8	
operations synergies	7	Synergies = 7.0
Technical Feasibility		
technical gap	9	
technical complexity	6	
technical uncertainty	9	Tech Feasibility = 8.0
Financial Reward		
expected profitability (magnitude; e.g. NPV)	9	
payback period	8	
certainty of return/profit estimates	7	Financial Reward = 8.0

Project Attractiveness Score = 75 / 100

EXHIBIT 10.4   Sample Criteria for Gate 3 and Scores for Hydro-P Project

Note: The should-meet items above are scored and added to yield factor average scores. They are added (weighted or unweighted) to yield the project attractiveness score. In this example, scales are 0–10; items and factors are added in an unweighted fashion. Total Project Score for Hydro-P = 45.5 out of a possible 60 points, which is 75.8%.

Impact on the Portfolio: Deciding the Project's Priority Level

The outcome of the project evaluation exercise at the gate is a decision: The project is either a "kill" (it fails the criteria and hurdles) or a "pass." Merely being a pass does not guarantee that the project will be immediately resourced, however. There is still the question of prioritization and finding the resources for the project before it can become a go.

The gate meeting is conceptually a two-part decision process (Exhibit 10.3). The first part rates and scores the project, leading to a kill or pass decision. The second facet of the gate meeting deals with prioritization and the decision to allocate resources to the go projects.

Assume that the project at the gate review passes the must-meet criteria, and its project attractiveness score clears the hurdles for the should-meet criteria. Will it be resourced? And where will the resources come from? These are the questions for the second part of the gate meeting (the second diamond in Exhibit 10.3).

To answer this question, management must look at the project in relationship to the list of active and on-hold projects; namely, the impact on the portfolio if the new project were to move ahead.

The first discussion question is:

* What is the value or attractiveness of the project relative to the rest of the projects? (That is, if you add this project, will it improve the overall value of your portfolio, or will it detract from your portfolio's value?)

To answer this question, management looks at the rank-ordered list of active and on-hold projects and considers where the new project would fit. Would its score place it toward the top of the list of active projects? Or would it fall nearer the bottom of the on-hold projects?

EXAMPLE: THE RELATIVE VALUE OF PROJECT HYDRO-P

Management considers the fairly good score of 75 for Hydro-P, this time not against the hurdle score of 60 but against the scores of the other new products that are active and on hold. Exhibit 10.5 shows the rank-ordered list of projects, ranked by project attractiveness scores. Note where Hydro-P would fit. It places fairly far up the list of active projects. That is, if L&P added this project, it would enhance the value of the portfolio. So far, the project looks like a good candidate for resourcing. But what will it do to the portfolio's balance and strategic alignment?

Next, the effect of adding the new project on the portfolio balance and strategic alignment are considered. Here the portfolio maps are reviewed. The question is posed: How does a go decision on this project affect the balance and strategic alignment of the total portfolio?

The approach here is to discuss the portfolio of projects—the list of active projects and the various maps or charts that display the portfolio—with and with-

Project Name	Total Project Score	Rank
✓ Project-D009	Must Do Project	1
✓ Project-D034	Must Do Project	1
Project Hydro-P (D501)	75	?
Project-D039	74	2
Project-D015	70	3
Project-D028	65	4
Projects on Hold		
Project-D041	74	1
Project-D040	71	2
Project-D042	66	3

EXHIBIT 10.5   Prioritized List of Active and On-Hold Projects (New Products Bucket Only)

Notes: ✓ Indicates a must-do project.

The new Hydro-P is placed in the rank-ordered list according to its project attractiveness score. It is not yet deemed a go project, however.

out the new proposed project. Note that discussion should focus only on the impact that the addition of this one project will have on the portfolio. This is not the venue to address the total portfolio of projects. Opening up this discussion at every gate meeting would lead to chaos!

Example: Recall from the last chapter that L&P's management had undertaken an exercise wherein they made some strategic splits in resources (strategic buckets). Each business area, including Product Group D, ended up with a strategic split in resources across projects types as well as across product groups. Exhibit 10.6 shows the split across project types for Business Group D. Management within Business Group D has also undertaken a few other splits and defined target spending splits across their market segments and product lines (see Exhibit 10.6). The target or desired splits are shown, along with actual spending splits, year to date. Note that already there are some gaps between target splits and actuals. For example, product line X accounts for about 67 percent of spending (versus a target of 75 percent). This 8 percent gap was relatively small as a percentage, so no corrective action had been taken.

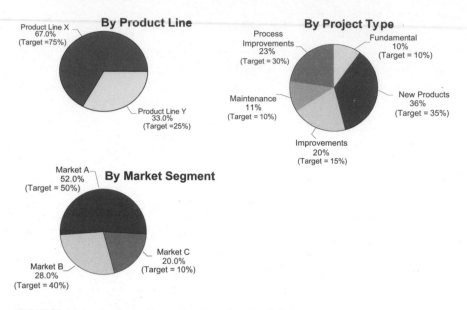

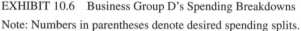

EXHIBIT 10.6   Business Group D's Spending Breakdowns

Note: Numbers in parentheses denote desired spending splits.

Now consider project Hydro-P. First it is a new product (as opposed to an im-provement or maintenance project). Second, it is targeted at Market Segment B, an area with a relative shortage of projects. So adding Hydro-P is apparently good for the portfolio because it helps to bring it into balance and strategic align-ment, at least on one vital dimension (market segments). Being in Product Line Y, the project has a fairly neutral effect in terms of product lines. There is no major shortage nor surplus of Product Line Y projects.

The decision: Hydro-P is a desirable project. It passes the key criteria. Its proj-ect attractiveness score is relatively good compared to the other projects, and it helps to balance the portfolio and improves its strategic alignment. The decision is a clear go.

Finding the Resources

If the decision is "go," then the gatekeepers must find the resources. Usually re-sources are not just lying around waiting to be allocated. Invariably people are very busy on other worthwhile projects and tasks! And many companies have a rule that other projects cannot be deprioritized between gates just to fund a rela-tive newcomer. Nonetheless, resources must be found. The potential sources of resources that gatekeepers must investigate include:

- resources already assigned to the project under review (normally, there are some people already working on the project who are available to continue this work)
- resources available in the very near future from projects completing certain phases, where certain people are no longer required on that team
- resources from projects in trouble, which should be shut down or curtailed (this could entail an "unscheduled" or emergency gate meeting in order to kill a project in trouble)
- resources from projects soon to be facing a gate meeting (Note that one rule is that, although resources are firm between gates, at gates each project is reviewed and may indeed be killed, thereby freeing resources for other projects.)
- new resources (for example, new hires, transfers, people who are between assignments)
- outside sources (for example, other divisions, corporate labs, strategic partners, universities, outside labs, consultants, or contract people).

If the resources cannot be found, then the project is placed in the hold tank. This should happen only after every effort has been made to support this worthwhile, high-scoring project.

Example: The decision for Hydro-P is "Go." Indeed, the decision is a fairly strong go, and resources are allocated right at the gate meeting. Resources are acquired from several sources. First, the two-person team already on the project is assigned to continue as key team players. Other technology players are added from another project soon to be entering the launch phase, where their services will not be required full-time. Finally, a project with several people assigned is approaching a Gate 4 meeting and may be canceled, potentially freeing up a few more people for Hydro-P.

So much for gates and decisions on individual projects—the fingers in Approach 1. Next we turn to the fist—the portfolio of all projects considered together.

Portfolio Reviews

Ideally, the portfolio review in Approach 1 should be merely a minor course correction. If the gating process and gate criteria are well designed and effectively applied, the portfolio meeting should not result in a major adjustment to the portfolio. The hope here is that the gates are working well and doing a good job of selecting and prioritizing projects throughout the year. Thus, instead of massive reallocations of resources occurring at the portfolio review—a 90-degree turn in direction—the desire is to have minor corrections to the portfolio of projects—a 5-degree course correction. Recall that maximizing the value, strategic fit and importance, and portfolio balance are very much the key criteria at the gates. Hence, projects selected at gates should automatically contribute to the overall portfolio.

POINTS FOR MANAGEMENT TO PONDER

Here are the key points from this section—food for thought:

1. You need to have an effective gating process in place—the right side of the PMP and Exhibit 10.1. Do not expect your portfolio reviews to correct the problems created by a broken gating process!
2. Gates should have clearly defined, consistent, prespecified, and visible criteria for making Go/Kill and prioritization decisions.
3. Consider using a set of must-meet questions to weed out the bad projects, followed by a set of should-meet questions to be scored via a scoring model. Use a scorecard.
4. Gates are a two-part decision process. If the project passes the must-meet and should-meet criteria, its impact on the portfolio is assessed (second diamond in Exhibit 10.3):

   • Does the project add to the value of the portfolio (how does its project attractiveness score compare to the other active and on-hold projects—Exhibit 10.5)?

   • Does the project help (or detract from) the portfolio balance and its strategic alignment (Exhibit 10.6)?

Steps in the Portfolio Review

The portfolio review entails the following steps:

1. Identify Strategic Imperatives.   First, there is a review of the business's strategy and an identification of any strategic imperatives; that is, projects that are absolutely essential to achieving the strategy.

EXAMPLE: PORTFOLIO REVIEWS IN PRODUCT GROUP D

Management conducts a portfolio review meeting twice a year in Business Group D. At the December portfolio review, each of the key strategic thrusts and arenas is discussed. One question focuses on the need to move ahead right now with any projects essential to the business's strategy. At this particular meeting, no such "Go" decisions are made: There are no strategically vital projects currently on hold.

Note: If you find that much of the portfolio review meeting is taken up discussing and approving must-do projects, then something is wrong with your gating process. The portfolio review in Approach 1 is not a substitute for effective gates!

2. Check Project Priorities—The Rank-Ordered List.   Next, there is a check that projects are ranked and prioritized appropriately: that the projects scoring highest on the key criteria—those with the greatest value to the corporation—are indeed being given top priority and maximum resources. If too many projects in the hold tank score higher than active projects, something is amiss!

The key criteria at the portfolio review are the same as those at the gate decision points. Indeed, the same scoring model or financial index should be used, but this time across all projects within a category. The scores or ratings given to projects at their most recent gate meetings are used at the portfolio review. For some projects, these scores are updated in the event of new information acquired since the gate meeting.

For new products, the project attractiveness score becomes the logical ranking criterion for use in a rank-ordered list of projects. For other types of projects, you can use other criteria, such as a financial index. This list is simply a prioritized list of active and on-hold projects.

EXAMPLE: REVIEWING THE RANK-ORDERED LIST OF PROJECTS

Business Group D's list of active and funded new product projects past Gate 3—the rank-ordered list—is reviewed (see Exhibit 10.5). In L&P Group D's case, recall that, a priori, management has split resources into five strategic buckets. One of these buckets is for genuine new products. (Exhibit 10.5 shows these projects; similar rank-ordered lists—not shown—are prepared for other project types: improvements and maintenance; cost reductions; and fundamental research.) The exhibit also shows projects in the hold tank below the horizontal line. The projects are ordered in this prioritized list according to the project attractiveness score from L&P's scoring model for new products (Exhibit 10.4).

Management now checks to ensure that projects at the top of the list are, indeed, given the appropriate priority in terms of resource allocation and scores. Several projects on hold have excellent scores; namely, projects D041 and D040. Indeed, they both have better scores than some active and funded projects, specifically projects D015 and D028. But both D015 and D028 are well on their way through testing and moving toward launch. Both still have good scores and continue to clear the gate hurdles. So the decision is to continue with both projects and to seek resources for the two top-rated on-hold projects, resourcing these as soon as people become available.

---

3. Check for Balance and Alignment.   Here the key question is, When all the active or go projects are considered together, is the resulting portfolio strategically aligned and properly balanced?

Various visual displays are recommended to portray the existing portfolio of active projects and to check for balance. Note that visual displays are best suited to portray balance in the portfolio (see Chapter 4):

- *Bubble diagrams:* This is a reward-versus-risk chart. Here the vertical axis is the probability of technical success; the horizontal axis is the reward measured via NPV (already adjusted for commercial risks); and the size of the circles denotes the magnitude of spending on that project (see Exhibit 9.9; see also Exhibit 4.1 for an interpretation of risk-reward bubble diagrams).

  If there is a fear of over-emphasis of financial measures (such as NPV), instead of using NPV, try a risk-reward diagram where reward is qualitatively assessed (such as in Exhibit 4.4). A more creative yet rigorous approach is to utilize the scores derived from the gate scoring model. Such a risk-reward bubble diagram is shown in Exhibit 10.7, whose axes are simply the weighted combinations of scoring model scores from Exhibit 10.4:

  - Reward is the horizontal axis and is composed of a weighted addition of market attractiveness, financial reward, and strategic fit.
  - Probability of success is the vertical axis and is made up of the weighted addition of product/competitive advantage, synergies (leverages core competencies), and probability of technical success.

  This risk-reward diagram (Exhibit 10.7) thus combines methods outlined in Chapter 4: the ease and attractiveness scored axes used by Reckitt-Benckiser (see Exhibits 4.7 and 4.8); Specialty Minerals' scored axes based on their gate scoring model (Exhibit 4.6); and ADL's nonfinancial approach to estimating reward (Exhibit 4.4).

Example: The bubble diagrams for Business Group D in L&P in Exhibits 9.9 and 10.7 portray the risk-reward snapshots of the portfolio. Note that these maps display all project types (some smaller projects are clustered). There are four clear Pearls—high-reward, high-probability projects. They also have four other Pearl projects, but they are not as strong—overall, a strong showing of Pearl projects. One fundamental project is a long shot, or Oyster, namely, D129. Bread and Butter projects are numerous and include one low-risk major new product with a fair-to-modest reward (Bundle D) and two major products (D214 and D408), a product improvement on an existing product, and a process improvement project. Smaller projects in this Bread and Butter quadrant are D034, D211, D215, and D331. There are no White Elephants.

Overall, management's assessment of the distribution of projects in the bubble diagram of Exhibit 10.7 is positive. The risk-reward pattern shows no obvious patterns for concern. For example, one long-shot Oyster project is deemed about right; management is pleased with the number of Pearls, and believes that the number of Bread and Butter projects is about right for their division.

- *Pie charts:* Pie charts show splits in such things as resources being spent, numbers of projects, key dimensions, or comparisons against desired spending patterns. Pie charts provide a check for strategic alignment.

Example: Business Division D's project spending breakdowns in Exhibit 10.6 reveal gaps between actual spending and desired spending splits. Recall that management had specified desired spending splits as part of the strategic planning exercise.

- *Product line split:* Exhibit 10.6 reveals that projects for product line X accounted for about 67 percent of spending (versus a desired 75 percent). This 8 percent gap was relatively small as a percentage, so no corrective actions were taken. Although product line Y accounted for 33 percent of the spending versus a desired spend of 25 percent, no corrective action was taken.
- *Market split:* Projects targeted at market B accounted for 28 percent of the spending; this is far short of the goal of 40 percent. Further, projects for market C accounted for far more than the goal (20 percent versus a target of 10 percent). Management agreed to increase funding preference for any new projects in market B and to be more critical of any new project proposals for market C until the imbalance is corrected.
- *Project type:* Strategic buckets were established a priori for the six project types. As shown in Exhibit 10.6, the desired spending levels had not been achieved. Too much was going to product improvements and not enough to process improvements. In spite of these imbalances management decided to remain with these desired splits for the short term.

Corrections and Adjustments

The portfolio review and discussion results in corrections to the mix of projects (that is, it corrects gate decisions already made) and in adjustments to the gating model or process itself (that is, it creates a shift in the mix of projects for the upcoming time period):

- *Kill decisions:* Some projects might be killed outright (for example, those with low scores or those voted not strategically important). In effect, the portfolio meeting overrides (or takes the place of) a gate meeting. The hope is that kill decisions here are rare, however. They should have been made at gate meetings! In other companies, the rule is that portfolio reviews should not be used to make kill decisions, but they might signal the need for an immediate gate review on some projects in trouble or in doubt.
- *Immediate go decisions:* Some projects are designated as strategic imperatives and elevated to go or top priority (maximum spend). Once again, in Approach 1 resist the temptation to use the portfolio review meeting to make the most of your go decisions. That is the role of gate meetings!

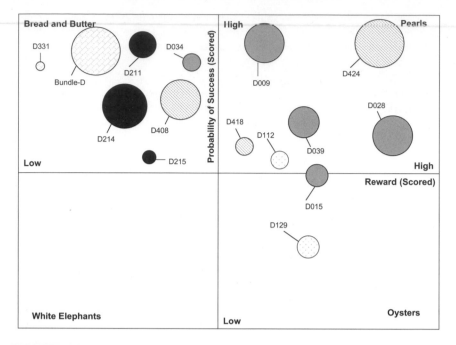

EXHIBIT 10.7   Alternative Version of Business Group D's Risk-Reward Diagram

Notes: Reward = 0.3Strategic Fit + 0.4Financial Reward + 0.3Market Attractiveness
Probability = 0.4Advantage + 0.25Synergies + 0.35Technical Success.
Factors are from scoring model.
Size = resources (annual); shading = project type. See Exhibit 10.4

SOURCE: Based on Specialty Minerals's model

- *Adjustments to the gating process*: A final result of the portfolio review is consensus on the need to adjust the balance of projects during the next period to better reflect both the desired balance and strategic priorities. For example, the decision might be that there are too many projects aimed at market C and not
  enough at market B. Next steps would aim to correct this imbalance over the following time period. For example, the gatekeepers (who are usually the same
  people as the portfolio reviewers) would agree to approve fewer projects aimed
  at market C (by increasing the hurdles, for example) and seek more projects targeted at market B.

Example: Business Group D's adjustment and correction decisions:

- There were no strategic imperatives.
- Nor were any projects on the hold list moved to active projects.
- A decision was made to seek resources for the two top-rated hold projects,
  D041 and D040.

- Management agreed to monitor the spending allocations in product line spending and, although no immediate action is needed, over time the imbalance would be corrected.
- It was agreed that market B projects were under-represented in the portfolio, and that market C projects were over-represented.

Recap: Approach 1—The Gates Dominate

To recap, the gates are where the day-to-day decisions are made on projects in Approach 1. Gates focus on individual projects—one at a time—and are in-depth reviews. At gates, each project is evaluated and scored before moving on to the next stage—a real-time decision process. At gates, poor projects are spotted and weeded out, and good ones are identified and prioritized accordingly. Note that resource decisions—committing people and money to specific projects—are made right at these gate meetings. Thus, the gates become a two-part decision process, with projects evaluated on absolute criteria (pass/kill decisions in Exhibit 10.3), followed by a comparison with other active and on-hold projects (go-versus-hold decisions). These gate decision points are real-time decisions.

Portfolio reviews, by contrast, are periodic meetings, held perhaps twice per year. They serve as a check on the portfolio and oversee the gate decisions being made. If the gates are working well, the portfolio reviews are largely rubber-stamp meetings.

Note that the portfolio reviewers and the senior gatekeepers are most often the same people. The result of the Stage-Gate™ or gating process working in tandem with the portfolio reviews is an effective, harmonized portfolio management process (Exhibit 10.8).

POINTS FOR MANAGEMENT TO PONDER

Here are the key points from this section:

1. In addition to a sound new product process with effective gates, you must also have periodic portfolio reviews. Recall that gates look at individual projects (the fingers), whereas portfolio reviews look at all projects together and in aggregate (the fist).

2. Here are the important steps in the portfolio review:
   - Check for strategic imperatives—"must-do-now" projects.
   - Check project priorities: Use the prioritized scored list and spot inconsistencies.
   - Check for balance and alignment: Use bubble diagrams, charts, and maps.
   - Define adjustments needed in the gating process.

3. Charts and maps to use at portfolio reviews might include:
   - The risk-reward bubble diagram (NPV versus probability, nonfinancial reward versus success probabilities, or scored axes)
   - Pie charts showing splits in resources (versus strategic buckets or target spending levels).

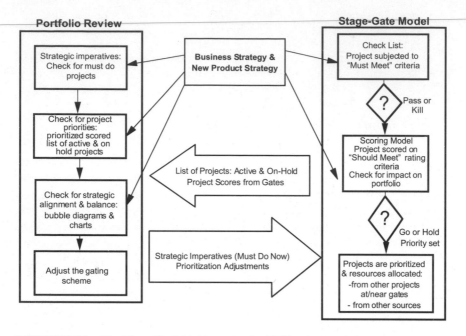

EXHIBIT 10.8   The Three Decision Processes for PMP—Approach 1

The portfolio review feeds the Stage-Gate™ model; and the Stage-Gate™ model feeds the portfolio review. Both schemes are in sync and driven by strategy.

Approach 2: The Portfolio Review Dominates

In Approach 2, the leadership team of the business makes Go/Kill and prioritization decisions at the portfolio reviews, where *all projects* are up for consideration. That is, a single decision on all projects replaces one of the gates in the gating process. And at this single decision point, every project must compete against all the others. This review typically occurs 3–4 times a year. The gates in the Stage-Gate™ process serve merely as checks on projects to ensure they remain financially sound and on schedule.

Approach 2 uses many of the same portfolio tools and models described above, but in a different way. The result is a more dynamic portfolio of projects. In this approach, the project enters the portfolio process, typically, after the first stage (at Gate 2 in Exhibit 10.9) when data are available.

The main difference from Approach 1 is that, early in the life of projects, a combined Gate 2 and portfolio decision meeting takes place. All new Gate 2 projects, together with all projects past Gate 2, are reviewed and prioritized against one another. Active projects, well along in their development, can be

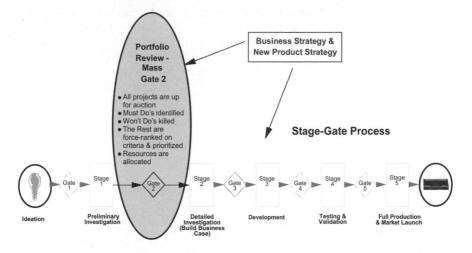

EXHIBIT 10.9 Approach 2—Portfolio Management Intersecting with New Product Process

Note: Projects are force-ranked against each other in the combined Gate 2/portfolio review. Prioritization is established, and resources are allocated here. Subsequent gates serve as checks.

killed or reprioritized here, and resources are allocated here rather than at gates.

The role of gates in Approach 2 is very different from that in Approach 1. Successive gates (after Gate 2) are merely checkpoints or review points. They

- Check that the project is on time, on course, and on budget
- Check quality of work done—the quality of deliverables
- Check that the business case and project are still in good shape.

If the project fails on any of these points, it could be killed at the gate, recycled to the previous stage, or flagged for the next portfolio review/Gate 2 meeting.

The major decisions, however, occur at the combined Gate 2/portfolio decision point, which is a more extended, proactive meeting than portfolio reviews in Approach 1. And although this is a periodic process, it is almost real-time because this portfolio/Gate 2 meeting is held every three to four months.

Example: EXFO Engineering (introduced in Chapter 3 and winner of the PDMA's Outstanding Corporate Innovator Award in 2000) has implemented both a Stage-Gate™ and portfolio management process, using Approach 2. Four times per year, the leadership team, chaired by the CEO, evaluates the complete slate of development projects during their portfolio review meetings. Any project at or beyond Gate 2 is included in this prioritization exercise. Projects are rated according to the following criteria:

1. Confidence in the project team and in their proposed costs, revenues, and schedules
2. Revenues (times a commercial risk factor) versus expenses (development and commercialization costs, including a technical risk factor) over a two-year period
3. Match to the strategic plan (specific growth directions, with a weighting factor on each)
4. Profitability index (return on investment)
5. Availability of technical resources and commercial strengths

Based on these criteria, projects are force-ranked against each other. The result is a prioritized list with some projects placed on hold. Note that EXFO is an entrepreneurial company, and one can see this reflected in the rating criteria used.

Details of Approach 2: The Portfolio Review Dominates

In this vital quarterly portfolio review/Gate 2 decision meeting, all Gate 2 and beyond projects are "on the table," meaning that any project can be killed or re-sourced at this key review meeting. Here are the steps in this crucial meeting:

Step 1: Review of All Projects.   All projects are discussed here. These include existing projects that are underway and already past Gate 2 (for example, already into the development or testing stages), projects on hold, and new projects approaching Gate 2. For existing projects, teams are asked to provide thumbnail updates. A good approach is to require that this update mirror the same criteria that you plan to use at the review meeting.

For convenience and to save time, some smaller projects—maintenance items and cost reductions—can be aggregated or rolled up into a group or cluster for discussion rather than discussing each and every small project individually. In order to make the exercise more visual, you may wish to have each project summarized on an $8\frac{1}{2}$ x 11 inch (or A-4) card, which can then be stuck on the wall. These cards also facilitate sorting exercises on a table.

Step 2: Identify the Must-Do's.   The portfolio managers (the leadership team of the business) first identify the must-do projects—the untouchables. They are typically of two types:

- *Projects that are already underway*—perhaps in Stages 3 or 4—that remain in good standing (Note that their scores or NPVs may not be the highest, but they are still good enough and it would be foolish to stop them.)
- *Projects that are strategic imperatives*—ones that you have to do in order to protect the business or even to stay in business.

Step 3: Identify the Won't-Do's. Next, management votes on and identifies won't-do's," which are killed outright. These are simply bad projects: Some might be new and are approaching Gate 2 for the first time. Others might be well underway and deserve to be killed. (Note that an effective Stage-Gate™ process should have spotted and have already killed them.)

Example of Approach 2. Ventura Inc.* is a medium-sized producer of electronic instruments used in a wide variety of industrial applications. The company is in a high-tech field (both hardware and software) and faces a dynamic market situation. Ventura has had in place an effective Stage-Gate™ process for several years (not unlike the five-stage process in Exhibit 10.2) and has adopted Approach 2 for its portfolio management process. Gate 2 is where the all-encompassing portfolio review takes place.

Senior management in the company (the CEO and heads of Marketing/Sales, R&D, Operations, Procurement, and Finance) meet four times per year to hold their portfolio review (really a portfolio review and Gate 2 meeting combined). The meeting typically lasts about two days, 12 hours per day. This is considered one of the most critical senior management meetings of the quarter.

The company has three categories of projects: platform developments, new products, and improvement projects (including fixes, updates, cost reductions, and modifications). Management has already been through a strategic buckets decision exercise to decide the split in resources and designated 50 percent for new product projects, 20 percent for platforms, and 30 percent for improvements.

This is the January 2 portfolio review/Gate 2 meeting. Let's consider only new product projects as an example. (A similar approach is used for other project types, except that different criteria are used to rate and rank them.)

- There are 20 new product projects already underway in Stages 2, 3, 4, or 5.
- An additional 5 are on hold. They are good projects, but there were not enough resources to approve them at the last portfolio review.
- Finally there are 5 brand-new projects—completing Stage 1 and approaching Gate 2 for the first time. These projects are not fully fleshed out but do have enough information for a project and portfolio review.

For all 30 new product projects, the teams have been asked to provide one-page updates or summaries. Four criteria are used to rate and rank new product projects at Ventura:

1. Strategic fit and importance
2. Competitive and product advantage
3. Likelihood of technical feasibility
4. Potential for reward (financial profitability)

---

* Ventura is a fictitious company, but the illustration is based on the experiences of a number of similar firms where Approach 2 has been implemented.

Project teams are asked to provide updates on each of the four criteria. For existing projects they must highlight any major changes from the last gate or portfolio review. Similar updates are provided for other types of projects—platform developments and improvements—but in a format relevant to the criteria used to rate those types.

The portfolio review begins with a discussion of all 30 projects. Some merit only minor comment; for others, especially those whose fortunes have changed dramatically or that are in trouble, the project team is asked to make a personal appearance to update management. Teams with new projects approaching Gate 2 for the first time also make brief presentations.

On day 2 the new product project cards are posted on the walls around the meeting room. The must-do projects are identified. These are either critical to the business or are well along (Stages 3, 4, or 5) and remain viable. In Ventura, each member of the leadership team is given large green adhesive dots, which they can stick to a posted project they wish to treat as a must-do. Then these are discussed and rated on the four criteria. At Ventura's portfolio review/Gate 2 meeting, of the 20 existing projects, 10 are designated must-do's. They are removed from the auction, along with their resource requirements for the quarter (that is, the pool of resources is reduced by the amount needed to undertake the must-do projects over the next three months). None of the new or on-hold projects is thought to be a must-do.

Next, Ventura management identifies the won't-do projects—the poor projects that must be considered for a kill decision. This time, management uses red dots to highlight the potential kills on the meeting room walls. These projects are debated and rated on the four criteria, much like a regular gate meeting. Team members are invited to the meeting to update management and to answer vital questions. Four projects are killed outright: 2 existing ones and 2 of the new ones. The resources that would have been used by the 2 existing projects are now available for other projects in the auction.

Ventura's remaining 16 projects represent the difficult decisions. Some are already on hold but are potentially excellent projects; a few are brand-new and look very promising, as it is often the case with new projects; and others are already underway but are discretionary (i.e., not essential and not the top-priority projects, but still worthy).

The same procedure is used for the other two project categories: platform developments and improvements. But the procedure is not quite as long. There are only a few platform projects to consider. Although there are many smaller improvement projects (updates, fixes, and cost reductions), many of them have been grouped together and presented as a cluster. The improvement projects rely on a financial index instead of a scoring model; as a result, the ratings and ranking on them are much quicker (project teams have already updated and inputted the financial numbers and indices).

Step 4: The Projects in the Middle.   Next, the projects in the middle are evaluated. There are various methods used here:

- For the portfolio review some firms use the same criteria they use at gate meetings, and in some cases, the most recent gate scores and ratings. For new products and fundamental or platform projects, where a scoring model is recommended, this means using the 0–10 scores and the project attractiveness score from the most recent gate meeting, updated as needed, to rank-order the projects. For smaller and more predicable projects, where you might use a financial criterion (NPV, EBIT, or some financial index), use the financial number presented at the most recent gate meeting to rank projects.

- Other companies rescore or rate the projects again at the portfolio/Gate 2 meeting. (If using a scoring model, they rely on a shorter list of criteria than the list found in the typical scoring model used at gate meetings. If financial criteria are used, the financial numbers are simply updated, agreed to, and used at the portfolio review.)
- Forced ranking on criteria is another method. Here management ranks the projects *against one another*—1 to N—on each criterion (where N is the number of projects). Again, a handful of major criteria are used, such as the five used by Kodak at its portfolio review[2]:

1. Strategic fit
2. Product leadership (product advantage)
3. Probability of technical success
4. Market attractiveness (growth, margins)
5. Value to the company (profitability based on NPV).

We recommend the forced ranking method because it yields better discrimination than a traditional scoring model, forcing some projects to the top of the list and others to the bottom. One of the weaknesses of a scoring model at a portfolio review is that projects tend to score middle-of-the-road (many projects score 50 to 70 out of 100).

Any of these three methods yields a list of projects rank-ordered according to objective scores or criteria. Projects are ranked (for example, using a spreadsheet displayed on a large screen) and funded until resources run out. This list is the first cut or *tentative portfolio.*

Some companies make a slight adjustment here to take into account the fact that some projects require far fewer resources than others—that they are *more efficient*. Note that two types of resources should be considered:

- Resources required to complete the entire project
- Resource requirements for the project for the next quarter—the constraining resource.

The goal here is to maximize the bang for buck. For that reason, some firms take the ratio of the criterion they are trying to maximize to the resources required to complete the project (for example, the ratio of the project attractiveness or the NPV to the resources required to complete the project). They then rank the projects on the basis of this ratio until resources for the next time period run out—this is the immediate constraint.

Example: Management at Ventura have tried using the gate scoring model at portfolio review meetings for new product projects, updating gate scores as needed. As is often the case, the scoring model was found to work very well at gate meetings, where the score is compared to some cutoff criterion;

but when looking at all projects together at the portfolio review, the project scores tended to bunch in the middle, and there really wasn't enough spread between projects. As a result, management has moved to *forced ranking* at the portfolio review/Gate 2 meeting, but using the same four criteria used at gates.

A visual and physical sorting technique is used at Ventura (which we recommend). The cards listing the 16 remaining projects—the ones in the middle—are dumped on a long conference-room table. Table #1 (the first sort) is the "strategic fit and importance" table. The senior management team now sorts the 16 remaining projects from "best" to "worst" along the table. Note that this is a ranking, not a rating process: There is a number 1 and there is a number 16 in terms of strategic fit and importance. There is much discussion and debate as the project cards are sorted and moved around on the table. This is a visual and active process, in which all senior management participates. The ranking on this first table is recorded.

Next, managers move to the next criterion: competitive and product advantage (Table #2). The same sorting technique is used, and the results are recorded. The procedure is repeated through the two remaining criteria—technical feasibility and potential for reward—with the rankings recorded after each sort.

Finally, a summary spreadsheet is projected for all to see. Here the 16 projects are shown in list format—numbers 1 to 16—based on the rankings in the previous four sorts* (see Exhibit 10.10). Also considered in this final ranking are development resources required to complete the entire project and those required for the next quarter**. Projects are ranked until resources for the next quarter run out (note that there is a resource limit per quarter for new products—the previously agreed-to strategic bucket). A line is drawn, and those projects above the line are designated as goes; those below the line are put on hold. The result is the *tentative portfolio,* or first-cut list of projects.

Step 5: Checking for Balance and Strategic Alignment. After this initial sort (your *tentative portfolio of projects*), it is necessary to check for balance and strategic alignment. So the proposed portfolio is displayed using some of the bubble diagrams and pie charts summarized in Exhibit 10.11. The purpose here is to visualize the balance of the tentative portfolio and to check for strategic alignment. If the tentative portfolio is poorly balanced or not strategically aligned, projects are removed from the list and others are bumped up. The process is repeated several times until balance and alignment are achieved: The result is the final portfolio of projects.

* This is done by simply taking the arithmetic means of the rankings across the four sorts and displaying the projects ranked by this mean in the table.
** Note that resources can be displayed in person-days or dollars. The next quarter is used here, as the exercise is repeated every quarter. You may wish to use a longer time period, such as six months. One year is too long for most businesses these days.

Project	Strategic Fit & Importance	Competitive & Product Advantage	Likelihood of Technical Feasibility	Potential for Reward	Final Project Ranking Score
AB-Togg	1	3	5	2	2.75
Wolf	2	1	3	1	1.75
Sunshine	3	2	4	5	3.50
Sol	4	5	2	4	3.75
PET-2	5	4	1	3	3.25
Fox 1	6	8	7	16	9.25
Rapid	7	6	11	14	9.50
Roto	8	9	8	6	7.75
Semi-One	9	7	10	13	9.75
Genie	10	16	6	8	10.0
Gemini	11	15	13	12	12.75
Gate	12	11	14	7	11.0
Fox 2	13	12	6	11	10.5
Endeavor	14	13	9	10	11.5
Wonder	15	10	15	9	12.25
Elec B	16	14	12	15	14.25

EXHIBIT 10.10   Ventura's Forced Ranking on Each Criterion

Example: "What does our portfolio of projects look like, assuming we go forward with this tentative portfolio?" asks management at Ventura. The process manager quickly inputs the projects selected and those that did not make the list (tentatively on hold), along with their respective resource requirements into the computer. Using portfolio software he then displays the various portfolio charts at the meeting to give management a feel for the portfolio they have just selected.

Management notices some imbalances. Even though they tried to be disciplined, they approved a few too many "improvement" projects. As well, too few resources appear to be going to Product Line X. There is some discussion, and a few adjustments are made to the portfolio. A few improvement projects are removed from the go list; and one new product project for Product Line X is bumped up from the on-hold list to go. The charts from Exhibit 10.11 are redrawn, and management is much happier with the result the second time around (chart not shown). The portfolio contains a set of high-value projects based on the scoring model and financial indices used to rank projects. It contains strategically aligned projects, and it has the right balance in terms of project types, market segments, and product lines. In short, the spending breakdowns mirror the strategic priorities of the business. The two-day portfolio review/Gate 2 meeting is adjourned. The portfolio of projects is decided.

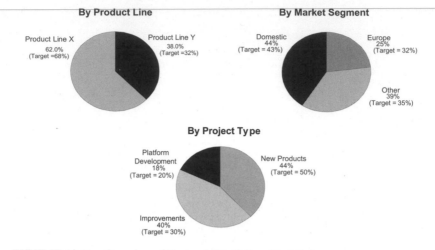

EXHIBIT 10.11   Overview of Ventura's Portfolio—First Cut

POINTS FOR MANAGEMENT TO PONDER

Here are the key points from this section—some more food for thought:

1. If you face a more dynamic or fluid market and industry situation, you should consider Approach 2 to portfolio management.

2. You must have a effective Stage-Gate™ process in place. Then select a gate—probably Gate 2—where portfolio management kicks in.

3. Gate 2 becomes an all-projects-combined portfolio review/Gate 2 selection decision meeting. All projects approaching or beyond Gate 2 are on the table and up for auction.

4. First select the must-do projects—likely those that are either strategic necessities or are well along and remain good projects.

5. Next kill the won't-do's.

6. Then prioritize the projects in the middle. Use a scoring model for new products and platform projects and a financial index for straightforward projects (improvements, fixes, modifications). Update the scores or values as needed. Or better yet, use a forced ranking process, as described in the example.

7. Rank or prioritize your projects until you are out of resources for that project type.

8. The same process applies to different types of projects—platforms, new products, and improvements. Usually it's best to handle each type separately (i.e., separate ranking exercises for each project type, and even using different ranking criteria).

9. The result is *your tentative portfolio* of projects—a rank-ordered list of active (go) and on-hold projects.

The Role of Gates in Approach 2

So what are the roles of the gate meetings if most of the decisions are made at this intensive portfolio review/Gate 2 meeting? The gates still play an important role in Approach 2, but not quite as much as in Approach 1. Projects still pass through the successive gates—Gates 3, 4, and 5 in Exhibit 10.2. And they are reviewed by the gatekeepers, who are usually the leadership team of the business. The questions are:

- Are the deliverables in place, and are they of sound quality—is the project team doing a good job (if no, the project can be sent back to the previous stage for "rework")?
- Is the project on time and within budget?
- Does the project remain a good investment—is the business case still solid, and does the project remain an attractive one?

Projects are rated on the gate criteria and must meet acceptable standards. If a project's business case becomes negative—for example, its NPV or project attractiveness score turns bad—then an immediate kill decision can be made at the gate (don't wait for the quarterly or semiannual portfolio review to shoot a bad project!). Resources are then freed up and reassigned to one or more projects previously approved but on the hold list. Thus, gates can approve continuation of resources for a project or may serve to kill a project. But, Approach 2 is unlike Approach 1 in that gates do not approve new projects or significant increases in resource commitments. That happens only at the portfolio review/Gate 2 combined meeting.

Recap: Approach 2—The Portfolio Review Dominates

The portfolio review/Gate 2 decision meeting is where key decisions are made in Approach 2. The portfolio review is really a Gate 2 and portfolio review all in one and is held three to four times a year. It is here that the key Go/Kill decisions are made and consequently is a senior management meeting. With all projects at or beyond Gate 2 on the table, the meeting:

- Identifies must-do and won't-do projects
- Scores (ratings or forced ranking) the ones in the middle
- Checks for balance and strategic alignment
- Decides the portfolio: which projects, what priorities, how much in resources.

In Approach 2, the gates serve mainly as a check. Projects are reviewed as they progress from stage to stage to ensure that they are on time, on budget, and worth continuing. Kill decisions are still made at gates to weed out poor projects. Gates rely on criteria, and the scores at the gates are often used as inputs to the portfolio review part of the meeting.

Approach 2, thus, lashes together the two decision processes: the gating process and the portfolio review. Gate 2 is really the integrative decision point in the scheme, and the point where the two decision processes intersect (Ex-

POINTS FOR MANAGEMENT TO PONDER

Here are the key points from this section—additional food for thought if you elect Approach 2:

Selecting your tentative portfolio based on a rating or ranking exercise is only the initial step at your portfolio review/Gate 2 meeting—it achieves the first goal of maximizing the value of the portfolio—but now you must check for balance and strategic alignment:

1. Create the various pie charts and bubble diagrams, displaying your tentative portfolio on dimensions that are relevant to you. Some good examples are shown in the preceding section.
2. Compare the actual split in resources with the desired split—spelled out either via your strategic buckets or target spending levels. And look at the bubble diagrams for the appropriate distribution of projects and resources.
3. Make whatever adjustments are needed to your tentative portfolio, bumping some desired projects up the list and removing others—perhaps ones that are overrepresented in your portfolio. Several iterations may be required.
4. Now you have your portfolio of projects.
5. Key points:

   • PMP Approach 2 takes a considerable time commitment on the part of senior management. The leadership team of the business must be prepared to meet for intense, attendance-mandatory decision meetings typically taking 2–3 days.
   • Gates in your Stage-Gate™ process still play an important role in Approach 2. Do not assume that because you implement Approach 2 you no longer need an effective gating process.

hibit 10.9). The result, like Approach 1, is a harmonized portfolio management process.

Pros and Cons of Approach 1 Versus Approach 2

Both approaches have advantages and disadvantages. Management indicates that it is easier to prioritize projects when looking at all projects on the table together, as in Approach 2 (rather than one at a time at real-time gates). In addition, some people have difficulty with the two-part gate scheme in Approach 1 (Exhibit 10.3); for example, how does one find resources for a good project when it is the only project being considered at the meeting? Finally, some managers like the notion that prioritization of all projects is done regularly—no project is sacred!

There are also disadvantages to Approach 2 and areas in which Approach 1 is superior. Many in management believe that if projects are to be killed, then project teams should be present to defend their projects (or at least to provide updated information), such as happens at an in-depth gate meeting. Another criticism is that Approach 2 requires a major time commitment from senior management. For example, senior management at EXFO takes three full days every quarter to conduct this portfolio/Gate 2 decision meeting! A further advantage of Approach 1 is that gate reviews provide a much more in-depth assessment than is ever possible when all the projects are considered at a single meeting.

In Conclusion: An Integrated Decision System

The portfolio management process ideally is an integrated decision system. The starting point is the strategy for the business or business unit. This is the driver, because strategy becomes real when you start spending money. So the choice of new product projects is the operationalization of strategy. Recall that strategy in our context includes the business and new product strategy for the BU. The latter specifies the new product goals for the BU, the arenas of focus (for example, markets, product types, and technologies), and the desired spending splits across these, or in terms of project types.

Next, there is the new product process or Stage-Gate™ model. Its focus is on individual projects: the "fingers." The gates in the new product process must be working well in order for the entire portfolio management process to perform. Note that for Approach 1, the gates are where most of the ongoing Go/Kill decisions are made, and where resources are allocated throughout the year. Gates can be constructed around a set of must-meet or culling (knockout) criteria and a set of should-meet items, which are scored and added via a scoring model. Criteria here include items that capture strategic fit and importance, value of the project to the business, and the likelihood of success. The project attractiveness score becomes the key input to the Go/Kill decision at the gate and also a key ranking criterion for use in prioritizing projects.

Then there is the portfolio review. If the gates consider the "fingers," then the portfolio review looks at the "fist." It is holistic in nature and enables management to stand back and consider all projects—those that are active versus those on hold—together. In Approach 2, this is where the key decisions are made, especially decisions to resource projects. Strategic imperatives may be identified. The prioritized list derived from gate decisions and the gate scoring model enable projects to be ranked against each other. Decisions may be made to deprioritize some projects and to elevate others. The balance of the portfolio is also reviewed with various bubble diagrams and pie charts. The risk-reward breakdown and spending breakdowns by project types, markets, products, technologies, project newness, and so on are topics of discussion here. Again, decisions may be made to reprioritize certain projects. Finally, adjustments are made to the gating process to favor certain types of projects.

If all three elements of the process exist—strategy, the Stage-Gate™ process, and the portfolio review (with its various models and tools)—then a harmonized system should yield excellent portfolio choices: projects that deliver economic payoffs, mirror the business's strategy, and achieve the BU's goals for new products. But if any piece of the PMP is not working—for example, if there is no clearly defined strategy or if the new product gating process is broken, or if portfolio reviews are not held—the results are less than satisfactory.

In the next chapter, we turn to the vital question: Now that you understand the elements and ingredients of a robust portfolio management process, how do you move ahead with the design and implementation of an PMP in your business?

Designing and Implementing the Portfolio Management Process: Some Thoughts and Tips Before You Charge In

Before You Charge In

The development of new products is one of the most important endeavors of the modern corporation. It is also the most difficult task to do successfully! Likewise, designing and implementing a portfolio management process (PMP) is one of the most difficult tasks in the corporation—both conceptually and operationally.

So think before you act. This is not the flavor of the month, nor will it take only a few weeks. Rather, designing and implementing an effective PMP is a major undertaking that will require the help and input of many people in your organization, including executive sponsorship and leadership. It may take several years before it is up and running successfully. So don't underestimate the costs and time required to do it right. Take care before you proceed, but do proceed. The stakes are too high and the payoffs too great to postpone taking action.

The design and implementation of a PMP is much like rolling out a new product. The difference is that you are developing a new management process rather than a new product and that the "customers" are internal—inside your own company—rather than external. Nonetheless, you can borrow many of the principles of product development when you design a new PMP. The first of them is that the design process proceeds stagewise, not unlike the five-stage, five-gate new product process outlined in Exhibit 10.2. We propose a four-stage method for the design and implementation of a PMP—see Exhibit 11.1:

- *Stage 1*: understanding the problem and defining the requirements for an effective PMP
- *Stage 2*: designing the PMP on paper, starting with a skeleton process and then fleshing out the details

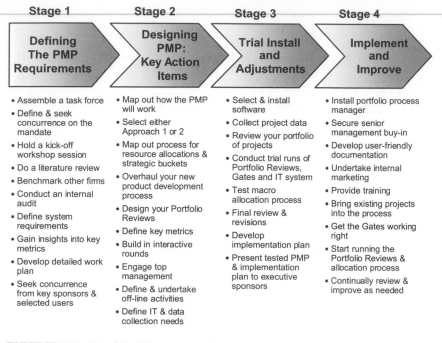

EXHIBIT 11.1   Portfolio Management System—Approach Plan

- *Stage 3*: installing the PMP on a trial basis, gaining some experience and making adjustments as needed
- *Stage 4*: implementing the process in the business: getting projects into the process, running portfolio reviews, making the gates work, and continually improving the process.

Stage 1: Defining the Requirements

Stage 1 entails defining the requirements for an effective PMP in your business. This is a first and necessary stage and one that is often skipped over by portfolio task forces with very negative results. Remember: Understanding the problem is the first step to a solution! Too often we witness well-intentioned portfolio task forces that meet in private, arrive at a solution, and then charge out with solution in hand, determined to change the way the company operates. When their initiative is greeted with less than the enthusiastic response they expected, doom sets in. Task force members become frustrated, and before long, it's another worthwhile initiative that went nowhere. Very often, the roots of disaster can be found right at the beginning: failure to do the upfront homework and to understand the needs and problems that the PMP must address.

The purpose of this definitional step is twofold:

1. To gain an understanding of the problems and issues faced in the business regarding portfolio management and project selection; in short, to identify what
   needs fixing
2. To map out the "specs" and requirements for the PMP—what the process must be
   and do, how it must function, and what its requirements should be.

Example: In a major international brewery, an in-depth audit of product development and project selection revealed several critical weaknesses. First, too many
projects were reaching the pre-launch decision point only to have senior management pull the rug out from under the project team, usually for strategic reasons. There simply were too many "eleventh-hour kills," often after several years
of work, and many dollars had gone into projects. Second, it was not evident that
the senior management had a clear or unified notion of their business's new product strategy: Arenas were not prioritized, nor had spending splits across arenas
been defined. (Perhaps this fuzziness helped explain why so many projects went
so far in the process before being killed.) Finally, while there was indeed a new
product process in place, it lacked specificity (for example, no clearly defined gate
criteria for making Go/Kill decisions), nor was the process being adhered to (due
to a lack of agreement on what projects went through the process).

From these problems the requirements for the new PMP for this business became clear:

1. The PMP must involve senior management earlier in the life of a project. They
   should be involved in the pre-development decision points. Portfolio reviews
   of active projects in the pipeline must also involve senior people, so that there
   are no eleventh-hour surprises.
2. Senior management must lead: They are the generals and their obligation to
   the business is to develop strategy. (In our first session with the executive
   group, they committed to fleshing out their business strategy and moving toward a new product strategy for the business: defined arenas, priorities on
   the arenas, and target spending levels by arena and project type).
3. The new product process must be revamped and fixed where needed; for
   example, gates must have visible criteria, there must be agreement on
   what projects are in the process, and so on.

Here are some of the key tasks or action items to be undertaken in Stage 1 to
define the requirements of your PMP:

1. Assemble a Task Force

The design of a company PMP is beyond the capabilities of one or two people. It
is not an easy task, and assigning it to a single person will lead to:

- a fairly narrow view of the problem (note that a variety of perspectives is required to
  fully understand the role and implications of portfolio management in the business)
- a lack of buy-in by those who must use the process.

We recommend that you assemble a portfolio task force charged with executing the steps outlined below, leading to the design and implementation of your PMP. Carefully select the task force members: thought leaders in the company with experience in new products (although not necessarily senior management); representative of different functions and businesses in the corporation, and if necessary, from different geographical areas; and with time available to do the work. The task force should have strong senior executive sponsorship (with a designated executive sponsor) and a respected task force leader with passion for and commitment to the task at hand.

2. Define and Seek Concurrence on the Mandate

The task force, together with the executive sponsor (or sponsoring group), should develop its mandate: what the task force is charged with doing, what it should not do, and what deliverables are expected by the sponsoring group. The sponsoring group (for example, leadership team of the business) should sign off on this mandate and also agree on their own roles and availability to the task force.

3. Hold a Kickoff Session—An Introduction to Portfolio Management

Consider inaugurating the task with a kickoff seminar/workshop—a one-day event. The session might be billed as a "best practices in portfolio management" seminar, focusing on project selection, portfolio management, and best-practice techniques (see Chapters 3–5 of this book). Invite a fairly large group, essentially those in your business who will become the "users" of the new process. Senior management should also be brought into the loop, either at this kickoff event or in a session tailored for them. This kickoff session helps in three ways:

- First, it creates awareness of the need for improvement. Observing best practices in other firms is an excellent start. Further, the seminar is the venue where the executive sponsors reiterate the business's new product goals and strategy. Usually this points to the need for a change in direction. Additionally, it is at the seminar that the executive sponsors announce the PMP initiative and introduce the task force members, thereby legitimizing their efforts on behalf of the company.
- Second, such a seminar/workshop helps identify the problems in project selection and prioritization that the business faces. For example, build a "problem detection" team exercise into the seminar. Thus the seminar/workshop can double as a "town hall meeting," enabling a wide audience to air their views, concerns, and suggestions.
- Finally, a kickoff seminar helps generate organizational buy-in. Remember: Obtaining organizational buy-in to new methods and practices is a formidable task. And organizational buy-in must begin in the first few days of the initiative. For example, build in a "what's the path forward?" team exercise toward the end of the kickoff event so that participants can advise the task force on the next steps to

define what is needed. Note that the task force members are the hosts at this kick-off session and must use it to full advantage to seek input and agreement on the road ahead.

4. Do a Literature Review

The task force should conduct a thorough literature review to find out what others have said and done. There is no sense reinventing the wheel. Authors and pundits have been writing about portfolio management, project selection, and new product resource allocation since the 1960s. As is often the case, many of the earlier works offer the best insights; but there have been new insights in recent years, so look into these articles and books too. Chapters 2 and 8 reviewed many of the works you might wish to seek out and provided references in the notes. Require that the task force immerse itself in the writings.

5. Benchmark Other Firms

This action item we suggest with some caution. First, thorough external benchmarking takes a lot of time. Second, some better-practice firms have been benchmarked so often that they are now resisting such overtures (or acquiescing but not providing full support). Finally, task force members are very often amateurs at business research and therefore are likely to do a mediocre job of benchmarking. Task force members often set out to benchmark others with great zeal but lose their enthusiasm when they quickly realize it is not so easy and they are not learning all that much. We offer two suggestions:

1. Seek professional help, especially in the design of your benchmarking methodology. There are numerous consultants who are experienced and capable at benchmarking exercises: use them!
2. Turn to the literature. Chapters 3–7 of this book provide results of a fairly comprehensive benchmarking of industry best practices. Your literature search may also turn up other reports of firms' practices in portfolio management.

6. Conduct an Internal Audit of Current Practices—Review Your Existing PM Process and Define the Problems

Undertake a study of current practices and deficiencies in your own business and company. This poses fewer problems than external benchmarking and should be an easier task. It is surprising that many task forces skip this, largely because they think they know the answers. Wrong! Every internal 3-P study we have been involved with—internal investigations into new product Practices, Performance, and Problems—has produced major revelations. That is, the findings of the study went far beyond the knowledge and understanding possessed by the task force; and there was definitely new information that the task force had to deal with. Don't skip this task. Here are some suggestions for how to proceed:

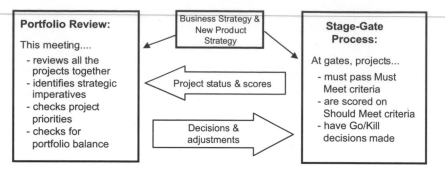

EXHIBIT 11.2   Three Decision Processes: NP Strategy, Portfolio Review, and Stage-Gating

- *Undertake a 3-P study*: We call this a 3-P study because it focuses on three Ps—practices, performance, and problems. We've even coined a term to capture the effort: *ProBE* or Product Benchmarking and Evaluation.* Our ProBE methodology is a questionnaire-based internal audit of a business's new product practices, performance, and problems and in part looks at portfolio management practices and related issues. ProBE then compares an individual company's results to the average business and against the top 20 percent. The method and database are based on our benchmarking study of a large sample of businesses. Alternatively, you can develop and conduct your own benchmarking questionnaire via individual interviews, e-mail surveys, or focus groups within your business. Try to uncover current project selection, prioritization, and resource allocation practices and deficiencies—what needs fixing and what seems to be working.
- *Focus on individual new product projects.* Dissecting a reasonable sample of past projects—both winners and losers—provides valuable insights into current practices and deficiencies, particularly in terms of the Go/Kill and prioritization decisions—the gating process (the right side of Exhibit 11.2). More specifically, require that teams from already completed projects undertake a retrospective analysis. That is, dissect each project, focusing first on mapping out just what happened from beginning to end, from idea to launch. Then lower the microscope on each of the key decision points in the process: how the Go/Kill decisions were made, who made them, what information was available (or should have been available), and what criteria were used. Assess the "goodness" of the decision points and resource allocation decisions, especially in the case of projects that should have been killed yet were allowed to proceed.

7. Define System Requirements and Develop Goals for Your PM Process

Write up the specs and requirements of your new PM process—what your process must be and must do. Integrate your many findings and conclusions from

---

* ProBE is available from the Product Development Institute in North America, Asia-Pacific, the UK, and Ireland: visit www.prod-dev.com; and in the rest of Europe from U3 Innovation Management: www.u3.dk.

Stage 1 into a set of specs and requirements for the PMP. For example, the task force at Hallmark came up with a detailed list for its project selection system (or PMP), including:

"Our [portfolio] process must . . .

- Promote objective Go/Kill decision-making, using common criteria, based on facts, and yielding consistency and continuity in decision-making.
- Improve resource allocation—better focus, sharper [project] prioritization, and the right people on projects."

The following sums up the types of requirements we have found in various firms: The new PMP process must:

- Provide for transparent decision making
- Ensure that all projects are evaluated fairly and consistently
- Encourage fact-based decision-making, based on objective Go/Kill and prioritization criteria
- Allocate resources correctly across the project types—not letting small, quick-hit projects crowd out longer-term but potentially more valuable ones
- Align the new business developments with company strategy
- Allocate and balance resources appropriately
- Ensure that all projects are on strategy and that our spending reflects the strategic priorities of our business
- Make sure that resources are allocated to the right business areas—the ones with the greatest potential and need for development resources
- Engage senior management in the decision-making process—resource allocation and project prioritization (but not micro-managing projects!).

8. Gain Insights into Key Portfolio Metrics

The detailed design of your PMP in the next stage requires the specification of metrics or measures—what you intend to measure and track for each development project. For example, besides the usual items—project name, type, and size—many businesses keep and track information such as the project's scores at gate meetings, its projected NPV, likelihoods of success, resource needs by department, and even the source of the idea. During Stage 1, you can begin to think about what metrics you plan to assemble and enter into the master database. That is, during your interviews and probing in Stage 1, begin to test the waters—identify what metrics might be useful, and whether they are readily available.

9. Develop Your Detailed Work Plan

This step in Stage 1 should map out a detailed work plan for the next phase of the effort; namely, the design of the various elements of your PMP. For example, if your business lacks an effective gating process, then its development becomes a major part of the work plan. Other action items for the work plan are outlined in the sections that follow.

10. Seek Concurrence from Sponsors and Selected Users

The specs of the PMP and the proposed work plan are now presented to senior management for their concurrence and signoff. This "gate" marks the end of the homework or audit phase and the entry into Stage 2. Selected and knowledgeable people who will be the eventual users of the PMP can also act as sounding boards here. While you might be tempted to hold a "town hall meeting" and get everyone who attended the initial kickoff event to review your specs and work plan, unfortunately you really have very little of interest to show people at this point. When you have the first draft of the PMP during Stage 2 is when you begin your iterations with users.

The ten action items in this section are not easy, nor can they be done overnight. However, they provide an excellent foundation to the design and implementation work that lies ahead.

POINTS FOR MANAGEMENT TO PONDER

Before you charge ahead, be sure to spend time defining the requirements of your portfolio management process. Remember: Understanding the problem is the first step to a solution. So take a little extra time here and lay the foundation carefully. Tasks you might consider in this Stage 1 definitional phase are

1. Assemble a task force with executive sponsorship
2. Define and seek concurrence on the mandate
3. Hold a kickoff workshop session—an introduction to portfolio management
4. Do a literature review
5. Benchmark other firms
6. Conduct an internal audit of current practices—review your existing PMP and define the problems
7. Define system requirements and develop goals for your PMP
8. Gain insights into key portfolio metrics
9. Develop your detailed work plan
10. Seek concurrence from sponsors and selected users

Stage 2: Designing the Portfolio Management Process—Key Action Items

The homework has been done, the problems are identified, and the specs or requirements for the ideal PMP for your business have been defined—what your PMP must be and do. Now it's time to begin designing the process in earnest.

1. Map Out System Design—How Your PMP Will Work

Design your PMP module by module. Begin with an overview or skeleton process, using Exhibit 10.1 and Chapters 9 and 10 as guides. Map out the key components and decide how they will work. For example,

- A process to decide macro resource allocations—across business areas, markets, and segments or across project types, etc. (strategic buckets). A suggested scheme was outlined in Chapter 9, along with a company example. You may wish to use Chapter 9 as a guide, adapting the suggested process to your own business. Note that the assumption is that you already have a business strategy and, embedded within it, a product innovation and technology strategy for your business. (If not, refer to Chapter 5 and the section "Developing a New Product Strategy for Your Business—A Quick Guide.")
- Your project selection and project prioritization process, including:

  - Your gating process (the assumption is that you have a Stage-Gate™ process in place!)
  - Your portfolio review process—see Chapter 10 for guidance
  - How portfolio management and the portfolio reviews will mesh with your gating review process.

2. Decide on Approach 1 or Approach 2— A Fundamental Question

Recall that two fundamental approaches were outlined in Chapter 10 for selecting specific new product and development projects:

- *Approach 1:* The gates dominate. Here the key Go/Kill and resource allocation decisions are made at the gates. Gates are a two-part decision process, with the first part focusing on the Go/Kill decision (does the project meet minimum acceptable standards?) and the second part dealing with resource allocation (the project's priority versus the other active and on-hold projects). In Approach 1, portfolio reviews are used as checks on the gate decisions—more as minor course corrections and address such questions as Do you have the right project priorities? Do you have the right balance of projects? Do you have a strategically aligned portfolio with projects on strategy and with spending breakdowns reflecting strategic priorities of the business?
- *Approach 2*: The portfolio review dominates. Here a single gate (probably Gate 2) and the quarterly portfolio review are combined. All active projects at or past Gate 2 are up for auction—they are all on the table. Projects are force-ranked against each other via a scoring model, or by using a ranking system. The key Go/Kill and resource allocation decisions are made at the mass Gate 2/portfolio review session. This is an intense and lengthy meeting, usually held 3–4 times per year, involving the leadership team of the business. In addition to force-ranking projects from best to worst, the portfolio reviews also deal with balance and strategic alignment is-

sues. Gates play a lesser role in Method 2. They are still important, but they are used more to spot and weed out bad projects and projects in trouble.

So take your choice. Many firms that already have a Stage-Gate™ process in place (and one that works!) elect Approach 1, simply by piggybacking portfolio reviews and an IT system atop an already proficient gating process. Approach 1 also seems to work well for slower-paced industries.

Approach 2 appears suitable for businesses in faster-paced industries and where the marketplace is quite fluid. This necessitates a more dynamic portfolio and project decision process where no project is sacred for very long! But it does require considerable commitment of time and effort by senior management—the 2–3 day portfolio meeting becomes the most critical senior management meeting of the quarter. After all, it decides the future of your business!

3. Map Out Your Process for Deciding Resource Allocations and Strategic Buckets

Chapter 9 outlined a method for making macro resource allocations—strategic buckets across business areas and projects types. Decide which dimensions are relevant to you and then develop your own strategic buckets process, using or adapting Chapter 9's scheme as a guide. Exhibit 11.3 shows some of the relevant dimensions other firms use for splitting resources, which you might wish to consider.

Here are the key steps from Chapter 9 that you can use as a guide for mapping your own process:

Step 1: Start with Current Portfolio Breakdown, the Status Quo.   Assess the current portfolio—a high-level or aggregate look at the current spending breakdowns or deployments: Where is the money going? The key dimensions of this assessment typically include resource allocation across:

- Business areas (could also be BUs; product groups or product lines; or market or industry sector groups)
- Project types (such as new products, product improvements and maintenance, etc.).

Step 2: Next, Move to a Top-Down or Strategic Allocation Process.   The prerequisite to the portfolio allocation exercise is having a solid understanding of your business strategy and, in particular, its product innovation and technology strategy. So if this strategy is not yet in place in your business, it must be developed (see Chapter 5).

Step 3: Do a First-Cut Allocation of Resources—Modified Delphi.   Make a first-cut allocation of resources across the business areas and also across the various project types. This is based on the strategic discussions, together with an understanding of the status quo or current spending. This is still very much a top-down approach; it is also fairly directional, beginning with the status quo or

Rank Order	Dimension
1	**Type of Market:** market a, b, c
2	**Type of Development:** maintenance, exploratory, frontier research, systems, line extensions
3	**Product Line:** product line a, b, c
4	**Project Magnitude:** minor/major project
5	**Technology Area:** base, enabling, new
6	**Platform Types:** new/old; product/technology
7	**Strategic Thrust** (against strategies in the plan)
8	**Competitive Needs:** quality, features, functions

EXHIBIT 11.3   Dimensions Used to Split Spending into Buckets

current splits and debating whether each business area or project type should have more or less. For this top-level, first-cut decision, we recommended a modified Delphi approach. The resulting decision is a first-cut matrix denoting desired resource splits across project types and across the business areas—the "what should be" split (Exhibit 9.6).

So far, everything has been "in aggregate" and top-level. Now it is time to lower the microscope and look at individual projects, a more bottom-up approach.

Step 4: Move to the Bottom-Up—Look at the Major Projects from Each Business Area.   Resource allocation, while strategic in nature, also depends on the specific opportunities; namely, the projects themselves. Each business area brings a list of preferred projects to the portfolio session. This list can be broken down into two types of projects:

- Must-do projects
- Should-do projects.

To arrive at this list, each business area has undertaken portfolio analysis and project selection within the business—a micro and project-selection exercise (the topic of Chapter 10). Smaller projects should be lumped together into categories or clusters and presented that way.

Step 5: Review Lists of Desired Projects Across the Business Areas and Roll-up. Next, scrutinize the lists of new product opportunities offered by each business area. Construct a rank-ordered list of the projects, including the must-do and should-do projects from each business area, but rolled up or combined. Prepare one list for each category of projects: fundamental research, new products, etc. (Exhibit 9.7).

Within each column in your table, the projects are rank-ordered from most attractive to least attractive. Use criteria to do the ranking, and develop different sets of criteria for different types of projects. Examples are:

- *Fundamental research projects*—a simple scoring model, with strategic criteria, impact on the corporation, and likelihood of technical feasibility as the key ranking criteria
- *New product projects*—again a scoring model, but this time employing more traditional new product criteria, such as strategic fit, competitive advantage, likelihood of technical feasibility, ability to leverage in-house resources, and risk/reward
- *Product improvements, fixes, enhancements, tweaks and maintenance items*—a financial metric such as NPV/R&D costs
- *Cost reductions*—again a financial metric.

Kill the obvious dogs outright. Then tentatively select the first-cut list of will-do projects by proceeding down each ranked list until the resources run out. Label projects above the line "go" and label those below "tentative list of will-do projects."

Step 6: Display What the Portfolio Would Look Like on the Basis of This Tentative Ranked List. Next consider what the portfolio would look like in terms of the various portfolio charts, assuming this "tentative list of will-do projects." Use the various charts in Chapters 3 to 5:

- Bubble diagrams of the "tentative list of will-do projects" (Exhibits 4.1 to 4.10)
- Pie charts, showing the breakdown of projects by business area and by project types, and by any other dimension that might be relevant to you (Exhibits 4.19 and 4.20)
- A breakdown table or resource matrix as in Exhibit 9.11.

Step 7: Start the Next Iteration(s) and Arrive at Next and Final Cut. Adjustments are required, and so Step 5 is repeated. The rank-ordered lists of all projects are displayed again, and there is some arbitrary adjusting and sorting— removing some projects from a business area that received too many, or bumping a project or two up the priority list. Even the first-cut Delphi splits—across business areas and project types—are questioned and adjustments are made as projects are added and deleted.

Several iterations of this step may be required, back and forth between the rank-ordered list of projects (Step 5) and looking at the resulting portfolio (Steps 6 and 7). The final iteration produces strategic buckets both by business area and by project type. It also goes a long way toward identifying which projects are to be done, at least the major ones, and their relative priorities. The resource matrix is finalized to reflect one row per business area (as in Exhibit 9.11).

4. Develop, Overhaul, or Refine Your New Product Process

This is the right side of Exhibit 11.2, namely, the gating process. An effective Stage-Gate™ process must be in place for a PMP to be effective, so you must tackle this task fairly early. If you already have a new product process in place, your audit may have identified weaknesses and things that need fixing (for example, gates that lack criteria or stages with unclear deliverables). So design the fixes here. Designing a new product process involves much more than merely sketching out a Stage-Gate™ diagram. Here are some of the elements (see also Appendix A):

- First, map the process—a flow diagram similar to Exhibit 10.2, with your stages and gates identified. Label each stage and gate with a name that connotes what the stage or gate does or stands for. Briefly characterize each stage and gate.
- Define the purpose, spirit, or flavor of each stage and gate.
      For example: Stage 1 amounts to a quick and inexpensive set of activities to gain a better understanding of the idea: that is, to identify which are the best ideas; to assess market potential and technical feasibility; to identify possible showstoppers; and to determine the need for further work. The spirit here is to make professional assessments and "best educated guesses"—a first cut—often with very limited data and in a very short time. Detailed assessments and studies are not expected in stage 1. The stage 1 work effort varies by project, but the order of magnitude is typically about 5 to 25 person-days of work, with elapsed time about one calendar month.
- For each stage, define the key tasks, actions, or activities and the resulting deliverables from these actions. Try to build in best practices here: sharp, early product definition, a strong market and customer orientation, the quest for product superiority, solid upfront homework, and so on (Appendix A).[1] For problematic actions and deliverables, or for unfamiliar ones, you may wish to develop guides, templates, or examples for users. Some firms also define who is accountable for seeing that these tasks are completed at each stage.
- For each gate, define the gatekeepers, the Go/Kill and prioritization criteria, and the gate outputs—what happens next. Exhibit 3.14 or Appendix B provides a good starting point for both must-meet and should-meet (scored) criteria for Gate 3. Early gates conveniently use a subset of these. For example, Gate 1 may use only the must-meet items as criteria for weeding out inappropriate ideas; Gate 2 may use the must-meet and a handful of should-meet or scored items (for example, the seven main factors in Exhibit 3.9).
- Capture the behavioral and organizational issues: team structure and leadership; the gatekeepers' roles, responsibilities and rules of the game; how gate reviews are to be conducted; rewards and recognition; and the need for and job description of a process manager or "gate meister."
- Define other peripheral but vital elements: which projects are "in the process"; flexibility and fast-tracking projects; improving idea generation and solicitation; developing an "open" idea vault and a convenient idea-handling system; and integrating the process with other company processes (for example, the capital expenditure process; or the release-to-plant process).

- Deal with and decide on some of the issues and challenges raised in Chapter 7 and Exhibit 7.1, for example:
  - What types of projects should your new product process handle? All developments or just some?
  - What information is required for each gate meeting? And how do you ensure quality or integrity of data?
  - How should you overcome the problem of imaginary precision?
  - How firm are resource commitments if made at gate meetings?
  - At what gate should the PMP kick in?
  - How should you correctly incorporate financial analysis methods into the gate and gate criteria? And how do you overcome the major problems with financial analysis outlined in Chapters 6 and 7?

5. Design Your Portfolio Reviews

Now it's time to turn to portfolio reviews, the left side of Exhibit 11.2. Designing the Portfolio Review process is a little more complex than it first seems. After all, what is involved in designing a review meeting to be held two to four times per year? Plenty, especially if you have elected Approach 2 for selecting projects, where the key decisions are made at the portfolio review! Here are some issues and challenges:

- Determine who the portfolio reviewers will be. Often this is controversial. In some firms, they are simply the leadership team of the business or the Gate 2 or Gate 3 gatekeepers (often these are the same people).
- Define the frequency of portfolio reviews. For Approach 2 and dynamic market situations, these can be as often as four times annually; for Approach 1, once or twice per year is more appropriate.
- Define what portfolio display models and charts will be used at this review. In Chapters 9 and 10, we offered some suggestions:
  - a prioritized scored list of active and on-hold projects (recall that this list is developed from the gate scores or from forced ranking at the portfolio review; see Exhibit 10.5)
  - a risk-reward bubble diagram (either with financial and probability axes; or with scored axes)
  - various pie charts: breakdown of spending by project type (the Mercedes star), by market, by product line, and so on (Exhibit 10.6).

  These are our suggestions, but every business and culture is different. You should review the various display models and methods outlined in Chapters 3–5 and select or modify them accordingly to suit your own decision styles, culture, and needs.
- Outline the structure, procedure, and flow of the meeting. For example, what materials will attendees receive ahead of time? In what standardized format? How will the meeting be conducted? If using Approach 2, the meeting might first identify the must-do's and won't-do's to get these projects and their re-

sources off the table. How? Will you use IT support at the meeting to assist in the decision making and review process—for example, to display alternate portfolio scenarios? What about other tools, such as projects on cards and using red and green dots to tag must-do and won't-do projects? Will there be a facilitator? (There should be.) How often will the portfolio review be conducted—quarterly, semiannually?

- Decide how the portfolio review will enable corrective action to be taken on the portfolio of projects. For example, in the event of an unbalanced portfolio or one that lacks strategic alignment, what happens? Do you kill some projects and approve resources for others during the portfolio review (as in Approach 2)? And how will you kill the projects? Or does the portfolio review merely send a signal to the gatekeepers to tighten up the criteria for certain overrepresented types of projects (as in Approach 1)? In short, what is the outcome of the portfolio review?
- Define the information flow into and from this portfolio review. For example, where and how are data obtained to generate the various bubble diagrams or pie charts? And will project teams deliver project updates? If so, in what format? Is a standardized project update form or template recommended?
- Define the IT support system required to store the vital data on each project and to effortlessly create the various displays you will need. IT support is such an important enabler to effective portfolio management that we devote a section to it—see action item 10 in this section.
- Deal with the remaining challenges and issues outlined in Exhibit 7.1. For example,

  - What types of projects should be considered in the PMP? (all projects that compete for resources? or only some?)
  - How do you intend to deal with that fact that there are too many projects for the resources available (a problem often encountered)?
  - What should be done with too many on-hold projects?
  - Why have a prioritized or rank-ordered list at all?
  - What happens if you end up with the wrong balance of projects—for example, too many small projects and not enough major hits?
  - Should your portfolio models provide information displays or be decision models?
  - How should gate decisions and portfolio decisions be best integrated?
  - How do you avoid information overload in the PMP (too many diagrams and charts)?

6. Define Key Portfolio Metrics

What measures and characteristics of projects do you intend to track? In Stage 1, we recommended that you start to identify them. But here in Stage 2, you must arrive at a comprehensive list. The metrics are the characteristics and measures of projects that you will use to create the many possible pie charts, ranked lists, and bubble diagrams. Probably you should create an all-encompassing list—err on the side of too many measures. Why? Because gathering the information on additional variables per project is relatively inexpensive; but if you have failed to

General:
- Project name
- Project identification
- Status: Active, On Hold, Other (or categories chosen by the user)
- Priority level of project
- Project leader
- Stage in Stage-Gate model
- Next gate and date
- Project type (e.g., platform, new product, improvement, maintenance, etc.)
- Project type: defensive, offensive, breakthrough
- Fit with business or corporate strategy (low, medium, high)
- Inventive merit and strategic importance to the business (low, medium, high)
- Durability of the competitive advantage (short-, medium-, long-term)
- Competitive impact of technologies (base, key, pacing, and embryonic technologies)
- Market or segment
- Product line
- Project size (minor, medium, major)
- Source of idea

Resources:
- Resources allocated ($)
- Resources allocated: FTEs
- Annualized resources ($)
- Annualized FTEs
- Total cost of project (now till launch) in $ or FTEs
- Time to completion (months)

Scores and Rankings:
- Ratings (0-10, most current) on key gate criteria
- Rankings (1-N) on key ranking criteria
- Project Attractiveness Score (based on ratings)
- Project Attractiveness Score (based on rankings)

Financials and probabilities:
- Projected NPV
- Probability of technical success
- Probability of commercial success
- Probability adjusted NPV
- ECV
- IRR %
- Payoff (a qualitatively scaled measure 0-10, modest to excellent)

EXHIBIT 11.4   Sample List of Key Metrics and Characteristics of Projects in the Master
Database

SOURCE: Taken from the NewPort Max software.

collect the data on a few items in the first place, it usually proves very time-consuming and expensive to go back and get it a second time.

Exhibit 11.4 provides a comprehensive list of many of the variables you may wish to keep for each project. Of course, you'll probably want to include some measures beyond this list, and most portfolio software will allow you to do so easily.

Most of the data on projects is obtained at gate meetings. Items ranging from the project's name and type through the projected NPV and gate scores on key factors are presented or available at the gate meeting. Often it is just a matter of ensuring that the process manager of your new product process attends every gate meeting and enters the data on each project discussed into the master database.

7. Build Several Rounds into Your Design Process—Make It an Iterative Process

To carry out this difficult design phase—action items 1 to 6 in this section—we recommend that your task force set aside blocks of time and meet in two-day sessions, roughly two to three weeks apart. Meeting an hour here and two hours there usually results in a lack of dedicated effort and too many people missing too many meetings. Set aside time blocks weeks ahead, and get the task force off premises! The two-to-three-week intervals are prescribed simply because that is approximately how long it takes to pull together the conclusions from each two-day session, disseminate it to team members, share it with others in the organization, and obtain the necessary feedback. In addition, there are other "off-line" activities underway by some task force members—subgroups of the task force—that often take a few weeks.

A word of warning: The toughest job by far is not the design of an effective PMP on paper; it is getting it implemented! For that reason implementation must be a primary concern all the way through this Stage 2 design phase. A fundamental truth is that people who have not had a hand in crafting something will invariably resist its implementation. Thus, the goal here is to involve as many of the potential users of the PMP as possible in its design. Clearly, a committee of 100 makes no sense, but feed-forward and feedback sessions are one method to solicit organizational buy-in long before formal implementation begins.

8. Engage Top Management As Part of This Design Effort

Top management involvement is critical throughout the entire Stage 2 design phase. The executive sponsors should stay very close to the task force and show up at many of the meetings (not for the full two days!). Some of the sponsors need to closely review the outcome of each session with the task force leader. Top management is involved more than simply as the sponsoring group, however. They must also take an active role in the design of the process:

- The development of a new product strategy for the business is one area where senior management's input, views, decisions, and approvals must be sought. Ideally they should lead the charge here.

- Another top management input is the development of criteria for use at the portfolio reviews and the gates they attend.
- Similarly, the development of rules of the game at portfolio reviews or gates should either be led by top management or, at least, their concurrence should be sought.

9. Undertake Some Activities Off-Line

Much work also goes on in the two-week intervals between the two-day task force sessions. This off-line work is undertaken by task force members working alone or perhaps in small groups on specific tasks defined by the task force. Some larger task forces define subgroups with leaders to accomplish certain tasks. Examples include:

- a subgroup to investigate and define IT needs and seek commercially available solutions
- a subgroup to start designing appropriate documentation for the new PMP (for example, instruction guides and templates)
- a subgroup to liaison regularly with the executive sponsor(s)
- a subgroup to work with the finance department to define the appropriate financial models, calculations, and spreadsheet
- a subgroup to handle communications to those who need to know throughout the business.

The point is that there is much work to be done, and not all can be accomplished in the two-day meetings. Organize to undertake some work off-line.

10. Define Data Collection and IT Needs

IT is a major enabler when installing and using your PMP. A master database to store and manipulate data on all projects along with user-friendly tools to display the data on portfolio diagrams are helpful in many facets of a PMP. For example, picture a portfolio review using Approach 2 where management ranks and reranks the list of projects several times, and each time wants to instantly see what their portfolio looks like on bubble diagrams or what the breakdown is in terms of pie charts. The ability to generate these charts and experiment with different portfolio scenarios greatly facilitates the portfolio review meeting.

IT has proven to be a problematic area, however. You have several IT choices:

- *No software at all.* Portfolio management is almost impossible to install without some type of software. At minimum, you'll need a database to keep vital portfolio information on all projects.
- *Use standard software and modify as needed.* For example, one approach we have used in some installations is to use MS-Office software. An Excel spreadsheet is used to store data on all projects (use an Access database for more sophisticated needs), and then PowerPoint is employed to display the many pie charts and bubble diagrams you need. One problem we have encountered here is the need to write macros, or programs, to manipulate and import the data into PowerPoint (otherwise the system is a very manual and tedious one). Writing

these macros can become quite expensive, and often the results are cumbersome and inadequate.

- *Purchase portfolio software*. This is the route we recommend, and indeed, we have developed software for our own use simply because we had so many problems with the two routes above. We designed NewPort Max™ to solve the problems of displaying portfolio data. NewPort Max™ features a full database, and it has great flexibility in displaying data in the form of rank-ordered lists, pie charts, and bubble diagrams. No macros are needed, and the system is totally automated for instantaneous displays. Finally, scenarios can be created and displayed, right at the portfolio reviews: What if you select this set of projects, what does the portfolio look like? Or what about another set, what will it look like then?

When you specify your portfolio management software requirements, here are some things it should be able to do:

- Keep a database of key metrics and characteristics on all projects, including their categories (active and on hold; platform developments, new products, improvements, etc.)
- Enable you to manipulate this data—for example computing new variables such as ECV or NPV/R&D
- Permit you to sort the data and projects—developing ranked lists or selecting only some projects for analysis
- Display a variety of portfolio charts from the database—pie charts, bubble diagrams, prioritized lists of projects—and without a lot of formatting instructions
- Permit the generation of scenarios: If this is your list of projects, then what does the portfolio look like in terms of the various charts? (very useful at the portfolio review meeting).

Results of Stage 2

The deliverables at the conclusion of step 2 includes a PMP "on paper" that has been reviewed by both users and management and meets their needs and demands: buy-in has already begun! This paper process is presented to the executive sponsors for approval of needed resources for the next stage, including decisions on acquiring IT support and software. Assuming executive concurrence is obtained, then it's on to Stage 3, Trial Installation and Adjustments!

Stage 3: Trial Installation and Adjustments

The purpose here is to try out your portfolio system just designed in Stage 2. You will probably find a number of glitches, and it's best to iron them out before formal roll-out of your PMP.

1. Select and Install Portfolio Software

A major task is selecting and installing the appropriate software. The requirements laid out in action item 10 in Stage 2 above provide guidance.

You will have to make some decisions on what data to keep on each project (action item 6 in Stage 2 above). Then set up your database. One nice feature of some software is that a standard database format comes built into the program, with "popular" or "frequently used stats" already set up. Exhibit 11.4 shows some popular data metrics to keep on projects.

2. Collect Initial Data on Projects (As Input to the Software)

Now comes the task of gathering data on many or all projects in order to test the software and, indeed, the entire PMP. The startup of your PMP will probably require a significant amount of data collection on all existing projects at the outset. You may not have the luxury of waiting for each project to pass through its next gate review to obtain data on it. So be prepared to assign someone to meet with each and every project team to explain the nature of the information needs and then to obtain the data firsthand. Tip: Sending out an e-mail to all team leaders asking for the types of data outlined in Exhibit 11.4 usually does not work: They either misunderstand some data requirements or politely ignore the request.

Step 1 here is to make a list of all projects that will make up this initial portfolio. For expediency, you may wish to leave out some project types. Next, provide operational definitions of each of the variables or metrics to be collected on each project. Recall that the list of metrics was developed in Stage 1, but now each metric must be defined with more care. Contact the project leaders of the identified projects and seek their agreement to help. And, finally, begin the data-collection process—face to face with project leaders or teams—via the assigned person.

3. Review Your Portfolio of Projects

One revealing task is to undertake a review of your current portfolio of active projects. Begin with characterizing the portfolio along key dimensions as outlined in action item 6 in stage 2—the portfolio metrics you've decided upon. That is, undertake a breakdown of either projects or project spending across important dimensions: by market segment, product lines, project types, technologies, and so on. Develop the appropriate pie charts, rank-ordered lists, and bubble diagrams to display the "what is" to management as part of your rollout of your new PMP. You can also develop breakdowns—both numbers of projects and spending—on other dimensions introduced in Chapters 4 and 5 and in Exhibit 11.4.

Assessing the value of the portfolio ought to be part of this task. That is, try to place a dollar amount on the current portfolio of projects using one of the financial methods outlined in Chapter 3. If the total value of the portfolio is less than what you have spent on it, then something clearly is amiss!

4. Conduct Trial Runs of Your Portfolio Reviews, Gates, and IT System

One part of trial installation amounts to running your first trial portfolio review meetings. If you elect Approach 1 for project selection, a trial portfolio review means a periodic check. Invite the right people—usually the senior gatekeeping group—and ensure that you have the right meeting procedure, format, and data available. You will find guidance in Chapter 10 for what happens during an Approach 1 portfolio review, but recall the key steps:

- Identify strategic imperatives
- Check project priorities (review the rank-ordered list of projects)
- Check for portfolio balance and strategic alignment (the various charts and diagrams)
- Make corrections and adjustments to the portfolio of projects and to the gating system.

Note the assumption is that you already have a gating process installed; hence, its implementation is not needed here. But if you lack a Stage-Gate™ process, it is necessary in Stage 2 above to design this process, and here in Stage 3 to begin its implementation via some trial or "welcome gates" along with some pilot projects.[2]

Even if your business has a Stage-Gate™ process, chances are that the structure and procedures at gate meetings will change as a result of adding your new PMP. For example, gates become a two-part decision process; gate criteria for prioritization of projects may be strengthened; and portfolio charts and diagrams—ranked lists, bubble diagrams, and pie charts—will be displayed at your gate reviews. These new features of your gate meetings should also be tested.

If you plan to use Approach 2 for project selection, then the portfolio reviews are even more critical, and their design and trial is vital. Again you can look to Chapter 10 for the details of what happens at a Approach 2 portfolio review, but the key steps are:

- Select the must-do projects (strategic necessities or good projects that are well along)
- Kill the won't-do's
- Prioritize the projects in the middle (a scoring model, financial index, or forced ranking)
- Rank or prioritize your projects until you are out of resources for that project type
- Apply the same process to different types of projects
- The result is *your tentative portfolio* of projects
- Then check for portfolio balance and strategic alignment (review the various charts and diagrams)
- Make final adjustments to the list of projects (may require several iterations).

Running these trial portfolio reviews also enables you to test your portfolio software as well as the types of charts and diagrams you plan to use in your PMP.

5. Test the Macro Allocation Process (strategic buckets)

This we recommend with some caution. The establishment of strategic buckets linked to strategy, outlined in Chapter 9, is a tough exercise. Nonetheless, management must undertake the task at some point, so you might do a trial allocation at this point. Alternatively, some task forces try to get the portfolio reviews along with the IT support up and running—it's perhaps a little easier and more visible—and then move to the macro resource allocation exercise later during Stage 4, Implementation.

6. Final Review and Revisions of PMP

Now your task force reviews the results of action items 1–5 in this section and makes the necessary corrections and adjustments. You will probably find that certain parts of the portfolio review meetings did not run perfectly, or that the wrong portfolio diagrams and charts were displayed or in the wrong format. Now is the time to take a hard, critical look at what you and your task force have designed and make the needed changes.

7. Develop Implementation Plan

One of the final actions in Stage 3 is the design of an implementation plan for the PMP. More on implementation in the next section.

8. Present Tested PMP and Implementation Plan to Executive Sponsors

The final "gate" of this staged approach to designing and implementing your PMP is management signoff. They have seen the process on paper, and they've participated in the trial gate reviews and portfolio reviews. They have witnessed the IT support and gained experience with the various charts and diagrams. They have even been through a prioritization exercise and, perhaps, even through the strategic buckets or macro resource allocation exercise. Now you present your results, conclusions, adjustments, and the implementation plan to the executive sponsoring group for full signoff and approval to implement.

Stage 4: Implementation and Improvement

Implementation of the PMP is perhaps the most challenging phase. Unfortunately, it is often underestimated and, consequently, poorly done in many companies. These key tasks will help ensure the quality of the process:

1. Install a Portfolio Process Manager

No process, however excellent its design and concept, ever implemented itself. And committees or task forces, again well-intentioned, have a history of being poor at implementation. They may do an excellent job on the design of the process, but once that task is finished, task force members seem to drift off to other work and fail to see the implementation through. One person must be charged with making the PMP happen: the process manager or process keeper (other titles might include gate meister, portfolio manager, and key master). Ideally this person is selected from among the task force members and is designated before implementation begins. His or her job is to ensure that the PMP is implemented; that is, that the steps laid out below are indeed executed. Where a company already has a Stage-Gate™ process with a new product process manager already in place, the process manager often takes on the added duties of PM process manager.

2. Secure Senior Management Buy-In

The PMP is doomed to failure unless senior management buy in and commit totally to it. In spite of the fact that senior management has sponsored the PMP initiative, and in spite of their apparent signoff on the process on paper at the end of each stage, in almost every organization we've worked with, there is still some hesitancy around total buy-in to the principles and methods of the PMP. They talk the talk, but they are not quite ready to walk the talk. Intellectually, senior management agrees with the concept of a PMP—a gating process with discipline and tough gates, and a portfolio review process based on facts, all driven by a new product strategy. The obstacle is that they do not realize the biggest change in behavior occurs at the top. Effective gate meetings demand different behavior on the part of senior people than they are used to. The gatekeeper rules of the game bring a certain discipline that is foreign to some senior groups. And portfolio reviews mean that all projects are subjected to the same scrutiny, so that even the general manager's pet projects are under the microscope.

Here are some ways we ensure senior management buy-in:

- First, involve senior management in the design of the process. For example, during Stage 2, ensure that a senior management session is built in where they help design the portfolio reviews or gates (for example, design the prioritization criteria, portfolio metrics, and the rules of the game).
- In Stage 3, run some pilots (for example, run a mock portfolio review with senior management as participants—ideally done in Stage 3).
- Provide a gatekeeper training session, where senior people can not only learn about the PMP, but can be briefed on expected behaviors and their rules of the game as well (particularly if you have selected Approach 2).

Example: When English China Clay introduced their gating process in the United States, the first group to take a training course was the executives, including the president of the company. This one-day training session laid out the details of the process, defined the gate criteria (which they had helped craft), and outlined the gatekeepers' rules (which they had already accepted). Then a mock gate meeting took place, using a real company case. Here the company president and some senior VPs played the roles of the project leader and team, while the more junior executives were the gatekeepers—a complete role reversal. The results were both humorous and instructive.

Example: At Reckitt-Benckiser, every executive right up to the CEO's office attended a two-day training program when their gating process was rolled out worldwide. The difference here was that the training session featured attendees from different levels in the company, so that managing directors sat on the same teams as junior product managers. This approach proved very instructive, especially to senior people who lacked the insights on the problems faced at the project team level.

---

3. Develop User-Friendly Documentation

Most documentation in support of new management processes is not very user-friendly. It is heavy reading, too long, and not very inviting. As a result, most manuals are never read! Too bad, because no doubt a lot of thought and hard work went into their preparation by some well-intentioned task forces. We recommend that you take a look at some of the manuals and guidebooks that have been developed for computer software programs in recent years. They certainly are a far cry from the deadly ones of the mid-1980s. Learn from their experience. We're not suggesting that you develop a guide that reads like "Portfolio Management for Dummies," but maybe a few ideas from this style of guide might be appropriate.

One way to handle the documentation is to develop several pieces or booklets with different levels of detail. Here are three we often use:

1. *Brochure*: A four-page, glossy, four-color brochure can outline the concept and purpose of the PMP. It would look much like a product sales brochure, and that's exactly what it is. First impressions count! Some companies also use this brochure as a selling tool with their customers and customer-partners, outlining how their new product process and portfolio management approach works. With the increasing number of product development efforts being conducted via strategic alliances, this type of communication becomes even more important.
2. *Guide*: A 10–15-page guidebook can provide a fairly in-depth description of the process: for example, prioritization criteria, various bubble diagrams and charts to be used at the portfolio review, outlines of the stages and gates in the new product process, and so on. But it is judicious and sparing in the detail it makes available.
3. *Manual*: The manual can be much longer and has much operational detail. (For example, the guide might list the prioritization criteria, much like Exhibit 3.10, while the manual provides operational definitions of the criteria, as in Appendix B.) The manual also contains examples, illustrations, and templates. The manual is what a project leader of a new product project would refer to as she or he provides input for a portfolio review or prepares for a gate review.

Many companies have elected to move to a paperless gating and portfolio management system. The entire process—from instruction manual to templates, scorecards, database, and metrics—is on the company Intranet system. We recommend such an approach, but we also warn that developing these systems from scratch is usually costly and takes longer than anticipated. Several off-the-shelf (but still flexible to your needs) comprehensive commercial systems are available—total packages that include not only portfolio management software but everything needed to manage your entire new product process.* In the long run, these commercially available models are usually less expensive, less trouble, and better than do-it-yourself efforts.

Although the development of documentation is a part of Stage 4, Implementation, this documentation work must begin much earlier—likely in Stage 3, as your PMP is being tested and finalized—in order to achieve a timely rollout.

* One system (the authors were involved in its design) is the *Accolade* software, a comprehensive system that supports the entire Stage-Gate™ process, including portfolio management. It is available from Sopheon (www.sopheon.com), or contact PDI at www.prod-dev.com.

4. Undertake Internal Marketing

Earlier in this chapter, we noted that rolling out a PMP is a bit like developing and launching a new product. So don't forget the marketing and selling! Here are some common marketing and promotional approaches:

Have an "announcement event" to roll out the PMP. This might coincide with some other company event. The goal is to have the executive sponsors place their blessing on the new PMP and announce that "effective March 1, this process is in place." Next, the task force presents some of the details of the PMP and outlines what will happen as rollout proceeds (for example, training, bringing existing projects in, and so on).

Use in-company communications; for example, your company newsletter, magazine, or e-mail. Inco (a major nickel producer), for example, found that corporate awareness and support for their new process was greatly enhanced after a newsletter was published with supporting quotes from key executives. It is excellent practice to keep the rest of the company informed of your task force progress all the way through Stages 2 and 3. Sometimes there is a long pause between the initial kickoff event and eventual rollout of the PMP, so you should be considering "news releases" and articles all the way along, not just as rollout begins. Someone on the task force can be appointed as "communications manager."

5. Provide Training on the PMP

Most companies underestimate the need for training when they roll out a new product process, a gating method, or a PMP. The assumption seems to be that "all this stage-gate and bubble diagram stuff is obvious, and anyone ought to be able to handle it by reading the manual." Wrong! First, many people don't read. Second, learning via reading is not everyone's forte. Third, this "stage-gate and bubble diagram stuff" is considerably more complex than you might expect. Finally, recall that buy-in is a critical goal. People will not use something new if they either fear it or do not understand it, no matter how loud the boss screams. So take every precaution to ensure that people appreciate the benefits of the new process (no fear!) and that they fully understand how it works. Training is essential for organizational buy-in.

6. Bring Existing Projects into the PMP

In Stage 3 above, an initial effort was made to collect data on projects; now it's time to revisit the data and include all projects with updated data in the database. First, assemble a list of the projects to be included in your PMP (this list should be available from Stages 2 and 3). Then update the projects list. Also, obtain and update the data on each project—data needed to characterize and describe each project—so that you can begin displaying the various portfolio charts at gate meetings and portfolio reviews. As in Stage 3, assign a person to do this face-to-face with project leaders.

7. Get the Gates Working Right!

Hold gate reviews soon! If you do not have a gating process in place and are concurrently installing a Stage-Gate™ process along with your PMP, it's essential that all projects move through at least one gate fairly quickly. Note that some of the required data on projects might be of doubtful validity; in addition, some data needed in certain portfolio models are not yet available (for example, project scores from gate reviews). Thus, the next challenge is ensuring that all projects pass through a gate review. This should be done as early as possible for two reasons:

1. The sooner all projects are "in" the Stage-Gate™ process, the better.
2. The gate reviews provide or validate much of the data needed for the portfolio models and portfolio review. For example, gates are where the gatekeepers accept the NPV values as valid; and gates are where project scores on key criteria are determined, at least in Approach 1.

An effective procedure here is to have a series of "welcome gates" to ensure that all projects pass through at least one gate within the first months of rollout. These welcome gates are somewhat gentler than real gates and require that project leaders declare in advance where they are in the process (what stage) and what they will deliver to the welcome gate. It is understood by gatekeepers that likely not all the desired deliverables will be available for the welcome gate. One output of the welcome gate is a decision on what and when the next "real" gate will be, and what deliverables will be available then. Another outcome of the welcome gate is the data—the NPVs, the approved expenditures, the project scores on key factors, probability estimates, and the like—needed for the portfolio database and model.

Another approach is to begin with some pilot projects. This can start in Stage 3 once a skeleton process is in place. That is, pick a handful of projects whose project leaders are willing (ideally their leaders might even be on the task force). These should be typical projects, perhaps at different stages. Then start running these projects through the gating process to test it, and in particular, to test the gate criteria and gate procedures. With a limited number of projects, you can also start to pilot the portfolio IT system and database and some of the portfolio models.

8. Start Running the Portfolio Reviews and the Macro Allocation Process

In Stage 3, you conducted a trial portfolio review meeting and, perhaps, even a trial macro allocation exercise, moving to the definition of strategic buckets. Now it's time to do these two exercises for real. Involve the senior people in the business, but remember it must be planned and executed proficiently. With the careful design in Stage 2, guidance from Chapters 9 and 10, and with benefit of the trial review results, Stage 4 should be relatively straightforward. But again, carefully orchestrate both meetings—the portfolio review and the macro allocation—mapping out the procedure carefully. And be sure to have the PMP manager direct and facilitate both sessions.

9. Continually Review and Improve Your PMP

Now that your PMP is fully operational remember that, as in the Stage-Gate™ process, there will inevitably be glitches and minor problems in the PMP. It is unlikely that you will have designed the perfect process. Instead, it will be "evergreen," improving as the organization learns how to use it. Many of these issues will reveal themselves only over time, as the process is fully utilized, and as projects make their way through the pipeline. For this reason, we recommend that the process manager set up a feedback mechanism to collect information about where the process is working well and where it might need improvement. For example, the PMP manager might hold an annual review meeting to solicit feedback on how the process could be improved; or, after the first PMP meeting, solicit feedback from the executives and other participants on how the meeting went and whether there are any improvements that they might like to see.

There is much work involved in the implementation of a PMP. If parts of the process are already in place (for example, you already have a new product strategy, or you already have a perfectly fine Stage-Gate™ process), then the task is certainly lighter. There are also many pitfalls along the way: see Exhibit 11.5, "Ten Ways to Fail," our tongue-in-cheek reminder list of some don'ts. We could continue with the warnings and cautions, but we think you get the point. Before you proceed, think through the design and implementation of a PMP carefully, and be prepared to make a major commitment here. But at all costs, do proceed! The costs of doing nothing are just too high.

POINTS FOR MANAGEMENT TO PONDER

Implementation can be a difficult stage, fraught with problems and miscues. But it need not be. If you've followed the task force action items in Stages 1 and 2, including seeking input and feedback from the users of your new PMP, and conducted the trials well in Stage 3, then implementation should be a matter of executing a well-thought-out plan. The key action items in this plan are:

1. Install a portfolio process manager
2. Secure senior management buy-in
3. Develop user-friendly documentation
4. Undertake internal marketing
5. Provide training on the PMP
6. Bring existing projects into the PMP
7. Get the gates working right!
8. Start running the portfolio reviews and the macro allocation process
9. Continually review and improve your PMP.

1. Design the portfolio management process on your own, in your own office, and in a vacuum. You know best — task forces are a waste of time!

2. Don't do any homework or auditing. You already know what the problem is in your company, so jump immediately to a solution.

3. Don't bother looking at other companies' methods — their approaches, IT, models, charts, criteria and scoring models, and so on. You have nothing to learn from them.

4. If you do assemble a Task Force, meet over several months in private. Then present "your grand design" and assume everyone in the company will applaud, even though they have not been involved in the design.

5. Don't seek outside help: just read the book and design your process based on the generic one. If you do seek help, hire a reengineering consultant who knows nothing about new product management or portfolio management.

6. Don't waste time testing and seeking feedback from others in the Company as your task force designs the process. After all, you're the Task Force. What do these "outsiders" know? Your "process design" is likely to be near perfect!

7. When others do have questions or criticisms, treat these people as "cynics" and "negative thinkers." Refuse to deal with these objections, and never, never modify the process. It's yours, and its cast in marble.

8. Don't provide training — most of this "portfolio management stuff "is obvious. Anyone ought to be able to do it, just by reading the manual.

9. Speaking of manuals, make sure the PMP guide is thick, full of checklists and forms. If in doubt, overwhelm the reader and user.

10. Don't bother installing a Process or Portfolio Manager — the process is so good, it will be automatically implemented.

EXHIBIT 11.5   Ten Ways to Fail at Portfolio Management Design and Implementation (Based on Experiences at Real Companies)

Winning at New Products

There are two ways to win big at new products: doing the right projects and doing projects right. This book is about *doing the right projects*. If you pick the right projects, then you are halfway to winning. You end up with an enviable portfolio of high-value projects: a portfolio that is properly balanced, and, most important, a portfolio that supports your business's strategy. Picking the right number of projects for the resources available—making sure that you don't overload your process and end up with pipeline gridlock—also has an added payoff in terms of doing projects right: Better portfolio management should positively affect the quality of execution of projects. The end result is higher success rates and shorter cycle times.

New products are the leading edge of your business strategy. The product choices you make today determine what your business's product offerings and market position will be in the future. Making the right choices today is critical. Portfolio management and new product project selection is fundamental to business success. How you invest your R&D and new product resources will shape the future of your business. Indeed, business history is littered with the remains of companies that failed at this task—failed to make the right strategic choices about what new products, developments, platforms, and technologies they wished to focus on. Over the next decade, some companies will win at new products and others will lose. The winners will be the next generation of Microsofts, GEs, 3Ms, and Pfizers. You won't hear too much about the losers as they fade away into obscurity. So take the needed steps to ensure that your business is on the winning side. Make sure that you have the tools you need to make the right choices—an effective portfolio management process—in your business!

Overhauling the New Product Process: Stage-Gate™ Methods—A Synopsis[1]

Goals of a New Product Process

Many companies have undertaken internal audits only to conclude that their new product process isn't working: Projects take too long; key activities and tasks are missing; and Go/Kill decisions are problematic. As a result, they have overhauled their process using a Stage-Gate™ approach. Numerous benchmarking studies and investigations into winners versus losers have pointed to the following goals for a successful new product process.

Goal 1: Quality of Execution

A quality-of-execution crisis exists in the product innovation process. The deficiency is evident in many benchmarking studies, including our own: Key activities are poorly done or not done at all; too many projects omit too many vital actions; and both quality of execution and thoroughness of the process are lacking. There is also clear evidence that the activities of the new product process—the quality of execution and whether these activities are carried out at all—have a dramatic impact on product performance.

This quality-of-execution crisis provides strong evidence in support of the need for a more systematic and high-quality approach to the way firms conceive, develop, and launch new products. The way to deal with the quality problem is to visualize product innovation as a process and to apply process management and quality management techniques to the process. Note that any process in business can be managed with a view to quality. Get the details of your processes right and the result will be a high-quality output.

Quality of execution is the goal of the new product process. More specifically, the ideal process should:

1. *focus on completeness*: ensure that the key activities that are central to the success of a new product project are indeed carried out—no gaps, no omissions—a "complete" process.

2. *focus on quality*: ensure that the execution of the key activities is proficient—that is, treat innovation as a process, emphasize DIRTFooT (doing it right the first time), and build in quality controls and checks.
3. *focus on the important*: devote attention and resources to the pivotal and particularly weak steps in the new product process, notably the upfront and market-oriented activities.

The new product process or Stage-Gate™ system is simply a process management tool. One builds into this process quality of execution in much the same way that quality programs have been successfully implemented on the factory floor.

Goal 2: Sharper Focus, Better Project Prioritization

Most firms' new product efforts suffer from a lack of focus: too many projects and not enough resources. Adequate resources have been identified as a principal driver of firms' new product performance, but a lack of resources plagues too many firms' development efforts. Sometimes the lack is simply because management has not devoted the needed people and money to the firm's new product effort. Often, the resource problem stems from trying to do too many projects, the result of inadequate project evaluations: the failure to set priorities and make tough Go/Kill decisions. In short, the "gates" are weak.

The need is for a new product funnel, not tunnel. A new product funnel builds in tough Go/Kill decision points (or bailout points throughout the process); the poor projects are weeded out; scarce resources are directed toward the truly meritorious projects; and more focus is the result. One funneling method is to build the new product process or game plan around a set of gates or Go/Kill decision points. The gates are the bailout points at which we ask "Are we still in the game?" They are the quality-control checkpoints in the new product process and focus on the quality, merit, and progress of the project.

Goal 3: A Strong Market Orientation

A market orientation is the missing ingredient in most new product projects. A lack of a market orientation and inadequate market assessment are consistently cited as reasons for new product failure. Moreover, the market-related activities tend to be the weakest in the new product process, despite the fact that they are strongly linked to success. While many managers profess a market orientation, the evidence—where they spend the time and money on projects—proves otherwise.

If positive new product performance is the goal, then a market orientation—executing the key marketing activities in a high-quality fashion—must be built into the new product process as a matter of routine rather than by exception. Marketing inputs must play a decisive role from beginning to end of the project. The following actions are integral and mandatory plays in the new product game plan (but they rarely are executed):

- *Preliminary market assessment*: a relatively inexpensive step very early in the life of a project, designed to assess market attractiveness and to test market acceptance of the proposed new product
- *Market research to determine user needs and wants*: in-depth surveys or face-to-face interviews with customers to determine customer needs, wants, preferences, likes, dislikes, buying criteria, and so on as an input to the design of the new product

- *Competitive analysis*: an assessment of competitors—their products and product deficiencies, prices, costs, technologies, production capacities, and marketing strategies
- *Concept testing*: testing the proposed product in concept form to determine likely market acceptance (Note that the product is not yet developed, but a model or representation of the product is displayed to prospective users to gauge reaction and purchase intent.)
- *Customer reaction during development*: continuing concept and product testing throughout the development phase, using rapid prototypes, models, and partially completed products to gauge customer reaction and seek feedback
- *User tests*: field trials using the finished product (or prototype) with users to verify the performance of the product under customer conditions, and to confirm purchase intent and market acceptance
- *Test market or trial sell*: a mini-launch of the product in a limited geographic area or single sales territory (This is a test of all elements of the marketing mix, including the product itself.)
- *Market launch*: a proficient launch, based on a solid marketing plan and backed by sufficient resources.

Goal 4: Better Upfront Homework and Sharp, Early Product Definition

New product success or failure is largely decided in the first few plays of the game—in those crucial steps and tasks that precede the actual development of the product. Solid upfront homework and sharp early product definition are key ingredients in a successful new product process and result in higher success rates and profitability. The upfront homework helps define the product and build the business case for development. Ironically, most of the money and time spent on projects is devoted to the middle and back-end stages of the process, while the upfront actions suffer from errors of omission, poor quality of execution, and underresourcing.

The ideal new product process ensures that the early stages are carried out and that the product is fully defined before the project is allowed to proceed—before the project is allowed to become a full-fledged development project.

Goal 5: A True Cross-Functional Team Approach

The new product process is multifunctional: It requires the input and active participation of players from many functions in the organization. The multifunctional nature of innovation coupled with the desire for parallel processing means that a cross-functional team approach is mandatory. Essential characteristics of this team are as follows:

- The team is cross-functional, with committed team players from the various functions and departments—marketing, engineering, R&D, manufacturing. Release time for the project is provided to team members.
- Every significant project team has a clearly defined team captain or leader. The leader is dedicated to the project (not spread across numerous other duties or projects) and is accountable from beginning to end of the project—not just for one phase.
- The leader has formal authority: This means co-opting authority from the functional heads. When senior management approves the team's action plan at gate

meetings, they also commit the resources—money, people, and release time—to the project leader and team; at the same time, senior management transfers decision-making power to the team. Expectations and the scope of this authority are made very clear to the team at the gate.

- The team structure is fluid, with new members joining the team (or leaving it) as work requirements demand. But a small core group of responsible, committed, and accountable team players should be present from beginning to end of the project.

Goal 6: Delivery of Products with Competitive Advantage—Differentiated Products, Unique Benefits, Superior Value for the Customer

Do not forget to build in product superiority at every opportunity. This is one key to new product success, yet all too often, when redesigning their new product processes, firms fall into the trap of repeating current, often faulty, practices: There's no attempt to seek truly superior products. And so the results are predicable: more ho-hum, tired products. Here is how to drive the quest for product advantage:

- Ensure that at least some of the criteria at every gate focus on product superiority. Questions such as "Does the product have at least one element of competitive advantage?" "Does it offer the user new or different benefits?" "Is it excellent value for the money to the user?" become vital to rating and ranking would-be projects.
- Require that certain key actions designed to deliver product superiority be included at each stage of the process. Some of these have been mentioned above (goal 3) and include customer-focused ideation; user needs-and-wants market research studies; competitive product analysis; concept and protocept* tests, preference tests, and trial sells; and constant iterations with customers during development via rapid prototypes and tests.
- Demand that project teams deliver evidence of product superiority to project Go/Kill reviews: make product superiority an important deliverable and issue at such meetings (rather than dwelling on the financial calculations).

Goal 7: A Fast-Paced and Flexible Process

The new product process must be built for speed. This means eliminating all the time wasters and work that adds no value in your current new product process. It also means designing a flexible process, one that accommodates the risks and nature of different projects. Some firms are moving toward a third-generation process,[2] which features three Fs:

- *Flexible*: The process is not a straitjacket or hard-and-fast set of rules; rather, each project can be routed through the process according to its risk level and needs; stages can be omitted and gates combined, provided the decision is made consciously, at gates, and with a full understanding of the risks involved.

---

*Protocept: Halfway between *concept* and *prototype*. For example, a crude mock-up or early prototype.

- *Fuzzy gates*: "Go" decisions can be conditional; the decision can be made in the absence of perfect information, conditional on positive results delivered later.
- *Fluidity*: The process is fluid and adaptable. For example, stages can be overlapped—a project can be in two stages at the same time; and activities are done concurrently within stages, much like a rugby approach (rather than a series or relay race scheme).

The Structure of the Stage-Gate™ Process

Fashion these seven key goals into a Stage-Gate™ new product game plan—a conceptual and operational model for moving a new product project from idea to launch. This Stage-Gate™ system is a blueprint for managing the new product process to improve effectiveness and efficiency.

Stage-Gate™ systems break the innovation process down into a predetermined set of stages, each stage consisting of a set of prescribed, cross-functional, and parallel activities (see Exhibit 10.2). The entrance to each stage is a gate: These gates control the process and serve as the quality-control and Go/Kill checkpoints.

The Stages

The Stage-Gate™ system breaks the new product project down into discrete and identifiable stages, typically four, five, or six in number. Each stage is designed to gather information needed to move the project forward to the next gate or decision point. Each stage is multi- or cross-functional: There is no "R&D stage" or "marketing stage." Rather, each stage consists of a set of parallel activities undertaken by people from different functional areas within the firm, but working together as a team led by a project team leader.

In order to manage risk via a Stage-Gate™ scheme, the parallel activities within a stage must be designed to gather vital information (technical, market, financial, and so on) in order to drive down technical and business uncertainties. Each stage costs more than the preceding one, and so the game plan is one of incremental commitment. As uncertainties decrease, expenditures are allowed to mount.

Finally, flexibility is built in to promote acceleration of projects. In order to speed products to market, stages can overlap each other; long lead-time activities can be brought forward from one stage to an earlier one; projects can proceed into the next stage, even though the previous stage has not been totally completed; and stages can be collapsed and combined.

The general flow of the typical or a generic Stage-Gate™ process is shown pictorially in Exhibit 10.2. In that exhibit, the five key and overlapping stages can be described as follows:

Stage 1. Scoping. Stage 1 is a quick investigation and scoping of the project. Typically, Stage 1 is undertaken by a very small core team of technical and marketing people; it includes the first-cut homework, such as preliminary market assessment, preliminary technical assessment, and preliminary business assessment.

Stage 2. Building Business Case. At Stage 2 the detailed homework leads to a business case. Stage 2 includes market research (a user-needs-and-wants study to identify requirements for the ideal product; competitive analysis; and a concept test to confirm purchase intent); detailed technical and manufacturing assessment; and a detailed financial and business analysis. Stage 2 should be undertaken by a core team of marketing, technical, and manufacturing people—the beginnings of the ultimate project team for Stage 3. The deliverables from Stage 2 include a defined product (on paper: target market, product concept and benefits, and product requirements); a business justification (economic and business rationale), and a detailed plan of action for the next stages (including resource requirements and timing).

Stage 3. Development.   During Stage 3 the actual design and development of the new product take place. Here the development plan is implemented; a prototype or sample product is developed; and the product undergoes in-house testing along with limited customer testing (for example, rapid prototypes and tests with potential users). In addition, the manufacturing process and requirements are mapped out; the marketing launch plan is developed; and the test plans for the next stage are defined. Stage 3 sees the project gain momentum, with a marked increase in resource commitment: Here the full cross-functional project team—marketing, technical, manufacturing, and perhaps quality assurance, purchasing, sales, and finance people—is in place.

Stage 4. Testing and Validation.   Stage 4 sees the verification and validation of the proposed new product, its marketing, and its production. This stage witnesses extensive in-house product testing; customer field trials or trials in the marketplace; pilot or preproduction trials in the plant; and even test marketing or a trial sell. The deliverable is a fully tested product and production process, ready for commercialization. The project team and leader from Stage 3 remain accountable for actions and deliverables in Stage 4.

Stage 5. Launch.   Stage 5 realizes full commercialization of the product. Stage 5 marks the beginning of full production and commercial selling. This stage sees the implementation of the marketing launch plan, the production plan, and the postlaunch activities, including monitoring and adjustment. While new members may be added to this "commercialization team" (for example, from the sales force and from operations), the core project team from Stages 4 and 5 remains in place and accountable for commercialization and beyond. There are no handoffs in this game!

Note that there are two homework stages in this process: Stage 1 is a quick homework phase and Stage 2 provides for a more detailed investigation. The result is superb upfront homework and sharp, early product definition (goal 4). In addition, constant customer contact and a market orientation are evident throughout all five stages: The actions outlined in goal 3 are heavily featured in the process. These actions heighten the odds of delivering a superior product with real value to the customer (goal 6). Finally, a cross-functional team approach is mandatory in order to successfully execute each stage (goal 5).

The Gates

Preceding each stage is an entry gate or a Go/Kill decision point, shown as a diamond in Exhibit 10.2. Effective gates are central to the success of a fast-paced new product process:

- Gates serve as quality-control checkpoints, where quality of execution is the focus: Is this project being executed in a high-quality fashion (goal 1)?
- Gates also serve as Go/Kill and prioritization decision points (goal 2). Gates provide for the funneling of projects, in which mediocre projects are successively culled out at each gate.
- Finally, gates are the points where the path forward for the next play or stage of the process is decided, along with resource commitments. Once again, quality of execution becomes a central issue.

Gate meetings are usually staffed by senior managers from various functions, who own the resources required by the project leader and team for the next stage.

Gates have a common format:

- *Inputs*: these are the deliverables to a gate review—what the project leader and team deliver to the meeting; they are the results of the actions of the previous stage and are based on a standard menu of deliverables for each gate.
- *Criteria*: these are questions or metrics on which the project is judged in order to make the Go/Kill and prioritization decision. They include both qualitative (for example, strategic fit; product superiority; market attractiveness) and quantitative criteria (financial return; risk via sensitivity analysis) and can include must-meet (mandatory) as well as should-meet (desirable) criteria (see Appendix B).
- *Outputs*: these are the results of the gate review—a decision (Go/Kill/Hold/Recycle); a prioritization level; resource commitments and action plan approved; and date and deliverables for next gate agreed on.

In the fastest Stage-Gate™ processes, gate decisions are made with incomplete information: This means that the project team is given a go decision, conditional on positive results occurring early in the next stage. In this way, the project is not held up while awaiting the completion of one or two tasks from the previous stage.

Understanding the critical success factors—what separates high-performing business units and winning new products from the rest—is the first step toward improving one's own performance. Overhauling your new product process, and incorporating these success factors into this Stage-Gate™ process, is the way many companies are now winning at new products.

Sample Gate 3 Screening Criteria (Scored)

Questions are scored on 0–10 scales and averaged to yield the six factors. The six factors are then added and averaged (final table) to yield the project attractiveness score.

Factor 1: Business Strategy Fit

Key Items	Rating Scale				Rating
	0	**4**	**7**	**10**	**Rating**
Congruence	Product has only peripheral fit with business strategies	Modest fit, but not with a key element of the strategy	Good fit with a key element of strategy	Strong fit with several key elements of strategy	
Impact	Minimal impact; no noticeable harm if product dropped	Moderate competitive, financial impact	Significant competitive and financial impact	Very strong positive impact on the business	

Factor 2: Product Competitive Advantage

Key Items	Rating Scale				Rating
	0	**4**	**7**	**10**	**Rating**
Customer Benefits	Product offers no unique benefits or features	Product offers some benefits, but not important to customer	Product offers unique features and benefits	Product offers positive, unique benefits and features	
Meets Customer Needs	Product is same as competitors in meeting customer needs	Product is marginally better than competitors in meeting customer needs	Product is better than competitors in meeting customer needs	Product is clearly superior than competitors in meeting customer needs	
Customer Value for Money	Product is same as competitors; poor value for money for the customer	Product provides better value for money for the customer	Product has good value for money for the customer	Product clearly has excellent value for money for the customer	

Factor 3: Market Attractiveness

Key Items	Rating Scale				Rating
	0	4	7	10	
Market Size	Very small market	Small market	Moderate sized market	Very large market	
Market Growth	No growth or negative market growth	Slow market growth; almost at GNP	Good market growth; better than GNP	Very fast market growth	
Margins in this Market (%)	Very small profit margins	Moderate profit margins	Good profit margins	Very large profit margins	
Competitive Situation	Many competitors; intense competition	Some competitors; fairly intense competition	Few competitors; not intense competition	Little or no competition; very positive competitive situation	

Factor 4: Leverages Core Competencies

Key Items	Rating Scale				Rating
	0	4	7	10	
Marketing Synergies (distribution, sales force)	No marketing expertise, experience or resources for this project	Some marketing expertise, experience or resources for this project	Considerable marketing expertise, experience or resources for this project	Leverages very well our marketing resources, expertise and experience	
Technological Synergies	Little or no experience or expertise in this technology; require hiring/acquiring new skills, technology	Some experience and expertise in this technology; require acquiring some new skills/technology	Experience in this area; somewhat leverages our existing technology	Highly experienced in this area; leverages well our existing technology	
Production/Processing Synergies	Little or no experience in this area; require new plant/facilities, training	Some experience in this area; require large modifications to current facilities	Experience in this area; require simple modifications	Highly experienced in this area; can use existing facilities with minimal modifications	

Factor 5: Technical Feasibility

Key Items	Rating Scale				Rating
	0	4	7	10	
Size of Technical Gap	Large gulf between current practice and objective; must invent new science	"Order of magnitude" change proposed	Step change short of "order of magnitude"	Incremental improvement; more engineering in focus	
Technical Complexity of Product	Many hurdles; undefined product	Some hurdles; defined product	A challenge, but "do-able"	Straight-forward	
Technical Uncertainty	Many, and major, technical uncertainties; difficult to define solution	Some significant technical uncertainties	Defined technical solution, but uncertainties remain	Defined technical solution is straight-forward and certain	
Demonstrated Technical Feasibility	Have not been able to demonstrate feasibility	Some demonstration, limited	Almost demonstrated; will be able to do early in Development	Technical feasibility demonstrated clearly	

Factor 6: Financial Reward

Key Items	Rating Scale				Rating
	0	4	7	10	
Expected Profitability (magnitude: NPV)	NPV <$1MM	NPV= $5MM	NPV= $50MM	NPV >$100MM	
Return (IRR%)	IRR<20%, Kill	IRR=25%	IRR=35%	IRR>50%	
Payback Period	>5 years	4 years	2 years	<1 years	
Certainty of Return/Profit Estimates	Uncertain of results	Moderately certain	Fairly certain	Positive of results	
Time to Commercial Start-Up	>5 years	4 years	2 years	<1 year	

Note: financial numbers are for illustrative purposes only and should be adjusted to reflect your business needs.

Summary Scores: Project Attractiveness Score

Key Items	Rating Scale				Rating
	0	4	7	10	
Business Strategy Fit					
Product Competitive Advantage					
Market Attractiveness					
Synergies (Leverage Core Competencies)					
Technical Feasibility					
Financial Reward					

NewPort Max™ Software
A Tool for New Product Portfolio Management

What Is NewPort Max™ Software?

NewPort Max™ software is a leading-edge portfolio management tool designed to enable tracking of key performance metrics and facilitate senior executive decision making. New-Port Max™ software is the result of years of consulting experience and research on a topic that continues to challenge many organizations.

NewPort Max™ software facilitates the identification of performance metrics, the tracking of these metrics, and ultimately the reporting of valuable decision-support information. The default presentation charts include an array of best practices from some of the world's leading companies.

NewPort Max™ Software: An Overview

NewPort Max™ software offers flexibility to its users. Users have the choice of implementing ready-to-use default performance metrics, charts, and presentation packages to help their organizations get started immediately, or to tailor the software to suit an organization's specific needs. Flexibility is further enhanced with the numerous options around organizing performance metrics and data, through to the customization of the presentation reports. NewPort Max™ software enables "what if" scenario testing to enhance senior executive decision making by providing a better understanding the impacts of their decisions prior to implementing them.

The Four Key Components of NewPort Max™ Software

The Data Pool. The data pool houses all your portfolio performance metrics and associated project metrics data. The default data pool contains more than 60 possible performance metrics and is easily customizable to suit individual organizational needs. Once designed, the data pool serves as the data-entry and data management tool.

The Template Set.   The template set produces subsets of the data pool to allow fast, effective analysis of a smaller set of data. The default templates produce numerous default charts for the corporate and business areas combined. A Template Editor supports the customization and further development of new templates, which in turn produces customized charts for presentation. This component also facilitates scenario testing while maintaining the integrity of the data pool.

The Chart Group.   The chart group can produce default charts from templates. It also allows for extensive customization. Chart Manager walks you through the steps to generate each display according to your organization's needs. Displays can be saved for future use, thus eliminating the need to recreate charts of similar types.

The Presentation Package.   The presentation package is the NewPort Max™ software finale. It pulls all the charts with the necessary information together into a packaged presentation for sharing with senior executive decision makers.

Benefits of NewPort Max™ Software

NewPort Max™ software was designed to work in concert with a company's portfolio management process and new product development process. The benefits of using New-Port Max™ software to help manage your company's portfolio include:

- analyzing and reporting key portfolio performance metrics from one database location
- running what-if scenarios
- analyzing portfolios from varied perspectives (e.g., product line, market, innovation type)
- linking with your Stage-Gate™ process
- providing charts for easy-to-understand visual presentation of portfolio status
- enhancing new product communication within your organization.

For more information on NewPort Max™ software, visit www.prod-dev.com.

The *NewProd*™ 3000 Model

The *NewProd™ 3000* model is a scoring model with a difference. It is based on the profiles and outcomes of hundreds of past new product projects. And it serves as both a diagnostic tool and a predictive model.

The *NewProd™ 3000* model is a computer-based scoring model that helps the project team understand their project much better—its strengths, its weaknesses, its risks, critical areas of ignorance about it, and what needs fixing. Thus it leads to a common understanding of the project, and it helps the project team develop an action plan for the project.

The *NewProd™ 3000* model also predicts the likelihood of commercial success and, therefore, is valuable as an input to the Go/Kill and portfolio management decision. For example, Procter & Gamble uses the *NewProd™* score—likelihood of commercial success—as one axis on their three-dimensional portfolio bubble diagram (see Exhibit 4.3).

The model is premised on the fact that the profile of a new product project is a reasonable predictor of success. It was developed from the experiences and outcomes of hundreds of past new product launches. Profile characteristics include measures of competitive and product advantage, leveraging of core competencies, market attractiveness and competitive situation, project innovativeness, and so on.

In use, up to twelve evaluators assess the project on each of thirty key questions, which are proven discriminators between winners and losers. The profile of the project, based on these ratings, is analyzed by computer and, in effect, compared with the profiles of hundreds of projects in the database that have known commercial outcomes. In this way, a likelihood of success and the project's strengths and weaknesses are determined.

Although originally developed for DuPont and Procter & Gamble, the *NewProd™ 3000* model is now commercially available and has been adopted as a selection and diagnostic tool in about 150 companies in Europe and North America. There are industry-specific versions, for example, for the chemical industry, the pharmaceutical industry, the service sector, and the consumer-goods industry. It has been successfully validated in the Netherlands, Scandinavia, and North America and yields predictive abilities in the 73 to 84 percent range—not perfect, but considerably better than the typical manager's ability to pick winners![1]

For more on the *NewProd™* model, visit www.prod-dev.com.

Reference Notes

Chapter 1

1. P. Roussel, K.N. Saad, and T.J. Erickson, *Third Generation R&D: Managing the Link to Corporate Strategy* (Boston: Harvard Business School Press & Arthur D. Little, Inc., 1991).

2. A. Griffin and A.L. Page, "An Interim Report on Measuring Product Development Success and Failure," *Journal of Product Innovation Management* 9, 1 (1993): 291–308. Also see A.L. Page, "Assessing New Product Development Practices and Performance: Establishing Crucial Norms," *Journal of Product Innovation Management* 10, 4 (1993): 273–90, and A. Griffin, *Drivers of NPD Success: The 1997 PDMA Report* (Mount Laurel, N.J.: Product Development & Management Association, 1997).

3. R.G. Cooper, *Winning at New Products*, 3d ed. (Reading, MA: Perseus Books, 2001).

4. R.G. Cooper, S.J. Edgett, and E.J. Kleinschmidt, "Portfolio Management in New Product Development: Lessons from the Leaders—Part 1," *Research-Technology Management* 40, 5 (1997): 16–28; "Portfolio Management in New Product Development: Lessons from the Leaders—Part 2," *Research-Technology Management* 40, 6 (1997): 43–57.

5. A study of portfolio management practices and what results were achieved. R.G. Cooper, S.J. Edgett, and E.J. Kleinschmidt, "Best Practices for Managing R&D Portfolios," *Research-Technology Management* 41, 4 (1998): 20–33. See also R.G. Cooper, S.J., Edgett, and E.J. Kleinschmidt, "New Product Portfolio Management: Practices and Performance," *Journal of Product Innovation Management* 16, 4 (1999): 333–51 (winner of PDMA's T.P. Hustad Best Paper Award, 2000). Also see R.G. Cooper, S.J. Edgett, and E.J. Kleinschmidt, *R&D Portfolio Management Best Practices Study* (Washington, DC: Industrial Research Institute, 1997).

6. R.G. Cooper, S.J. Edgett, and E.J. Kleinschmidt, "New Problems, New Solutions: Making Portfolio Management More Effective," *Research-Technology Management* 43, 2 (2000): 18–33.

7. R.G. Cooper, S.J. Edgett, and E.J. Kleinschmidt, "Portfolio Management—Fundamental to New Product Success," *PDMA New Product Development Tool Book* (New York: Wiley & Sons, 2002).

8. See the portfolio study cited in note 5.

9. See the portfolio study cited in note 5.

Chapter 2

1. N. Archer and F. Ghasemzadeh, "Project Portfolio Selection Techniques: A Review and a Suggested Integrated Approach," Innovation Research Centre Working Paper No. 46, McMaster University, 1996; N.R. Baker, "R&D Project Selection Models: An Assessment," *IEEE Transactions on Engineering Management* EM-21, 4 (1974): 165–70; N. R. Baker, and W.H. Pound, "R&D Project Selection: Where We Stand," *IEEE Transactions on Engineering Management* EM-11, 4 (1964): 124–34; N. Danila, "Strategic Evaluation and Selection of R&D Projects," *R&D Management* 19, 1 (1989): 47–62; M.J. Liberatore, "A Decision Support System Linking Research and Development Project Selection with Business Strategy," *Project Management Journal* 19, 5 (1988): 14–21.

2. S. Liyanage, P. Greenfield, and R. Don, "Towards a Fourth Generation R&D Management Model—Research Networks in Knowledge Management," *Project Management Journal* 18, 3/4 (1999): 372–93. The authors refer to more than 200 quantitative and qualitative methods for selecting R&D projects.

3. J.F. Bard, R. Balachandra, and P.E. Kaufmann, "An Interactive Approach to R&D Project Selection and Termination," *IEEE Transactions on Engineering Management* 35, 3 (1988): 139–46. Parts of this discussion are taken from J.E. Matheson, M.M. Menke, and S.L. Derby, "Improving the Quality of R&D Decision: A Synopsis of the SDG Approach," *Journal of Science Policy and Research Management* (in Japanese) 4, 4 (1989). See also P. Evans, "Streamlining Formal Portfolio Management," *Scrip Magazine*, Feb. 1996.

4. Liyanage, Greenfield, and Don, "Towards a Fourth Generation R&D Management Model." See also N.R. Baker, "R&D Project Selection Models: An Assessment," *IEEE Transactions on Engineering Management* EM-21, 4 (1974): 165–70; M.R. Baker and J. Freeland, "Recent Advances in R&D Benefit Measurement and Project Selection Methods," *Management Science* 21 (1975): 1164–75; D.L. Hall and A. Nauda, "An Interactive Approach for Selecting IR&D Projects," *IEEE Transactions on Engineering Management* 37, 2 (1990): 126–33; P. Roussel, K. Saad, and T. Erickson, *Third Generation R&D, Managing the Link to Corporate Strategy* (Boston: Harvard Business School Press and Arthur D. Little, 1991); D.A. Yorke and G. Droussiotis, "The Use of Customer Portfolio Theory: An Empirical Survey," *Journal of Business & Industrial Marketing* 9, 3 (1994): 6–18.

5. J.L. Ringuest, S.B. Graves, and R.H. Case, "Formulating R&D Portfolios That Account for Risk," *Research-Technology Management* 42, 6 (1999): 40–43; and W.E. Souder and T. Mandakovic, "R&D Project Selection Models," *Research Management* 29, 4 (1986): 36–42.

6. The use of *Crystal Ball* is described in T. Stevens, "Picking the Winners," *Industry Week* 249, 5 (2000): 27–30. See also I. Noor and T. Rye, "Guideline for Successful Risk Facilitating and Analysis," *Cost Engineering* 42, 4 (2000): 32–37, explaining the use of Monte Carlo simulation and *Crystal Ball.*

7. P.V. Rzasa, T.W. Faulkner, and N.L. Sousa, "Analyzing R&D Portfolios at Eastman Kodak," *Research-Technology Management* Vol. 33, no. 1 (Jan.–Feb. 1990): 27–32; D.V. Kleinmuntz, C.E. Kleinmuntz, R.G. Stephen, and D.S. Nordlung, "Measuring and Managing Risk Improves Strategic Financial Planning," *Healthcare Financial Management*, June 1999, pp. 50–58.

8. T. Faulkner, "Applying 'Options Thinking' to R&D Valuation," *Research-Technology Management* Vol. 39, no. 3 (May–June 1996): 50–57; T. Stevens, "Picking the Winners," *Industry Week* 249, 5 (2000): 27–30; W.L. Miller and M. Langdon, *4th Generation R&D—Managing Knowledge, Technology, and Innovation* (New York: Wiley & Sons,

1999; and M. Schilling and C. Hill, "Managing the New Product Development Process: Strategic Imperatives," *Academy of Management Executive*, Aug. 1998, 67–81.

9. W.E. Souder, "A System for Using R&D Project Evaluation Methods," *Research Management* 21 (Sept. 1978): 21–37; and W.E. Souder and T. Mandakovic, "R&D Project Selection Models," *Research Management* 29, 4 (1986): 36–42.

10. F. Zahedi, "The Analytic Hierarchy Process—A Survey of the Method and Its Applications," *Interfaces* 16, 4 (1986): 96–108; and E. Van Dyk and D. Smith, "R&D Portfolio Selection by Using Qualitative Pairwise Comparison," *Omega* 18, 6 (1990): 583–94.

11. See www.expertchoice.com.

12. L.L. Lapin, *Quantitative Methods for Business Decisions*, 6th ed. (Fort Worth, TX: Dryden Press, 1994).

13. S. Alter, *Information Systems—A Management Perspective*, 2nd ed. (Menlo Park, CA: Benjamin/Cummings, 1996), p. 225.

14. F. Ghasemzadeh and N. Archer, "Project Portfolio Through Decision Support," *Decision Support Systems* 29 (2000): 73–88.

15. Parts of this are taken from P. Chu, Y. Hsu, and M. Fehling, "A Decision Support System for Project Portfolio Selection," *Computers in Industry* 32 (1996): 141–49; S. Graves, J. Ringuest, and R. Case, "Formulating Optimal R&D Portfolios," *Research-Technology Management* 43, 3 (2000): 47–51; M. Iyiguen, "A Decision Support System for R&D Project Selection and Resource Allocation under Uncertainty," *Project Management Journal* 24, 4 (1993): 5–13; and J. Ringuest, S. Graves, and R. Case, "Formulating R&D Portfolios That Account for Risk," *Research-Technology Management* 42, 6 (1999): 40–43.

16. Parts of this are taken from J.E. Matheson, M.M. Menke, and S.L. Derby, "Improving the Quality of R&D Decision: A Synopsis of the SDG Approach," *Journal of Science Policy and Research Management* (in Japanese) 4, 4 (1989). See also R. Evans, "Streamlining Formal Portfolio Management," *Scrip Magazine*, Feb. 1996; J. Matheson and M. Menke, "Using Decision Quality Principles to Balance Your R&D Portfolio," *Research-Technology Management* 37, 3 (1994): 38; and P. Roussel, K. Saad, and T. Erickson, *Third Generation R&D, Managing the Link to Corporate Strategy* (Boston: Harvard Business School Press and Arthur D. Little, 1991).

17. R.G. Cooper and E.J. Kleinschmidt, "Benchmarking Firm's New Product Performance and Practices," *Engineering Management Review* 23, 3 (1995): 112–20; R.G. Cooper and E.J. Kleinschmidt, "Winning Businesses in Product Development: Critical Success Factors," *Research-Technology Management* 39, 4 (1996): 18–29.

18. See, for example, N. Danila, "Strategic Evaluation and Selection of R&D Projects," *R&D Management* 19, 1 (1989): 47–62; A. De Maio, R. Verganti, and M. Corso, "A Multi-Project Management Framework for New Product Development," *European Journal of Operational Research* 78, 2 (1994): 178–91; T. Erickson, "Worldwide R&D Management: Concepts and Applications," *Columbia Journal of World Business* 25, 4 (1990): 8–13; D. Hall and A. Naudia, "An Interactive Approach for Selecting IR&D Projects," *IEEE Transactions on Engineering Management* 37, 2 (1990): 126–33; R. Khorramshahgol and Y. Gousty, "Delphic Goal Programming (DGP): A Multi-Objective Cost/Benefit Approach to R&D Portfolio Analysis," *IEEE Transactions on Engineering Management* EM-33, 3 (1986): 172–75; M.J. Liberatore, "An Extension of the Analytic Hierarchy Process for Industrial R&D Project Selection and Resource Allocation," *IEEE Transactions on Engineering Management* EM-34, 1 (1987): 12–18; W.E. Souder and T. Mandakovic, "R&D Project Selection Models," *Research Management* 29, 4 (1986): 36–42; R. Weber, B. Werners, and H. Zimmermann, "Planning Models for Research and Development," *European Journal of*

Operational Research 48, 2 (1990): 175–88; S.C. Wheelwright and K.B. Clark, "Creating Project Plans to Focus Product Development," *Harvard Business Review* 70, 2 (1992): 70–82; A. Gupta, D. Wilemon, and K. Atuahene-Gima, "Excelling in R&D," *Research-Technology Management* 43, 3 (May–June 2000): 52–58; Z. Liao and P. Greensfield, "The Synergy of Corporate R&D and Competitive Strategy: An Exploratory Study in Australian High-Technology Companies," *Journal of High Technology Management Research* 11, 1 (2000): 93–107; S. Liyanage, P. Greenfield, and R. Don, "Towards a Fourth Generation R&D Management Model—Research Networks in Knowledge Management," *Project Management Journal* 18, 3/4 (1999): 372–93; M. Schilling and C. Hill, "Managing the New Product Development Process: Strategic Imperatives," *Academy of Management Executive*, Aug. 1998, pp. 67–81; J. Davidson, A. Clamen, and R. Karol, "Learning from the Best New Product Developers," *Research-Technology Management* Vol. 42, no. 4 (July/Aug. 1999): 12–18; H. Gokhale and M. Bhatia, "A Project Planning and Monitoring System for Research Projects," *International Journal of Technology Management* 15, 3 (1997): 159–63; T. Stevens, "Balancing Act," *Industry Week* 246, 6 (1997): 40–48.

19. N. Danila, "Strategic Evaluation and Selection of R&D Projects," *R&D Management* 19, 1 (1989): 47–62.

20. T.J. Erickson, "Worldwide R&D Management: Concepts and Applications," *Columbia Journal of World Business* 25, 4 (1990): 8–13.

21. M. Czinkota and M. Kotabe, "Product Development the Japanese Way," *Journal of Business Strategy* Nov.–Dec. 1990, pp. 31–36.

22. D.A. Yorke and G. Droussiotis, "The Use of Customer Portfolio Theory: An Empirical Survey," *Journal of Business & Industrial Marketing* 9, 3 (1994): 6–18.

23. V. Belton, "Project Planning and Prioritization in the Social Services—An OR Contribution," *Journal of the Operational Research Society* 44, 2 (1993): 115–24; R.G. Cooper, "Third-Generation New Product Processes," *Journal of Product Innovation Management* 11 (1994): 3–14; M. Czinkota and M. Kotabe, "Product Development the Japanese Way," *Journal of Business Strategy*, Nov.–Dec. 1990, 31–36; N. Danila, "Strategic Evaluation and Selection of R&D Projects," *R&D Management* 19, 1 (1989): 47–62; D. Hall and A. Nauda, "An Interactive Approach for Selecting IR&D Projects," *IEEE Transactions on Engineering Management* 37, 2 (1990): 126–33; R. Khorramshahgol and Y. Gousty, "Delphic Goal Programming (DGP): A Multi-Objective Cost/Benefit Approach to R&D Portfolio Analysis," *IEEE Transactions on Engineering Management* EM-33, 3 (1986): 172–75; M.J. Liberatore, "An Extension of the Analytic Hierarchy Process for Industrial R&D Project Selection and Resource Allocation," *IEEE Transactions on Engineering Management* EM-34, 1 (1987): 12–18; D. Yorke and G. Droussiotis, "The Use of Customer Portfolio Theory: An Empirical Survey," *Journal of Business & Industrial Marketing* 9, 3 (1994): 6–18; J. Davidson, A. Clamen, and R. Karol, "Learning from the Best New Product Developer," *Research-Technology Management* Vol. 42, no. 4 (July–Aug. 1999): 12–18; A. Gupta, D. Wilemon, and K. Atuahene-Gima, "Excelling in R&D," *Research-Technology Management* 43, 3 (May–June 2000): 52–58; P. Rzasa, T. Faulkner, and N. Sousa, "Analyzing R&D Portfolios at Eastman Kodak," *Research-Technology Management* 33, 1 (Jan.–Feb. 1990): 27–32.

24. J. Bard, R. Balachandra, and P. Kaufmann, "An Interactive Approach to R&D Project Selection and Termination," *IEEE Transactions on Engineering Management* 35, 3 (1988): 139–46.

25. R.G. Cooper, *Winning at New Products*, 3d ed. (Reading, MA: Perseus Books, 2001); and R.G. Cooper, "Product Innovation and Technology Strategy," in the Succeeding in Technological Innovation series, *Research-Technology Management* 43, 1 (Jan.–Feb. 2000): 28–44.

26. M. Liberatore, "An Extension of the Analytic Hierarchy Process for Industrial R&D Project Selection and Resource Allocation," *IEEE Transactions on Engineering Management* EM-34, 1 (1987): 12–18.

27. J. Matheson and M. Menke, "Using Decision Quality Principles to Balance Your R&D Portfolio," *Research-Technology Management* 37, 3 (1999): 38; P. Rzasa, T. Faulkner, and N. Sousa, "Analyzing R&D Portfolios at Eastman Kodak," *Research-Technology Management* Vol. 33, no. 3, Jan.–Feb. 1990, 27–32; and M. Schilling and C. Hill, "Managing the new product development process: Strategic imperatives," *Academy of Management Executive,* Aug. 1998, pp. 67–81; W. Miller and M. Langdon, *4th Generation R&D—Managing Knowledge, Technology, and Innovation* (New York: Wiley & Sons, 1999); J. Davidson, A. Clamen, and R.A. Karol, "Learning from the Best New Product Developers," *Research-Technology Management* Vol. 42, no. 4 (July–Aug. 1999): 12–18; A. Gupta, D. Wilemon, and K. Atuahene-Gima, "Excelling in R&D," *Research-Technology Management* 43, 3 (May–June 2000): 52–58; J. Ringuest, S. Graves, and R. Case, "Formulating R&D Portfolios That Account for Risk," *Research-Technology Management* 42, 6 (1999): 40–43.

28. N. Danila, "Strategic Evaluation and Selection of R&D Projects," *R&D Management* 19, 1 (1989): 47–62; W. Souder and T. Mandakovic, "R&D Project Selection Models," *Research Management* 29, 4 (1986): 36–42; J. Taggart and T. Blaxter, "Strategy in Pharmaceutical R&D: A Portfolio Risk Matrix," *R&D Management* 22, 3 (1992): 241–54. For the pharmaceutical industry, see R. Henderson, "Managing Innovation in the Information Age," *Harvard Business Review*, Jan.–Feb. 1994, 100–105.

29. N. Danila, "Strategic Evaluation and Selection of R&D Projects," *R&D Management* 19, 1 (1989): 47–62.

30. J. Taggart and T. Blaxter, "Strategy in Pharmaceutical R&D: A Portfolio Risk Matrix," *R&D Management* 22, 3 (1992): 241–54.

31. J.F. Bard, R. Balachandra, and P.E. Kaufmann, "An Interactive Approach to R&D Project Selection and Termination," *IEEE Transactions on Engineering Management* 35, 3 (1988): 139–46; T. Erickson, "Worldwide R&D Management: Concepts and Applications," *Columbia Journal of World Business* 25, 4 (1990): 8–13; D. Hall and A. Naudia, "An Interactive Approach for Selecting IR&D Projects," *IEEE Transactions on Engineering Management* 37, 2 (1990): 126–33; M. Liberatore, "An Extension of the Analytic Hierarchy Process for Industrial R&D Project Selection and Resource Allocation," *IEEE Transactions on Engineering Management* EM-34, 1 (1987): 12–18; W. Souder and T. Mandakovic, "R&D Project Selection Models," *Research Management* 29, 4 (1986): 36–42; R. Weber, B. Werners, and H. Zimmermann, "Planning Models for Research and Development," *European Journal of Operational Research* 48, 2 (1990): 175–88.

32. M. Liberatore, "An Extension of the Analytic Hierarchy Process for Industrial R&D Project Selection and Resource Allocation," *IEEE Transactions on Engineering Management* EM-34, 1 (1987): 12–18.

33. W. Souder and T. Mandakovic, "R&D Project Selection Models," *Research Management* 29, 4 (1986): 36–42.

34. T. Erickson, "Worldwide R&D Management: Concepts and Applications," *Columbia Journal of World Business* 25, 4 (1990): 8–13.

35. M. Liberatore, "An Extension of the Analytic Hierarchy Process for Industrial R&D Project Selection and Resource Allocation," *IEEE Transactions on Engineering Management* EM-34, 1 (1987): 12–18.

36. J. Bard, R. Balachandra, and P. Kaufmann, "An Interactive Approach to R&D Project Selection and Termination," *IEEE Transactions on Engineering Management* 35, 3

(1988): 139–46; V. Belton, "Project Planning and Prioritization in the Social Services—An OR Contribution," *Journal of the Operational Research Society* 44, 2 (1993): 115–24; D. Hall and A. Naudia, "An Interactive Approach for Selecting IR&D Projects," *IEEE Transactions on Engineering Management* 37, 2 (1990): 126–33; R. Weber, B. Werners, and H. Zimmermann, "Planning Models for Research and Development," *European Journal of Operational Research* 48, 2 (1990): 175–88; A. De Maio, R. Verganti, and M. Corso, "A Multi-Project Management Framework for New Product Development," *European Journal of Operational Research* 78, 2 (1994): 178–91.

37. J. Bard, R. Balachandra, and P. Kaufmann, "An Interactive Approach to R&D Project Selection and Termination," *IEEE Transactions on Engineering Management* 35, 3 (1988): 139–46; V. Belton, "Project Planning and Prioritization in the Social Services—An OR Contribution," *Journal of the Operational Research Society* 44, 2 (1993): 115–24.

38. A. De Maio, R. Verganti, and M. Corso, "A Multi-Project Management Framework for New Product Development," *European Journal of Operational Research* 78, 2 (1994): 178–91.

39. S. Alter, *Information Systems—A Management Perspective*, 2d ed. (Menlo Park, CA: Benjamin/Cummings, 1996).

40. R. Weber, B. Werners, and H. Zimmermann, "Planning Models for Research and Development," *European Journal of Operational Research* 48, 2(1990): 175–88.

41. A. De Maio, R. Verganti, and M. Corso, "A Multi-Project Management Framework for New Product Development," *European Journal of Operational Research* 78, 2 (1994): 178–91; R. Schmidt, "A Model for R&D Project Selection with Combined Benefit, Outcome and Resource Interactions," *IEEE Transactions on Engineering Management* 40, 4 (1993): 403–10; R. Weber, B. Werners, and H. Zimmermann, "Planning Models for Research and Development," *European Journal of Operational Research* 48, 2 (1990): 175–88; S. Wheelwright and K. Clark, "Creating Project Plans to Focus Product Development," *Harvard Business Review* 70, 2 (1992): 70–82.

42. R. Schmidt, "A Model for R&D Project Selection with Combined Benefit, Outcome and Resource Interactions," *IEEE Transactions on Engineering Management* 40, 4 (1993): 403–10.

43. A. De Maio, R. Verganti, and M. Corso, "A Multi-Project Management Framework for New Product Development," *European Journal of Operational Research* 78, 2 (1994): 178–91.

44. R. Weber, B. Werners, and H. Zimmermann, "Planning Models for Research and Development," *European Journal of Operational Research* 48, 2 (1990): 175–88.

45. S. Wheelwright and K. Clark, "Creating Project Plans to Focus Product Development," *Harvard Business Review* 70, 2 (1992): 70–82.

46. S. Cooley, J. Hehmeyer, and P. Sweeney, "Modelling R&D Resource Allocation," *Research Management* 29, 1 (1986): 40–49; M. Liberatore, "An Extension of the Analytic Hierarchy Process for Industrial R&D Project Selection and Resource Allocation," *IEEE Transactions on Engineering Management* EM-34, 1 (1987): 12–18; S. Wheelwright and K. Clark, "Creating Project Plans to Focus Product Development," *Harvard Business Review* 70, 2 (1992): 70–82.

47. S. Cooley, J. Hehmeyer, and P. Sweeney, "Modelling R&D Resource Allocation," *Research Management* 29, 1 (1986): 40–49.

48. M. Liberatore, "An Extension of the Analytic Hierarchy Process for Industrial R&D Project Selection and Resource Allocation," *IEEE Transactions on Engineering Management* EM-34, 1 (1987): 12–18.

49. B. Jackson, "Decision Methods for Selecting a Portfolio of R&D Projects," *Research Management* Vol. 26, no. 5 (Sept.–Oct. 1983): 21–26; P. Morris, E. Teisberg, and A. Kolbe, "When Choosing R&D Projects, Go with the Long Shots," *Research-Technology Management* 34 (1991): 35–49; J. Taggart and T. Blaxter, "Strategy in Pharmaceutical R&D: A Portfolio Risk Matrix," *R&D Management* 22, 3 (1992): 241–54; Y. Wind and V. Mahajan, "New Product Development Process: A Perspective for Reexamination," *Journal of Product Innovation Management* 5, 4 (1988): 304–10.

50. J. Taggart and T. Blaxter, "Strategy in Pharmaceutical R&D: A Portfolio Risk Matrix," *R&D Management* 22, 3 (1992): 241–54. See also Y. Wind and V. Mahajan, "New Product Development Process: A Perspective for Reexamination," *Journal of Product Innovation Management* 5, 4 (1988): 304–10.

51. P. Morris, E. Teisberg, and A. Kolbe, "When Choosing R&D Projects, Go with the Long Shots," *Research-Technology Management* 34 (1991): 35–49.

52. J. Davidson, A. Clamen, and R.A. Karol, "Learning from the Best New Product Developers," *Research-Technology Management* Vol. 42, no. 4 (July/Aug. 1999): 12–18; A. Gupta, D. Wilemon, and K. Atuahene-Gima, "Excelling in R&D," *Research-Technology Management* 43, 3 (May–June 2000): 52–58; S. Liyanage, P. Greenfield, and R. Don, "Towards a Fourth Generation R&D Management Model—Research Networks in Knowledge Management," *Project Management Journal* 18, 3/4 (1999): 372–93; W. Miller and M. Langdon, *4th Generation R&D—Managing Knowledge, Technology, and Innovation* (New York: Wiley & Sons, 1999).

53. See note 52.

Chapter 3

1. The Productivity Index method is proposed by the Strategic Decisions Group (SDG). For more information, refer to D. Matheson, J.E. Matheson, and M.M. Menke, "Making Excellent R&D Decisions," *Research-Technology Management* Vol. 37, no. 6 (Nov.–Dec. 1994): 21–24; and P. Evans, "Streamlining Formal Portfolio Management," *Scrip Magazine*, Feb. 1996.

2. R.G. Cooper, *Winning at New Products: Accelerating the Process from Idea to Launch,* 3d ed. (Reading, MA: Perseus Books, 2001).

3. For more information on this issue and options pricing in general, refer to R. Deaves and I. Krinsky, "New Tools for Investment Decision-making: Real Options Analysis," McMaster University Working Paper, Apr. 1997; T. Faulkner, "Applying 'Options Thinking' to R&D Valuation," *Research-Technology Management* Vol. 39, no. 3 (May–June 1996): 50–57; T. Luehrman, "What's It Worth? A General Manager's Guide to Valuation," *Harvard Business Review,* May–June 1997, pp. 132–42.

4. T. Faulkner, "Applying 'Options Thinking' to R&D Valuation," *Research-Technology Management* Vol. 39, no. 3 (May–June 1996): 50–57; S. Hemantha, B. Herath, and C. Park, "Economic Analysis of R&D Projects: An Option's Approach," *Engineering Economist* 44, 1 (1999): 1–35.

5. Industrial Research Institute CTO (Chief Technology Officer) Forum, Oct. 2001, Washington, D.C. Unpublished proceedings.

6. R. More and B. Little, "The Application of Discriminant Analysis to the Prediction of Sales Forecast Uncertainty in New Product Situations," *Journal of Operations Research Society* 31 (1980): 71–77.

7. G. Haley and S. Goldberg, "Net Present Value Techniques and Their Effects on New Product Research," *Industrial Marketing Management* 24 (1995): 177–90.

8. Taken from a presentation by H. Korotkin—controller for the new product process at Polaroid Corporation—at the Portfolio Planning and Management for New Product Development Conference (held by the Institute of International Research and Product Development Management Association, Dec. 1996).

9. R.G. Cooper, S.J. Edgett, and E.J. Kleinschmidt, "Best Practices for Managing R&D Portfolios," *Research-Technology Management* 41, 4 (July–Aug. 1998): 20–33; R.G. Cooper, S.J. Edgett, and E.J. Kleinschmidt, "New Product Portfolio Management: Practices and Performance," *Journal of Product Innovation Management*, 16, 4 (1999): 333–51 (winner of T.P Hustad Best Paper award, 2000).

10. See R.G. Cooper, "Benchmarking New Product Performance: Results of the Best Practices Study," *European Management Journal* 16, 1 (1998): 1–7; R.G. Cooper and E.J. Kleinschmidt, "Winning Businesses in Product Development: Critical Success Factors," *Research-Technology Management* 39, 4 (1996): 18–29; R.G. Cooper and E.J. Kleinschmidt, "Benchmarking Firms' New Product Performance and Practices," *Engineering Management Review* 23, 3 (1995): 112–20; S.J. Edgett, "The New Product Development Process for Commercial Financial Services," *Industrial Marketing Management* 25, 6 (1996): 505–15.

11. A listing of success factors is found in R.G. Cooper, "The Invisible Success Factors in Product Innovation," *Journal of Product Innovation Management* 16, 2 (Apr. 1999): 115–33. See also R.G. Cooper, "New Products: What Separates the Winners from the Losers," in *PDMA Handbook for New Product Development*, ed. Milton D. Rosenau, Jr. (New York, Wiley & Sons, 1996); and R.G. Cooper and S.J. Edgett, "Critical Success Factors for New Financial Services," *Marketing Management* 5, 3 (1996): 26–37.

12. One major consumer goods firm undertook a major study of predictors of new product success. The conclusion: Of six predictors, the NPV calculated prior to the development phase was the poorest predictor of eventual profitability—there was actually a fairly low correlation between predicted NPV and actual NPV. Other factors, such as product superiority and purchase intent, were more strongly linked to profit performance.

13. R.A. Karol, "Integrating the Selection Process to Stage Gates," *Proceedings, Portfolio Management for New Product Development* (Ft. Lauderdale, FL: Institute for International Research and Product Development & Management Association, Jan. 2001).

14. S. Bull, "Innovating for Success—How EXFO's NPDS Delivers Winning Products," *Proceedings, Portfolio Management for New Product Development* (Ft. Lauderdale, FL: Institute for International Research and Product Development & Management Association, Jan. 2001).

15. Source: S. Bull, see endnote 14.

16. R.L. Englund, "Implementing a Prioritization Process That Links Projects to Strategy," *Proceedings, Portfolio Management for New Product Development* (Ft. Lauderdale, FL: Institute for International Research and Product Development & Management Association, Jan. 2001).

17. The reported correlations are from R.G. Cooper and E.J. Kleinschmidt, *New Products: The Key Factors in Success* (Chicago: American Marketing Assn., 1990). For other studies of success factors, see A.M. Sanchez and L.N. Elola, "Product Innovation Management in Spain," *Journal of Product Innovation Management* 8 (1991): 49–56; and M.M. Montoya-Weiss and R.J. Calantone, "Determinants of New Product Performance: A Review and Meta Analysis," *Journal of Product Innovation Management* 11, 5 (1994): 397–417.

18. Kodak's portfolio management approach is described in E. Patton, "The Strategic Investment Process: Driving Corporate Vision Through Portfolio Creation," pp. 43–55 in *Proceedings, Product Portfolio Management: Balancing Resources with Opportunity* (Boston: Management Roundtable, 1999).

19. For more information on the *NewProd™3000* model, see www.prod-dev.com. See also R.G. Cooper, "Selecting Winning New Products: Using the NewProd System," *Journal of Product Innovation Management* 2 (1987): 34–44; and R.G. Cooper, "The NewProd System: The Industry Experience," *Journal of Product Innovation Management* 9 (1992): 113–27.

20. For example, Procter & Gamble uses the *NewProd* model and reports a predictive ability of about 84 percent. See R.E. Davis, "The Role of Market Research in the Development of New Consumer Products," *Journal of Product Innovation Management* 10, 4 (1993): 309–17; see also J.J.A.M. Bronnenberg and M.L. van Engelen, "A Dutch Test with the NewProd Model," *R&D Management* 18, 4 (1988): 321–32.

21. The P&G results—84 percent predictive using the NewProd scoring model—were reported in R.E. Davis, endnote 21.

22. W.E. Souder, "A Scoring Methodology for Assessing the Suitability of Management Science Models," *Management Science* 18 (1972): 526–43.

23. R.G. Cooper, S.J. Edgett, and E.J. Kleinschmidt, "Best Practices for Managing R&D Portfolios," *Research-Technology Management* 41, 4 (July–Aug. 1998): 20–33.

Chapter 4

1. P. Roussel, K. Saad, and T. Erickson, *Third Generation R&D, Managing the Link to Corporate Strategy* (Boston: Harvard Business School Press and Arthur D. Little, 1991).

2. Roussel, Saad, and Erickson, *Third Generation R&D*.

3. Taken from the Strategic Decisions Group (SDG). For more information, refer to D. Matheson, J.E. Matheson, and M.M. Menke, "Making Excellent R&D Decisions," *Research-Technology Management* Vol. 37, no. 6 (Nov.–Dec. 1994): 21–24; and P. Evans, "Streamlining Formal Portfolio Management," *Scrip Magazine*, Feb. 1996.

4. Gary L. Tritle, "New Product Investment Portfolio," internal 3M document.

5. From discussions with Tom Chorman, Corporate New Ventures Group, Procter & Gamble.

6. Roussel, Saad, and Erickson, *Third Generation R&D*.

7. E.B. Roberts and C.A. Berry, "Entering New Businesses: Selecting Strategies for Success," *Sloan Management Review,* Spring 1983, pp. 3–17.

8. H. Weintraub and C.M. Berke, "Make Portfolio Planning a Sustainable Business Process," in *Proceedings, Portfolio Management for New Product Development* (Ft. Lauderdale, FL: Institute for International Research and Product Development & Management Association, 2001), p. 6.

Chapter 5

1. For more detail on the development of a product innovation and technology strategy, see R.G. Cooper, *Winning at New Products*, 3d ed. (Reading, MA: Perseus Books, 2001). See also R.G. Cooper, *Product Leadership: Creating and Launching Superior New Products* (Reading, MA: Perseus Books, 1998) and R.G. Cooper, "Product Innovation and

Technology Strategy" in the Succeeding in Technological Innovation series, *Research-Technology Management* 43, 1 (Jan.–Feb. 2000): 28–44.

2. Parts of this section are taken from R.G. Cooper, *Winning at New Products*, 3d ed. (Reading, MA: Perseus Books, 2001).

3. R.E. Albright, "Roadmaps and Roadmapping: Linking Business Strategy and Technology Planning," *Proceedings, Portfolio Management for New Product Development* (Ft. Lauderdale, FL: Institute for International Research and Product Development & Management Association, Jan. 2001).

4. Charts are from Albright, "Roadmaps and Roadmapping," endnote 3.

5. "Thomson Solutions Process" (internal company document), used with permission. Thanks to Ro Pavlick and Dodge Bingham, who modified the typical Stage-Gate™ process by adding their "Discover Stage," a strategy development stage designed to identify strategic new product projects.

6. M.E. Porter, *Competitive Advantage: Creating and Sustaining Superior Performance* (New York: Free Press, 1985).

7. O. Gadiesh and J.L. Gilbert, "How to Map Your Industry's Profit Pool," *Harvard Business Review*, May–June 1998, pp. 3–11.

8. C.M. Christensen, *The Innovator's Dilemma* (New York: HarperCollins, 1997).

9. R.N. Foster and R.H. Waterman, *Innovation: The Attacker's Advantage* (Fort Worth, TX: Summit Books, 1998).

10. G. Getz, "Looking Ahead at the Front End," *Proceedings, Portfolio Management for New Product Development* (Ft. Lauderdale, FL: Institute for International Research and Product Development & Management Association, Jan. 2001).

11. For more information on the use of lead users in idea generation, see E.A. Von Hippel, M. Sonnack, and J. Churchill, *Developing Breakthrough Products and Services: The Lead User Method* (Minneapolis, MN: LUCI Press). See also C. Herstatt and E.A. Von Hippel, "From Experience: Developing New Product Concepts via the Lead User Method: A Case Study in a 'Low Tech' Field," *Journal of Product Innovation Management* 9 (1992): 213–21; G.L. Urban and E.A. Von Hippel, "Lead User Analyses for the Development of New Industrial Products," *Management Science* 34, 5 (May 1988): 569–82; E.A. Von Hippel, *The Sources of Innovation* (New York: Oxford University Press, 1988); and E.A. Von Hippel, S. Thomke, and M. Sonnack, "Creating Breakthroughs at 3M," *Harvard Business Review*, Sept./Oct. 1999, pp. 47–57.

12. Getz, "Looking Ahead at the Front End," endnote 10.

13. The example is taken from C.M. Christensen, *The Innovator's Dilemma* (New York: HarperCollins, 1997).

14. *PDMA Handbook for New Product Development*, ed. M. D. Rosenau, Jr. (New York: Wiley & Sons, 1996).

15. Much of this section on roadmapping is taken from Lucent Technologies (Bell Labs). See R.E. Albright, "Roadmaps and Roadmapping: Linking Business Strategy and Technology Planning," in *Proceedings, Portfolio Management for New Product Development* (Ft. Lauderdale, FL: Institute for International Research and Product Development & Management Association, Jan. 2001).

16. E.B. Roberts and C.A. Berry, "Entering New Businesses: Selecting Strategies for Success," *Sloan Management Review*, Spring 1983, pp. 3–17.

17. P.V. Rzasa, T.W. Faulkner, and N.L. Sousa, "Analyzing R&D Portfolios at Eastman Kodak," *Research-Technology Management* 33, 1 (1990): 27–32.

18. R.A. Proctor and J.S. Hassard, "Towards a New Model for Portfolio Analysis," *Management Decisions* 28, 3 (1990): 14–17.

Chapter 6

1. Much of this chapter is taken from an article by the authors: R.G. Cooper, S.J. Edgett, and E.J. Kleinschmidt, "Best Practices for Managing R&D Portfolios," *Research-Technology Management* 41, 4 (1998):20–33.

2. R.G. Cooper, S.J. Edgett, and E.J. Kleinschmidt, "Portfolio Management in New Product Development: Lessons from the Leaders—Part I," *Research-Technology Management* 40, 5 (1997): 16–28. See also: R.G. Cooper, S.J. Edgett, and E.J. Kleinschmidt, "Portfolio Management in New Product Development: Lessons from the Leaders—Part II," *Research-Technology Management* 40, 6 (1997): 43–52.

3. See R.G. Cooper, S.J. Edgett, and E.J. Kleinschmidt, "Portfolio Management for New Product Development: Results of an Industry Best Practices Study," *R&D Management*, Vol. 31, no. 4 (Fall 2001).

4. R.G. Cooper, "New Products: What Separates the Winners from the Losers," in *PDMA Handbook for New Product Development*, ed. Milton D Rosenau Jr. (New York: Wiley & Sons, 1996).

5. Section taken from R.G. Cooper, S.J. Edgett, and E.J. Kleinschmidt, "New Product Portfolio Management: Practices and Performance," *Journal of Product Innovation Management* 16, 4 (1999): 333–51.

6. Section taken from R.G. Cooper, S.J. Edgett, and E.J. Kleinschmidt, "Portfolio Management for New Product Development: Results of an Industry Best Practice Study," *R&D Management,* Vol. 31, no. 4 (Fall 2001).

Chapter 7

1. R.G. Cooper, "The Invisible Success Factors in Product Innovation," *Journal of Product Innovation Management* 16, 2 (1999): 115–33.

2. The popularity of NPV use is based on a study of portfolio management practices and what results were achieved (IRI member companies). See R.G. Cooper, S.J. Edgett, and E.J. Kleinschmidt, "Best Practices for Managing R&D Portfolios," *Research-Technology Management* 41, 4 (1998): 20–33.

3. Similar observations are reported in C.M. Crawford, "The Hidden Costs of Accelerated Product Development," *Journal of Product Innovation Management* 9, 3 (1992): 188–99.

4. Exxon Chemical, Product Innovation Process (company brochure).

5. R.G. Cooper, S.J. Edgett, and E.J. Kleinschmidt, "New Problems, New Solutions: Making Portfolio Management More Effective," *Research-Technology Management* 43, 2 (2000): 18–33.

6. Parts of this section are taken from Cooper, Edgett, and Kleinschmidt, "New Problems, New Solutions," pp. 18–32, endnote 5.

7. New product success factors are reported in R.G. Cooper, "New Products: What Separates the Winners from the Losers," *PDMA Handbook for New Product Development*, ed. M.D. Rosenau, Jr. (New York: Wiley & Sons, 1996).

8. Success factors are defined in R.G. Cooper, *Winning at New Products: Accelerating the Process from Idea to Launch* (Reading, MA: Perseus Books, 2001); and R.G. Cooper and S. Edgett, *Product Development for the Service Sector* (Reading, MA: Perseus Books, 1999). Also, an excellent review of success/failure studies is M.M. Montoya-Weiss and R.J. Calantone, "Determinants of New Product Performance: A

Review and Meta Analysis," *Journal of Product Innovation Management* 11, 5 (1994): 397–417.

9. See Cooper, *Winning at New Products*; Cooper and Edgett, *Product Development for the Service Sector*; and Montoya-Weiss and Calantone, "Determinants of New Product Performance," endnote 8.

10. R.G. Cooper, "Developing New Products on Time, in Time," *Research & Technology Management* 38, 5 (1995): 49–57; and R.G. Cooper, and E.J. Kleinschmidt, "Determinants of Timeliness in New Product Development, *Journal of Product Innovation Management* 11, 5 (1994): 381–96.

11. Parts of this section are taken from Cooper, Edgett, and Kleinschmidt, "New Problems, New Solutions," 20–30, endnote 5.

12. Parts of this section are taken from Cooper, Edgett, and Kleinschmidt, "New Problems, New Solutions," 18–25, endnote 5.

13. See, for example, R.G. Cooper and E.J. Kleinschmidt, "Benchmarking Firm's New Product Performance and Practices," *Engineering Management Review* 23, 3 (1995): 112–20; R.G. Cooper and E.J. Kleinschmidt, "Winning Businesses in Product Development: Critical Success Factors," *Research-Technology Management*, 39, 4 (1996): 18–29; S.J. Edgett, "The Development of New Financial Services: Identifying Determinants of Success and Failure," *International Journal of Service Industry Management* 5, 4 (1994): 24–38; R.G. Cooper and S.J. Edgett, "Critical Success Factors for New Financial Services," *Marketing Management* 5, 3 (1996): 26–37; and Montoya-Weiss and Calantone, "Determinants of New Product Performance."

Chapter 8

1. Reasons for poor data and a lack of homework are taken from R.G. Cooper, "The Invisible Success Factors in Product Innovation," *Journal of Product Innovation Management* 16, 2 (Apr. 1999): 115–33.

2. R.G. Cooper, *Winning at New Products: Accelerating the Process from Idea to Launch,* 3d ed. (Reading, MA: Perseus Books, 2001).

3. For an overview of past success and failure studies see R.G. Cooper, *Winning at New Products: Accelerating the Process from Idea to Launch,* 3d ed. (Reading, MA: Perseus Books, 2001); and R.G. Cooper and S.J. Edgett, *Product Development for the Service Sector* (Reading, MA: Perseus Books, 1999).

4. C.M. Christensen, *The Innovator's Dilemma* (New York: HarperCollins, 2000).

5. For a short review of different trend analysis techniques, see M.R. Czinkota, M. Kotabe, and D. Mercer, *Marketing Management: Text and Cases* (Oxford, Eng.: Blackwell Business, 1997), 181–87; and F.G. Bingham, Jr., and B.T. Raffield III, *Business to Business Marketing Management* (Homewood, IL: Irwin, 1990), 223–25.

6. This section is adapted from R.G. Cooper, *Winning at New Products: Accelerating the Process from Idea to Launch,* 3d ed. (Reading, MA: Perseus Books, 2001).

7. Parts of this section on scenarios are based on P. Schwartz, "The Official Future, Self Delusion and Value of Scenarios," *Financial Times,* 2 May 2000, "Mastering Risk" section, pp. 6–7. Schwartz also WROTE *The Art of the Long View* and is the former head of scenario planning at Royal Dutch Shell.

8. J.A. Bers, G.S. Lynn, and C.L. Spurling, "A Venerable Tool for a New Application: Using Scenario Analysis for Formulating Strategies for Emerging Technologies in Emerging Markets," *Engineering Management Journal,* June 1997, 33–40.

9. See Bingham and Raffield, *Business to Business Marketing Management*, 222–23.

10. See Christensen, *Innovator's Dilemma*, endnote 4.

11. Christensen, *Innovator's Dilemma,* p. xviii, endnote 4.

12. See Christensen, *Innovator's Dilemma*, endnote 4.

13. K. Brady, "Concept Testing Should Measure More Than the Intent to Purchase," *Marketing News*, 3 Jan. 1986, p. 63. The author suggests that specific behavioral questions are needed to turn intent-to-buy measures into usable estimates for market penetration data.

14. See, for example, L. Fitzpatrick, "Qualitative Concept Testing Tells Us What We Don't Know," *Marketing News*, 9 June 1997, 26–28, for guidelines on how to write effective concept statements.

15. A.L. Page and H.F. Rosenbaum, "Developing an Effective Concept Testing Program for Consumer Durables," *Journal of Product Innovation Management* 9, 4 (1992): 267–77.

16. K. Maddox, "ARF Forum Examines Internet Research Effectiveness," *Advertising Age* 70, 2 (1999): 28; S. Rhea, "Training an IT Nation," *Black Enterprise* 30, 7 (2000): 69–70; and J. Rubin, "Online Marketing Research Comes of Age," *Brandweek* 41, 42 (2000): 26–28.

17. E. Dahan and V. Srinivasan, "The Predictive Power of Internet-Based Product Concept Testing Using Visual Depiction and Animation," *Journal of Product Innovation Management* 17, 2 (2000): 99–109.

18. Rubin, "Online Marketing Research Comes of Age," endnote 16.

19. P. Kotler, P.H. Cunningham, and R.E. Turner, *Marketing Management*, 10th ed. (Toronto, ON: Prentice-Hall, 2000), p. 333; for concept testing of consumer products, see also Rubin, "Online Marketing Research Comes of Age."

20. S.C. Choi and W.S. DeSarbo, "A Conjoint-Based Product Designing Procedure Incorporating Price Competition," *Journal of Product Innovation Management* 11, 5 (1994): 451–59; P.E. Green, A.M. Krieger, and T.G. Vavra, "Evaluating New Products," *Marketing Research* 9, 4 (1997): 12–21; J.R. Dickinson and C.P. Wilby, "Concept Testing With and Without Product Trial," *Journal of Product Innovation Management* 14, 2 (1997): 117–26; and Dahan and Srinivasan, "Predictive Power of Internet-Based Product Concept Testing."

21. Part of the discussion is based on D.A. Aaker, V. Kumar, and G.S. Day, *Marketing Research*, 6th ed. (New York: Wiley & Son, 1998), p. 745.

22. J.E. Cox, Jr., "Approaches for Improving Salespersons' Forecasts," *Industrial Marketing Management* 18, 4 (1989): 307. The author reports that 62 to 71 percent of all companies use the sales force composite approach for forecasting sales for existing products.

23. R. Subramanian and S.T. IsHak, "Competitor Analysis Practices of US Companies: An Empirical Analysis," *Management International Review* 38, 1 (1998): 7–23.

24. D. Gerwin, "Integrating Manufacturing into the Strategic Phases of New Product Development," *California Management Review* 35, 4 (1993): 123–32; and L. Wah, "MR Research," *Management Review* 88, 8 (1999): 18–21.

25. R.M. Fulmer and A.A. Vicere, "Executing Development: An Analysis of Competitive Forces," *Planning Review* 24, 1 (1996): 31.

26. H. Simon and U. Munack, "Setting the Right Price, at Internet Speed," *Brandweek* 41, 33 (2000): 22–27.

27. R.G. Cooper and E.J. Kleinschmidt, "Success Factors in Product Innovation," *Industrial Marketing Management* 16, 3 (1987): 220.

28. R. Cooper and R. Slagmulder, "Develop Profitable New Products with Target Costing," *Sloan Management Review* 40, 4 (1999): 23–33; and S.A. Butscher and M. Laker, "Market-Driven Product Development," *Marketing Management* 9, 2 (2000): 48–53.

29. E. Shim and E.F. Sudit, "How Manufacturers Price Products," *Management Accounting* 76, 8 (1995): 37; Simon and Munack, "Setting the Right Price"; and Butscher, and Laker, "Market-Driven Product Development," endnotes 28, 26.

30. C.M. Suttner, J.T. Akridge, and W.D. Downey, "Value-Based Pricing (part 3)," *Agri Marketing* 31, 9 (1993): 20–22; and Butscher and Laker, "Market-Driven Product Development."

31. D. Gerwin, "Integrating Manufacturing into the Strategic Phases of New Product Development," *California Management Review* 35, 4 (1993): 123; and G. Boer and J. Ettlie, "Target Costing Can Boost Your Bottom Line," *Strategic Finance* 81, 1 (1999): 49–52.

32. R.W. Koehler, "Triple-Threat Strategy," *Management Accounting* 73, 4 (1991): 30; T.H. Stevenson, F.C. Barnes, and S.A. Stevenson, "Activity-Based Costing: Beyond the Smoke and Mirrors," *Review of Business* 18, 1 (1996): 25–31; Y.R.O. Lobo and P.C. Lima, "A New Approach to Product Development Costing," *CMA* 72, 2 (1998): 14–17; M. Smith, "Innovation and Great ABM Trade-off," *Management Accountant* 76, 1 (1998): 24–26; S.G. Shina and A. Saigal, "Technology Cost Modeling for the Manufacture of Printed Circuit Boards in New Electronic Products," *Journal of Manufacturing Science Engineering* 120, 2 (1998): 368–75; and E. Shim and E.F. Sudit, "How Manufacturers Price Products," *Management Accounting* 76, 8 (1995): 37.

33. Shim and Sudit, "How Manufacturers Price Products"; Boer and Ettlie, "Target Costing Can Boost Your Bottom Line"; and Simon and Munack, "Setting the Right Price," endnotes 29, 31, 26.

34. R. Hales and D. Staley, "Mix Target Costing, QFD for Successful New Products," *Marketing News* 29, 1 (1995): 218; Cooper and Slagmulder, "Develop Profitable New Products with Target Costing"; and Boer and Ettlie, "Target Costing Can Boost Your Bottom Line," endnotes 28, 31.

35. Boer and Ettlie, "Target Costing Can Boost Your Bottom Line," endnote 31.

36. Gerwin, "Integrating Manufacturing into the Strategic Phases," endnote 31.

37. R. Cooper, "Japanese Cost Management Practices," *CMA* 68, 8 (1994): 20; and Cooper and Slagmulder, "Develop Profitable New Products with Target Costing," endnote 28.

38. Cooper and Slagmulder, "Develop Profitable New Products with Target Costing."

39. S.W. Anderson and K. Sedatole, "Designing Quality into Products: The Use of Accounting Data in New Product Development," *Accounting Horizon* 12, 3 (1998): 213–33.

40. Cooper, "Japanese Cost Management Practices," endnote 37.

41. C.D. Shepherd, "Strategic Alignment of New Product Development (NPD) Frameworks," unpublished Ph.D. diss., University of Bradford, Bradford, England, 2000, pp. 535–44.

42. For more information on NewProd, see R.G. Cooper, "The NewProd System: The Industry Experience," *Journal of Product Innovation Management* 9 (1992): 113–27. For information on NewProd 3000, see www.prod-dev.com.

43. R.E. Davis, "The Role of Market Research in the Development of New Consumer Products," *Journal of Product Innovation Management* 10, 4 (1993): 309–17.

44. J. Bronnrenberg and L. van Englelen, "A Dutch Test with the NewProd-Model," *R&D Management* 18, 4 (1988): 321–32.

45. P.G. Smith, "From Experience: Reaping Benefits from Speed to Market," *Journal of Product Innovation Management* 16, 3 (1999): 222–30.

46. The ensuing discussion is largely based on: A. Griffin, "The Effect of Project and Process Characteristics on Product Development Cycle Time," *Journal of Marketing Research* 34, 1 (1997): 24–35.

47. R.J. Calantone, J.B. Schmidt, and C.A. Di Benedetto, "New Product Activities and Performance: The Moderating Role of Environmental Hostility," *Journal of Product Innovation Management* 14, 3 (1997): 179–89; and A.K. Gupta and W.E. Souder, "Key Drivers of Reduced Cycle Time," *Research-Technology Management* 41, 4 (1998): 38–43.

48. C. Karlsson and P. Ahlstrom, "Technological Level and Product Development Cycle Time," *Journal of Product Innovation Management* 16, 4 (1999): 352–62.

49. For additional information, see T. Campbell and J. Madura, "Forecasting Financial Budgets with Monte Carlo Simulation," *Journal of Accounting and EDP* 5, 1 (1989): 28; R. Bon, "Replacement Simulation Model: A Framework for Building Portfolio Decisions," *Construction Management* 6, 2 (1988): 149; F.W. Barnett, "Four Steps to Forecast Market Demand," *Harvard Business Review* 66, 4 (1988): 28; M.A. Cohen and N. Agrawal, "An Analytical Comparison of Long and Short Term Contracts," *IIE Transactions* 31, 8 (1999): 783–96; C.F. Kelliher and L.S. Mahoney, "Using Monte Carlo Simulation to Improve Long-Term Investment Decisions," *Appraisal Journal* 68, 1 (2000): 44–56; R.J. Gerth and T. Pfeifer, "Minimum Cost Tolerance Under Uncertain Cost Estimates," *IIE Transactions* 32, 6 (2000): 493–503; L.L. Brennan and R.A. Orwig, "A Tale of Two Heuristics: Conflicting Work Allocation Approaches in Engineering Consulting," *Engineering Management Journal* 12, 3 (2000): 18–25; and M. Labbe, J.-F. Thisse, and R.E. Wendell, "Sensitivity Analysis in Minisum Facility Location Problems," *Operations Research* 39, 6 (1991): 961–70. The text discussion is largely based on C.F. Kelliher and L.S. Mahoney, "Using Monte Carlo Simulation," p. 56.

50. For more information on tornado diagrams see: Jackson, J., Kloeber, J., Ralston, B. and Deckro, R., "Selecting a Portfolio of Technologies: An Application of Decision Analysis", Decision Sciences, 30(1), pp. 217–238, 1999; Eschenbach, T., Risk Management Through Sensitivity Analysis", AACE Transactions, D&RM.4, 1996.

Chapter 9

1. The GE/McKinsey matrix is based on the original Boston Consulting Group four quadrant stars, cash cows, dogs, and wildcats portfolio allocation model. Here BUs are plotted. For more information, see G. Day, *Analysis for Strategic Marketing Decisions* (St. Paul, MN: West Publishing, 1986); and La Rue Hosner, *Strategic Management* (Englewood Cliffs, NJ: Prentice-Hall).

2. Day, *Analysis for Strategic Marketing Decisions*, endnote 1.

Chapter 10

1. Much of this section is taken from R.G. Cooper, S.J. Edgett, and E.J. Kleinschmidt, "New Problems, New Solutions: Making Portfolio Management More Effective," *Research-Technology Management* 43, 2 (2000): 18–33.

2. E. Patton, "The Strategic Investment Process: Driving Corporate Vision Through Portfolio Creation," *Proceedings: Product Portfolio Management: Balancing Resources with Opportunity* (Boston: The Management Roundtable, 1999), pp. 43–64.

Chapter 11

1. For a list of the critical success factors and best practices in product development, see R.G. Cooper, *Winning at New Products: Accelerating the Process from Idea to Launch,* 3d ed. (Reading, MA: Perseus Books, 2001); see also R.G. Cooper and S.J. Edgett, *Product Development for the Service Sector* (Reading MA: Perseus Books, 1999); R.G. Cooper, *Product Leadership: Creating and Launching Superior New Products* (Reading, MA: Perseus Books, 1998); and R.G. Cooper, "New Products: What Separates the Winners from the Losers," *PDMA Handbook for New Product Development*, ed. Milton D Rosenau, Jr. (New York: Wiley & Sons, 1996).

2. For details on the implementation of a gating process, see Cooper, *Winning at New Products,* and Cooper and Edgett, *Product Development for the Service Sector.*

Appendix A

1. Much of this appendix has been adapted from R.G. Cooper, *Winning at New Products*, 3d ed. (Reading, MA: Perseus Books, 2001), and R.G. Cooper, "Overhauling the New Product Process," *Industrial Marketing Management* 25 (1996): 465–82. For the service sector, see R.G. Cooper and S.J. Edgett, *Product Development for the Service Sector* (Reading, MA: Perseus Books, 1999).

2. These concepts were first introduced in R.G. Cooper, "Third-Generation New Product Processes," *Journal of Product Innovation Management* 11, 1 (1994): 3–14.

Appendix D

1. For more information, see R.G. Cooper, "Selecting Winning New Products: Using the NewProd System," *Journal of Product Innovation Management* 2(1987): 34–44; R.G. Cooper, "The NewProd System: The Industry Experience," *Journal of Product Innovation Management* 9 (1992): 113–27. For further information on the P&G experience, see R.E. Davis, "The Role of Market Research in the Development of New Consumer Products," *Journal of Product Innovation Management* 10, 4 (1993): 309–17. For the Netherlands study, see J.J.A.M. Bronnenberg and M.L. van Engelen, "A Dutch Test with the NewProd Model," *R&D Management* 18, 4 (1988): 321–32.

Index

About the Authors

Dr. Robert G. Cooper is a world expert in the field of new product management and the U.S. publication, *Journal of Product Innovation Management* has labeled him "the quintessential scholar" in the field of new products. He is president of Product Development Institute, Inc., professor of marketing at Michael G. DeGroote School of Business, McMaster University, Ontario, Canada, and on the faculty of the ISBM at Penn State University's College of Business Administration. He is also Crawford Fellow of the Product Development & Management Association (PDMA), and a fellow of the Canadian Academy of Engineering.

Bob is considered the father of the Stage-Gate™ process, now widely used by leading firms around the world to drive new products to market. His NewProd series of research—an extensive investigation over the past 20 years into the practices and pitfalls of product innovation in hundreds of companies and over 2,000 new product projects—has been widely cited. He has published more than 85 articles and six books on new products, including the popular *Winning at New Products: Accelerating the Process from Idea to Launch*, third edition.

Bob's dynamic talks have captivated thousands of businesspeople in North America, Europe, and the Pacific. He has consulted in the field of new product management for leading companies worldwide, including Air Products, Alcan, American Express, Bell-Canada, BF Goodrich, BP (U.K.), Carlsberg Breweries, Corning, Courtalds (U.K.), DuPont, Emerson Electric, Exxon Chemicals, Glaxo, Goodyear, Guinness Breweries, Hallmark, Hoechst (U.S.), IBM, ITT, Inco, Kodak, Lego, Nortel, Pfizer, Pillsbury, Polaroid, PPG Industries, Procter & Gamble, Reckitt-Benckiser (U.K. and U.S.), Rohm and Haas, SC Johnsons Wax, Shell, the Royal Bank of Canada, US West, and W.R. Grace. Many of these companies have implemented his Stage-Gate™ approach to accelerating new products to market.

Bob holds bachelor's and master's degrees in chemical engineering, an MBA, and a Ph.D. in business.

Dr. Scott J. Edgett is an internationally recognized expert in the field of new product development and portfolio management. He is CEO and cofounder of the Product Development Institute and an associate professor of marketing at the Michael G. DeGroote School of Business, McMaster University, Ontario, Canada. Scott is also on the board of directors of the Product Development Management Association and vice president of publications.

Scott is a noted speaker and consultant who has conducted executive seminars and consulting projects in Canada, the United States, Europe, and Japan. Some of his recent clients include Amway, ABB, Abitibi-Consolidated, Alcan, American Express, Amoco, Clorox, Delta Airlines, Dianippon Ink & Chemical, Diageo, Dofasco, DowElanco, E.B. Eddy Paper, Gennum, Grace Davison, Hallmark, Hollister, ICI, John Hancock, Kelloggs,

Kennametal, Invitrogen (Life Technologies), Nova Chemicals, NSP, PECO Energy, Pennzoil-Quaker Oil, Pepsico, Hydro-Quebec, Roche, Rohm and Haas, the Royal Bank of Canada, R.W. Johnson Pharmaceutical, Sun Life, Toray, U.S. Filter, Warner Lambert, W.R. Grace, and Xerox.

He has published more than 60 articles and papers, including the "Best Practices" series. He has also co-authored four books.

Scott holds a bachelor of business administration in accounting, an MBA in marketing/finance and a Ph.D. in marketing (new product development).

Dr. Elko J. Kleinschmidt is a leading expert on the process of new product development, portfolio management of new products, and success factors for new product development programs. He is a professor of marketing and international business and director of the Engineering and Management Program at McMaster University.

He is a recognized researcher in the field of new product development, portfolio management for new products, and the impact of the international dimension on new products. He has written over 60 publications. He, together with his two colleagues (Cooper and Edgett), received the Thomas P. Hustad Best Paper Award for 1999 of the *Journal of Product Innovation Management* for the article "New Products Portfolio Management: Practices and Performance." His current ongoing research project is benchmarking global new product development with companies in North America, Europe, and NZ/Australia.

Elko has international working experience in Europe, North America, Australia, and Africa. He has given numerous seminars to companies in North America, Europe, Asia (China), and NZ/Australia, primarily in the areas of new product development, portfolio management, and marketing.

His consulting activities have included market forecasts, new product management, benchmarking analyses, portfolio management for new products, and developing new product processes for companies.

Elko holds a mechanical engineering degree, as well as an MBA and a Ph.D. in business administration. His practical work experience includes engineering tasks, investment analysis for technical projects, and technical marketing.